Lowland Outcrops

D1639185

Compiled by
Tom Prentice and Grahame Nicoll

With additional contributions from
Roger Everett, Bruce Kerr, Andrew Fraser
and others.

Edited by Roger Everett

SCOTTISH MOUNTAINEERING CLUB
CLIMBERS' GUIDE

Published in Great Britain by the Scottish Mountaineering Trust, 1994
Copyright © The Scottish Mountaineering Club

British Library Cataloguing in Publication Data
Nicoll, Grahame
  Lowland Outcrops
  I. Title II Prentice, Tom
  796.522309411

  ISBN 0-907521-43-6

Maps drawn by Grahame Nicoll and Bruce Kerr
Diagrams by Mary Benstead, Grahame Nicoll, Bruce Kerr,
Tom Prentice, Ken Crocket and Donald Bennet
Production by Scottish Mountaineering Trust (Publications) Ltd
Typeset by Westec, North Connel
Colour separations by Par Graphics, Kirkcaldy
Printed by St Edmundsbury Press, Bury St Edmunds
Bound by Hunter and Foulis, Edinburgh

Distributed by Cordee, 3a DeMontfort Street, Leicester, LE1 7HD

Contents

List of Illustrations

List of Diagrams and Maps

The Climber and the Mountain Environment

With increasing numbers of walkers and climbers going to the Scottish hills, it is important that all of us who do so should recognise our responsibilities to those who live and work among the hills and glens, to our fellow climbers and to the mountain environment in which we find our pleasure and recreation.

The Scottish Mountaineering Club and Trust, who jointly produce this and other guidebooks, wish to impress on all who avail themselves of the information in these books that it is essential at times to consider the sporting and proprietory rights of landowners and farmers. The description of a climbing, walking or skiing route in any of these books does not imply that a right of way exists, and it is the responsibility of all climbers to ascertain the position before setting out. In cases of doubt it is best to enquire locally.

During stalking and shooting seasons in particular, much harm can be done in deer forests and on grouse moors by people walking through them. Normally the deer stalking season is from 1st July to 20th October, when stag shooting ends. Hinds may continue to be culled until 15th February. The grouse shooting season is from 12th August until 10th December. These are not merely sporting activities, but are essential for the economy of many Highland estates. During these seasons, therefore, especal care should be taken to consult the local landowner, factor or keeper before taking to the hills.

Climbers and hillwalkers are recommended to consult the book HEADING FOR THE SCOTTISH HILLS, published by the Scottish Mountaineering Trust on behalf of the Mountaineering Council of Scotland and the Scottish Landowners Federation, which gives the names and addresses of factors and keepers who may be contacted for information regarding access to the hills.

It is important to avoid disturbance to sheep, particularly during the lambing season between March and May. Dogs should not be taken onto the hills at this time, and at all times should be kept under close control.

Always try to follow a path or track through cultivated land and forests,and avoid causing damage to fences, dykes and gates by climbing over them carelessly. Do not leave litter anywhere, but take it down from the hill in your rucksack.

The number of walkers and climbers on the hills is leading to increased, and in some cases very unsightly erosion of footpaths and hillsides. Some of the revenue from the sale of this and other SMC guidebooks is used by the Trust to assist financially the work being carried out to repair and maintain hill paths in Scotland. However, it is important for all of us to recognise our responsibility to minimise the erosive effect of our passage over the hills so that the enjoyment of future climbers shall not be spoiled by landscape damage caused by ourselves.

As a general rule, where a path exists walkers should follow it and even where it is wet and muddy should avoid walking along its edges, the effect of which is to extend erosion sideways. Do not take short-cuts at the corners of zigzag paths. Remember that the worst effects of erosion are likely to be caused during or soon after prolonged wet weather when the ground is soft and waterlogged. A route on a stony or rocky hillside is likely to cause less erosion than on a grassy one at such times.

Although the use of bicycles can often be very helpful for reaching remote crags and hills, the erosion damage that can be caused by them when used 'off road' on soft footpaths and open hillsides is such that their use on such terrain must cause concern. It is the editorial policy of the Scottish Mountaineering Club that the use of bicycles in hill country may be recommended on hard roads such as forest roads or private roads following rights of way, but it is not recommended on footpaths or open hillsides where the environmental damage that bicycles cause may be considerable. Readers are asked to bear these points in mind, particularly in conditions when the ground is wet and soft after rain.

The proliferation of cairns on hills detracts from the feeling of wildness, and may be confusing rather than helpful as regards route-finding. The indiscriminate building of cairns on the hills is therefore to be discouraged.

Climbers are reminded that they should not drive along private estate roads without permission, and when parking their cars should avoid blocking access to private roads and land, and should avoid causing any hazard to other road users.

Finally, the Scottish Mountaineering Club and the Scottish Mountaineering Trust can accept no liability for damage to property nor for personal injury resulting from the use of any route described in their publications.

The Mountaineering Council of Scotland is the representative body for climbers and walkers in Scotland. One of its primary concerns is the continued free access to the hills and crags that we now enjoy. Information about bird restrictions, stalking and general access issues can be obtained from the National Officer of the MCofS. Should any climber or walker encounter problems regarding access, they should contact the National Officer of the MCofS, whose current address is published in CLIMBER AND HILLWALKER magazine.

Acknowledgements

Like all others, this guide has used much information from previous guides, including the old *Western Outcrops*, *Glasgow Outcrops*, *Eastern Outcrops* and *Creag Dubh* guides, whose major authors were Ken Crocket, John Kerry, Ken Johnstone, John Mackenzie, Chris Chapman and Martin Plant. Although much of the text in this guide has been updated, it was originally based on *The Climbers' Guide to Central and Southern Scotland*, whose authors were Rab Anderson, Bob Campbell, Ron Cowells, Ken Crocket, Bob Duncan, Andrew Fraser, Jerry Handren, Ken Johnstone, Tony Kay, Bruce Kerr, Gary Latter, Tom Prentice, Mike Thompson, Duncan McCallum, Craig Macadam, John Mackenzie, Kenny Spence, and Bill Wright.

We are particularly grateful to Mary Benstead and Bruce Kerr for producing a new series of excellent diagrams, which are both visually pleasing and more informative than those in previous editions. We are also grateful for the contributions of Andrew Fraser to the South-West section, and for the Fast Castle sea-cliff section of Bruce Kerr.

A large number of other people have contributed valuable information on the crags and climbs, or have made informed comments on the text. They include Jamie Andrew, Rab Anderson, Kenny Brookman, Graham Campbell, Rick Campbell, Alex Coon, Melanie Crowther, Graham Dudley, Mike Dunn, Dairena Gaffney, Andy Gallacher, Grahame Johnstone, Graham Little, Craig Macadam, Al Matthewson, Robin McAllister, Dave McGimpsey, George MacIntyre, John Mackenzie, Nick Milton, Stuart Murdoch, Kirsty Noble, Ray O'Hara, Adrian Plumb, Stephen Reid, Burnitt Rudd, Neil Stevenson, George Szuca, Ian Taylor, and Jamie Taylor.

Introduction

This guide is a new edition of the previous guidebook to Central and Southern Scotland, giving comprehensive coverage of the Lowlands, the Southern Uplands and the South-West peninsula of Scotland. The Establishment (in the form of the SMC) have now taken over full responsibility for the production of the Outcrop Guides, which means we can now aim at a better production standard, colour photographs and easier revision and reprinting.

Although it is only eight years since the previous edition of the guide was published, so much has changed that in many places it has been necessary to produce a completely revised version. The mountain walkers in the SMC make much fun over the way the Munros seem to move a little up and down, and even from side to side, depending on Ordnance Survey revisions. Well, the climbers can go one better: in this area, whole crags disappear (in fact or in practice), reappear, are discovered for the first time, and (as anyone who has climbed on the dolerite quarries can confirm), they move all over the place. The climbs themselves tend to undergo similar technical rearrangements, which can be most embarrassing if you find out that your pleasant E2 has become a necky E5, only after committing yourself to the crux.

All these changes are recorded here. In the obituary section, we are saddened to report the loss of Lennie, Ravelrig and various minor quarries, which have been filled-in for ever. Limekilns is in a state of limbo, existing yet unavailable. Other good crags, notably Ratho Quarry, have been reprieved, but perhaps only temporarily. But on the happier side, these losses have been offset by a host of new discoveries, of which the best are probably amongst the South-West and Fast Castle sea-cliffs.

Climbers operating at the highest levels have been at least partially catered for by the (controversial) bolt routes at Dumbarton, and the less controversial ones at Dumbuck, Dunglas and North Berwick Law. Several extremely hard traditional routes have been forced in Roslin Glen.

Rearrangement of existing climbs has sometimes left rather exciting and worthwhile new problems; these are legion in the dolerite quarries. In fact, large chunks of Auchinstarry have, for better or worse, been remoulded to leave many new opportunities in various states of stability. This leads me to a heart-felt request. While there are many new lines remaining in these quarries, if you want to produce a new route PLEASE do it properly. Abseil down with brush and crowbar and remove ALL the loose junk thoroughly; I wouldn't like the authors of the next edition to have as many near miss incidents as I did while checking routes for this guide.

The guide has been divided into several chapters, starting in Glasgow, proceeding north to Lomond and the Trossachs, then south to the balmy sea-cliffs of Galloway. Returning to the central valley again, we go past the erstwhile 'sandbag city' at Cambusbarron (now re-graded, but not I hope a 'handbag city') through Central Region to Edinburgh. After a trip north to Fife, we finish in East Lothian and on the Berwickshire coast.

The climbing in the Lowlands and Southern Scotland is fabulously varied, an excellent resource for the locals and a worthy venue for migrating visitors from further afield. Go out and enjoy it.

Roger Everett. January 1994

History

Glasgow Outcrops: 1891 to the 1950s *by Ken Crocket*

"A precipice 20 feet high does not sound very serious, but there may be more fun and real climbing in getting up or down such a place than there is in ascending the 4,406 feet of Ben Nevis ... A quarry face is by no means bad fun, if one can either find a place free from onlookers, or can turn a deaf ear to their somewhat personal remarks about the sundry coppers missing from the shilling ..."

This comment about outcrop climbing was by Gilbert Thomson, one of the founder members of the Scottish Mountaineering Club. It was published in January 1892, by which time various rock athletes from that club – themselves young at some point in their lives – had scurried up quite a few crags. On Saturday, December 12 1891, the day following that Club's Third Annual Dinner, a team of hard men paid a visit to The Whangie. This was the third visit to that crag, the party on this day consisting of: Horace Walker, President of the Alpine Club: Professors Ramsay and Veitch; Messrs Maylard, Munro, Naismith, W.A.Ramsay, and Thomson. Despite snow on the moor and ice-filled cracks, some time was "very enjoyably spent in various pieces of fancy climbing."

The following July, Maylard, Naismith and Thomson attacked The Whangie with two 40-foot ropes; joining them together and climbing the isolated pinnacle now known as The Gendarme by techniques dubiously modern. Crag climbing had arrived in Central Scotland. In September 1892 the crags saw the first climbing accident, also on The Whangie, as loose rock precipitated a climber off the top of the ridge. He lived, thanks to his roped companion.

Other crags were being visited at this time; Craigton, Pillar Crag, Salisbury Crags glowering over Auld Reekie, and Loudoun Hill in Ayrshire. About this time also, in the mid-1890s, started the east-west rivalry which in one form or another persists to this day. Ben An in The Trossachs came under siege in May 1896, by that crag-rat Thomson, H.C.Boyd and his brother the Rev Arnold Boyd. The lower rocks appeared too steep and difficult, the party tackling instead two vegetatious gullies. These remain vegetatious, the cleaner, steeper rocks in the interim having given many enjoyable routes.

Thomson and his friends thus recorded the first route on Ben An with the 30m Left-Hand Gully (Very Difficult). The other gully, on which they failed that day, was climbed two years later by Naismith, Douglas and Maclay, on New Year's Day, 1898. On January 22 1898, Harold Raeburn and J.S.Napier visited the crag and recorded the Oblique Crack, a Very Difficult on the upper tier of rocks.

Loudoun Hill meanwhile had been visited by Naismith as long ago as 1895, when he had attempted to solo a route up the Central Wall. Returning alone by cycle in April 1896, he managed to reverse his line, finding great difficulty climbing in the rain wearing cycling shoes. His route, more of a scramble, starts under The Edge and traverses up and right.

The rocks at Dumbarton Castle were known of by those pioneers, but footwear then was too inadequate for the technical gems waiting to be found on the boulders. Outcrops in any case were regarded by most as a convenient means of obtaining fitness with amusement at the same time, an attitude which persisted for over 70 years. This early, casual approach to the crags has inevitably led to a dearth of recorded history. With a few exceptions, most of the routes climbed before the 1970s have no sure claimant. Only since the early 1970s has a section of climbers attached more importance to the outcrops, recording routes in minutiae, leading or soloing routes and problems previously top roped, freeing aid routes.

The initial phase of exploration by the SMC died out during the first three decades of the present century. Only with John 'Jock' Nimlin in 1930 can we put a date on the renaissance. In that year W.White led the Ash Wall on Ben An, graded then as an 'Amiable Severe'. Nimlin that same year recorded several other excellent routes, including the Birch Wall, The Last 80, and The Rent, the latter Severe or Very Severe, depending on one's jamming abilities.

With mass unemployment in the 1930s great numbers of young people took to walking, the cheapest sport available. For some, climbing naturally followed, many new clubs forming. Jock Nimlin from Glasgow was the force behind the Ptarmigan Club, while Andy Sanders formed the Creagh Dhu. The Lomond M.C. also came into being at this time. Nimlin recorded his climbs on Ben An, but on the lowland crags nobody bothered, being intent on a friendly spirit of competition.

With the end of the Second World War The Whangie especially took a beating, the talents of the Creagh Dhu and the Glencoe M.C. being prominent. Hamish MacInnes left a visiting card with several peg routes; to be freed many years later. Craigmore was also visited by the Creagh Dhu – this area was where they first explored the outdoors after all – but not being accustomed to digging for their routes they soon left that future crag in peace, though not without in all probability first climbing the prominent Craigmore Corner. John Cullen edited the first outcrop guide to appear with The Whangie, in 1950; significantly, that crag already appeared mature, with some 76 routes.

Loudoun Hill saw further activity in the 1930s, following on Naismith's visit in 1895. In an article in SMCJ Vol. XX (1935), Douglas Scott describes climbs which later became known as Pulpit Arete, Left Crack, Foxglove Chimney, Jackdaw Chimney and Dusk Route. Hamish Hamilton climbed The Edge on a top rope during this period. However, the most significant advances here came when the late John Jackson and friends climbed many of the most obvious lines. These routes were recorded in a small private guide, which was preserved by John Jackson's father. This records a remarkable series of ascents, which included Slings (climbed with some aid), and Lunge. The description of the latter makes no mention of aid if so, this must have been one of the hardest climbs of the period; it is now a tough E3 6a! During the 1970s and 1980s, Kenny McClusky and Rab Sandilands freed Slings and Epitaph Variation, and added Senile Slab and Chalkster.

The Quadrocks were being developed round about the 1960s, with members of the Greenock M.C. prominent. 'Big' Bill Skidmore recorded the lines in an interim guide.

Glasgow Outcrops: 1960s to 1986 *by Gary Latter*

Probably as rock boots began to find their way over the channel, Dumbarton Rock began development. The leading light there was the late Neil MacNiven, killed in the Alps in 1963 at the age of 21. His brilliance at the 'Rock' led to ascents of such routes as Stonefall Crack, Stonefall Crack Direct, and the aid route Chemin de Fer. MacNiven also climbed about half of the boulder problems, including Pas Encore, Route Royale (with Brian Shields), Suckers Slab, B.N.I., and Nemesis.

Brian Shields, Michael Connolly and others climbed the remainder of the Dumbarton routes in the early 1960s, Shields being responsible for recording them. Climbs put up by Shields included: Longbow (with Jimmy Houston, using 7 pegs and 8 wedges), Windjammer Crack, and Monsoon Gully, the latter seeing a failed attempt on a direct finish by MacNiven and Shields. Many of the boulder problems fell to Shields, including Short Notice, Skint Knuckles (one sling), and Switch Direct (in Vibrams). Shields was also responsible, with Connolly, for the big aid route Requiem, the finish up the headwall requiring expansion bolts. The other aid route from Shields was The Big Zipper, with A.Baillie.

This wave of activity passed, though the comparative trough was to be short-lived, as a new group of climbers was spawned at the 'Rock'. The 'Dumbarton Boys', whose core included 'Big' Ian Nicolson, Rab Carrington, John Jackson, 'Wee' Ian Fulton and others, found newer and harder boulder problems, some of which took weeks to work out. All this was at the end of the 1960s and into the 1970s. Shields had two more routes to record however, with the aid route Cyclops, and with Desperado. Court Knowe in Glasgow's suburban south was explored by the Crocket brothers in the late 1960s, Wullie's Crack and other routes being soloed.

At the beginning of the 1970s a visiting gritstone climber, Steve Belk, began to investigate the 'Rock'. This led to Bobtail, the first free ascent of Longbow, and the top rope ascent of Grey Wall. On January 3 1971, Belk and Ken Crocket climbed Requiem, with Belk making a superb lead on tied-off blade pegs at the top of the wall, where the wide crack fades. No signs of any bolts were found on this ascent, supposedly the third.

Craigmore began to have its concealing cover of turf removed in secret, the diggers being expatriate Welshman John Kerry and Gordon Jeffrey. The latter had climbed on Craigmore in the late 1960s. John Mackenzie was also living in Glasgow at this time, his enthusiastic explorations finding many lines on Craigton, Pillar Crag and Dunglas, the latter with Colin Garthwaite. Craigmore was such a well-kept secret that it was not included in the first outcrop guide to be published for this area – Ken Crocket's *Western Outcrops* (Nevisport, 1975). This beat the rival *Glasgow Outcrops* (Highrange, 1975) into print by about six months.

Auchinstarry Quarry was rediscovered in 1975 by Ken Johnstone, and was included in a second volume of the Glasgow Outcrops. Johnstone recorded the first routes here with Trundle and Mascarade. Kerry soon homed in on this old quarry, finding such popular routes as Spirogyra, Thumbelena, and Red Lead. Pete Greenwell found Knife Edge, while Willie Todd climbed the thin arete of Nijinski, employing a runner on the neighbouring Promontory Direct, having first top-roped the route. In 1982 Dave Cuthbertson cleaned the arete by abseil then made the first lead with no side runner. Deep Throat was top-roped then led by Johnstone.

Back at Dumbarton, Andy Kelso recorded Ciamar a Tha Sibh and a short aid route, later freed by Todd to give Snowhite. Two fine aretes succumbed, Nick Colton's Fever Pitch and Todd's Gaucho. Johnstone was also busy here, with ascents of Slainte, Drizzle, Rough Sea, and the fine crack of Antigrav, using two aid points. This was later freed by Todd, with several yo-yos. Modern attempts to free the classic aid routes saw Murray Hamilton climb the Big Zipper with only two bolts for aid. At this time too (1977), Kerry and Johnstone put up most of the routes on Cowden Hill, while the latter produced the first route on Girnel Quarry with Obelisk and most of the routes on the West Face of Craigmuschat.

The boulder problems at Dumbarton, the 'black Fontainebleu', were gradually being expanded in 1978, with Mark Worsley on Supinator, Greenwell on Gorilla, and Todd on Good Nicks. Auchinstarry saw further developments from Rob Kerr with Power Play and Soft Machine. Two years on, both top-roped routes on the Trundle Slab were soloed to give Walk on the Wild Side and Midas Touch.

In 1981 Tom Prentice, Callum Fraser and Dave Cuthbertson visited Johnstone Quarry, Cuthbertson leading Tom's Crack. Two years on saw much activity at Auchinstarry, with Jerry Handren producing The Dream Machine, Blade Runner, and Death is the Hunter. Ben Masterton boldly climbed Balance of Power while Gary Latter made a two-day ascent of Carouselambra. Duncan McCallum solved 'the last great problem' in the quarry with his ascent of the blank-looking wall of Surface Tension.

It somehow seems appropriate to conclude this abbreviated and of necessity incomplete history of the Glasgow and West of Scotland outcrops, with mention of deeds at Dumbarton Rock. On the boulder front, Latter added Mestizo, Toto and Physical Graffiti. The old peg problem Pongo was freed. But the big guns were aimed at the aid routes of the face. Cuthbertson worked hard in the spring of 1980, recording Woops, an alternative, fingery start to The Big Zipper. The same climber also succeeded in freeing Chemin de Fer, over the course of several evenings, ropes and runners being left in situ overnight. Kerr climbed Datura at the far right of the West Face.

Cuthbertson returned in 1981, freeing the uncompromising corner of Cyclops, taking successive falls on to a preplaced peg runner. Two years later Masterton made a direct start to Requiem, while Latter climbed the excellent Rock of Ages, and made the first lead of Grey Wall. Latter went on to free the two aid bolts on The Big Zipper, taking six day's work spread throughout the summer. The last great problem on Dumbarton Rock was the great crack of Requiem. This fell at last to Cuthbertson after a heroic struggle encompassing six weeks of humid climbing in the summer of 1983. At the time of climbing, this was Scotland's hardest pitch. Finally, in the spring of 1984 Latter climbed Rising Power and Samora.

The art and practice of outcrop climbing has travelled far and hard since Gilbert Thomson's days. Long looked on as a useful adjunct to bigger things, many now find much pleasure in the short, but difficult problems described in this volume. It is hoped this guide will help climbers of all abilities to continue to find pleasure in these rocks.

The South-West: 1906 to 1986 *by Craig Macadam*

Investigating the development of climbing in the south-west does not yield any dramatic results nor any complete heritage. The early history is one of possibilities rather than events: the few articles from the turn of the century, though they mention all the crags in the Galloway Hills, describe no real climbing. Indeed, in the SMC Journal of 1906, which gives the first comprehensive round-up of walking and climbing in this area, the Climbs section points the prospective climber to the steepest and most continuous crags but, perhaps in character, records no routes.

Rock climbing in the south-west was given an obtuse start when E.C.Thomson and company, discovering Benbeoch, soloed the easiest line in the centre of the crag in 1932. The general tone of the early articles is apologetic and pleading, perhaps because the south-west has always been something of an unknown quantity. The pleas having been largely unheeded, this tone is still apparent in 1958 when A.G.Waldie wrote of the first climbing in the district: "The disconsolate climber, enervated by the balmy climate of Galloway and preserving his nails on its lush vegetation, might well consider selling his rope to the Solway boatmen". Waldie nevertheless goes on to give a series of reasons, in the shape of sea cliffs and outcrops, as well as the crags of the Galloway Hills, that might persuade the climber to hold on to his rope. Recording the first routes in the Galloway Hills, Waldie tells of climbing on most of the major crags including the Cooran Buttress on the Dungeon of Buchan, Craig an Eilte, and the Clints of Dromore. From this time on, local knowledge has it that climbing continued, though without any recording of routes or any direct contact between those taking part. The lack of a tradition or the relative youth of the climbers is perhaps the reason for this.

Waldie notes a further area of development, what is now known as the Dumfries Outcrops. Again, the inquisitive climber can only discover the number of routes that were climbed, as opposed to locating any one of them. Sixteen climbs are mentioned at Clifton, from Easy to Very Severe. This means progress has to be gauged in numbers and grades: there are now 48 routes on this cliff, up to E4. This increase in activity started in 1976, when Craig and George Macadam were pointed to the cliff. Technical standards began to move and the following year the first Extremes were climbed. Jugular Vein was the first to fall, then Wall Street was exposed from behind a tenuous line of ivy on the first ascent. Finally, the Toddamundo arete was soloed, after a quick brushing. 1978 saw the first 5c in The Arete, and in 1979, the first 6a climbs, Fingerlust, and

Lemur. However, unknown to the local climbers, and predating the first climbs at Clifton, the larger sea-cliffs south of Kirkcudbright were being developed. Bill Cheverest had started climbing at Meikle Ross in 1972. His first route, Limehouse Blues, climbed in April of that year, is not the most obvious when an entire cliff is available. Limehouse Blues, however, was climbed in the days before precleaning was common-place as it is now, and this route stays naturally clean. This was the same with K.9, Cheverest's other major climb, which also has a similar structure: from a straightforward slabby start, the route steepens to an exposed and technical crux finish. These routes were the first advance in standards for 20 years.

Cheverest, significantly, wrote the first article on climbing in the south-west since A.G.Waldie. This was published in *Rocksport*, and brought the attention of a number of other climbers to this area. After a two-year lull, John Kerry was brought south from Glasgow by the Rocksport article. He gardened and climbed a series of major routes in the period from March 1975 to September 1977, which were recorded in the Glasgow Outcrops, Volumes 1 and 2. Initially, Kerry's attention was focused on the eye-catching crack lines, which are a feature of these cliffs. Salty Dog (HVS 4c) was climbed in March 1975, the same day as Kerry led the twin bulges of Mellow Yellow, in Little Zawn. However, excellent as these routes are, Kerry's real interest was in the longer layback grooves of the main cliff. Galloway Corner, climbed in early 1975 by Andy Hunter, though favoured at the time, is not of the same quality as Side Track, which, by climbing direct to the first stance, avoids a 15m walk and gives the route a more sustained interest and difficulty. The first pitch of Side Track is part of a natural groove line, 60m high. Kerry returned in May 1977 and completed this route, Back Track, E1 5a the boldest in the area at that time.

Craig Macadam was alerted to these sea-cliffs through the 'Glasgow Outcrops' guide. However, as an inexperienced climber, these more intimidating cliffs proved more of a test than the local outcrops. Kerry's technical high-point, Bloody Crack (E1 5b), climbed in January 1976, was not surpassed in the 1970s. Excellent routes were found by a thorough examination of the cracks and spaces on Limehouse Blues Cliff, but the hardest and best of these, the wall of Finesse, climbed in October 1978, is only just inside the Extreme category.

Late in 1979, the discovery of Burrow Head turned attention away from the locally established crags. The steeper smoother greywacke has meant that the routes are more strenuous and more sustained than those of the Ross. Conquistador, climbed in January 1980, was the first E2 on the sea-cliffs. However, the pace of development, while constant, was never quickened by the threat of competition. Seven months later, Naked Fun, another sustained E2, was climbed on the best-looking face in the south-west.

The period from 1975 to 1980 was one of great activity, with the discovery of four new crags and the consequent surfeit of unclimbed rock. The same has not been true of the years from 1981 to 1985. There are a number of reasons for this. A lack of information deterred potential first ascentionists from further afield; and, as most of the major lines had been climbed, there was not the same scope for the few that knew of the latest developments.

These years did see major new additions on all the main crags, and a small increase in the number of active climbers. Two years behind Clifton, Macadam climbed the first E3s at Meikle Ross in 1981. The smooth corner of Fil d'Or, with its difficult initial bridging, is particularly of note. Burrow Head was visited the following year by Ian Duckworth and Macadam, then Stirling-based. The result was Mirror, Mirror, E3 5c, by a direct start – a bold on-sight lead by Duckworth.

A border raid by Pete Whillance and Jim Fotheringham was the only activity of 1982. Of their three routes, The Highwayman had been climbed by G.Little in 1968, exemplifying the recording problems in this area. Of the other routes, Saddle Tramp, at E2 5c the hardest route in the Galloway Hills, makes excellent use of the terraced buttress it climbs.

Nothing of any importance was climbed in 1983, but 1984 more than compensated for this, After a four-year gap, the first new routes were put up on Clifton. Derek Austin climbed through the curving overhang of Moonshine to make Beyond the Terminator, and Macadam, after one fall, completed Toddamundo by forcing the headwall above the initial arete, the first E4 in the south-west.

Meikle Ross was closely scrutinised, and a number of possibilities were spotted. Austin climbed the deceptive crack of Corridor of Power, E3 5c. This climb is unusual as it is formed by the edge of the bedding planes, the first climb to do this, but surely not the last, Catalysed by this activity, Macadam returned to the Ross and forced the smooth wall right of Mellow Yellow. Called Sunshine Superman, E4 6a, this is the boldest climb in this section.

Glasgow Outcrops and South-West Scotland: 1986-1993 by Tom Prentice and Roger Everett

After the publication of the 1986 guide, new route activity started again when Tom Prentice started excavating some new lines at Auchinstarry Quarry. Altogether seven Extremes were climbed, most of which have been modified by subsequent rockfall (either deliberate or accompanied by some unfortunate climber). The best that remain are probably Race Against Time and Shot in the Dark.

The same year Simon Yates and Davy Gardner visited Creagan Tom Dubh, the obvious wall on the hillside above the east bank of Loch Lomond. Two more extremes were added three years later. Also active on the loch shores in 1986 was John Christie, who discovered the slate quarry at Ross Point and climbed the excellent Crystal Junction (E4), adding two more routes the following year. The crag now has seven routes. Around this time Craig Macadam climbed the impressive Craig's Wall right of Layback Crack at Craigmore.

In search of some less transitory routes, Prentice turned his attention to the sea-cliffs of the south-west and in particular the Mull of Galloway. Portobello was found in 1986 and Laggantalluch Head with Simon Richardson in 1987. That same year a small group of Glasgow climbers spent a leisurely time climbing some 20 of the most obvious lines at both areas including The Man From Del Monte (E3), Thunderbolt (HVS), Laggantalluch Corner (HVS), Ape Escape (E2) and Freewheeling (E2).

The following year attention turned to the adventurous sandstone of the Mauchline Gorge, spurring local climber Stuart Lampard onto the main line on River Buttress; Bridge Over Troubled Water (E4). Prentice was more than happy to settle for Ayrheid (E2), and Games of Chance and Sandancing (E2).

Satisfied with their achievements at Portobello and Laggantalluch, the Glasgow climbers passed the crags to irrepressible south-west activist Andrew Fraser and members of the Ayr-based Kyle Club. The results were dramatic: 34 new routes at Portobello between 1989 and 1992 and 27 at Laggantalluch between 1991 and 1992. Among the best are St Elmo's Fire (E3) and The Cruel Seaside (E2) at Portobello and Davy Jones's Locker (E1) and Heart of Darkness (HVS) at Laggantalluch.

1990 was a year of controversy. After two bolt routes were placed on Dumbarton Rock, the owners, Historic Scotland, took action and had the bolts and other *in situ* protection removed. For a while threatening noises were made about enforcing the ban on climbing at the Rock. It remains to be seen what will become of the subsequent bolt lines which were placed during 1992 and 1993. Although these routes provide entertainment and a needed resource for local sports climbers, they present a dilemma in terms of the question of bolting on a largely traditional crag. With the new MCofS policy on bolts now widely accepted, it is hoped that future bolting developments will be sensitive to the wishes of both sports and traditional climbers.

Glasgow's sports climbers have also been looking for alternative venues. The overhang at Dumbuck was bolted to give three routes, the best of which is Awaken (F8a), and then in 1992, attention turned to Dunglas. The small steep wall on the west face between Deviant and Wall of Horrors had already received two new routes – The Beef Monster (E5) from Bruce Kerr and Steel Finger (E3) from Graham Dudley. Three bolt routes were added to the collection, of which the best is Airhead (F7a).

Inland, the potential at Dungeon of Buchan in the Galloway Hills had been known for some time, but it was left to a group of Lake District climbers, inspired by Stephen Reid, to take up where Pete Whillance and Jim Fotheringham had left off in 1982. During the spring and summer of 1991 they utilised mountain bikes to make no less than eight visits to the area, cleaning and recording 15 routes. Of these, Heir Apparent (HVS) and Colonel's Corner (HVS) on the 100m main buttress are worth particular mention, as is Parcel of Rogues (E3) on the immaculate granite of the smaller Dungeon Buttress. Many of these climbs are of excellent quality in beautiful mountain *situations* and stand head and shoulders above many routes in this guide. However, a long drive followed by a 2 hour walk, seasonal restrictions and the vagaries of Scottish weather mean that only time will tell whether north-looking Scots climbers give these routes the traffic they deserve.

Fired up by their new routes on the sea-cliffs, Kyle Club members, most notably Robin McAllister, Dave McGimpsey and, of course, Andrew Fraser, refused to let lichen grow between their toes. In 1992 Money Head was found, resulting in 14 routes and the same year the excellent Crammag Head, the granite headland just south of Laggantalluch, offered up 24 enjoyable outings, the best of which are Molotov Cocktail (E1) and Yosemite Sam (HVS). Meanwhile, Graham Dudley had visited Laggantalluch Head and swiped the obvious and much-eyed crack line in the overhanging prow, to give Quick Seal (E3).

Between sea-cliff sojourns, members of the Kyle team were poking round the accessible inland crags climbing the odd route at Clints of Dromore and Craigencallie. This latter crag already had three routes, climbed, but not recorded, by Graham Little in 1977, and a few more had been added in the early 1980s. The hardest of their new routes was Across The Barricades (E3) by Fraser, McAllister and McGimpsey in 1992.

In 1977 Little had been similarly active in Glen Afton, but again failed to record his routes. With the new guidebook nearing completion, the crags came under renewed scrutiny, resulting in a number of fine routes including Stone Circle (E1) from McAllister. In 1992 McAllister took a deep breath and added Sweet Liberty (E3) and Delirium (E4), two of the hardest routes to be climbed in Ayrshire. Fairly quick access from Glasgow and a selection of star quality Extremes should establish Glen Afton on the map. Unfortunately the crag is fairly slow to dry.

Back in the Galloway Hills, 1992 was also Mullwharchar's year, with the Kyle team adding nine new routes. Despite the quality of Behind The Mask (E1), and the fine situation, it's hard to know whether these remote, frequently seeping and rather heather-strewn mountain crags will become popular. Spurred on by his achievements the previous year, and aware of the impending guidebook, Stephen Reid returned from the Lakes to add five routes at Craignelder, but then put himself out of action in a mountain biking accident.

In late 1992 and early 1993 tragedy struck the local Glasgow climbers, when Kilsyth District Council were advised by their insurers to instigate an attempt to stabilise Auchinstarry Quarry. This followed a serious accident when Crazy Paving collapsed with a climber attached. Plans were drawn up and both MCofS and SMC representatives were consulted. However, despite clear recommendations on how to proceed with minimal impact on the climbing potential of the quarry, the contractors ignored all the advice and devastated parts of the main quarry. Unaccountably, several of the better and more solid climbs were totally destroyed. The middle grade climber will lament the loss of Fusion and Sandman, while in the higher grades the destruction of Balance of Power, one of the best dolerite quarry climbs anywhere, is simply sabotage of our national heritage. As a consolation, a number of new worthwhile climbs have been created from the rubble. With a bit of traffic, many of the old and new climbs could become clean and solid, and the quarry should once again become popular.

Most of the best new routes in the Glasgow area must now have been climbed. However, the past few years have shown that there are still lots of excellent climbs to be found by those interested or motivated enough to leave their familiar haunts. New crags are known to lie just around the corner, while challenging lines still wait to be climbed on existing crags.

The bulk of the new development in this section of the guide has occurred in the mountains or on the sea-cliffs of the south-west. Alas, the latter are frequently dismissed because of their distance from Glasgow, lack of stature, poor rock and bird life. However, climbers who make an effort will revel in the many easily accessible diamonds in the dirt and an absence of crowds in beautiful scenery. They will also find that the birds are far less numerous than on the East coast, that much of the greywacke is surprisingly solid, and that granite of Laggantal-luch is as good as many well known venues. A steady flow of excellent and hard new climbs has been produced at Portobello by Andrew Fraser, Robin McAllister and Mike Reed, amongst others. As we go to press, this team continues to find excellent routes of increasing difficulty – The Waster at Portobello seems destined to become a test-piece with a reputation. The lightning development of the strangely-named Kiln O' The Fuffock illustrates the possibility that whole crags with excellent climbs on good rock may remain undiscovered in hidden inlets along the coast. The impressive Delta of Venus (E4) at Craigencallie is also a pointer to the potential remaining in the Galloway Hills. For those willing to go a little bit further, the crags of Dungeon of Buchan have it all – including midges!

The Central Outcrops: 1970-1993 by Craig Macadam and Roger Everett

Though the rambling cliffs of the Ochils have been scrambled upon in the dim and distant past, the first real climbing in the area took place in the mid-1970s when Bob Conway and friends from the naval base at Rosyth climbed a series of routes on The Wallace Monument cliffs. During one cleaning session how-ever, a large block ended up on the road below the cliff with the result that climbing was banned. The ban continues to this day, a sad loss as many of the lines were good.

In the late 1970s Ian Duckworth, Allan Pettit and Pete Billsborough adopted Wolfcrag Quarry as their local training ground. The walls of this small quarry were very steep and sheltered, and therefore it made a fine bouldering area. Unfortunately, the rock is also very smooth, and so to increase the amount of climbing available they chipped lines of holds all over the wall. Ian Duckworth led Leonardo and Ian's Wa', then Tony Kay took over as the main activist with ascents of Up on the Catwalk, Experiments in Incest and (after some jiggery pokery) Tribal Look. More recently, Craig Macadam soloed Waterfront and The Outsider (one of the quarry's few all-natural routes) and Ron Cowels led Lock-it and Thirty Frames a Second.

In the early 1980s more cliffs were discovered. Ron Cowels in particular deserves credit for the discovery of North Third, Limekilns and Cambusbarron Quarry, the three best cliffs in the area. At North Third, Cowels was responsible for cleaning and climbing most of the routes to give a fine series of crack climbs. The real prize, however, was the superb diagonal crack of Red Shift. This particular climb repulsed numerous attempts from a variety of climbers until it was eventually led free by Gary Latter in 1984. The direct start had been climbed by Kenny Spence on an earlier, abortive attempt.

Limekilns was a unique find – two limestone blocks hidden in the woods beside the Firth of Forth. The first route here was Humbug by Martin Bennett in 1981. Then Tony Kay, Neil Morrison and Neil Paxton swooped in to exploit the potential. Morrison led Cruel Summer, New Gold Dream, Colours Fly and The

Struggler whilst Tony Kay added most of the eliminate lines on the Humbug face and the fine arete of Methods of Dance. Cowels eventually got in on the act with Marley's Ghost but by now all eyes had turned to the two superb cracks splitting the overhanging north face of the Sentinel. These held out until early 1984 when Kenny Spence led Velvet Glove and John MacKenzie led Iron Fist. The most recent routes here are Tony Kay's alternative finish to Methods of Dance and Allan Pettit's Elgin's Wall, the first route on the Gellet Block.

Cambusbarron Quarry received its first route in 1983 when Tony Kay and Ron Cowels climbed Big Country Dreams, with one rest point. This very fine climb soon attracted other climbers to the quarry. In early 1984 Murray Hamilton free-climbed Big Country Dreams and went on to add Formica Crack, and Murray's Corner, while Rab Anderson added Fuel for Thought. An intense May Day weekend's activity led to Oink Oink, Quantum Grunt (since made harder by the unnatural disappearance of a small tree which the first ascentionists used to start the climb) and the intriguing Both Ends Burning being created by Duncan McCallum, Graham Pedley and Kenny Spence. Craig Macadam led Visions of Monaco and Purr-Blind Doomster, the latter being straightened out by McCallum before being led without the *in situ* protection by Spence. The last big climb of the summer was Gary Latter's route Power of Endurance. As well as these full length climbs Graham Livingstone added a number of worthwhile boulder problems, of which Spanking the Monkey is particularly bold and impressive.

Of the less important cliffs Dollar Quarry is perhaps the best. It was developed by Jamie Main in 1981 and though of limited potential it did give some very worthwhile climbs, particularly Applause from The Gallery and Energy Transfer.

The poor weather during 1985 limited further development of the Central Outcrops. By far the greatest activity was at the Gellet Block at Limekilns, which now boasts over 20 routes, many being the work of D.Baker, A.Borthwick, A.McCord, D.Moffat and M.Russell. Of the harder routes, the generally acknowledged classic would seem to be Duncan McCallum's Ivy League, Murray Hamilton being responsible for The Charleston to the left. At Cambusbarron McCallum was again busy, sticking his neck out on The Crowd, while Rab Anderson also helped to fill in the remaining lines with Economy Drive.

Since the publication of the last guide, new route activity has been rather sparse in the Central Outcrops. Rab Anderson added three routes at Cambusbarron, including the aptly-named Thug of War (E4), but undoubtedly the most significant development has been the landscaping of the quarry behind Cambusbarron. This has created a sheltered, sunny and fast drying crag with a pleasant outlook – quite unlike most of the quarries! It provides many excellent routes in the middle grades, most of which are unusually dependent on jamming. Scope remains for more, especially if work on the scale required to construct Chisel (a blatant rock sculpture!) is applied on more of the thin crack lines.

The Eastern Outcrops: 1890-1986 *by Jerry Handren*

Most of the early activity in the Edinburgh area centred around the cliffs of Holyrood Park. Indeed until the late 1940s this area was the scene of a series of developments which marked it as one of the main forcing grounds in Scotland.

Harold Raeburn was the first to explore the possibilities. The 1896 SMC Journal includes an article and map by him detailing some 20 climbs on the Salisbury Crags. Around 1900 he made ascents of Fallen Column climb and the vicious central crack on the Dassies, while on Salisbury Crags he found a fine route up the buttress to the right of the Cat Nick. W.Inglis Clark, in the SMCJ of 1900, used photodiagrams for perhaps the first time for a Scottish outcrop, and included a photograph of an early ascent of Raeburn's Cracked Slabs Route. These routes, together with Collier's climb up the left-hand buttress of the Cat Nick, paved the way for the epic ascent of Great Buttress (originally 'Eastern Buttress of the Great Quarry') in 1902. Climbed by Morrison, Newbigging and the Swiss guide Briquet, this route caused quite a stir at the time, not so much for the difficulty of the climbing as for the steep, exposed and loose rock.

The 1914-18 war left a long shadow over Scottish climbing and it was not until the 1930s that activity began to pick up again. Around this time Jimmy Hewit, Alan Horne and Archie Hendry added a series of routes to the area around the South Quarry on Salisbury Crags. Hewit's Groove, Horne's Slab and Archie's Slab all gave climbing at VS/HVS standard at a time when few cliffs in Scotland could offer any routes harder than Severe. Apart from the usual problems of dubious rock and no protection these climbers now had to contend with a ban on climbing which had come into operation after the Great War, and which has undoubtedly contributed to the general lack of awareness of the historical significance of the climbing here. In 1939 Hewit wrote a guide to the Crags, unfortunately never published, but which formed the basis of the comprehensive guide of the late 40s by J.G.Parish, C.G.M.Slesser and D.H.Haworth, and also of a selective E.U.M.C. guide of around 1950.

As the 1940s approached a strong group of climbers from Edinburgh University appeared on the scene. The main activist was D.H.Haworth. Despite being a relatively obscure character nowadays, he made an important contribution to Scottish climbing, with a string of classic routes throughout the mountain areas. He made many first ascents in Holyrood Park, the finest of which was undoubtedly Steeplejack's Staircase, the original route in The Great Quarry at Salisbury Crags. As with many other hard routes of the day it was top-roped prior to its ascent; nevertheless it was probably the hardest route in the country at the time, and went unrepeated for nearly 15 years before Jimmy Marshall and Robin Smith made the second and third ascents. Both found the route very near their limit at the time.

In the early 1950s Geoff Dutton discovered the pleasant crags on the southern flank of Traprain Law and with the Edinburgh J.M.C.S. climbed a few of the easier lines. In 1955, Robin Smith, the Marshall brothers and the 'Currie Boys' began to take an interest and soon the cliff was covered with a network of pleasant routes on good rock. Smith led Burp and Chute and Jimmy Marshall led Wobble, and Piglet by its left-hand variation. As well as these harder routes many of the classic easier routes such as Great Corner, Left Edge and M.S. Route were first climbed during this period. The same group also explored the cliffs of Dalmahoy Hill, but unlike Traprain the routes here were rather loose and vegetated and the cliff was quickly forgotten.

After this brief period of activity things remained quiet until new faces began to emerge in the early 1960s. Dave Bathgate, Bugs McKeith, Brian Robertson and Ian MacEacheran formed the nucleus of a group of climbers that later became The Squirrels. In 1962 they discovered and developed The Hawkcraig, a steep sea-cliff on the Fife coast. MacEacheran climbed Gaucho, Cranium Crack and The Beast, while Bathgate made ascents of Squirrel Slab, Diptera and, with McKeith, the High Girdle. Neil MacNiven climbed Pain Pillar, still the classic route of the cliff, and Jim Brumfitt climbed Guano, which was probably the hardest of those earlier routes.

During the mid-1960s climbers began to explore the more extensive sea-cliffs of the Fast Castle area. Ian Campbell had described some scrambling traverses by the Fast Castle in 1935, but the first real development was a series of routes on Fast Castle Head itself, climbed by a group of Newcastle climbers led by Gordon Davidson. That same year (1965) Dave Bathgate climbed the impressive sea-stack of The Souter by its landward face, and a year later returned with the rest of the Squirrels to climb some interesting routes in the very secluded bay to the east of the Brander. John Cleare visited the area while researching for his book 'Sea-Cliff Climbing in Britain' and added a route up the seaward face of The Souter. Despite all this activity the climbing on this stretch of coast did not become popular with the majority of local climbers, and the area was not included in Graham Tiso's guide to *Creag Dubh and the Eastern Outcrops*, published in 1967.

After the publication of this guide only a few minor routes were added to the traditional crags, though 'Lord' John Mackenzie's free ascent of Beatle Crack at Traprain was a fair achievement. It soon became obvious that Traprain and Hawkcraig had little more to offer as far as new routes were concerned and development remained at a standstill, until attention turned to the many dolerite quarries dotted around the region.

In 1972 local climbers from Rosyth began to develop Rosyth Quarry, a small dusty crag just north of the Forth road bridge. Ravelrig Quarry was a better find. This was developed during 1973 by members of the M.E.S.L. Mountaineering Club, with Chris Masterton in particular being responsible for many of the routes. Routes such as Headline, Beeline and Demo Route were found to give good climbing on solid rock, and the cliff quickly became popular. Pete Myles and Alistair Borthwick climbed Plumbline using a few nuts for aid, and Masterton later made a free ascent to establish one of the best routes in the area. Unfortunately in 1979 the local landowner blew up the Plumbline wall, totally destroying Plumbline and its neighbouring routes.

Around the same time members of The Jacobite M.C. began to add routes at Rosyth Quarry. Willie Jeffrey was the main activist with routes such as Waullie, Iconoclast and Inspiration, which all gave quite hard climbing. The Jacobites also made the first inroads into Ratho Quarry, perhaps the biggest and most imposing of the local quarries. Willie Jeffrey again made some good ascents including Shear Fear. This and Murray Hamilton's free ascent of Rained In at Ravelrig at about the same time were the first routes in the area to improve on the standard set by Haworth in 1946.

In 1975 members of the Edinburgh J.M.C.S. re-discovered the cliff on Dalmahoy Hill. After an extended gardening session they completed around 20 routes, most of which gave good climbing on rough rock. The only evidence of the passing of the 'Currie Boys' some 20 years previously was a couple of rusty pitons on what is now called Resurrection.

Despite all this activity the quarries had so far only yielded rather scrappy and uninteresting routes (apart from the better climbs at Ravelrig). Climbers lost interest and once again development stood still. During the next five years, while the rest of Scotland was being shaken by an explosion of new routes and rising standards, the Edinburgh cliffs remained quiet. Combinations of Rab Anderson, Dave Brown and Murray Hamilton climbed Grinding, Wheelchair Route and Snowflake Crack at Ravelrig, and Murray Hamilton and Dave Cuthbertson added a few eliminate lines at The Hawkcraig, but otherwise little was achieved.

In 1980 the quiet was rudely shattered when Pete Hunter made a superb series of ascents at Ratho. Doomed Oasis covered some impressive ground but Diverticulitis and Pettifer's Wall were really fine routes, giving the hardest and best climbing in the area at the time. The following year he returned to add Sahara, Ouroborus Eliminate and Pete's Wall. In March and April 1981, unknown to local climbers, a group of Northumberland based climbers added a fine series of routes to the Brander area of Fast Castle. Kevin Howett, in particular, made some fine ascents with routes such as Blue Moves, Sea Sprite and the suicidally loose Lucky Day. Though these events passed more or less unnoticed, local climbers began to re-assess the area and soon came to realise that there was plenty of scope for good new routes.

In March 1982 the short walls surrounding The Souter saw a sudden burst of activity. Kenny Spence was the first to spot the potential, but it was John 'Spider' MacKenzie who grabbed the best routes with his ascents of Fast Bleeder and Walnut. Rab Anderson, Bob Duncan, Jim Melrose, Jerry Handren and Alan Taylor got involved and in the space of a few weekends about 20 routes had been climbed. Though many of these are quite short, they give good steep climbing in an unusual setting, and perhaps deserve to become more popular.

That summer Gordon Bisset climbed the excellent Golden Brown at Ravelrig and on the same crag Pete Hunter freed the old bolt route to give The Prowler. At Ratho Rab Anderson led Slow Strain and in the East Bay, Kenny Spence climbed a very fine and unusual route which he later named Gruel Brittania. By now it was obvious that there really was a great deal to be done and a gold rush mentality began to develop. In August Spence, Hamilton, Anderson and Handren added another batch of routes to The Souter area. The best of these was Souterrain by Spence, though Hamilton climbed a serious route up the wall to the right of Walnut to give Porker's Wall – the first E4 in the area. A point worth mentioning is that the routes at Fast Castle and Ratho required mammoth gardening to reveal solid rock before ascents were possible. The lessons learned in the process were put to good use in the development of other areas.

Spence scoured the countryside for new rock and came up with Benarty Hill. That September he climbed Cubism to give the crag its first route and at the same time cleaned off several other lines. During the winter months Salisbury

Crags are often to be found bone dry and basking in the sun. That winter the temptation of so much rock so close at hand proved too much, and after a series of night-time gardening sessions Jerry Handren added three routes to the area around Steeplejack's Staircase. This effort proved worthwhile and, despite the attentions of the Park Police, these routes have since become very popular.

1983 was a bumper year for the Edinburgh outcrops. Again it was Kenny Spence who led the field. In early April he led Wally 1 at Ratho and with Rab Anderson began to snatch up the remaining lines. Anderson led Welcome to the Cruise, Ane Ledge and Rebel without Claws, but it was Spence who took the best lines with his ascents of Wally 2 and 3, Artho, and the superb This Septic Heil — the hardest route in the quarry. The only climbers to intrude on this monopoly were Jim Melrose with Time's Last Gift, and Jerry Handren with The Lone Groover. Pete Hunter's routes at last got the popularity they deserved and almost all the new routes saw several repeat ascents. Thus in the space of a few months Ratho had become one of the best and most popular crags in the area.

Spence returned to Benarty Hill to climb the lines which he had cleaned the previous year. Dolly Parton followed a horrific wide crack, not dissimilar in appearance to the great lady's cleavage. The two other routes, Ram and A Fist Job, were both led by John MacKenzie.

That summer, Spence tackled the tremendous north side of The Souter, a line which had been looked at by several other notables. The resulting route — Squid Vicious — turned out to be one of the best in the area, giving a very strenuous and serious climb. Towards the end of the summer the pace of development began to slow down a little. During work for the guide Bruce Kerr led two old top-rope problems at Ravelrig to give Men at Work and Overkill. Jerry Handren climbed Prime Cut to give Queensferry Quarry its first route and in October added three more routes at Salisbury Crags to give Transatlantic Trip, Black-dance and After the Axe.

During the autumn yet another new crag was developed. This time it was Rab Anderson and Duncan McCallum who cleaned and climbed the first routes at Lennie Quarry. Though only six miles from the centre of Edinburgh, an evil pool at the base of the main wall had discouraged many would-be explorers. Never-theless routes such as Dive in Movie, Think Sink and Dunker's Delight gave good climbing in an exciting position.

By 1984 activity seemed to have slowed down as climbers began to explore other areas, particularly the newly developing Stirling outcrops. Perhaps the most notable event was the draining of Lennie Quarry, which immediately became very popular. New routes soon followed with Duncan McCallum leading Staying Alive and Chris Dale The Creature from the Black Lagoon. Later in the year Rab Anderson led White Tide and Murray Hamilton led Hard Contract, a very fine climb which had stopped several strong attempts and been the scene of at least one spectacular failure. In early 1985 Lennie received another batch of new routes, but the most important event was undoubtedly John MacKenzie's superb lead of Staying Alive without using the two bolts that McCallum had placed for protection.

The summer of 1985 was very poor and few routes were added. At Lennie Quarry Murray Hamilton added Tar McCallum, a hard layback problem, while at Ratho Quarry the wall left of Godzilla finally received an ascent by Duncan McCallum, resulting in The Blob. The bouldering areas saw a large proportion of the climbing activity in the east in 1985, the indefatigable Kenny Spence being responsible for yet another significant addition with the cleaning of the Lennie bouldering wall.

The Eastern Outcrops: 1986-1993 *by Grahame Nicoll*

When the previous edition of this guide appeared in 1986, the authors were unaware of the developments that had been taking place in Roslin Glen. In June 1985, Kenny Spence and Gerry Rooney had started their explorations, and it was not until January 1987 (40 routes later) that the area was publicised in Mountain magazine. John 'Spider' MacKenzie and Rab Anderson had been let into the secret, but it was Spence who had picked the plums – Hanging Rock, The Wrinklies, Plunging Neckline, Piano Player and Duncrankin are all his work. However, two of the best routes, Beyond Traprain and Gaping Gap, were later found to have been climbed (but not recorded) by Pete Hunter in 1980. This was around the same time that he put up Diverticulitis and Pettifer's Wall at Ratho. Beyond Traprain, at E4 6b, was an outstanding achievement for 1980. It is also worth mentioning that Willie Jeffrey had put up the first recorded route (Centre Line) four years before, and it seems likely that there were other unrecorded ascents even earlier.

Rosyth Quarry was thought unworthy of inclusion in the last edition of the guide. However, the quarry has some good routes, and it has remained popular despite the lack of information. A few additions have been made over the years, but 1986 saw the best and certainly the hardest with Ian Cropley's free ascent of Matinee Cracks, now renamed The Stinking Swordsman.

Undoubtedly the most significant events in the late 1980s in the Edinburgh area, from the rock climbing point of view, has been the loss of several crags. In particular, 1987 was a black year. Firstly, access to the blocks at Limekilns was denied by the landowner. This was sparked off by extensive gardening of the Gellet Block, further exacerbated by litter and offensive graffiti – a prime example of a minority of mindless climbers spoiling it for everyone. Graham Little made strong representations to the owner on behalf of the MCofS, but to no avail, and finally a fence was erected and all the holds within reach of the ground daubed with grease!

Lennie Quarry, which had become very popular since being drained, began to get filled in, and over the following four years the routes diminished in height until only the top few moves were available as boulder problems. In September 1987 Tarmac applied for planning permission to start quarrying at Ravelrig and Dalmahoy. Permission was granted, and Ravelrig was soon filled in with waste. The cliffs at Dalmahoy survive, but in a markedly inferior environment. The only good news was that Traprain Law was bought by East Lothian District Council, thereby securing its future as a climbing venue.

The expected popularity of Roslin Glen, after its divulgence in Mountain, failed to materialise. The climbing is an acquired taste, not to everyone's liking. However, a few enthusiasts (notably Rick Campbell and Owen Hayward) continued development through 1988, raising standards in the process. The high point was Hayward's lead of Roslin Roulette, after extensive top-rope practice. This ethic has become the norm on Roslin's friable and poorly protected sandstone.

In the spring of the following year, Rab Anderson started the development of North Berwick Law (although it was Spence who had first noted its potential). The first route followed a line of old bolts of unknown origin, then a further six routes were added on the steep main wall, mostly with bolts for protection. These bolts seem to have been cordially accepted, and the crag has become very popular. More recently, a couple of eliminate routes have been added, and more bolts placed at the top to aid lowering off. Unfortunately, during 1993 the hangers were stolen from the two routes on the slab, a selfish and pointless act as there have never been any traditional routes here. In contrast to the bolted lines at North Berwick Law, two very bold new routes were also established in 1989. After a long cleaning session, Bruce Kerr led the friable Twilight Hour on the Cockleshell Fin at the Fast Castle sea-cliffs, and Rick Campbell soloed the short but very hard Hezbollah at Roslin, after top rope practice.

In April 1990, the Crimpanzie Fin at The Souter (Fast Castle) was discovered, and by August seven fine little routes had been completed, all the work of Malcolm Smith, Paul Thorburn, Rick Campbell and Ian Dawson. On another sea-cliff, The Hawkcraig at Aberdour, Psylocibie was squeezed into the gap between Gaucho and Rebel's Groove. This is typical of several poor eliminates that continue to be claimed at both Aberdour and Traprain Law, but many of these have almost certainly been climbed previously and thought unworthy of recording.

New route activity increased in 1991, perhaps due to the rumour that a new guide was to be produced! Jamie Andrew, unemployed at the time, was particularly productive. Having climbed most of the existing routes at Holyrood Park, he started adding routes of his own, and together with Al Matthewson he filled in many of the gaps at Roslin Glen. Most of these were the easier lines which had been overlooked by previous parties. Down at Fast Castle, the wide space at the right-hand end of The Brander was filled by Matthewson's Bouma Sequence and Up-helly-aa, and Andrew's Ancient Mariner – three fine but not too well protected routes that deserve to become popular.

The bad news in 1991 came when Wimpey Asphalt applied for planning permission to in-fill Ratho Quarry. The MCofS and many individuals submitted objections, and for once the outcome was favourable: Wimpey withdrew their application in April 1992. Another notable event at Ratho took place soon afterwards, when Jamie Andrew managed to re-climb Sahara, an excellent route that had remained unclimbed since the loss of a crucial flake. This is now the toughest route in the quarry.

Meanwhile, at Roslin, the 'stick men' Paul Thorburn and Rick Campbell were working on a string of exceedingly difficult new routes, which culminated in Thorburn's ascent of Walk on By, probably the hardest route in the Eastern Outcrops. Mention must also be made of the first ascent of the impressive Lover's Leap Cliff by Jamie Andrew. More good routes were also being done at The Brander, particularly Drop the Pilot by George McIntyre and Voyage of the Mad Manxman by Bruce Kerr. McIntyre also completed the first route at Midden Craig, just north of Fast Castle. However, perhaps the most important event of 1992 was the opening of the excellent new climbing wall at Dunfermline, in October.

In comparison, 1993 was a quiet year for new routes, although access issues were once again to the fore. The Deep Sea World at North Queensferry Quarry opened for business, effectively halting climbing there, and Ratho was once again under threat, this time from the M8 extension. On a brighter note, discussions regarding access to Salisbury Crags were underway, and hopefully by the time this guide is published an access agreement will have been formulated.

Notes on the Use of the Guide

Grading of Rock Climbs

The normal British grading system of Easy, Moderate, Difficult, Very Difficult, Severe, Very Severe (VS), Hard Very Severe (HVS) and Extremely Severe has been used. The Extreme grade is sub-divided into E1, E2, E3, E4, E5, E6 and E7.

Technical grades have been given where known. The normal range of technical grades expected on routes of the given overall grade are as follows: VS – 4b, 4c, 5a; HVS – 4c, 5a, 5b; E1 – 5a, 5b, 5c; E2 – 5b, 5c, 6a; E3 – 5c, 6a; E4 – 5c, 6a, 6b; E5 – 6a, 6b. Routes with a technical grade at the lower end of the range will be sustained or poorly protected, while those with grades at the upper end of the expected range will have a short and generally well protected crux section.

Although the British system is thought second to none by those who use it, it is known to confuse visitors from abroad. For their benefit, it can be assumed that 5a, 5b, 5c and 6a correspond approximately to the American grades of 5.9, 5.10a/b, 5.10c/d and 5.11a/b respectively. Eurocraggers should note that there is little or no fixed protection on most of the climbs here, and that if they are used to cruising bolted French 6c, they may suffer some distress while attempting the corresponding 6a pitches on traditional routes, having to stop and fiddle in gear.

In some places, the grades used in the previous edition of this guide have been modified, based on the authors' personal experiences. We have made every effort to grade climbs for an on-sight lead without prior knowledge, pre-placement of protection or dogging. It is sometimes hard to grade climbs on local outcrops, where familiarisation can lead to underestimation of the real difficulties. So, if you think that a favourite test-piece has been unnecessarily upgraded, please try and remember how hard you found it the first time.

A small number of climbs have been given the grade of "Scottish VS". This indicates that the climb was first done in an era before the HVS and Extreme grades were introduced, and that (usually for obvious reasons) more recent information is lacking. Climbers attempting such routes should do so with caution. We will be happy to include updated information in future editions.

A few bolt protected climbs have been produced in the last few years. These have been given French grades, which are more suitable for this style of hard climb. As a rough guide, F6b is approximately British 5c and F6c is British 6a; F6c climbs would be in the E3 and E4 range. At higher French grades the situation becomes more complicated, but if you can climb at that standard you'll know all about it anyway.

Graded Lists

A graded list of climbs at some of the more popular and more extensive crags can be found near the back of this book. Due to the differences in rock types and climbing styles between different areas, this list is organised crag by crag. We recognise that, as with all lists of this type, the information is very subjective. In addition, we accept that it is also incomplete. We hope that publication of this list will stimulate lively discussion so that more accurate and more complete lists can be included in future editions of this guide.

Grading of Winter Climbs

In exceptional conditions, a small number of routes in this guide can be climbed in winter conditions. The traditional Scottish winter grading system has been used: Grade I indicates simple snow climbs, with perhaps a corniced exit; Grade II includes gullies with either individual or minor pitches, or high angled snow with difficult cornice exits, and the easier buttresses under winter conditions; Grade III incorporates gullies which contain at least one substantial ice pitch, and sustained buttress climbs without great technical difficulty; Grade IV gullies may include nearly vertical ice sections, while the buttresses will require a good repertoire of techniques; Grade V icefalls and gullies include steep and sustained ice pitches, while the buttresses will involve hard technical climbing. There are insufficient hard winter climbs in this area to merit application of the two tier grading system.

Bolts

After extensive consultation with all interested parties, the Mountaineering Council of Scotland has issued a policy statement on the use of bolts in Scotland. This policy is endorsed by the Publications Sub-Committee of the Scottish Mountaineering Club.

"The MCofS acknowledge that there is a place for bolts in the future development of Scottish climbing. However, to ensure that the highly regarded ethos of, and future development of, traditional climbing (involving the use of leader-placed and second-removed protection) is not threatened, it is felt that the use of bolts should be limited to the production of sports climbs. There should be no retrospective bolting of established climbs for protection or belays, and there should be no minimalist bolting.

The production of sports climbs with bolts is acceptable on natural rock only when all the following conditions have been satisfied:

(1) On low-lying cliffs, provided that such development is not against the wishes of the landowner. Bolts are inappropriate on mountain cliffs and sea-cliffs.

(2) On routes where natural protection is absent or is inadequate for the repeated falls that such routes necessitate.

(3) Where the rock is steep and provides climbs of a high order of difficulty, at the forefront of developments of the day.

(4) Where there is no historical or local anti-bolt ethic.

Concerning quarried rock, it is felt that any future development should be constrained only by points (2) and (4) above.

Finally, it is felt that bolts should be located to ensure minimum visual impact and should be placed according to current best practices.

It is intended that these principles are not seen as simply restrictive rules, but as a guide to promote the positive development of Scottish climbing, where sports climbing, rather than becoming a substitute for traditional climbing, grows alongside it."

It is also important to note that any pegs referred to in this guide may not always be present, and that (particularly on sea-cliffs) they may be in a poor state.

Inner City Climbing
It has long been common practice to use railway bridges and walls, and other structures built for different purposes, as convenient training grounds. Unfortunately, this practice is increasingly frowned apon by the authorities, and we have been asked by British Transport Police and the District Councils to erase all mention of these venues from this guide.

Terminology
Left and right refer to a climber facing the cliff or facing downhill in descent. In cases of potential ambiguity a compass direction is also given. Pegs and other fixed gear are for protection only, except where specifically stated that they are for direct aid. Do not assume that they will either be in place or in a safe state of repair.

Diagrams
The cliffs on some of the cliffs have been numbered. This indicates that there is a diagram depicting at least part of the cliff. This will be found close to the relevant text. The numbers in the text correspond to the numbers on the diagrams. If a numbered climb is not shown on the diagram it will be located in relation to the numerical order of those that are.

Recommended Routes
No list of recommended climbs is given, instead a star grading system for quality has been used. Three stars indicates a route of the highest quality. If a route has no star this does not necessarily mean that it is poor, it may also indicate that insufficient is known about that route properly to assess its quality. Star ratings may be found to be inconsistent. It is hoped that climbers using this guide will inform the authors of such inconsistencies so that future editions of the guide can be improved.

First Ascensionists
The year of first ascent, where known, is given in the text. The full date and pioneers are listed in chronological order, area by area, at the back of the guide. Further relevant details of the first and subsequent ascents where known are also listed in this section. Much of the information about first ascensionists has been lost, so we recognise that this list is incomplete. We welcome any further information which could be included in future editions of this guide.

Maps and Other Sources of Information

Place names and map references have in general been taken from the OS 1:50000 Landranger Series maps. The sheets required are 57, 58 and 63 to 67 for the Glasgow, Stirling and Edinburgh areas, and 71, 77, 78 and 82 to 84 for the crags in Ayrshire, Galloway, Dumfries and the South-West sea-cliffs. The 1:250000 OS Routemaster Series Sheet 1 map of Southern Scotland is very useful to put into context the whole of the area.

The meanings and pronunciations of local place names can be found in *Scottish Hill and Mountain Names* by Peter Drummond, published by the Scottish Mountaineering Trust (1991). Much useful information can be found in the Scottish Mountaineering Club District Guides to *The Southern Uplands* (1992) and *The Southern Highlands* (1991), published by the Scottish Mountaineering Trust.

Mountain Rescue

In case of an accident requiring rescue or medical attention, contact the Police. Try to leave someone with the victim, who should in any case be made as comfortable as possible. Some knowledge of rudimentary first aid is a desirable thing for a climber to have, so it is wise to consult one of the large number of suitable books on mountaineering first aid and rescue techniques.

The Glasgow Outcrops

This chapter describes the climbing which is available in and around Glasgow north of the Clyde, starting in the west at Dumbuck and Dumbarton, then proceeding eastwards as far as the Kilsyth quarries. All the crags described in this chapter can be found on OS Sheet 64.

DUMBUCK   *(Map Ref 420 748)*

Dumbarton Rock's neighbouring volcanic plug overlooks the A82 at the east side of the town. Like Dumbarton the crag is basalt, but the attentions of a quarrying company have left it looking like a large molar in need of serious treatment.

The routes, which are the result of the work of Andy Gallagher during the early 1990s, all climb the large roof high on the west face, and though the rock requires a little care, this is more than made up for by the quick-drying westerly aspect and natural shelter from the rain. Lower-off points exist at the top of the crag. So far the quarry company has turned a blind eye to climbers and with discretion this will continue.

Heading north on the A82, continue past the quarry entrance for 1km, then take the first turning on the right. Follow this road to a bend at the top where parking is possible. Walk east through two fields, then slant up and right to the crag. All the routes have five bolts, and they have been given French grades only. They are described from left to right.

Awaken   10m   F8a ***
Follow the groove to a jug at half-height. Float past a few hard moves to better holds.

If Six Was Nine   10m   F7c **
Good undercuts lead to a resting place. Move onto the slab with difficulty and finish delicately.

Gentle Mass Touching   10m   F8a *
Thin moves and small holds lead to a handrail. Another hard move leads to easier climbing.

DUMBARTON ROCK   *(Map Ref 400 745)*

Glasgow's best outdoor training and bouldering area has a climber loyalty that dwarfs other crags in this guide. But for as many who love the seriousness and technicality of the many boulder problems, there are lots of climbers whose blood runs cold at their mere mention.

Dumbarton isn't a crag for the weak-fingered or the weak-hearted, but perseverance will strengthen both. The rock is a fine-grained basalt with reasonable friction in the dry, but lethal in the damp. During the summer the rock dries very quickly after rain and the open western aspect allows climbing to sunset.

The leading routes are much less popular than the problems, a pity because some are memorable experiences and among the best climbs in this guide, while others like Chemin de Fer and Requiem rank among Scotland's finest. Many of the climbs follow cracks and corners, with reasonable but often fiddly protection. In comparison, the walls are compact and badly protected.

It should be remembered that Dumbarton Rock is an Historic Monument. Please do not climb into the castle grounds and remember that climbing here is a privilege, not a right.

From Glasgow follow the A814 to Dumbarton and take the second on the left after Dumbarton East railway station. Follow this to a small car park on the right. From here a path leads under the North Face to the Boulders and the main face. There are frequent trains from Glasgow.

NORTH FACE

This is the steep black wall above the access path. The grassy slopes above the routes are disgusting and difficult to descend, and the best way down is to ascend to the top of the Gully Wall, traverse right and descend carefully down the gully. The routes are often more enjoyable than they look, and continued traffic would make them much better.

1   Alpha   20m   HVS 5a
Climb the twin cracks high on the left-hand end of the face to a belay well back.

2   Beta   20m   E1 5b
The central crack to the right is approached by sloping rock, belay well back.

3   Gamma   20m   E1 5c
Climb sloping rock to the steep crack just left of the left-hand of two right-slanting mossy ramps.

4   Uisge Beatha   25m   HVS 5a
The left-hand of the two slanting ramps gives a botanical romp.

5   Rising Power   35m   E2 5b   (1984)
Start as for Uisge Beatha, but follow the obvious right-slanting fault to the foot of the Antigrav crack. Climb the crack to the good hold and continue traversing right to finish up Crackerjack. Good climbing but quite mossy and eliminate.

6   Bohert   30m   HVS 5a
Sloping rock leads to the right-hand slanting ramp which gives mossy climbing. Finish up a crack.

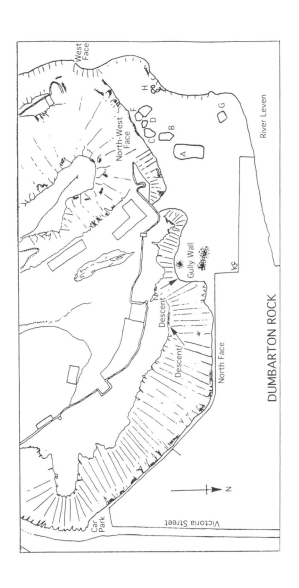

West Face

North-West Face

H

F

D

C

B

A

G

River Leven

Descent

Descent

Gully Wall

North Face

Car Park

Victoria Street

N

DUMBARTON ROCK

7   Antigrav   30m   E3 **   (1970s)
A superb route with a strenuous crux, frequently viewed from a sitting position.
The crack is very well protected in contrast to the poky wall below. Very high in
the grade (if you can do this one on sight without weighting gear you're in good
shape for E4).
1. 20m 6a   Start below the hanging crack and climb the wall to a recess below
the roof. Pull through the roof and continue up the crack with difficulty.
2. 10m 4c   Finish up the crack behind to a belay well back.

8   Slainte   30m   E2 5c   (1970s)
This follows the right-hand of two hairline cracks, right of Antigrav. Climb the wall
to the crack, and up this turning the small overlap on the right.

9   Crackerjack   30m   E1 5b **
The main feature of this route is an entertaining well protected crack after a bold
start. Start immediately below the vertical finger crack right of the hairline cracks
of Slainte. Go up the wall to a small ledge at about 8m. Step left and follow the
crack and its continuation.

10   Drizzle   30m   HVS 5a *   (1970s)
Another good route. To the right, an obvious left-slanting crack starts from a
small recess. Follow this to an awkward move onto a sloping ledge below a
shallow corner. Climb the corner for a few moves, then move left to the arete.

11   The Neilweg   30m   E1 5b *   (1964)
Climb the corner above and right of the slanting crack of Drizzle, with a mossy
exit onto a ledge and possible belay. The crack above provides an airy finish.

12   Big Ears   35m   E1 5b   (1981)
A poor route taking the rock right of The Neilweg. From the ramp, enter the
triangular niche and climb the groove above, finishing by a thin crack.

13   Boulevard   30m   VS 5a *   (1963)
Gain the obvious ramp below the triangular niche with difficulty, then climb
rightwards to a grassy finish.

14   Hailstone Climb   30m   Severe 4a   (1960s)
Climb the wall to the right via corners, grooves and the line of least resistance
to a grassy finish. Not recommended.

15   Left Edge Route   30m   VS   (1960s)
This takes a line up the left edge of Monsoon Gully. Start at the middle of a short
wall and follow a direct line, aiming for the arete above. Climb the arete until a
steep section forces a move out left to a finishing crack.

16   Monsoon Gully   35m   Severe 4b *   (1963)
A delightful neo-Victorian gully for sub-aqua devotees and ecologists. At the top
of the gully move left to gain the grass. The direct finish gives HVS 5a climbing
up the steep crack on the right wall at the top of the gully.

17   Supple as a Brick   35m   E4 *   (1988)
Steep and technical with just adequate protection.
1. 15m 5c   Climb Monsoon Gully until a good jug gives access to the slim
groove in the right wall. Follow the groove to a finger slot at the top. Move onto
the wall on the left and use an overlap to reach better holds up and left.
2. 15m 5a   From the ledge move 2 metres left and climb interesting grooves
and walls to the top.

18   Nameless Crack   25m   Very Difficult   (1964)
Start 10 metres right of Monsoon Gully and climb the pleasant grassy left-slanting crack line.

19   Alleyway   25m   VS 5a   (1960s)
Start at the base of Nameless Crack, but climb the narrow right-slanting shelf to
grass. Step left and finish up mixed ground.

20   Sunset Groove   30m   VS 5a   (1970s)
At the right end of the face is a foul-looking chossy groove. Climb it if you dare.

21   Angel's Pavement   90m   5a **   (1964)
A low-level girdle of the complete face, usually less than 3m up, gives pleasant
bouldering with little chance of breaking an ankle. However, there's a high
chance of being stung to death. The section below Boulevard provides the crux.

THE GULLY WALL
To the right is a grassy gully. The next few routes climb the west-facing wall
recognised by the large mass of ivy on its left. Descent is by traversing right from
the top of the routes and carefully down the gully.

22   Ganglion Grooves   20m   VS 4c   (1964)
Just right of the ivy is a bulging groove. Climb this for 5m then, using a dubious
flake, pull right onto a slab. Continue up the grassy groove and crack to the top.

23   Ciamar a tha Sibh   25m   E2 5b *   (1970s)
The short corner on the left side of the wall gives enjoyable open climbing. Follow
Ganglion Grooves for 5m, then go up the narrow slab on the right (poor
protection) to the short corner, which is climbed until forced left to the arete.

24   Snowwhite   20m   E2 5b ***   (1970s)
A superb pitch giving bold and strenuous climbing with improving protection.
Start right of the corner of Ciamar a tha Sibh below a crack in the upper wall.
Step left onto a slab (small wires), then go back right and up steep rock to the
base of the crack. This gradually eases towards the top.

25   Rag   15m   Severe 4a   (1970s)
Climb the large grassy groove right of Snowwhite.

26   Tag   15m   HVS 5a   (1970s)
Up and right of Rag is a series of short discontinuous cracks. Climb the twin
left-hand cracks and the wall above, then finish up the groove on the left side of
the block overhang.

27   Bobtail   12m   HVS 5a   (1970s)
Start at the far right-hand end of the face. Follow a short crack to a groove, make
an awkward move to gain the continuation groove and step left at the top.

NORTH-WEST FACE
This awe-inspiring sheet of rock, split by the impressive crack lines of Chemin
de Fer and Requiem, offers some desperate exercises in stamina and jamming.
The surrounding corners give tamer but no less impressive routes.

28   Route Three   20m   HVS 5b ***   (1965)
At the left-hand side of the wall is a crack topped by an overhang. Climb the crack
below the left end of the overhang, traverse right below the roof and finish up the
wider crack.

29   Stonefall Crack   20m   HVS 5a **   (1963)
The wider crack on the right leads to a left-trending line of holds. Follow these to
below the overhang, traverse right and finish up the wider crack.

30   Stonefall Crack Direct   20m   HVS 5a *   (1963)
Climb directly up the wider crack, which is poorly protected in the middle section.

31   Woops   10m   E4 6a *   (1980)
Technical climbing up the short overhanging finger crack just right of Stonefall
Crack. Climb the crack to gain the obvious traverse right into The Big Zipper
corner. Finish up this.

32   The Big Zipper   30m   E3 ***   (1964/83)
After a serious first pitch, the corner gives a stunning exercise in bridging and
jamming with good protection.
1. 15m 5b   Climb Stonefall Crack Direct until it is possible to traverse right
round the arete (serious and unprotected) to a belay at the foot of the corner.
2. 15m 5b   Continue up the magnificent corner. Abseil descent.

33   Omerta   30m   F7c ***   (1993)
A stunning and exposed route. Climb the obvious direct start to The Big Zipper,
then continue up the right arete of the corner.

34   Chemin de Fer   30m   E5 6a ***   (1964/80)
One of the finest crack pitches in Scotland and a site of frequent derailments.
Gain the crack and follow it with extra hard moves at the bottom, the middle and
the top, the latter probably being the crux.

35   Requiem   45m   E7 6c ***   (1965/83)
With only a couple of ascents to date (1992), this remains a major undertaking,
requiring a determined approach and considerable stamina. From a bolt belay
on the halfway ledge, follow the central crack and the right-trending line of holds
up the headwall to a crux near the top. There are one, or sometimes two, manky
in situ nuts *en route* and a bolt belay and chain at the top. Abseil descent.

The wall right of Requiem has been bolted, but it remains a project in late
1993. The grade is expected to be as high as F8c!

36   Rock of Ages   15m   E3 6a **   (1983)
The right-rising traverse from Chemin de Fer to the halfway ledge is technical
and poorly protected. One wobbly peg runner *in situ*. Abseil from the bolt on the
halfway ledge.

37   Requiem Direct Start   15m   E3 5b   (1983)
A bold and serious pitch up the lower wall. Climb the wall direct to turn a small
overlap on the left.

38   Cyclops   45m   E5 *   (1974/81)
Technical bridging and rarely repeated. Start beneath a series of ledges at the
right-hand end of the slabby lower wall.
1. 20m 5a   Go up ledges and the wall above, by-passing a large dubious block,
to belay on the halfway ledge.
2. 15m 6b   Difficult bridging leads to a poor peg at 5m. Make a few moves on
the left wall, then regain the corner and follow this and the crack in the right wall
to a block belay (abseil descent possible from here).
3. 10m 5a   Step left and go up the short groove to a nut belay well back. (Abseil
from the bolts at the top of Requiem).

The overhanging wall to the right has been climbed by two routes whose bolts
have been removed. The left-hand route was **Sufferance** (F7c+) and the
right-hand one **Tarrier** (F7c+). The wall round to the right is easily identified by
three steep corners. The best descent from the top of these routes is to abseil
from the top of the Cyclops corner (large sling).

39   Fever Pitch   30m   E4 5c *   (1970s)
An exciting but serious pitch with poor protection, some dirty rock and a few rattly
holds. The crux is much harder than anything else on the route. Start just right
of the left arete of the buttress. Climb straight up to a resting place on the left at
half-height. Continue past the overhang and finish rightwards up the wall above.

40   Longbow   30m   E1 5b ***   (1964)
Exhilarating and well-protected climbing up the steep left-hand corner, with an
exciting finish. Considerably better than it looks from below. Climb the corner to
exit right at the top.

41   Appliance of Violence   F7b **   (1993)
This is the obvious bolted extended boulder problem which climbs the leaning
arete. Lower off at the top.

42   Desperado   30m   HVS 5a *   (1970s)
Good climbing up the central hanging corner, but with poor protection in the
middle section. Climb Windjammer Crack for 10m to a sloping ledge. Traverse
left into the corner and follow it past a rotting peg.
Variation: **Eldorado**   E3 5c
Climb the overhanging arete until a swing right is possible to gain the left traverse
of Desperado.

43   Gaucho   30m   E2 5c   (1970s)
A rather pointless eliminate on Desperado, but if anyone is brave enough to take
the challenge of the left arete direct it would make a fine and very bold outing.
Climb the shallow groove left of Windjammer to gain the left traverse of Desperado. Move diagonally left to the arete, then go up and right to the lowest part of
a small overlap. Move right into Desperado, continue to the large overhang and
traverse left to finish at the same point as Longbow.

44   Windjammer Crack   30m   HVS 5a ***   (1964)
An excellent sustained pitch up the right-hand corner. Once again the climbing
is considerably better than it looks. Take a Friend 3½ for the polished lower
section.

45   Rough Sea   30m   E2 5b   (1970s)
The arete right of Windjammer Crack gives scrappy and poorly protected
climbing. Follow Windjammer until it is possible to traverse right via hollow flakes
to the arete. Climb the wall on the right to the top.

The wall to the right of Rough Sea has been bolted to give three good hard
routes. From the left these are: **Bad Attitude** (F7b * 1993), **Half Breed** (F7b **
1993) and **Unforgiven** (F7b *** 1993). All are fully bolted and lead to a lower-off.

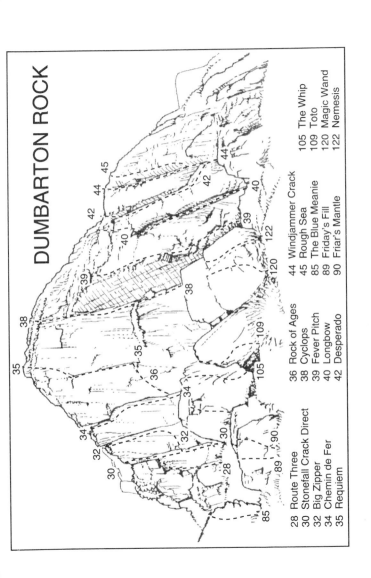

DUMBARTON ROCK

28 Route Three
30 Stonefall Crack Direct
32 Big Zipper
34 Chemin de Fer
35 Requiem

36 Rock of Ages
38 Cyclops
39 Fever Pitch
40 Longbow
42 Desperado

44 Windjammer Crack
45 Rough Sea
85 The Blue Meanie
89 Friday's Fill
90 Friar's Mantle

105 The Whip
109 Toto
120 Magic Wand
122 Nemesis

46   Benny's Route   7m   F7c
This takes the bolted wall below and right of Windjammer crack and above the descent to the West Face. Apart from being perma-dry, it apparently has little else going for it. Slap desperately upwards on slopers; it would help to have your legs amputated first.

WEST FACE

A rather broken and unsatisfactory area of rock with an open aspect down the Clyde. To the right of and below Windjammer Crack a short ridge of poor rock leads to the beach. West Face Gully is the large grassy cleft below and left of the castle wall.

47   Dumbarton Chimney   30m   VS 4c
The obvious chimney left of West Face Gully gives a disgusting climb.

The left wall of West Face Gully contains a few routes.

48   Silly Thing   40m   HVS
This climbs the rightmost corner in the wall.
1. 25m 4b   From the gully traverse easily left to the foot of the corner and follow it to a block belay at the foot of a steep crack.
2. 15m 5b   Climb the crack and belay well back.

49   Frendo   30m   VS 4c   (1963)
Higher up the gully is a slab bordered by a narrow ramp. Climb the ramp for 10m or so. After a short section of mixed ground make a short right traverse over loose blocks to another slab. Easy for the grade.

50   Grey Slab   25m   VS 5a   (1964)
Above and right of Frendo, near the finish of the gully, is a steep slab. Climb it direct to finish up Frendo.

51   West Face Gully   30m   Severe 4a   (1965)
The overgrown gully - yuck.

52   Plunge   30m   Difficult **   (1960s)
Traverse right from the old mooring ring and climb the right-trending rib to the castle wall. Good climbing.

53   Red Slab   10m   Hard Severe 4b
To the right of Plunge is a cracked red slab, bulging at the top.

54   Old Socks   10m   VS 4c   (1965)
Takes a direct line up the crack and overhang, about 4 metres right of Red Slab.

55   Poison Ivy   10m   VS 5a   (1964)
Delicate climbing up the steep red slab, topped with ivy, some 7 metres right of
Old Socks.

56   Sea Traverse   140m   4c   (1960s)
This traverse lies between the foot of West Gully and the park railings on the
south side of the Rock. The route is usually less than 5m above the beach. For
most of its length the traverse is about Difficult, but about midway there is a 10
metre stretch containing the crux. More enjoyable at high tide!

The next two routes lie on the small crag below the castle wall, up and right
of Poison Ivy.

57   Pinky   12m   VS 4b
From a start just left of the small central overhang, gain the shallow groove and
finish up this.

58   Perky   12m   Hard Severe 4b
Follow the groove just right of Pinky, passing the small overhang on the right.

Further right at the same level and below the castle wall is a small grey-green
wall with a prominent black groove on its left-hand side. Ivy is slowly re-claiming
some of the routes.

59   Banana Rib   15m   Very Difficult   (1970s)
Climb the rib left of the black groove.

60   Banana Groove   15m   VS 4c   (1970s)
Follow the black groove, moving right at the top to finish.

61   Banana Slide   15m   E1 5a
An eliminate line. Start just right of the black groove and climb the wall until
forced on to the arete. Make a few moves up the arete then traverse right to
finish.

62   Grey Wall   15m   E4 5c *   (1983)
A serious pitch up the centre of the grey wall, with no protection and a crux near
the top. Follow holds past an obvious hanging flake at about half-height.

63   Datura   12m   E3 5c   (1980)
Start about 3m uphill from Grey Wall, below a small downward-pointing flake.
Climb the wall direct past two ledges.

64   Samora   12m   E3 5c   (1984)
Start a few metres right of Datura and follow holds to gain the ledge at its right
end, then finish directly.

THE BOULDER PROBLEMS

All the problems are graded for on-sight ascents, although the sequence nature of the moves and frequently hidden holds mean on-sight climbing should be undertaken with caution. Dumbarton problems don't give up without a fight.

Chalk is essential, but thankfully the frequent rain leaves few clues. A fine covering of lichen remains on the routes after winter, but this soon disappears as the summer progresses. In past years trees have been cut down for a few more routes. This is totally unacceptable; anyway they soon grow back, so don't bother.

A BOULDER - EAGLE ROCK

This is the first boulder reached from the approach path below the North Face and clearly identified by its slabby east face. Descent is by the easy south-east arete facing the castle. The routes are described anti-clockwise, starting with the large slab right of the descent route.

65   Rankin's Bajin   3b *
Start about 1 metre right of the descent route and climb the slab on good holds.

66   Soixante-Neuf   4b *
The line of least resistance straight up the slab about 2 metres right of the descent route.

67   Pas Mal   4b *
Straight up the slab just left of No.1 Route.

68   No.1 Route   3a *
The obvious left-slanting ramp and groove gives the easiest route on the slab.

69   Left Direct   4a
From the halfway ledge on No.1 Route, climb straight up on good holds.

70   Centre Direct   5a *
Delicate climbing with few holds up the wall midway between Left and Right Direct.

71   Right Direct   4b
Follow a line to the left of the flake on No.2 Route.

72   No.2 Route   3a
Take the fault line on the right of the slab, finishing via a flake.

73   No.2 Route Direct   4c
Climb the short white groove in the small overhanging wall. Walk off left.

74   Pullover   5a *
About one metre to the right is a fault line in the overhanging wall. Climb this to a jug on the lip of the wall, pull over and finish directly above. Short, but sharp.

75   Zigzag   5b ***
This weaves its way through the stepped roofs 3 metres right of Pullover. Reach a large flake hold and pull onto a stance. Make an awkward step left, finishing directly. Excellent varied climbing.

76   Tam's Route   5c **
The overhanging wall 5 metres right of Zigzag is sometimes ascended via poor flat holds, finishing right on small lichenous holds. Scary.

77   High Flyer   6b *
Start from the ledge on the left side of the cave. Make a high jump for a good hold and continue out right to the lip of the overhang.

78   Shadow   6c **
Just right of Tam's Route is an overhanging black groove. Follow this to make an awkward slap left and finish straight up to a small slab.

79   Trick of the Vale   6c **
Start at the same point as the previous route and climb the overhanging wall direct. Spare underpants recommended.

The west face is characterised by a wildly overhanging north-east arete and a long gently overhanging wall.

80   Gorilla   6b ***
Thrills and spills up the wildly overhanging arete. Either statically or dynamically gain a large but smooth layaway on the wall above the cave. Swing left to a good hold on the lip, pull over this and finish up the slab.

81   Cautious Lip   6b **
Similar to but harder than Gorilla. Climb Gorilla to the layaway then go straight up to finish up the slab. On second thoughts, perhaps it's easier than Gorilla when you know the secret!

82   Supinator   6a **
The devious overhanging crack in the centre of the wall leads to an unsettlingly hard exit.

83   2HB   6a ***
Start just left of the tree at an undercut hold. Climb the overhanging wall up and right to an orange bulge and commit yourself to the finishing moves. A refined falling technique is needed to secure a safe landing on the slope below the route.

84   A Ford Flash   6c **
Start just right of the tree below a small groove. Climb straight up and make a long reach left to a good hold and mantel it to finish. Cracked ribs have been experienced.

85   The Blue Meanie   5c ***
At the top of the path and just left of the boulder's descent route is a steep orange and black wall with paint splashes at its base. Climb the wall above the slabby rock on the path, 1½ metres left of the yellow paint. It is possible to finish out left along a line of jugs.

86   P.T.O.   5a **
The short wall and overhang above the yellow paint.

87   1920 Traverse   4a
Start up the descent route, then traverse the east face at mid-height, finishing up No.2 Route.

88   1990 Traverse   6c *
From the tree below 2HB, traverse right to finish up The Blue Meanie.

B BOULDER
This boulder lies down and right of A Boulder and has one fine wall which faces down the Clyde.

89   Friday's Fill   4a
A long stretch and strenuous pull are needed to finish the broken crack on the left.

90   Friar's Mantle   5b **
Surprisingly delicate climbing up the obvious stepped central line.

91   Ungava   5a *
The steep wall on the right is climbed without using the right edge.

C BOULDER - HOME RULE BOULDER
This lies above and right of B Boulder and is characterised by a graffiti-covered wall, facing the descent from A Boulder. Descend by reversing the steep south-east arete, facing the castle (The Beast). All lines (save the first) are described anti-clockwise from The Beast.

92   The Beauty   5a
Climb the overhang and the bulging wall just left of the south-east arete on good holds.

93   The Beast   4b *
Pull up onto the arete, turn the nose on the left and follow the arete to the top.

94   The Brute   5a
The wall just right of the arete is gained from the smaller of two rocks below the boulder.

95   Valkyrie   5a *
Above the smaller of the two rocks under the boulder is a shallow corner. Climb it and finish rightwards up the slab.

96   Pas Encore   5b **
From the larger rock pull strenuously straight over the bulge.

97   Head Butt   6c *
Start at the same place as Pas Encore, but pull right round the overhang to a small corner.

98   Mugsy   6c **
Right of the larger rock, but left of the arete flanking the graffiti-covered wall, is an impressively steep black wall. Levitate to a good incut on the left and pull right into the upper groove. The climbing is tenuous and the landing awkward.

99   Mestizo   6a ***
Forceful climbing up the arete flanking the graffiti-covered wall on the left. Gain a good hold high on the arete and move left to finish boldly up a shallow groove.

100   Physical Graffiti   6b **
Bold and fingery climbing directly up the left side of the graffiti-covered wall.

101   Home Rule   6a **
A one-time test piece. Climb the wall right of Physical Graffiti to the handrail, traverse right and finish past the jammed block. The platform below the wall can be dangerously slippery. A direct finish is possible at the same grade, mantel-shelfing onto the handrail and finishing by avoiding holds on the arete.

102   Home Rule Traverse   6a ***
A superb fingery and very sustained problem. Start up Home Rule and make a devious traverse left at the height of the handrail to the arete. Now do battle with Mestizo!

103   Presence   5c *
From the platform below the graffiti-covered wall climb the right arete with increasing exposure - polished.

The following two problems lie on the large face right of Presence.

104   Route Royale Direct   6a **
Intimidating and committing climbing up the weakness in the centre of the lichenous wall, stepping right at the top. The original route traversed in from the platform on the left below Home Rule.

105   The Whip   5b **
From the hanging blunt arete right of Route Royale, small sloping ledges lead up and right to a shallow groove. Delicate climbing leads to the top.

The next two problems lie on the slabby west-facing wall, right of the upper part of The Whip and facing D Boulder.

106   The Switch   5a *
Take a left-slanting line between the shallow groove of The Whip on the left and Valhalla on the right. A 5b finish is possible by climbing the bulge on the right, instead of veering left at the top.

107   Valhalla   4c *
The shallow fault is followed to an awkward move at the top.

D BOULDER - SUCKER'S BOULDER

The next problems climb the Dumbarton-facing wall, immediately right of The Whip and the cave formed between C and D Boulders.

108   P.S.   5a
Strenuous jamming up the cleft between C and D Boulders.

109   Toto   6b ***
Right of PS is a left-slanting crack giving an archetypal boulder problem; short, technical, going nowhere and frequently failed on. Excellent! A rather dirty direct finish has been made at the same grade. It is also possible to finish rightwards from the wee nicks.

110   Snooker Shelf   5a
At the right end of the face is a left-slanting shelf. Pull up on small holds and follow the shelf leftwards until it's possible to climb easily up wall above - a bit dirty.

Four problems can be found on the slabby west face above the crevasse between D and F Boulders. Approach from left of The Beast.

111   Mosca   3b
Climb the left arete on small holds.

112   Antimatter   5b **
A thin eliminate line immediately right of the arete.

113   Suckers Slab   5b **
Faith and friction straight up the centre of the slab. Rather polished.

114   Volpone   3b *
The thin crack.

E BOULDER

Right of Snooker Shelf is another cave-like passage between Boulders E and F. The wall to the right is characterised by the ridiculously overhanging crack of Pongo. Descend via the hole on the west face between Boulders E and F.

115   Chahala   5c **
The logical position for this route, although it's technically on Boulder F. Start just right of Snooker Shelf, below a trio of good incuts. Gain the first by a leap and continue, finishing right. Difficult for shorties.

116   Skint Knuckles   5b **
Standing at the cave-like passage between Boulders E and F, use a small side pull on the right wall to pull up to a good layaway. Gain a standing position on the sloping ledge using the edge above.

117   Slap Happy   6c
Climb directly up the overhanging wall right of Skint Knuckles with two hard moves to finish.

118   Pongo   6b **
Swing in from the left and, providing contact can be maintained for more than a second, climb the crack. Otherwise, kiss the glass in the grass.

Right of Pongo is a bushy tree. The next problems climb the undercut slab to its right.

119   Sorcerer's Slab   5a *
Pull onto the slab and follow a left-trending line.

120   Magic Wand   5b
Climb straight up from the start of Sorcerer's Slab.

121   Slant   5b *
Follow the short groove just right of Magic Wand.

The following six problems lie to the right on the west side.

122   Nemesis   5b *
Fingerjam with difficulty over the bulge to an easy slab.

123   Narcosis   5b *
Start just right of Nemesis and climb a short shallow groove.

124   Lunik   5b *
Start at the same point as Narcosis, but go right to finish up the arete above Cheddar Direct.

125   Cheddar Direct   4b *
The steep blunt arete is climbed from the right.

126   Hard Cheddar   5c **
Start at Cheddar Direct, but follow the hanging bulging rib rightwards until a pullover is possible onto the slab.

127   Juggie   4b *
The bulging black arete left of the polished hole between E and F Boulders is climbed via a steep pull on two small holds.

128   EBGB   6b *
A low-level traverse right from Sorcerer's Slab to finish up Hard Cheddar.

F BOULDER - BNI BOULDER
Characterised by the impressive hanging BNI slab which faces the Longbow and Windjammer corners. The initials BNI reputedly stand for "Bloody Nigh Impossible". Reverse Astronomy to descend or, if you feel lucky, jump from the top onto the ledges of the main face. The first four problems face Dumbarton and form the V-junction with Boulder E. They can be approached via the hole right of Juggie on Boulder E.

129   Harvester of Eyes   4a
The open groove on the left.

130   Astronomy   4a
The blunt rib in the centre gives a sensible descent.

131   Deo Gratis   5b *
A hard move at half-height gives interest to the wall right of Astronomy.

132   Imposter Arete   5a **
Small but good holds up the arete bounding the BNI slab on the left.

133   BNI Direct   5c **
Start below the arete, step onto the slab and traverse to an obvious sharp foothold. Make thin moves up left, then finish straight up more easily (avoiding holds on the arete).

134 BNI 5c ***
Delicate and committing. From the start of the Direct, make thin moves up right, using a small flake, to gain the semi-detached block of Pendulum.

135 Good Nicks 6a ***
The right arete of the BNI slab gives an excellent technical problem. A short undercut crack leads to a niche. Span and smear left and make a committing move up the rib to the top.

136 Pendulum 4c ***
Climb onto a ledge and face into a series of bulges on the left. Pull up and swing round, using a jug, onto the slab. Mantelshelf onto the flake or finish on small holds. A bold variation finish is possible from halfway along the flake by reaching right into the short V-groove and finishing on good holds (5a).

G BOULDER - THE SEA BOULDER
Regardless of the tide, this Boulder gives the safest landings at Dumbarton (providing you can swim) but there again, the pollution may kill you. The water's action has given it a finely polished bottom.

137 White Streak 6a *
Climb directly up the narrow wall facing the approach path, without hesitation, deviation or resource to holds on either arete. Eliminate.

138 Steptoe 4c ***
Climb the right arete without using the lump of lead.

139 Red Streak 5c **
Just right of the arete are some faint streaks of red paint. Follow them directly, avoiding holds on adjoining routes (and the lump of lead).

140 Chowbok 4c *
Climb the centre of the seaward wall, via a thin crack.

141 Erewhon 5c **
Manic smearing up the right arete of the north wall eventually leads to good holds. Easier for the tall.

142 Tuesday Treat 5b
Thin climbing up the wall facing down the Clyde, just right of Erewhon, without using holds on that route. So eliminate it hardly exists.

143 Commercial Route 4c *
The small corner to the right.

144   Wednesday Wail   4c
An eliminate line just right of Commercial Route, avoiding holds on adjacent routes.

145   Silver's Route   4c
Sidepulls give access to the slabby wall on the right. Finish by moving left and up, or more directly.

146   Gardner's Girdle   5a **
Circumnavigate until tired. At least three stars when the tide's in, but if you wear your wellies you'll probably need them.

H BOULDER
The small trio of broken boulders, below E Boulder. Care should be exercised to avoid becoming just another piece of flotsam on the beach below.

147   Long Reach   5c *
Climb the wall just right of Short Notice and pull into the scoop avoiding the right arete, then finish directly. Eliminate.

148   Short Notice   5b
The nose of rock facing Dumbarton. Step onto the slab below the nose and pull up.

149   Short Sight   4a
Climb the short east-facing wall left of Short Notice.

If that isn't enough, the lower sections of Longbow and Windjammer give excellent though rather polished bouldering - follow the chalk at will. Down and right of this area is a steep black wall which gives numerous short polished problems and traverses from 5a upwards.

DUNGLAS (Map Ref 575 789)

This conical volcanic plug is situated 2km east of Blanefield in open countryside at the foot of the Campsie Fells. The rock is micro-prophyritic basalt with marked hexagonal columns on the north and east faces. Most of the climbing is on the west face where the rock takes a sheet-like structure. The routes are up to 30m high and take about two sunny days to dry. In recent years only the routes on the west face have remained popular.

From Glasgow take the A81 towards Blanefield, turning east onto the A891 at Strathblane. The crag is soon seen on the right side of the road. The farm track leading to it is private, but there is a lay-by 700 metres before the track, on the right. Cross the field and a disused railway track, then go right to the crag. Recently the farmer has sometimes objected to climbing during the lambing season.

EAST FACE

This is the left-hand face, as seen from the approach path. It is large and rather featureless, with a big corner in the centre. The unsoundness of some of the rock and areas of steep grass have restricted development. The first two routes are on an easy-angled rib of reasonable rock left of the corner.

1   Rubbish   30m   Difficult   (1977)
Climb the groove left of the rib to finish on easy ground.

2   Ribbish   30m   Severe   (1977)
Start below the rib at a boulder. Climb the rib to a small overhang and take this by a groove on the right, past a spike. Continue up the slabby rib to a grass ledge, step right and go up slabby rock to a steeper exit.

3   Dunglas Corner   30m   Severe   (1975)
Climb the central corner left of the broad rib, trending right at the top past small trees to finish by the loose corner above.

4   Overlord   30m   E1 5c   (1982)
This takes the prominent nose formed by the junction between the east and north faces. Start 10 metres right of Dunglas Corner and climb a shattered rib into a scoop and go up to a peg runner. Move left and up to bulging rock, then go right to gain a corner crack. Wend through bulges, step right and move up to the top.

5   North-East Arete   25m   E2 5c   (1976)
The steep edge bordering Dunglas Corner. Start right of the edge then climb it trending right beneath an overhang and a jug. Surmount the overhang (crux), then follow easier rock to join Dunglas Corner.

NORTH FACE

A rather menacing part of the crag with much unstable ground. A large scree-covered ledge splits the face into two tiers, with impressive corners above and overhangs below. The routes take lines on the lower tier.

6   Joker's Groove   25m   VS 4c   (1975)
This climbs the corner right of the overhangs. Climb the rib and enter the corner. Trend left past flakes and finish up the wall on left (crux). The rock is loose.

7   Bite them Bequerels   20m   E3 5b   (1987)
Serious and exciting. Start at the obvious rock scar right of the massive scar. Pull up on large holds to a foot ledge and poor peg runners on the left. Move right across the wall and up on better holds to the trough. Follow this leftwards and up to below the overhangs. Traverse right, taking care with the rock to belay pegs. Abseil descent.

8   The Nightmare   20m   E2 5c   (1976)
This takes the hexagonal slabs right of the massive rock scar. Start at the inset corner on the left of the slabs. Climb this and a steeper corner over slabs above (crux) to a small ledge and shattered blocks. Traverse left along shattered rock to the edge. Move up to a ledge and climb the wall above. An apt name.

WEST FACE

This sunny wall contains some of the most solid rock and has the most popular routes on the crag, although lack of traffic has allowed the moss to reclaim many of the easier lines. The obvious features are a right-slanting ramp, Curioser and Curioser, and a cross-shaped crack in the centre, The Cross. At the left end there is the remains of an old fence; the first route starts about 40 metres left of this.

9   The Gentle Touch   20m   HVS 5b   (1976)
A rib, about 8 metres left of the shallow corner of Pullover, marks the start. Move up shelves past a spike and surmount an overhang (crux) to reach a belay. Traverse right to a break and climb the centre of the arete on large holds to an awkward exit.

10   Pullover   20m   VS 4c   (1976)
About 5 metres left of the remains of the fence is a shallow corner. Climb the corner past a peg runner, pull up and traverse a few metres left along a shelf. Continue up and right past blocks to exit up the groove above.

11   Curioser and Curioser   40m   VS 4c   (1975)
This follows the slanting ramp, starting as for Pullover. Move up then across right to a small ledge. Cross the wall to a second ledge, then up right to basin hold. Traverse right past a narrowing to the second cave. Step right, surmount the overhang and finish up a crack.

12   Skirmish   25m   VS 5a   (1975)
The original route on the crag has some bold climbing. Climb the wall about 5 metres right of the remains of the fence, trending slightly left to a ledge and caves. Go through the overhang left of The Cross and continue leftwards to a thin crack and horizontal break, traversing left (crux) to finish. A direct start climbs the wall above the old fence at the same grade.

13   The Cross   20m   E1 5b *   (1975)
Good climbing. Follow Skirmish to the cave. Move right and follow the crack through the overhang to the top.

14   A Feet of Arms   20m   HVS 5b   (1976)
Some athletic moves in well protected situations. Start below a slanting crack about 8 metres right of the fence. Climb a wall to the base of the crack, then go up this and the wall on the right to a ledge, finishing up the deceptive wall.

DUNGLAS WEST FACE

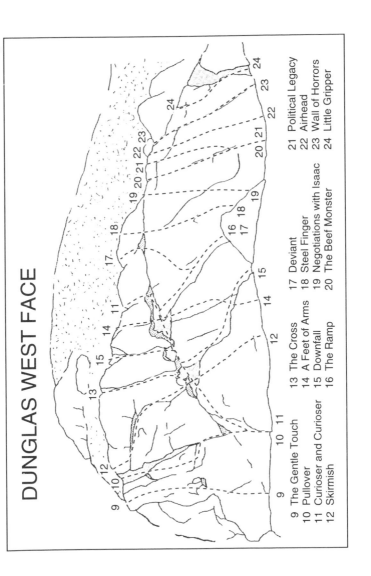

9 The Gentle Touch
10 Pullover
11 Curioser and Curioser
12 Skirmish
13 The Cross
14 A Feet of Arms
15 Downfall
16 The Ramp
17 Deviant
18 Steel Finger
19 Negotiations with Isaac
20 The Beef Monster
21 Political Legacy
22 Airhead
23 Wall of Horrors
24 Little Gripper

15   Downfall   35m   HVS 5b   (1975)
This follows the obvious left traverse line about 10 metres right of the old fence.
Climb up to the traverse and follow it to the cave. Traverse right past a narrowing
and a ledge and go over the overhang right of The Cross. Climb the wall trending
left to finish by a V-break and drooping spike.

16   The Ramp   13m   Moderate   (1975)
The slanting break right of Downfall provides easy access to the upper wall.

17   Deviant   15m   E1 5b *   (1987)
Interesting climbing. Follow The Ramp for a few metres until it is possible to get
established on a parallel ramp line above, which leads to a second cave.
Traverse right across the horizontal break to a niche, finishing above.

18   Steel Finger   15m   E3 6a *   (1991)
Start 2 metres right of The Ramp and climb the strenuous steep wall and thin
crack.

19   Negotiations With Isaac   15m   F6c *   (1992)
Climb directly up the left end of the overhanging wall via two bolts.

20   The Beef Monster   15m   F6c+ **   (1989)
Start right of Negotiations With Isaac at the base of a left-slanting crack. Climb
straight up past a horizontal break, move up and right, continue up a thin crack
to gain the niche-break, then go right and up the wall to the top.

21   Political Legacy   15m   F7b *   (1992)
Start up The Beef Monster, then follow two bolts and holds leftwards.

22   Airhead   15m   F7a **   (1992)
Tackle the bulging wall left of Wall of Horrors past two bolts.

An eliminate may be climbed at F6a/b between Airhead and Wall of Horrors.

23   Wall of Horrors   10m   E3 5c *   (1977)
Near the right-hand end of the face is an overhanging wall with a thin crack.
Climb up very steeply on good holds to a small niche and a jug. Continue past
a flake and through the easier overhang at the top. The main problem is hanging
on while getting the runners in.

24   Little Gripper   10m   VS 5a   (1975)
The overhanging rib right of Wall of Horrors. Climb the bulging wall to exit via a
jammed flake on the right. Traverse left, go up the wall to a ledge, then move up
and left to finish at a break.

25   Moss Flop   8m   Difficult   (1976)
The shallow corner right of Little Gripper, finishing right.

26   Last Grasp   8m   Severe   (1976)
Start at the blunt rib right of the last route. Climb the wall, step left to a block and finish up grass shelves.

27   A Dream of Brown Trousers   VS 5b   (1976)
A low level left to right girdle with interesting moves in entertaining positions. Climb to a height of 5m at the extreme left end. Follow a line to The Ramp then past shelves to some difficulties by Little Gripper and the crux beyond Moss Flop. Finish on grass.

CRAIGTON   *(Map Ref 517 766)*

Craigton is a pleasantly situated outcrop of rough basalt similar to Craigmore. Facing north-east it takes a couple of days to dry after summer rain. Most of the climbs are short, but seem longer due to the steep bank below. Unlike nearby Craigmore, peace and quiet are guaranteed.

The outcrop faces Hilton Park Golf Club, high on the west side of the A809 Glasgow to Drymen road. From the club car park the crag can be seen right of the wooded hillside and behind the electricity pylons. It is closer than it looks.

CRAIGTON QUARRY

The quarry at the left end of the crag contains one route.

Chasing the Dragon   E2 5c
The obvious finger crack in the steep slab in the top right-hand corner of the quarry.

MAIN CRAG

Jughandle Corner   4m   3b
At the left end of the outcrop is a small buttress topped by a wind-swept tree. Climb the short corner crack left of the alcove.

Elbow Crack   4m   4c
The crack in the alcove's left wall. Better in autumn!

Machiavelli's Crack   6m   5c *
The steep crack in the left side of the next buttress.

Jam Crack   4m   4b
The cracked corner on the right.

The Rasp   5m   4a
The painful wide crack on the left side of the next buttress.

Mantelshelf Wall   6m   5c
The mantelshelf and slab.

Hairy Mary   6m   5a *
The left-hand groove topped by a chockstone.

Easy Lady   6m   3a
The right-hand groove.

Two Hand Crack   4m   4b
Twin cracks up and further right.

Boa Constrictor   10m   4c
A tight off-width behind the flake.

Farewell Groove   10m   4c
The narrow ramp behind the flake.

The Screaming   12m   6a **
This takes the obvious line of weakness up the smooth wall left of The Clam.
Start beside a boulder and climb to a horizontal break. Continue up the crack
(crux), then go direct to the top. An easier variation avoids the crux by traversing
the break (5c).

The Clam   12m   5b **
The chimney-crack through the overhang.

Octopus   10m   5c **
The right end of the overhung recess leads to an off-width crack. Or, traverse
into the crack from the right (5b).

Chockstone Groove   4m   4a
The V-groove on the right.

Lone Tree Groove   3m   4a
The next crack.

Gremlin's Groove   10m   5b *
The overhanging groove further right. A bit nasty.

Lazy Layback   10m   3a
Some broken rock leads to the next buttress. This takes the broken groove and
wide layback crack.

Affront 10m 4c
Climb the rib and cracked arete further right.

Sidestep 10m 4c
Climb the crack on the left, step right and climb the crack above.

The Groove 10m 4c
Climb the big groove.

The Doddle 10m 5c **
A bulging wall is split by a sloping ledge. Climb the centre of the wall direct.

Two routes climb the broken rock to the right: **Isolated Buttress** (4b) is a thin groove, and **Deception** (4c), a small wall.

Deceiver 4m 5b
This is the obvious deep groove in the large block separated by deep cracks.

Shield Right Edge 4m 5b *
The right edge of the obvious shield-like flake gives surprisingly good climbing.

The small walls and cracks to the right are taken by: **Route 1**, (4b); **Route 2**, (2a); **Twisted Crack**, (4c); **Black Crack**, (5b); **Ledge Wall**, (4a); **Small Wall**, (4b) and **Small Wall Groove**, (4c). Their names are description enough.

CRAIGMORE   *(Map Ref 527 797)*

Solid rock and numerous routes throughout a wide variety of grades make this 10m to 15m escarpment one of the most popular outcrops in the Glasgow area. The rough basalt gives excellent friction (although some routes are becoming quite polished) with generally positive face holds but rounded cracks. However, it can be quite slippery when wet and the routes can get a bit dirty. The crag faces north-east and can be slow to dry after rain. Midges are rife in the summer.

A general lack of protection, especially on the harder routes means that solo climbing and top-roping has developed as the local ethic and accordingly, routes only have a technical grade. Leading is quite acceptable, but what isn't is the placing of bolts and pegs. Hopefully climbers will continue to remove them as soon as they appear. With more than 80 routes there is no excuse for cutting down "offending" trees for the sake of yet another scrappy and escapable problem.

From Glasgow take the A809 Glasgow-Drymen road. Just past the Carbeth Inn turn right and take the B821 Blanefield road for 1km. Park on the verge on the left by a stile; the crag is visible among trees to the left. By public transport take the Drymen bus from Glasgow Buchanan St Bus Station and walk from Carbeth Inn. The local farmer is understanding; please help to maintain this state of affairs.

THE CHIMNEY AREA

Following the path through the field, this is the first area reached and it marks the furthest left end of the crag. The most obvious feature is a body-sized chimney. Some poor and now overgrown routes have been made to its left, but the real climbing starts with:

1   Chimney Arete   8m   4c
The left arete of The Chimney.

2   The Chimney   8m   4a **
Climb the body-munching chimney, staggering leftwards to finish.

3   Polo   8m   5b
A problematic start gains the short crack right of The Chimney.

4   Polover   8m   6a *
Climb the wall just right of Polo via thin cracks and a long reach to finish.

5   Silver Arete   8m   4a *
Follow the arete right of Polo direct, then go up a slab and exit left.

6   Glug   8m   3b
The groove adjacent to Silver Arete, finishing up that route.

7   Grooved Arete   10m   4c *
Climb into the hanging groove right of Glug and gurgle up the arete to exit at tree. Or, if you've got an itch to scratch, start up the wide crack to the right (4b).

8   Kit Kat   10m   3b
Follow the obvious curving groove right of the block to a ledge, then the continuation groove above.

9   Legless   10m   6b *
Start just right of the Kit Kat groove and make hard moves up and then right to join Wide Eyed.

10   Wide Eyed   10m   6b ***
An excellent route up the zigzag crack. A long reach gains a horizontal break, marginal laybacking up the crack brings better holds, but not that quickly.

Mosca, Dumbarton Rock (Climber, Mark Ryle)

11   Harmless   10m   6a *
To the right a short crack leads to a rounded spike. Finish up the ramp of Arrowhead Left-Hand.

12   Arrowhead Left-Hand   10m   4b **
Right again is a small pinnacle. Start on its left side and climb left-slanting ramp to finish with a short left traverse. Continuing up the outside of the pinnacle from the ramp is 4a.

13   Arrowhead Right-Hand   10m   3b
Climb the wide crack on the right side of pinnacle.

14   Chimney Area Girdle   30m   4c
A low level traverse starting at Chimney Arete and finishing by a hand traverse of the block of Kit Kat.

MAIN AREA
This extends from the corner with what was once a healthy holly tree and is now just a stump, past a number of grooves to an obvious undercut boulder next to the path. The first route starts on the left wall of the corner with the tree stump.

15   Cariad   15m   5b
Takes the first crack line right of the pinnacle. Go up the wall to gain a shallow groove, climb this and the crack on the right, avoiding grass ledges.

16   Magic Crack   15m   5b **
The prominent crack in the wall left of Holly Tree Corner. An enjoyable direct finish is possible through the overhang on the right at the top of the corner.

17   Holly Tree Corner   15m   4b **
Climb the corner to the tree stump, step left onto the wall, then go diagonally left until it is possible to traverse right on the slab above the overlap. A fine airy finish can be had by traversing horizontally right below the overlap to finish up a short arete (4c).

18   The Beast   15m   5c ***
Start below the groove in the arete of Holly Tree Corner. Pull directly into the groove and follow this to a slab, finishing up the wall on the left, avoiding the right arete.

Leech Direct, Craigmore (Climber, Cameron Bell)

19   Slingsby's Crystal   15m   6a **
Climb the wall between the start of The Beast and Jolly Green Dragon (eliminate). Continue up the slab above (treating the eponymous crystal with care) without using the arete of the groove of The Beast. Finish directly up the upper wall using as few holds as possible. Amazingly, climbed by Slingsby in the early 1900s, but not recorded.

20   Jolly Green Dragon   15m   5c **
Start two metres right of The Beast. Gain the shallow groove without using the boulder and pull round right into a short finger crack. Make a hard move onto the ledge and finish up a short groove.
Variation: 15m   6a
Using any start that seems appropriate, climb the arete between Slingsby's Crystal and Jolly Green Dragon via a superb and unlikely rockover. Done properly it is quite independent.

21   Craigmore Corner   15m   5b ***
The classic of the crag, taking the big corner capped by an overhang. Climb the corner to the overhang, trend right and go up to a ledge, then finish up a groove. Alternative finishes go left of, or straight over, the overhang.

22   Tom and Jerry Wall   15m   5a ***
Another very fine route, with a problematic start. Start below the arete. Move up and left to reach a good pocket, then continue more easily up the wall to reach the arete. Finish up a short groove.

23   Rampage   15m   4b **
Start below a curving crack right of the arete. Go up and left to cracks, climb these and the ramp above to a large ledge overlooking Craigmore Corner. Traverse left to the arete on the skyline and finish up this.

24   Curving Groove   15m   5b *
Gain and climb the groove direct to join Rampage. Follow this and the groove above.

25   Hamilton's Arete   15m   6b ***
Climb the arete between Curving Groove and Daylight Robbery on its left side, finishing by a short crack. Delicate, fingery, technical and strenuous.

26   Daylight Robbery   12m   4c
The next mossy groove along is climbed all the way.

27   Basil Brush   12m   5b
Just right of the last route is an overhung vegetated niche. Climb this leftwards, then go back right into a narrow mossy groove. Or, from the slim groove on the ordinary route pull into and follow the slanting crack on the right to finish at the same grade.

CRAIGMORE – CHIMNEY AREA

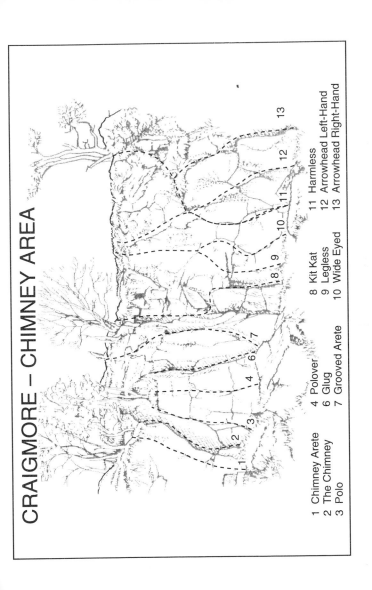

1 Chimney Arete
2 The Chimney
3 Polo

4 Polover
6 Glug
7 Grooved Arete

8 Kit Kat
9 Legless
10 Wide Eyed

11 Harmless
12 Arrowhead Left-Hand
13 Arrowhead Right-Hand

28   The Niche   10m   4c ***
Start just right of the last route below an obvious niche. Climb up into the niche, pull out right and climb cracks to a block, then layback to easier ground. An inferior finish is possible out left from the niche to join a sloping crack (5a).

29   Crib   10m   5a
Start below the small overlap right of The Niche by a rock scar. Climb to the easy-angled arete then go up this, avoiding the crack on the right.

30   Rampant   10m   4a *
Follow the ramp throughout; popular, polished and dirty.

31   Grotty Groove   10m   4a
Climb Rampant for 3m then go right onto a ledge, then climb the groove to the top. Not as popular or as polished, but dirtier!

32   Sunday Wall   12m   5b **
Start 2 metres right of Rampant. Climb the wall direct to a horizontal crack, then pull up the wall to the top. The horizontal crack can be traversed right (5b) to finish up the arete of Hot Dawg.

33   Hot Dawg   10m   5c
Right of Sunday Wall is a block. From the top of this gain a hold on the arete, then balance precariously up.

To the right is a horrible green groove, **Gregor's Groove** (4a), and right again a smaller pinnacle-like buttress. **Mirage** (4b) takes the crack on the left side of the buttress, and **Solo** (4b) the right arete and the arete above. The dirty broken groove to the right is **Nap** (3b).

LAYBACK CRACK AREA
Right of the undercut boulder is a fine wall which extends rightwards to a pinnacle split by an obvious hand jamming crack.

34   Terror   5m   5c **
A good problem up the overhung right arete of the boulder.

35   Bwana   13m   5b
Above the boulder and below and right of the beech tree is a wide blocky overhanging crack.

36   Spinal Wall   15m   5c **
Climb horizontal cracks in the wall right and above the overhung boulder and left of the White Hope groove.

CRAIGMORE – MAIN AREA

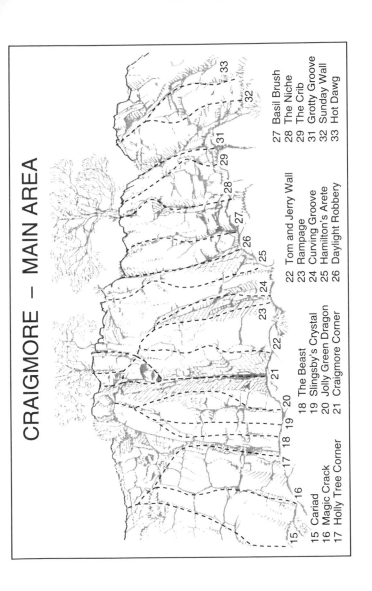

15 Cariad
16 Magic Crack
17 Holly Tree Corner
18 The Beast
19 Slingsby's Crystal
20 Jolly Green Dragon
21 Craigmore Corner
22 Tom and Jerry Wall
23 Rampage
24 Curving Groove
25 Hamilton's Arete
26 Daylight Robbery
27 Basil Brush
28 The Niche
29 The Crib
31 Grotty Groove
32 Sunday Wall
33 Hot Dawg

37   White Hope   15m   5c ***
The groove to the right is climbed until it is possible to move right to finish up the slanting crack of Layback Crack.
Variation: 15m   6a
It is possible to climb the wall between the arete and the groove direct from ground level.

38   Layback Crack   15m   5c ***
A popular classic taking the fine crack in the centre of the wall. Climb the strenuous flake crack, then make a hard move up and left for a jug. Finish up the left-slanting crack above. The True Finish takes the right-slanting finger crack at 6a ***, from where the normal route escapes left. The Superdirect still needs finishing off!

39   Craig's Wall   15m   6c ***
Climb directly up the wall right of Layback Crack to a good hold. Levitate up right to a desperate finish.

40   Crag Mate   12m   5a
About 5 metres right of Layback Crack is a brown sentry-box with a crack. Follow this and the left-slanting groove above.

41   Salamander   10m   5b
Start just right of Crag Mate. Climb into the scoop without using holds on adjoining routes, step up left and ascend the wall on the right to a rib and finish up this.

42   Not Another Eliminate   10m   6b *
Start as for Salamander, then go straight up over the overlap.

43   Samson   10m   5b
Start 2 metres right of Salamander, below a crack. Climb the crack to an inverted-V then go up into a groove.
Variation: 6b *
An excellent problem. Gain the inverted-V from the right.

44   Sabre Crack   8m   4c **
Climb the crack above the boulder and finish up the arete. The grade is lowered to 4b if the boulder is used.

45   Stiletto Crack   8m   4c **
Hand jam the crack to the right of Sabre Crack.

46   Rapier Arete   8m   5b
The arete just right of Stiletto Crack is climbed direct, avoiding both adjacent cracks.

CRAIGMORE – LAYBACK CRACK AREA

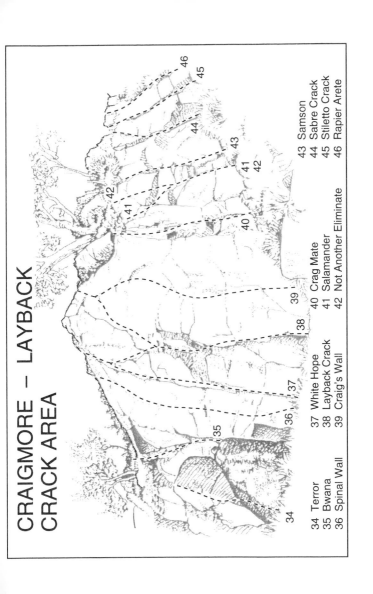

34 Terror
35 Bwana
36 Spinal Wall

37 White Hope
38 Layback Crack
39 Craig's Wall

40 Crag Mate
41 Salamander
42 Not Another Eliminate

43 Samson
44 Sabre Crack
45 Stiletto Crack
46 Rapier Arete

BLADE AREA

Right of Stiletto Crack is an area of more broken rock, then a large elliptical boulder known as The Blade, whose left and right sides have been climbed at 4a and 2a. Right again is another boulder taken by Tae a Moose, then an area of higher rocks bounded on the right by an arete.

47   White Streak   5m   5b
From the top of the Blade, climb the wall above trending left.

48   Preliminary Exercise   10m   5c
Climb the overhanging twin cracks right of White Streak without using the pinnacle.

49   Tae a Moose   3m   4a *
Climb the crack on the boulder below and right of The Blade.

50   Tic Tac   3m   5b
Climb the wall right of the previous route, only using the right-hand rib.

51   Bugs Bunny   6m   3b
Climb the foul gully behind the last two routes. For the desperate only.

52   Weasel   10m   5b
Start in the niche at the left end of the area of higher rocks. Pull up onto the left-sloping ramp. From its end move right onto the wall and go up to a ledge. Finish up the wall above.

53   Stoat   10m   5b *
Follow the previous route to a ledge above the niche, step right then go straight up to a ledge. Finish up the rib.

54   Autobahn   10m   5a **
Climb the nice groove in the centre of the wall to its top. Move left to another groove and finish up this.

55   All Hope   10m   5a **
Start just right of Autobahn at a crack. Climb this to a ledge on the right, step left and climb the groove and crack to the top.

56   Hendo's Obsession   8m   5c
Climb the arete then follow All Hope to the top.

57   Elk   6m   3a
Climb the mossy groove to the top.

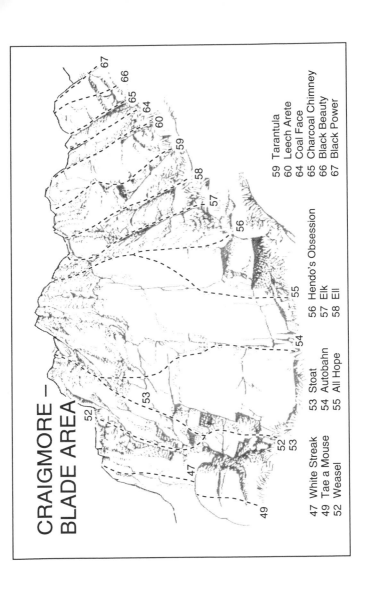

CRAIGMORE –
BLADE AREA

47 White Streak
49 Tae a Mouse
52 Weasel

53 Stoat
54 Autobahn
55 All Hope

56 Hendo's Obsession
57 Elk
58 Ell

59 Tarantula
60 Leech Arete
64 Coal Face
65 Charcoal Chimney
66 Black Beauty
67 Black Power

58   Ell   6m   4a
The crack and wall just right of the previous route; dirty.

59   Tarantula   6m   5b **
Just right of Ell is an obvious nose of rock above a steep scooped wall. Climb to the nose, pull over and continue up the groove above.

60   Leech Arete   6m   6b *
Pull onto the arete on the left via small holds and finish straight up.

61   Leech Direct   5m   6a **
Round and right is a short vertical wall. Climb the centre of this wall direct, avoiding holds on adjoining routes.

62   Leech   5m   5b *
The original line. Start up the corner of Eel, then hand traverse left to finish above the crux of the Direct.

63   Eel   5m   4c
Climb the corner to a hard finish.

64   Coal Face   5m   4b *
The cracked wall right of Eel.

65   Charcoal Chimney   5m   4a **
The prominent chimney.

66   Black Beauty   5m   5a **
The cracked wall right of the chimney, avoiding holds on that route.

67   Black Power   5m   4c
The arete right of Black Beauty.

68   Mat Black   3m   4b
The wall immediately right of the arete.

Going uphill from here the height of the crag decreases to about 3m. At the highest point of the path is a useful descent route. The small walls and corners give a variety of short problems as easy or as hard as desired.

LITTLE BUTTRESS
The path then leads downhill to the foot of a small buttress with two wide blocky cracks. The first route starts at the left side of the buttress halfway up.

69   East Wall   3m   5a
Move right onto the buttress from the grass, then go up to the top.

70   Pinnacle Wall   7m   4c **

Climb the face of the buttress, left of the double cracks, without straying from the straight and narrow.

71   Donald Duck   5m   4a

The left-hand crack.

72   Mickey Mouse   5m   4b

The right-hand crack.

73   Piglet   5m   5a

Climb the wall just right of Mickey Mouse, avoiding all holds on that route.

74   Pigs Ear   6m   5a

Start as for Piglet. After 1 metre move right to the arete and finish up this.

75   Silk Purse   6m   5b

Climb the start of the arete to Pigs Ear and finish up a slab; dirty.

76   West Wall   6m   5b

The wall right of the last route, finishing up the slab.

To the right are some unappetising vegetated grooves, best left to herbivores.

EXTREME RIGHT-HAND SLAB

Continuing rightwards a small buttress is passed (wot no routes?), then more broken rocks until after about 50 metres an obvious slab left of a pinnacle is encountered.

77   Tree Wall   5m   5a

Climb the short wall left of the slab, avoiding the right arete and the tree above.

78   Left Arete   10m   4b

Start left of the obvious crack in the slab. Pull up to gain the left edge of the slab, then follow the edge and the short wall above.

79   Cracked Slab   10m   3b *

Climb the obvious crack splitting the slab, taking the right-hand branch to finish up the wall above to the left.

80   The Slab   10m   4a **

Climb cracks in the slab right of the large crack of Cracked Slab, avoiding the right edge and the crack on the left. Finish up the wall above at its highest point.

81   Right Arete   6m   4a

Pull up to gain the right edge of the slab, then climb this direct.

82   Cave Route   5m   3a ***
Just right of the slab is a short chimney. The cave inside gives an underground excursion, or you could just climb the chimney. No place for fatties.

83   Slab Traverse   12m   4a
Start as for Tree Wall. Climb the wall for a few moves, gain the arete on the right, traverse right across the slab to Right Arete and finish up this.

84   The Wizard   6m   6b ***
Powerful and impressive climbing up the left arete of the flat-topped pinnacle right of the slab. Starting from the top of the chockstone in the short chimney reduces the grade to 6a.

85   Tarot   6m   3b
The right edge of the pinnacle.

Right of the pinnacle is an unattractive short wall with some routes recorded at 4a and 3b; climb at will.

86   Suzy Q   6m   5b
Some 4 metres right of the pinnacle is an arete right of an obvious wide crack. Step on to the ledge from below, then follow the crack above.

87   Victory V   5m   4c
About 3 metres right of Suzy Q is a grotty crack with boulders at its base. Pull out onto the capped block on the right of the crack (without using the back wall or standing on the block), then go up and over the block above.

88   Wopitee   5m   5b
Start below the obvious roofed niche to the right of Victory V. Bridge up and gain the wall above the roof, then continue directly to top.

89   Expo   5m   5b
Follow the right edge of the niche to reach flat holds above. Finish up left edge, avoiding vertical cracks. Or start in the niche and traverse horizontally right (5b), or climb the wall below the tree stump, avoiding the left arete and the crack on the right (5a).

90   Toad   8m   4c
Climb the crack below and right of Two Tree Wall to reach a ledge. Finish up the wall above.

91   Rizla   3m   3a
Just right of the final wall of Toad is a groove. Climb it.

92   Amphitheatre Girdle   15m   5a
This wall has been girdled starting from the short wall right of Tarot, crossing Suzy Q and going below the roof of Wopitee (crux), then round the corner and right below the tree stump.

PINE TREE BOULDERS
Some 15 metres right is a pile of scattered boulders below a Scots Pine which give assorted bouldering and routes, of which the best are:

93   Vanguard   3m   5a
Climb the narrow wall just left of the wide crack above the three-tiered slab.

94   Sunshine Arete   3m   5a *
Below the Scots Pine is a fine arete which is climbed direct. The slabby left wall of the arete gives a thin and fingery 6a if holds on adjoining routes are avoided.

95   Sunburn   3m   3a
The pile of blocks right of Sunshine Arete is climbed on the left-hand side.

96   Jamie's Overhang   3m   6a **
The cave-like overhanging wall opposite Sunshine Arete can be climbed by starting in the centre at an incut on the lip. A problem with a secret! The overhanging nose to the left is 5c.

PILLAR CRAG   *(Map Ref 541 795)*

This small but enjoyable crag of columnar basalt offers generally well protected crack climbing. It faces north, but is lichen-free and dries quickly. Although a good alternative to crowded Craigmore, it is rarely climbed on. This is a pity considering the average Scots climber's inability to climb cracks! Most routes can be top-roped.

   The crag lies in trees on the south side of the B821 about 1km east of Craigmore, before the winding descent into Blanefield. There is a small parking place on the north side of the road on the edge of the wood. The crag lies opposite and is reached by crossing a marshy field and scrambling through the trees.

In the Groove   4m   5a
The first groove at the left-hand end.

Moss Crack   5m   2b
The broad crack.

Keystone Corner   4m   2a
The jammed boulder corner.

Serpent's Chimney   6m   4a
The obvious chimney, finishing left,

The Ride   6m   5a *
The arete to the right of the Serpent's Chimney.

Twin Roots Chimney   6m   3b
The next chimney on the right, with a low chockstone.

Club Foot   10m   6a *
The thin cracks right of Twin Roots Chimney.

Butterfingers   10m   5c **
The fine thin crack.

The Slot   10m   5a *
Right again is a corner crack with a hard start.

Sidestep Wall   10m   5a
The next thin corner.

The Horror   10m   5b
Climb one of two jam cracks to a ledge, then the groove above on the left.

Melting Pot   12m   4c **
An expanding jam crack on the right leads to a higher ledge and a chimney.

Pinnacle Chimney Direct   10m   4b
A groove followed by a crack on the left.

Pinnacle Chimney   10m   3a
Climb the right side of the pinnacle and the groove above.

Damocles Groove   10m   4c *
Follow the groove below the single poised block. This is a good reference point for starting to locate the climbs.

Pillar Groove   10m   5a *
The groove right of the poised block.

Candle Snuffer   10m   3b
An apt name for the chimney formed by three large sections of column.

Pillar Front   10m   5a
Climbs the front edge of the fallen column.

Chockstone Chimney Direct   10m   4b
The left of two cracks leads to a chimney right of the fallen column. The right-hand crack is 5a.

Mick   10m   3b
A wide pod-shaped crack.

Lurcher's Chimney   10m   4c
The nasty-looking inverted-V groove.

Manky Crack   10m   4b
A crack with a small tree.

The broken area on the right is taken by two routes; **Grand Slam** (5a) and **Fingerlicker** (5c).

Avalanche Chimney   10m   4c
A wide crack right of the broken rock, with a tree at the top.

Cracker Crack   10m   4c **
A cracking jam crack.

Hiroshima Groove   10m   5b **
The smooth groove.

Twiggy's Crack   10m   3b
Climb the crack right of the tree, then the cracked groove on the left.

Up and right are three dirty grooves: **Woody Groove** (2a); **Thunder Block Groove** (2b); and **Pinnacled Groove** (4a).

Right-Hand Crack   4m   4b **
A good short jamming crack.

Right-Hand Wall   4m   4c
The wall right of the crack.

THE WHANGIE   *(Map Ref 496 806)*

Only Ben An bears comparison to The Whangie's inspirational outlook across Stockie Muir to Loch Lomond and the Southern Highlands. Situated on the flanks of Auchineden Hill, the crag faces west and gets a lot of sun, making it particularly enjoyable on summer evenings.

A unique basalt outcrop, The Whangie is similar to Craigton and Slackdhu, but, unlike these areas, the faces have been cleaved from the hillside to form interesting pinnacles and ridges. In 1892 the cragging pioneer Gilbert Thomson described the rock at The Whangie as "rather treacherous, being mainly shaky". His words ring true today and care should be taken when leading or soloing.

The popular routes are generally the more stable and better protected crack lines, the faces often being steep, a bit loose and quite bold. All the hard routes should be approached with great caution. Unfortunately a lack of finishing belays makes top-roping extremely difficult in places.

From Glasgow take the A809 Drymen road to Queen's View car park (Map Ref 511 807). From here, follow the path up and around the hillside for about 25 minutes to a high point at a small tree and a rock-step. Descend to a lower path (muddy) and the crag is reached in a further 5 minutes.

THE GENDARME

This is the first group of pinnacles met when approaching on the path from the north. In 1892 Gilbert Thomson and companions made the "first ascent" of The Whangie by throwing a rope over The Gendarme and "ascending" the wall right of Heartbreak Corner.

The first routes are on the Inside Face and are described from right to left. The face gets some sun at midday and the rock is slabby and pleasantly solid, but a bit polished in places.

1   Spider Slab   4m   Severe 4a
Rather artificial climbing up the short slabby wall at the north end of The Gendarme.

2   Blaeberry Crack   4m   Very Difficult
Climb the line of polished holds left of Spider Slab.

3   Mossy Slab, Right   4m   Severe *
A deceptive route, climbed mainly on small holds.

4   Mossy Slab, Left   4m   Difficult **
Straightforward and pleasant.

5   Staircase Crack   4m   Easy
A convenient descent route.

6   The Bulge   4m   Hard Severe 4b *
The small bulge left of Staircase Crack gives a technical high step.

7   Bird's Nest   5m   Very Difficult ***
An obvious line of good holds lead left above the prominent slanting corner.

8   Red Crack   5m   Very Difficult
Follow the slanting corner to an awkward steepening and finish right. A direct start can be made up polished red holds below the steepening (**Red Slab**, Very Difficult), or to the left again, (**Windswept Wall**, Severe 4a), or via the corner left of Upturned Flake and a right traverse (**Upturned Left**, Very Difficult).

9   Upturned Flake   5m   HVS 5a *
Start immediately left of the edge. Thin moves lead to a good undercut, then climb the smooth wall and crack in the headwall.

The next routes are on the Outside Face of The Gendarme, again described from right to left. This face gets the afternoon and evening sun, but the rock requires care.

10   Angel Corner   7m   HVS 5a
Climb the right arete of The Gendarme.

11   Angel Direct   6m   HVS 5a *
The corner left of the arete gives a short sharp shock.

12   Heartbreak Corner   5m   E1 5b **
Smear and layaway up the fine corner in the middle of the face, until it is possible to move right and up past loose rock. Steep and technical.

13   Knife Edge   5m   E2 5b
A long reach and crank should solve this problem up the arete immediately left of Heartbreak Corner.

14   Hangover Overhang   5m   VS 4b
Poor climbing up the poorly-defined curving corner left of Knife Edge.

15   Whodunnit   5m   E2 5c
Not many; not surprising. The steep blocky wall left of Hangover Overhang may have already lost all the essential holds.
Variation: 5m   5c
Climb the bulging broken rib to the left, avoiding the boulder and holds on the left.

16   Trench Wall   5m   Very Difficult *
A slabby start up the detached flake leads to a steep juggy finish on the wall above.

17   Barrowland Bulge   4m   Severe 4a
Athletic moves overcome the bulging wall left of the gap.

18   Backsnapper Crack   4m   Very Difficult
The wide crack dividing the two small pinnacles gives a poor loose route.

19   Gendarmerie   25m   4a
A low-level circumnavigation of The Gendarme, clockwise from Spider Slab.

NUMBER ONE FACE

The west face of the main crag faces Loch Lomond and has some excellent steep routes and a number of horror shows. The Lomond faces of the boulders in front of the cliff have a few short problems.

20   Triangle   3m   VS 4c *
At the north end of the face is a small triangular wall. A good finger pocket starts a strenuous sequence.

21   Thin Crack   4m   VS 5a
Right of Triangle is a thin finger crack. A difficult start leads to a loose finish.

22   Finger Exercise   8m   E1 5b
Climb the blunt arete to finish just left of Recess Route.

23   Recess Route   8m   VS 4b *
A good exciting line, though with some loose rock. Gain the obvious recess and swing left and up.

24   Cave Crack   10m   VS 4c
Follow the chimney, which narrows to a crack. Climb a gently overhanging wall to finish more easily.

25   Grim Wall   10m   HVS 5a
From the lowest point of the wall climb up and right to a ledge. Gain the arete, then swing left and finish up poor rock.

26   Sou'West Rib   10m   Very Difficult
Loose rock abounds on the rounded arete at the end of this section of the face.

27   Snowy Traverse   12m   4a
A low-level traverse going left from the start of Sou'West Rib.

28   Cave Chimney   10m   Very Difficult *
The wide chimney right of the arete leads past a small cave and chockstone.

29   Easy Chimney   8m   Difficult
To the right is a large open chimney.

30   Easy Wall   7m   Very Difficult
Climb the short wall right of the chimney by a choice of lines.

31   Easy Groove   7m   Difficult
Useful for beginners or as a descent route. Climb the polished left-slanting groove.

THE WHANGIE – LEFT-HAND SECTION

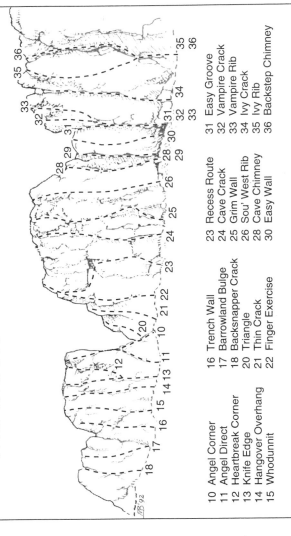

10 Angel Corner
11 Angel Direct
12 Heartbreak Corner
13 Knife Edge
14 Hangover Overhang
15 Whodunnit

16 Trench Wall
17 Barrowland Bulge
18 Backsnapper Crack
20 Triangle
21 Thin Crack
22 Finger Exercise

23 Recess Route
24 Cave Crack
25 Grim Wall
26 Sou' West Rib
28 Cave Chimney
30 Easy Wall

31 Easy Groove
32 Vampire Crack
33 Vampire Rib
34 Ivy Crack
35 Ivy Rib
36 Backstep Chimney

32   Vampire Crack   10m   VS 4c **
Start up Easy Groove, but continue up the curving hand and fist crack. Popular and well protected.

33   Vampire Rib   10m   HVS 4c
Climb to the base of Ivy Crack, place a high runner, then traverse right onto the arete and continue to the top. Short and a bit eliminate.

34   Ivy Crack   10m   Hard Severe 4b ***
A superb route, one of the best climbs at The Whangie. The prominent steep corner crack capped by a chockstone is technically interesting, sustained and well protected.

35   Ivy Rib   10m   E1 5a
Serious climbing on poor rock with little protection. Follow Backstep Chimney for a few moves, then make a committing traverse left on rattly holds and follow a wall and rib of deteriorating rock.

36   Backstep Chimney   12m   Hard Severe 4b **
A classic of its kind, the key is in the name. The moves are polished and a bit brutal, but thankfully quite short! Finish up the pleasant chimney.

.37   Backbreak Wall   13m   VS 4c
Gain the small sloping ledge on the wall to the right. Climb the bulge above on creaking holds, traverse left and finish up Backstep Chimney. Continuing up the poorly protected exfoliating wall pushes the grade to E2 5a (Horror Route!)

Just to the right is a steep bulging wall with a thin crack, previously taken by the aid route **Bluebottle**. The previous edition of this guide describes the route as free at E2 5b. This seems unlikely, and the present writer invites stronger and more talented climbers to settle the question.

38   Sudden Death   15m   E3 6a   (1985)
Rarely climbed, let alone led. Steep, strenuous and friable with poor protection, what more could you ask for? About 6 metres right of Backstep Chimney is a thin curving crack with a peg stump in it. Follow this for about 4m to a move left on dubious rock to a high jug. Continue up the crack line, past a sapling to a loose rightward finish. Belay on the pathetic "tree".

39   Flakealong   10m   Severe 4a
A low-level traverse going right from the foot of the large prominent flake right of Sudden Death.

THE WHANGIE – RIGHT-HAND SECTION

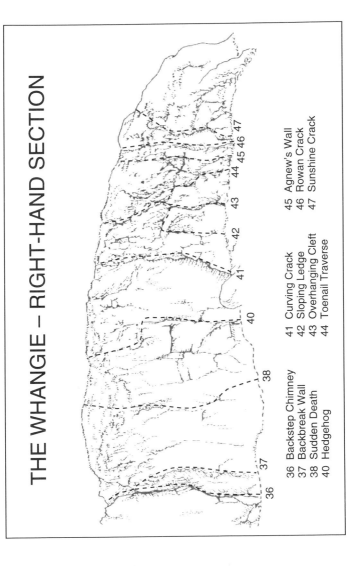

36 Backstep Chimney
37 Backbreak Wall
38 Sudden Death
40 Hedgehog

41 Curving Crack
42 Sloping Ledge
43 Overhanging Cleft
44 Toenail Traverse

45 Agnew's Wall
46 Rowan Crack
47 Sunshine Crack

40   Hedgehog   15m   E2 5c *
The crack to the right below the *in situ* tat is the most amenable of the hard routes, but even then it's not to be sniffed at - it might fall down! Strenuous climbing leads past a reasonable peg to a suspicious spike. Commit yourself to this and continue up protectable cracks to the pegs and tat. Lower off or grunt past another peg to the top. Belay on the right (Friend $3\frac{1}{2}$ useful). The second is advised to stand well away from the route.

41   Curving Crack   15m   HVS 5a ***
Good climbing. A corner leads to the striking curved crack. Step right onto the white rib, move up to a ledge, then go left and over a bulge to finish (Friend $3\frac{1}{2}$ useful for belay).

42   Sloping Ledge   15m   Hard Severe 4b *
A crack splits the white wall right of Curving Crack. Climb this to the sloping ledge, traverse right and climb the exposed left-slanting fault on dubious holds.

43   Overhanging Cleft   10m   HVS 5a *
Jam and bridge up the technical bulging crack. Move left and finish up the left-slanting fault of Sloping Ledge.

44   Toenail Traverse   12m   VS 4c
Climb ledges on small holds and move left to finish as for Overhanging Cleft.

45   Agnew's Wall   10m   VS 4b
Start as for Toenail Traverse, then climb a right-trending crack to a holdless slab. Finish up the bulging wall.

46   Rowan Rib   8m   VS 4c **
Dynamic climbing up the rib left of Sunshine Crack leads to a traverse right to finish.

47   Sunshine Crack   8m   VS 4c *
A deceptive little number. Enter the recess and climb the crack above.

NUMBER TWO FACE
Although the rock is quite solid, the sunless "back side" of the main crag is dark and dank, and understandably the least popular bit of rock at The Whangie. The routes are described from left to right.

48   Be-Bop   7m   Very Difficult *
Starting about 4 metres in from the south end of the passage, climb a small wall on good holds to a groove.

49   Monk's Wall   7m   E1 5b
Climb the steep wall on the right to a sharp pocket, the finish up and left.

50   Ladybird Layback   8m   Very Difficult *
Follow the obvious right-slanting ramp.

51   Ladybird Direct   7m   E1 5b
This climbs the left arete of the large overhung recess, finishing as for the normal route (a bit artificial).

52   Militant Tendency   7m   E1 5b
Follow the crack at the back of the large overhung recess to a roof, pull left and finish up Ladybird Layback.

53   Nocibur Wall   10m   VS 4b **
A good interesting route. Bridge up between the two walls at the narrowest part of the passage, transferring onto the left wall to finish.

54   Ruth's Route   10m   VS 4c **
About 2 metres right of the narrowing, where the path rises, a line of holds lead to a thin crack. Step left and up to finish.

55   Whippenwoof Wall   10m   Severe 4a *
Starting just right of the last route, climb a shallow groove to a ledge, followed by a wall.

56   Gremlin Groove   10m   Very Difficult *
Pleasant climbing up the obvious groove 5 metres right of the narrows in the passage.

57   Mantelshelf Wall   10m   Severe 4a *
To the right, the path starts to level off. Climb the broad rib, with an interesting move to gain a large hold on the left a few moves up.

58   Varsity Groove   10m   Very Difficult
Start at the same place as Mantelshelf Wall, but move right into a shallow groove. Follow this to a grass ledge finishing up poor rock.

59   McBain's Wall   10m   VS 4c **
Some 10 metres right of the narrows in the passage is a steep crack. Gain a handhold with difficulty and climb slabby rock on the left past a spike to easier ground. The easier original line started to the left.

60   Rowan Tree Groove   12m   Difficult *
Good holds lead up the obvious right-slanting groove on the left side of an arete.

61   Fallen Tree Arete   12m   Very Difficult *
Make a difficult move onto the right-facing arete to finish more easily.

62   Fallen Tree Groove   12m   Severe 4a
Above where the path starts to descend and right of the arete is a corner. Climb it, awkward at the top, finishing through vegetation.

63   Young's Route   12m   Severe 4a *
About 3 metres right of Fallen Tree Groove is a nose of rock above smooth wavy rock. Climb the slabby wall to the left of the nose, step right and finish up the wall.

64   Allison's Route   12m   VS 4b *
The path starts to level out about 5 metres to the right of the nose of Young's Route. This route climbs the steep wall between the sections of wavy rock, moving right at the top to a vegetated finish.

65   Ripple Wall   12m   HVS 5a
Start as for Allison's Route. Climb the left edge of the smooth wavy rock to join Allison's Route at the top.

66   Long John's Wall   12m   HVS 5a
Sustained climbing on small holds up the steep wall with a thin crack, where the path starts to rise towards The Gap.

67   Hutch's Route   8m   Severe
Right of Long John's Wall the angle eases; climb the wall.

68   Needle Route   7m   Moderate
Climb the arete left of the wide crack which forms the descent route from Backstep Chimney.

The following routes lie on the buttress right of The Gap.

69   Novice Overhang   6m   Difficult
Climb the steep rib left of a prominent recess on good holds.

70   Novice Crack   6m   Moderate
Grassy climbing up the wide crack on the left side of the detached pillar.

71   Jughandle Arete   7m   Moderate
Pleasant climbing on good holds up the prominent arete 6 metres right of the recess.

72   Arrowhead Arete   15m   Difficult
Follow the arete dividing Number One and Number Two Face.

73 Tidemark 45m E1 5a
A girdle of Number Two Face.

NUMBER THREE FACE

A number of routes have been recorded on the loose slimy front face of Auchineden Hill. They were fully documented in the previous edition of this guide; if you're that keen to climb here you can probably dig up a copy from the local library. The wall is best left to the adventurous or sad of heart. However, a low level traverse of the face gives some 60 metres of 5b entertainment.

SLACKDHU *(Map Ref 558 816)*

The crags on this south-facing dolerite escarpment provide the only worthwhile climbing in the Campsies. Much of the rock is inherently unstable (like The Whangie), but it gets much less traffic, so great care should be taken. Coffin Gully is the deep black cleft in the centre of the main face above Blanefield. Lower and to the right is a small compact crag, Jenny's Lum, which gives the most stable climbing hereabouts. The outlook is suburban stockbroker belt, but very fine. Definitely worth a visit on a lazy Sunday afternoon.

Park at the war memorial in Blanefield, near the start of Campsie Dene Road (Map Ref 556 767). Follow the road to open hillside, and the crag can be seen up and on the right at the lowest part of the escarpment. The prominent two-tier crag at the right end is The Black Craig; it is very loose.

Jenny's Lum Arete 10m Hard Severe 4b *
The arete and crack to the right give an excellent route.

Tendons 10m HVS 5a (1992)
Follow the broken twin cracks in the wall 2 metres right of the arete.

Rusty Pegs 10m HVS 5a
About 2 metres left of the waterfall is an obvious crack-chimney line, normally fern-filled in summer.

To the right of the waterfall are broken buttresses, then a prominent pinnacle with an obvious block-filled chimney on its left.

Blocker 8m Severe 4a (1992)
Bridge up the large chimney, climb the pinnacle on the right and make an exciting step back to terra firma.

Classic Crack 8m Severe 4a (1992)
The crack in the pinnacle right of the chimney.

Pinnacle Arete 8m Severe 4a *
Climb the arete face of the pinnacle.

About 40 metres further right is another smaller tower called Jacob's Ladder.

Jacob's Crack   5m   VS 4b
The mossy crack.

Moss Kills   5m   Very Difficult   (1992)
Climb the broken right side of the pinnacle.

A number of routes have been climbed in this area over the years, but only the best are described above. Other scrambling and bouldering possibilities exist. Two traditional routes, which combine loose and wet rock and turf in equal measures, climb the main face left of Jenny's Lum. **The Long Gully** (135m Moderate) takes the first prominent gully right of Dumgoyne. **Coffin Gully Buttress** (75m Very Difficult) takes a line to the left of Coffin Gully.

AUCHINSTARRY QUARRY   *(Map Ref 719 771)*

Once one of the best quarries within easy reach of Glasgow, recent "safety" work by the local council has left large parts of Auchinstarry vandalised from the climbing point of view. However, things are not quite as black as it seemed at first. Following an accident involving loose rock, the council's insurers requested that work be done to make the quarry safer for climbing. Despite consultation with MCofS and SMC representatives, who made clear requests and recommendations on how to implement the planned work with minimum impact on the better routes, a number of important climbs have been lost. The classic test pieces Balance of Power and Knife Edge (to name but two) are no more, and a host of excellent middle grade routes such as Fusion and Sandman now lie in rubble. Taking Monty Python's advice to "always look on the bright side of life", it must be said that the climbs near the car park remain mostly unaffected, and that some of the destroyed climbs in the main quarry have been re-established as worthwhile routes.

The quarry faces south, and still offers some excellent climbing, including some hard test-pieces. The quartz-dolerite rock dries quickly after rain and allows climbing for most of the year. The original landscaping has produced a pleasant atmosphere which is enjoyed by climbers, fishermen and others who come to while away the hours. The best of the climbs that remain are on sound clean rock, although loose holds may be found even on popular climbs. Once the ground at the top of the crag has dried out in summer there is a tendency for sand to trickle down some areas and collect on the holds. For this reason, a few of the harder climbs are best brushed before an attempt. In general, good protection is available with an average rack of nuts and Friends, but some routes require large numbers of micro nuts. There is a risk that the council may decide that further safety work is required, so visitors should be aware that the validity of the descriptions that follow may be temporary.

The quarry is on the southern outskirts of Kilsyth. There are a multitude of approaches, but from Glasgow it is probably best to take the M8 eastwards, then the M80 and A80 towards Stirling. At the first roundabout after the Moodiesburn traffic lights, an exit onto the B8048 leads to a confusion of roundabouts; follow the signs to Croy and Kilsyth. Once through the obstacle course that comprises the main street of Croy, turn right at the junction, go down the hill and over the bridge; the quarry is just off a nasty left-hand bend. The nearest rail station is at Croy (2km), while Kilsyth is served by bus from Buchanan Street.

A number of fine routes start straight from the car park. Those in the main section of the quarry must be reached by scrambling down. The best descents are down the broken ground left of Stir Crazy and the slopes to the right of Dream Machine. Helmets are a sensible precaution as the younger locals frequently toss stones and other rubbish over the top.

The climbs are described starting in the Promontory area, which rises above the car park. They include some of the best in the quarry. At the far west end of the car park is a tree-shrouded bay. A path goes up to the top from the left end of the tapering wall. The left end of this wall provides a number of short problems, but they are steadily becoming overgrown. The first real route is the corner at the junction of the tapering wall and what becomes the main face.

1 Green Onion   10m   HVS 5b   (1980)
Climb the groove and corner.

2 I-Spy   10m   E2 5c *   (1980)
Start up Green Onion, then gain and climb the curving flake. Subtract one point if you touched the ledges on the left.

3 Mr Men   10m   VS 4b **   (1980)
A serious lead up the delightful short arete on good holds.

4 First Footer   15m   E1 5c **   (1978)
The fine clean open groove to the right of the dirty corner gives an enjoyable problem with a delicate reach in the lower section, but the finish is on poor rock.

5 Access Route   15m   Difficult ***
The rib and groove left of the smooth slab gives a splendid climb, popular with beginners.

The smooth slab itself can be climbed direct at 5c by those with blinkers. The flake crack to its right is taken by:

6 Scream   15m   Hard Severe 4b   (1977)
The crack gives interesting and well protected climbing.

7 Anarchist   15m   Very Difficult
The obvious line up the broken buttress right of Scream, passing a small tree.

8   Tar   15m   Severe   (1976)
Climb Anarchist for 5m, then trend right to the top.

9   Knock Back   15m   E1 5b **   (1977)
The slabby corner right of Tar is climbed to an overhang at half-height. Break left
and follow the shallow groove and crack with interest.

10   Slinky Lizard   15m   Hard Severe 4b *   (1977)
This steady route follows the slabby corner all the way to the top.

The buttress on the corner provides some of the best and most technical
routes in the quarry. The most prominent line is the fine arete of Nijinski.

11   Cat's Whiskers   15m   E2 5b
Start below the tree, 5 metres left of the arete. Climb cracks to a step right near
the top. Either traverse to finish up the arete or climb more directly to the tree
stump.

12   Death is the Hunter   15m   E4 6b ***   (1980s)
Brilliant technical climbing, best brushed before a sight lead. First arrange
protection (RP3) in a tiny crack level with the crux, by leaning across from an
horizontal break after the first few moves of Cat's Whiskers. Start at the bottom
of the faint arete. The fun soon begins. A series of humorous moves up the
apparently blank wall may lead to an awkward mantel onto the first real holds.
Climb the thin crack above (numerous small wires) and finish direct.

13   Nijinski   15m   E5 6a ***   (1982)
Another tremendous route. Balance up the bold arete to a good hold, then move
up and left to the thin crack of Death is the Hunter. Fill this with small wires, step
back down, then move up and right to the arete. The bold and committing
climbing above (crux) is best finished direct.

The next four routes share a common start up the groove some 4 metres right
of the arete.

14   Blade Runner   15m   E4 6a **   (1980s)
This takes the wall right of Nijinski. Climb the groove to a good ledge at its top.
Continue briefly up the wall of Promontory Direct to arrange protection, then
descend to just below the good ledge. Swing left below the small overlap and
mantelshelf with difficulty to a reasonable rest. The short thin crack above takes
up to five good micro wires. A difficult sequence leads to much easier climbing
for the last few feet. If you can climb the thin direct start (6b) and continue straight
over the overlap without deviation, award yourself five points.

15   Promontory Runner   15m   E4 6b   (1989)
An almost circular variation. Climb Blade Runner to the rest by the small wires,
then crank up and right to join Promontory Direct.

AUCHINSTARRY QUARRY – CAR PARK AREA

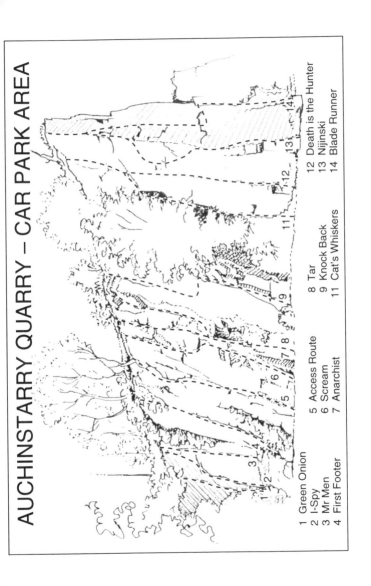

1 Green Onion
2 I-Spy
3 Mr Men
4 First Footer

5 Access Route
6 Scream
7 Anarchist

8 Tar
9 Knock Back
11 Cat's Whiskers

12 Death is the Hunter
13 Nijinski
14 Blade Runner

16   Promontory Direct   15m   HVS 5a ***   (1976)

An excellent route. Follow Blade Runner to the good ledge, then make a couple of awkward moves up the wall above. Step left and climb the prominent hand crack, which is set in a little corner in its lower half.

Right again is a thin crack which gives a good 5c extended boulder problem which leads to the good ledge of Promontory Direct. The same point may be reached by an easy scramble round to the right, an alternative start to the next climb.

17   Spirogyra   15m   VS 4c   (1976)

Follow Blade Runner to the good ledge, climb the short wall of Promontory Direct, then move up to ledges which lead right across the overhanging wall. Where they stop, climb a short awkward groove to the top.

18   Carouselambra   15m   E5 6b **   (1980s)

The obvious crack in the overhanging wall below Spirogyra gives a desperate problem with overhead protection, although most normal mortals will be faced with a choice between ethics and runner placements. After reaching the huge hold at half-height (unaccountably savaged by council navvies), somewhat easier climbing leads left and up to the last moves of Spirogyra.

A route has been climbed which starts from the top of the tree below the traverse of Spirogyra, hand traverses right to join and follow Carouselambra for a short distance, then finishes up and rightwards up the wall (**In Through the Out Door**, E5 6a, 1993). To the right of Carouselambra the rock becomes greener and poorer. While they may once have been fine outings, the older climbs here are in a poor state and may now be much harder than when they were first graded (which was presumably after a thorough cleaning). Public spirited enthusiasts are invited to return them to their former glory.

19   Fish Rising   E2 5b

Climb the green arete right of the open groove right of Carouselambra.

20   Twilight Zone   15m   E4 6a *   (1992)

This route climbs the sharp arete right of Fish Rising directly past a peg runner, making the crux move to finish onto an easy slab.

21   Tit for Tat   E2 5c

Climb the shallow groove capped by an overhang, round to the right of Twilight Zone.

22   The Surf Shack   15m   E5 6b   (1992)

Start next to the corner of the old building. Climb with difficulty past two peg runners to reach a jug. Make another hard move to reach better holds and a welcome runner. Finish awkwardly and strenuously.

AUCHINSTARRY QUARRY – MASCARADE BUTTRESS

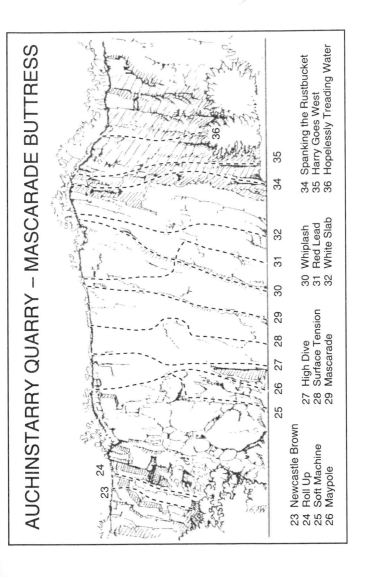

23 Newcastle Brown
24 Roll Up
25 Soft Machine
26 Maypole

27 High Dive
28 Surface Tension
29 Mascarade

30 Whiplash
31 Red Lead
32 White Slab

34 Spanking the Rustbucket
35 Harry Goes West
36 Hopelessly Treading Water

The dank overgrown section behind the building has been climbed by a number of routes, but they are in such a poor state that they are not worth describing. Once out of the trees, a rather better buttress lies up on the left.

23   Newcastle Brown   15m   E1 5b   (1978)
A steep slabby wall about 20 metres right of the building is split by two cracks. Climb the left-hand crack and the awkward groove above finish on recently-exposed rock.

24   Roll Up   15m   VS 4c
The obvious layback crack, joining Newcastle Brown for a step before finishing on the right.

To the right is a large area of recent excavation, with debris descending to the water's edge.

25   Soft Machine   20m   E2 5c   (1978)
Scramble a few metres at water level to a ledge beneath a shallow groove. Climb the groove (poorly protected) to a roof, then step right to join Maypole. A serious route, at the upper limit of its grade.

26   Maypole   20m   HVS 4c   (1976)
Right again is a short vertical groove. Climb it to a ledge, over an awkward bulge to a small ledge. Move left to finish up the groove above. Poorly protected.

27   High Dive   25m   E3 5c *   (1980s)
Gain the slim groove starting at water level at the left end of the smooth wall. Climb the groove to a ledge (RP2 runner) then make a very long and frightening reach up and right to better holds. Finish directly.

The next six routes are on Mascarade Buttress. They are approached by a low level traverse from the right.

28   Surface Tension   25m   E5 6b ***   (1980s)
An awe-inspiring pitch taking the centre of the smooth wall, which is best brushed on abseil before an attempt. Traverse in above the water to a tiny stance and belay at the foot of a long groove (Mascarade). Move left below an overlap, and make hard moves up to a peg. Lunge up and right to a resting place. Step left and up (small wires), then climb the centre of the wall to the top. Leaders contemplating a swim may be reassured to learn that local urchins have been known to jump from the top (yes, the water's deep enough).

Hedgehog, The Whangie (Climber, Ron Stevenson)

29   Mascarade   25m   E1 5c   (1975)
Approach as for Surface Tension and climb the long vertical groove in the centre of the buttress. Variations are possible on the right wall.

30   Whiplash   25m   E1 5b   (1976)
The smaller bottomless groove right of Mascarade. Climb to the top of a pinnacle, then follow the groove and shallow scoop above.

31   Red Lead   25m   VS 5a ***   (1977)
An enjoyable route with a finely placed crux. Climb the centre of the white slab to a horizontal break. Step down and left to a hidden layback crack. Follow the crack and traverse left across Whiplash to a thin diagonal crack. Climb this (crux) and the vertical crack above, finishing at the same point as Mascarade.

32   White Slab   25m   Hard Severe 4b   (1977)
Traverse left just above the water to the foot of the white slab, crux. Climb up to a hand-sized crack, continue to a ledge and finish up the shallow scoop of Whiplash on the left.

33   Demons and Dead Lizards   30m   HVS 5a
Follow the thin crack right of White Slab to a ledge, then climb newly-exposed rock to the top.

The area right of Mascarade Buttress is known as Little Amphitheatre. The next three routes take lines on the steep left wall. The top sections of the first two have been severely affected by the council trundlers, but they should still be possible at their original grades.

34   Spanking the Rustbucket   25m   E3 5c   (1990)
Climb the obvious awkward clean-cut white groove just right of the water's edge (bold and difficult) until moves up left gain a steep wide crack. Climb this to a ledge, then continue up the rock scars to the top.

35   Harry Goes West   25m   E2 5b   (1990)
Follow the cleaned line of good holds up the wall right of the white groove (bold) to gain a small pillar. Climb the crack on the left to the large ledge of the previous climb, then finish up newly-exposed rock.

36   Hopelessly Treading Water   10m   E4 6a   (1990)
A serious route on less then perfect rock. Start at the left end of a higher ledge at the junction of the left and main faces. Climb to and past the peg runner at 4m, using hidden holds in a slanting line just left of the peg. Gain a small ledge (sideways Rock 5 placement) and continue with difficulty to the top.

The Edge, Loudoun Hill (Climbers, Jim Blyth and Dave McGimpsey)

The back wall of Little Amphitheatre was one of the areas most affected by the stabilisation work. It is now smaller and scarcely more stable; hardly worth climbing on. Most of the routes were destroyed, but if you're really desperate a few climbs in the lower grades might be constructed. Approximately in the middle of this sector, a rather better piece of rock is taken by the following climb:

37   The Seven Year Plan   10m   E2 5c *   (1992)
Climb a short grey wall to a ramp (peg runner). Finish directly over an overhang.

38   Cracked Arete   15m   VS 4c **   (1977)
Climb the fine arete in the buttress which marks the right end of Little Amphitheatre. Finish up the prominent crack.

The obvious corner to the right was Fourth Wave, but it most of its holds have been removed by order of the council. It may still provide an interesting climb after cleaning.

39   Caftan   15m   HVS 4c   (1977)
There are three vertical bore holes in the wall right of the warning sign. Climb the bold wall to a good hold at a protruding block. Step left and climb the wall to the top.

40   Bazaar   15m   HVS   4c   (1977)
Climb Caftan to the protruding block, then step right and go up right to the top.

41   Ice Edge   10m   VS 4c
Start up Mastalgia and climb its left arete. Rather artificial.

42   Mastalgia   10m   VS 4c *
The steep corner with a smooth right wall some 10 metres right of Bazaar gives good climbing.

43   Higher Beginning   10m   Very Difficult
Climb the wall right of Mastalgia.

The area to the right provides the easiest descent into the quarry. The next climbable feature, a smooth slabby wall to the left of a deep corner, is most easily reached by traversing in from halfway down the descent.

44   Stir Crazy   10m   HVS 5a
Climb the centre of the slab left of Lion Cub.

45   Lion Cub   10m   Hard Severe 4a *   (1977)
Climb the right edge of the slab, bold at the top.

46   Lion   10m   HVS 5b **   (1977)
Climb the obvious corner right of the slab. The top section gives technical but
well protected bridging.

Right of the corner of Lion there is some sound rock at the top of the crag,
once climbed by **Chevron** (E1 5b) and **Scrumpy** (HVS 5a). Unfortunately the
blocks at the bottom comprise what used to be their lower reaches; diligent
cleaning may yet reinstate these routes. The fine-looking buttress just to the right
used to house **Thumbelena**, a notoriously unstable route. The following climb
approximates to the line of **Moonshine**, which also fell victim to the blasting.

47   Sunshine   25m   HVS 5a **   (1993)
Start just left of the toe of the buttress. Climb steep rock on the left-hand side to
a flake crack. Step right to a ledge, then move over the overhang to deep cracks.
Step left to climb thin cracks before moving back right to finish on the arete.

48   Kelvin Way   25m   E1 5a   (1976)
Start up the grey wall at the foot of the buttress, then move right into the open
groove. Move up, then take the left wall for a few feet (or climb direct, 5c) before
returning to the groove for an overhanging sand exit.

The next three routes start from a terrace, reached by a scramble up blocks
15 metres right of Kelvin Way.

49   Mac's Wall   20m   HVS 5a
From the terrace, scramble carefully over blocks to the crest of the prow which
overlooks Kelvin Way. Climb the cracks in the prow directly to the top.

50   Short Reach   15m   E1 5b **   (1976)
Start up the wide chimney some 10 metres right of Mac's Wall, then climb the
thin groove to a small overlap, step right and go for the top.

51   Pigeon Hole   15m   VS 4c   (1977)
Starting about 10 metres right of Short Reach, climb blocks to a ledge and finish
up the corner above.

52   Exorcist   5m   HVS 5b
Below the terrace a short overhanging crack faces the pool. Climb the crack to
an awkward mantle finish.

53   Separated Edge   25m   HVS 5a   (1977)
Further right a long groove runs up to a fine prow. This route climbs its left arete.
Climb the wall left of the groove to good holds, then continue more easily to
below the prow. It is probably easiest to step into Pigeon Hole to finish.

The long groove itself used to be taken by **Talisman** (VS 4c), but the top section has been removed and a hideous earth cornice remains. The right arete of the groove was the start of **Knife Edge** (E2 5c), which finished up the fine prow. The vital hold was a wee bit loose, and the council has protected you from the folly of its use. The prow may still be possible at a much higher grade. Most of the other climbs in this area have been demolished, the only survivor takes the next obvious groove which runs the full height of the quarry.

54   Christmas Corner   25m   HVS 5a *   (1976)
The corner gives a varied and interesting climb.

The buttress to the right once housed some of the finest routes on quarried dolerite. Stand on the pile of rubble and inspect the thin and frightening crux of **Balance of Power** at close quarters. It would still be possible to climb this to ledges in the middle of the wall, and a possible finish up Christmas Corner, but the runner placements are no longer high enough above the ground to prevent a Desmond. The new smooth corner to the right has been revealed by the complete removal of **Fusion** and **Sandman**.

55   Glass   25m   E1 5c   (1993)
What you get when you fuse sand! A hard start leads to better holds and an interesting excursion on the right wall to gain the upper groove. Scrabble past another hard reachy move to an exit on the right arete.

56   Dream Machine   25m   E4 6a/b ***   (1983)
This fine problem takes the right arete of the buttress. Although the upper section is on newly-exposed rock, the climbing here is straightforward. Even before the bogeymen came, a crucial foothold had disappeared from the lower section, turning a hard problem into one that is very difficult to flash. Climb delicately to a good layback hold. Place a vital Rock 2 runner in the thin crack above with care, then make a series of hard moves up the arete. It is possible, but extremely precarious and strenuous, to place excellent protection. Don't use a Friend behind the good hold, as a fall will snap it off.

Further right the cliff becomes broken, and there is an easy descent at the top right-hand corner of this section. At the top of the quarry, just right of the descent, is a short problem up a blunt arete left of a vertical bore-hole (**Model T**, HVS 5b). The other climbs further right on this upper wall have been destroyed, but it may be possible to find some short but worthwhile replacements. The next prominent feature is a square-cut pinnacle, one of the most obvious landmarks of the quarry. On its left side is a short but merry problem:

57   Think of England   10m   E2 5c **   (1980)
Bridge up over the waiting pool to reach the hanging crack. Then just lie back and …

58   Quick Buck   10m   VS 5a *
The leftmost of the cracks in the pinnacle's right wall.

Right again a splendid slab descends to the edge of the pool. This provides some of the best middle grade routes on dolerite. Although the routes can be finished via any of the easier obvious lines in the upper section, it is common to traverse off left along the ledges at two-thirds height. There is a rather pointless girdle traverse at about half-height of the lower wall, going from left to right and finishing up Gold Rush (**Southern Man**, E2 5b 1981).

59   Replicant   30m   E3 5c
Start at the far left side of the slab below a steeper prow. Climb up and boldly right below a white-speckled wall to easier ground to the right of the prow. The crux holds come to light only at the last moment.

60   Trundle   30m   VS 4c ***   (1977)
The crack up the left side of the slab is enjoyable and well protected.

61   Walk on the Wild Side   30m   HVS 5a ***   (1980)
The faint crack line in the slab right of Trundle gives a steady lead. After an initial bold section the microwire protection is excellent.

62   Midas Touch   30m   E1 5b ***   (1980)
Climb the right edge of the slab to a faint groove in the arete, which is taken direct, with runners in the crack on the left.

63   The Gold Bug   30m   E3 5c   (1988)
Climb the wall left of Gold Rush by a boulder problem start, then by using the left arete. Pull left onto Midas Touch 5m from the top.

64   Gold Rush   30m   E1 5b ***   (1975)
Another outstanding climb which takes the striking groove right of Midas Touch.

65   After the Gold Rush   30m   E2 5a   (1977)
Mantleshelf onto the ledge just right of the corner, then climb the centre of the wall direct on creaking flakes.

66   After the Grave Dig   30m   E1 5a **
A more sensible alternative to the above. From the ledge, trend up right to the arete and climb cracks in its left side.

About 20 metres further right is another fine buttress. Although all the climbs have been affected by recent excavation, the best of them are still possible.

67   Deep Throat Revived   30m   E5 6a ***   (1977/91)
A climb with a history. The original was protected by pegs, but natural rockfall removed the placements and the crux holds. The line was then repeated with a poor replacement peg runner, but this failed during a later attempt. At present, it is virtually unprotected, but it would be possible to place a good peg runner in a horizontal crack at 10m. There is no record of a successful lead in its current pegless state, hence the grade. Start at the foot of the left arete of the buttress, and climb to a step right into a vague niche at 10m. Move left beneath the overhang, then make a series of precarious hard moves on slowly improving holds to a good ledge. Climb the left arete of the wall above.

68   Power Play   30m   E1 5b *   (1976)
Start in the overhung bay right of the corner to the right of Deep Throat Revived. Climb up awkwardly through a small overhang to easier ground and a block belay. Continue up the groove slightly to the right, then traverse left below the final overhangs to the top of Deep Throat Revived.

69   Foxy Woxy   15m   E3 5c **   (1976/93)
Remember the big blocks that you used to bridge from to start this one? Well, they've gone! From the belay of Power Play, place an unconvincing Friend 3 in the bore-hole then step down and onto the wall. Balance precariously left (nasty fall potential) to holds in the groove on the left. Climb the groove to join and finish up Deep Throat Revived.

Right of Power Play is a smooth wall with strange circular striations, and right again is an area ravaged by rockfall both natural and unnatural. About 10 metres right of the smooth wall, twin cracks can be seen high on the lower section of the quarry.

70   Crazy Daisy   25m   HVS 5a
Climb a grassy groove and move right to climb the cracks. Find a way through the recent debris to reach the top, or face a horrible scramble back down to the left.

71   Think Positive   5m   E2 6a
A good little problem which smears up the slabby arete right of Crazy Daisy. Finish up the cracks of Crazy Daisy.

72   Shot in the Dark   15m   E1 5a *   (1986)
Start up the centre of the white-speckled slabby wall about 10 metres further right. Trend right to an interesting finish up a small groove.

73   Evasive Action   15m   VS 4c
Climb the corner groove just right of Shot in the Dark, exiting right.

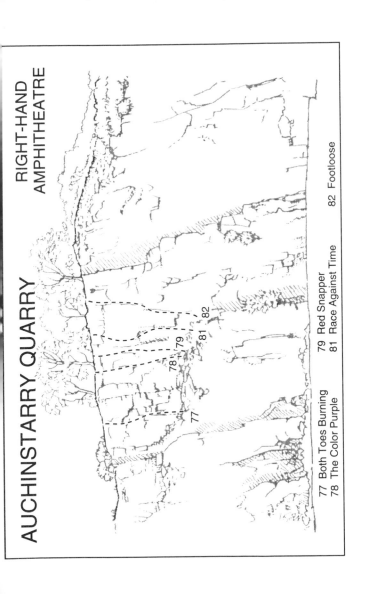

AUCHINSTARRY QUARRY

RIGHT-HAND
AMPHITHEATRE

77 Both Toes Burning
78 The Color Purple

79 Red Snapper
81 Race Against Time

82 Footloose

The area to the right is The Right-Hand Amphitheatre, which is split into three distinctive sections: the lower cliff right of Evasive Action, identified by the 'ear' of Urea, the upper cliff above the terrace and the wall at the far right of the quarry. The routes on the lower section degenerate into vague scrambling at half-height.

74   B.C.'s Return   25m   E1 5b   (1981)
Left of Urea lies a squat pinnacle. Climb the blunt arete to a horizontal break. Move up and step right onto the prow, then continue to easy ground.

75   Urea   25m   VS 4c   (1976)
Climb the diagonal crack on the right of the prominent 'ear' (about 10 metres right of B.C.'s Return), to a wide crack and easier ground. Climb a slab and scramble through the upper walls.

The climbs further right on the lower tier have all been substantially modified and are probably not worth re-investigating. The next routes are on the upper tier, best reached by taking the path round the top of the quarry on the right and then scrambling down with care (to the west of the climbs) to good ledges at half-height. The rock here is intrinsically loose; take care. Ironically this part of the quarry (except for the descent, which is much harder) has not been much affected by the stabilisation work.

76   Stool Pigeon   15m   E3 6b
The left side of the upper tier wall is defined by an orange groove, the result of recent excavations. To its right is a smooth convex wall. Climb the centre of the blank wall, with side runners in the next route.

77   Both Toes Burning   15m   E2 6a   (1986)
Start at the right side of the convex wall. Climb a short groove and vertical crack line through two small roofs, finishing up an easier groove.

78   The Color Purple   15m   E1 5b   (1986)
Climb the obvious jamming crack about 5 metres left of the corner. The top section has been affected by council crowbars.

79   Red Snapper   15m   E2 5c   (1986)
A technical and poorly protected route up the corner, where the crag turns right.

80   Band Aid   15m   E3 5c   (1986)
Climb the thin crack in the white wall with difficulty, past a peg runner, to a loose finish.

81   Race Against Time   15m   E3 5c   (1986)
Step right from the foot of Band Aid into a shallow corner. Layback this, surmount the roof and continue up the wide crack to another loose finish (very nearly the scene of the demise of the guidebook checking team!). Use of holds on Band Aid makes this easier, and vice versa.

82   Footloose   20m   HVS 5a
Start on terrace down and right of Race Against Time. Climb the crack line to the right of the smooth open (unclimbed) corner. Again, great care is needed at the top.

The buttress to the right is one of the largest in the quarry, but it is very loose and unsatisfactory. Climbs have been found starting from water level on the left-hand side, and also up the ramp on the right-hand wall. Both are dangerously loose and best avoided.

JACKDAW AND CROY QUARRIES   *(Map Ref 722 761)*

JACKDAW QUARRY
This is the hole in the ground beside the B802 on the outskirts of Croy, 1km south of Auchinstarry. Approach as for Auchinstarry. Park on the north side of the road beside Croy Tavern, and cross a style beside a double gate. Walk down the tarmac track; the quarry is on the left after 100 metres.

The Dispossessed   20m   E2 5c   (1985)
Climb the left-hand of two cracks in the steep black wall.

The Trouble   20m   E2 5c   (1992)
The right-hand crack.

CROY QUARRY
There is lots of rock here, but it is north-facing and rather lichenous. The quarry has two tiers, and the following route takes a slabby rectangular wall in the middle of the upper tier, roughly opposite the largest quarry entrance. Park as for Jackdaw Quarry and continue down the track; the quarry is on the right.

Tazy Lady   15m   E3 5c   (1987)
Climb the obvious line starting at the bottom left-hand end of the buttress. Move up and right to a horizontal crack. Make a hard move up and right to gain a standing position in the horizontal fault. Follow the obvious ramp up and left to a good foothold. Make an awkward move up and right to a horizontal crack, then follow this to the right to good Friends. Climb up and right to a vague scoop. It is best to leave a rope in position for the easy but loose top section.

COWDEN HILL QUARRY   *(Map Ref 769 798)*

Not even the 1986 guide managed to revive the fortunes of this pleasant enough quarry, so it continues to be infrequently visited. Like Auchinstarry, the rock is quartz-dolerite and the south-facing routes dry quickly after rain. With a general absence of traffic the rock should be treated with care, although the faces are sounder than Auchinstarry. Descent is possible down broken ground right of the routes. Birds of prey nest here from April to June.

The quarry lies 5km east of Kilsyth. From Glasgow, approach as for Auchinstarry, but continue into Kilsyth and follow the A803 east towards Bonnybridge. Take the third turning on the left after Kelvinhead, easily missed, and park on the right after an old railway bridge. Follow the track which leads up and left into the quarry. The climbs are on the south face, which faces the entrance to the quarry.

Earth Summit   30m   E4 6a   (1992)
This route follows the obvious flake up the black wall at the back of the quarry, passing two pegs. Move right below a small roof to the top of a small pinnacle. Finish directly up the wall, passing another peg runner.

Lorraine   35m   VS 4b   (1976)
Start 10 metres left of the lowest part of the cliff. Climb the short wall to a ledge, then go left up a blunt rib. Follow grooves on the right past a pinnacle to the top.

Ostrich   35m   HVS 5a   (1977)
From the lowest part of the face, climb the short broken wall to a ledge, then a shallow groove, just right of Lorraine, to a small ledge. Traverse left to a bore-hole then go up and left over short walls.

Kerrygold   35m   HVS 5b
Start about 3 metres right of the lowest point of the face. Climb the narrow diagonal slab and the parallel diagonal cracks above. Step right to a slab and finish up the short corner above the terrace.

Ground Control   35m   E1 5a
The next obvious feature is a short overhanging groove. Climb the shallow groove just left to a ledge, go up and left to make an awkward and poorly protected mantelshelf to the base of the groove. Follow the groove to the top.

D-Day   25m   HVS 5b   (1976)
Climb the overhanging groove then the shallow groove to a ledge above and right. Climb the groove above or swing right round a loose block. Finish up the wall just left of a gorse bush.

Newton Blues   25m   E1 5c   (1976)
About 7 metres right of D-Day is an obvious square-cut corner reached by a short scramble. Climb the corner and the groove above.

Ladybird   35m   E1 5b **   (1976)
Start below a small corner crack about 10 metres right of Newton Blues. Go up a short wall to a ledge just right of the block crack. Continue to the top of the detached block, then right and up corner to another ledge. Make a diversion on the left wall until the corner can be re-entered. Walk right for 10 metres and climb the wall right of corner to the top.

Klingon   35m   E2 5b
Start just right of Ladybird. Climb grooves to a ledge halfway up the wall. Continue up the wall with an awkward move right below a small overhang near the top. Finish up the corner above.

Hole in the Wall   15m   E1 5b   (1976)
Start 4 metres right of Klingon. Gain the obvious scoop in the blank wall from the right, then finish more easily.

Narita   10m   E3 5c   (1986)
Start as for Hole in the Wall, then take a faint right-trending line to the top.

GLASGOW MINOR CRAGS

CRAIG MINNAN   (Map Ref 641 322)

A steep little outcrop in a fabulous setting. Approach from Muirshiel Country Park, 3km north-west of Lochwinnoch. Follow the signs to Windy Hill from where the crag can be seen. Climb at will.

JOHNSTONE QUARRY   (Map Ref 429 613)

This quarry is the higher of two off Craigbog Road opposite the public park and named "High Craig" in the Geographia street atlas of Glasgow. One climb has been recorded: **Tom's Crack** (20m, E3 6a **) is an esoteric gem taking the obvious crack on a compact buttress of quartz dolerite in the trees above and overlooking the forecourt. Approach through wood to the left.

WINDYHILL QUARRY   (Map Ref 435 614)

A rather overgrown north-facing quarry which holds some potential for the green fingered. Legend has it there was a 25m pinnacle here before the quarry was filled in. So much for legends! **Hide-and-Seek** (12m, E2 6a) climbs the obvious cleaned crack and groove line in the middle of the wall. The groove on the left is a poor VS, and the small tower on the right is VS 4c. On the north side of the road is a small bouldering cliff. Approach from the road.

KILPATRICK HILLS

Various routes have been done at Loch Humphrey Head (Map Ref 453 745) and Lang Crags (Map Ref 433 767), but the rock is structurally unsound on a major scale. (See SMCJ 1973, 1974).

BOWLING CRAG   *(Map Ref 442 738)*

A pleasant little crag with a couple of routes and some bouldering. Approach along the old railway line which is now a walkway and cycle path.

THE CAMPSIE FELLS

Apart from Jenny's Lum crag on Slackdhu, there is little worthwhile climbing in the Campsies. A few routes have been done on **Crichton's Cairn** near Campsie Glen (Map Ref 610 800), and the north-facing **Corrie of Balglass** (Map Ref 589 849) has some impressive crags, plus a lot of steep grass and loose rock.

KELVIN HALL WALL   *(Map Ref 570 662)*

This Bendcrete wall is situated on the balcony of the Kelvin Hall International Sports Arena on Argyle Street, opposite the Museum and Art Galleries. If you like climbing walls, this one is quite good (but no competitor for Dunfermline). There is ample opportunity for problems varying from about 4a to the extremely silly, and the overhanging sections offer excellent stamina training. At peak times it is crowded (a good time to observe interesting problems), but it is usually quiet during lunch (a good time to get them well wired). Except when there are major events occurring in the main arena, it is open every day from 9am to 10pm. Tel: 041 357 2525.

Loch Lomond and The Trossachs

This chapter describes the climbing on the crags near the east shore of Loch Lomond, most of which is relatively recent, and also crags both old and new in The Trossachs. The crags on the west side of Loch Lomond are in the area covered by the *Arran, Arrochar and the Southern Highlands* guide. The OS maps required for the crags in this chapter are sheets 51 for the minor crags at the northern limit of this area, 56 for the Loch Lomond crags, and 57 for The Trossachs.

CREAGAN AN AMAIR GHLAIS   *(Map Ref 488 063)*

This is an impressive-looking mica schist crag on the east flank of Ben Venue, overlooking the south-east end of Loch Katrine. Unfortunately it faces north-east, gets a fair amount of drainage and is rather slow to dry.

From the Loch Achray Hotel on the A821, 7km north of Aberfoyle, follow the forest track behind the hotel westwards for 1½km. On leaving the forest, cross the stile and head steeply up the slope to the crags.

Root Beer   10m   E1 5b   (1992)
The lower wall is steep and lichenous, and may be recognised by its light green colouration. This route follows a discontinuous crack at the right-hand end of the wall, with some loose holds. Start in an alcove at the right-hand end and climb steeply above to an obvious crack. Finish with a hard move at the top on sloping holds.

Sarsaparilla   15m   E2 5b   (1991)
This takes the most direct line up the clean slabby middle wall, which lies some 200 metres up the slope behind a terrace with trees. Start in a small niche on the grassy ledge, just left of the lowest rocks. An awkward move onto a ramp leads slightly left to the main slabby wall (poor peg runner possible), then climb direct to the steep upper wall and finish using shallow cracks leading to a grassy terrace and tree belay.

ACHRAY WALL   *(Map Ref 504 066)*

About half a dozen routes have been done on this small steep mica schist crag, but only the best two have been recorded.

From Glasgow follow the A81 to Aberfoyle then the A821 over the Duke's Pass. Park in a small lay-by opposite the crag on the banks of Loch Achray, about 280 metres north-east of the Loch Achray Hotel.

The Bow   25m   HVS 5a   (1983)
Start at the open groove at the lowest part of the crag, facing the road. Climb the
groove to a niche, move up the slabby ramp to the left, then go right to the top.
A bit dirty at the top.

The Arrow   20m   E2 5c **   (1983)
Climb the vague hanging groove to the right of The Bow, past a protection peg.
Steep and strenuous, but with big holds.

BEN AN   *(Map Ref 505 082)*

Ben An epitomises the best of the mountain cragging offered in this guide. The
routes are short but memorable, the pocketed mica schist delightful to climb on,
the landscape relaxing, and to sift out the weak of spirit, the routes require more
than a 500m uphill walk from the car.
   The crags lie at about 300m on the south side of the hill, facing Ben Venue
and overlooking the eastern end of Loch Katrine. However, many of the walls
face roughly south-east, so sunshine can't be guaranteed for an evening's sport.
The rock is quite solid, though mossy and quite polished in places, so care
should be taken in damp conditions.
   From Glasgow follow the A81 to Aberfoyle, then the A821 over the Duke's
Pass. Shortly after the turn-off for Loch Katrine and 100 metres before The
Trossachs Hotel turn right into a car park. Opposite this, a signposted path leads
uphill and into the forest. After 15 to 20 minutes a grassy area with boulders is
reached, from where the crags can be viewed. Where the main path steepens,
a small path leads off left to the base of the Lower Tier.

LOWER TIER
A steep buttress with an impressive corner is encountered first. Left of this is a
rocky gully then a long undercut wall which ends at an ash tree. The first se*ven*
*route*s are described right to left.

1   Preamble   13m   Severe
Starting just right of the lowest point of the crag climb a small overhang. Finish
as for The Edge, or more easily by moving right.

2   The Edge   13m   VS 4c *
Good airy climbing up the right arete of the corner. Swing strenuously over the
bulge at the start and move up and left to overlook the corner. Finish up the crack
and edge above.

3   Tricky Vicky   12m   E4 6a *   (1985)
Technical unprotected climbing up the right wall of the corner.

4   Club Corner   12m   E3 5c *
The steep corner gives a strenuous bridging problem with little protection. Faith
and friction lead to the thank God hold and a finish up The Edge.

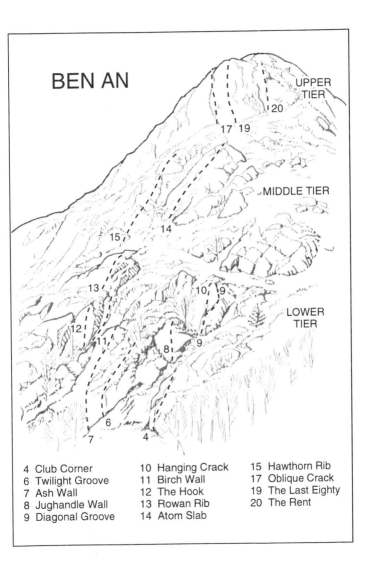

BEN AN

UPPER TIER

MIDDLE TIER

LOWER TIER

4 Club Corner	10 Hanging Crack	15 Hawthorn Rib
6 Twilight Groove	11 Birch Wall	17 Oblique Crack
7 Ash Wall	12 The Hook	19 The Last Eighty
8 Jughandle Wall	13 Rowan Rib	20 The Rent
9 Diagonal Groove	14 Atom Slab	

5   The First Thirty   10m   Difficult
Left of the obvious corner is a wall forming the right side of the gully. Good but polished holds lead to the top.

6   Twilight Groove   20m   HVS 4c *
A short corner is the main feature on the long undercut wall left of the gully. The corner is awkward to enter, protection difficult to arrange and contact with the rock surprisingly tenuous. May raise a few goose pimples.

The wall to the right has been top-roped. **Blind Faith**, 6a. Start right of Twilight Groove, and trend right on thin holds.

7   Ash Wall   30m   Severe 4a **   (1930)
This takes a well worn line behind the ash tree, about 12 metres left of the rocky gully splitting the first tier. Gain the top of the polished flake and step left into the groove. Move up this to a slab which is followed for about 15m until it is possible to reach a rib on the left edge. Follow the rib to finish just right of a prominent tree.

The next three routes take lines on the left wall of the gully splitting the Lower Tier.

8   Jughandle Wall   13m   Difficult
Opposite the top of The First Thirty is a slabby wall. Take the line of least resistance via an outrageous jug.

9   Diagonal Groove   10m   Severe 4a *
Higher up the gully is an impressive crack. Climb to below the crack, then follow the ramp rightwards to a 'balancy' move round the corner.

10   Hanging Crack   10m   VS 4c **
Despite its brevity, the crack is shockingly steep with a high fall potential. Start as for Diagonal Groove, but gain the niche then layback boldly up the crack.

The next two routes lie above and slightly left of the finish of Ash Wall. They can also be gained by a left traverse from the gully splitting the Lower Tier.

11   Birch Wall   13m   Hard Severe 4a *   (1937)
Behind the tree is an obvious polished corner. Smear into the corner and wobble upwards on gradually improving holds.

12   The Hook   10m   E3 5c ***
Forceful climbing with poor protection up the right side of the steep wall left of Birch Wall. Move up to a vertical pocket and continue with difficulty above. Often top-roped, rarely led.

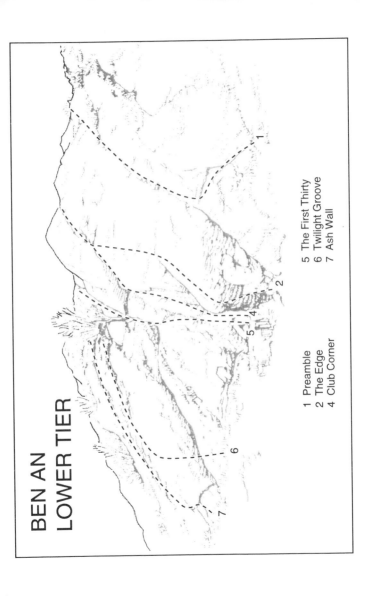

BEN AN
LOWER TIER

1 Preamble
2 The Edge
4 Club Corner

5 The First Thirty
6 Twilight Groove
7 Ash Wall

The centre of the wall left of The Hook has been top-roped – **Crunchy**, 5c.

13   Rowan Rib   10m   Difficult *
Directly above the finish to Birch Wall is a polished bulge with a metal spike. Pull over awkwardly to a hidden jug and continue more easily to belay at a large boulder.

CENTRAL TIER
This is characterised by indefinite rock ribs on the left, divided by vegetated gullies.

14   Atom Slab   5m   Severe
Above and right of Rowan Rib is a minute crag with assorted problems and a polished top wall.

15   Hawthorn Rib   40m   Difficult
Across the scrub left of the top of Rowan Rib is an indefinite rib line. This is the cleanest rock on the central tier and the way followed by most parties heading for the upper tier.

To the left of Hawthorn Rib are two vegetated gullies, **Right-Hand Gully** and **Left-Hand Gully**, both Very Difficult. They were first ascended in 1898 and 1896, but are rarely climbed now.

UPPER TIER
Directly below the summit, this tier contains some good routes in a superb position and is easily recognised by a quartz banded face, flanked on the right by striking crack lines and on the left by the deep slanting chimney of The Oblique Crack. The climbs are described from left to right.
    Left of the deep chimney are a number of gullies, probably best left for enthusiastic botanists; **McLay's Chimney**, Very Difficult and **Right-Hand Gully Continuation**, Severe.

16   Spare Rib   25m   Severe
Left of the deep chimney is a rib. Climb this up and left to an edge, then finish more directly.

17   Oblique Crack   20m   Very Difficult *   (1898)
Follow the left-slanting chimney - very character building.

18   Coriander   25m   VS 4c **   (1970)
Right of the chimney is an impressive open face covered in quartz. This route climbs grooves on the left edge. Climb the overhanging crack right of the start of The Oblique Crack, or from the start of the chimney reach out right to a large quartz hold and swing on to the edge. Either way, climb the slab above and follow poorly protected grooves always to the left of The Last Eighty.

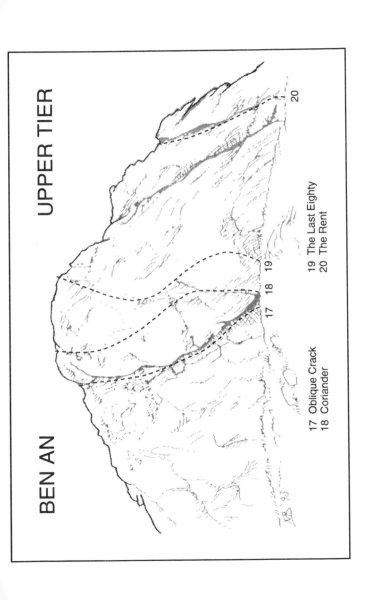

BEN AN

UPPER TIER

17 Oblique Crack
18 Coriander

19 The Last Eighty
20 The Rent

19   The Last Eighty   25m   Severe 4a ***   (1930)
Enjoyable climbing on interesting and ever-steepening rock. Start below a small
overhang, just left of the lowest part of the buttress. Pull over the bulge on good
holds and continue fairly directly on well-marked rock, to finish up a steep corner
at the top. The first roof can be avoided by traversing in from the right.

20   The Rent   25m   VS 4c *   (1934)
To the right of the quartz face is a vertical crack which gives a more elegant and
delicate climb than expected.

As if the view wasn't enough, the summit of Ben An provides a final party piece
with the **Record Slab**, the apex of which actually forms the summit. From a
standing start with toes touching the lowest part of the slab, timed ascents can
be made to both feet on the summit.

LOCH LUBNAIG CRAG   *(Map Ref 586 100)*

This small south-facing crag of slabby mica schist may give some brief entertainment at the end of a day. From Callander follow the A84 north through the
Pass of Leny towards Loch Lubnaig. The crag lies below Anie Farm, facing the
road. Park in the lay-by opposite, then walk north along the road for 110 metres
to a gate. Follow the farm track until it is possible to cross the river on the left
and enter a field. Walk along the right edge of the field between the corridor fence
and a stone wall. The routes are described from left to right.

Upright and Up   15m   Severe   (1985)
The initial bulge on the left is climbed on thin holds, then follow the sloping ledge.
Traverse right and finish up a slab.

Ramp Route   15m   VS 4b   (1985)
Follow the ramp to twin heathery cracks. Climb these and the slab above.
Alternately start directly by climbing a bulge to join the end of the ramp.

Clean Cut   10m   Very Difficult   (1985)
Climb the mossy left wall to a tree belay.

Zigzag   15m   Hard Severe 4a   (1985)
Climb the buttress on the right with a detour at the top.

CASHEL QUARRY   *(Map Ref 395 942)*

Opposite the north end of Cashel campsite is a small slate quarry with an
impressive arete. The harder routes have little or no protection and are usually
top-roped.

From Glasgow follow the A809 to Drymen, the B837 to Balmaha and the minor road towards Rowardennan. The quarry lies about 4½km from Balmaha on the edge of Loch Lomond. Park in the forecourt.

Left Wall   5b/c
Climb the clean streak in the left wall. A route whose crux and grade changes with every ascent. Top-roped.

Polly   VS 4c   (1989)
The corner at the back of the quarry.

Heel Hooker   E4 5c   (1991)
Left of the arete is a large flake. Climb this strenuously, then make difficult moves up and right to finish up the arete.

Arete   6a **
The impressive arete gives some interesting radical slate climbing, with the crux near the bottom.

CARN NA MUICE   *(Map Ref 385 951)*

Despite appearances and a pleasant location on the east bank of Loch Lomond, this is a very disappointing crag. The exposure of quality mica schist is limited and most routes deteriorate in quality and increase in vegetation after steep starts. In summer the midges seem to be DEET immune.

From Glasgow follow the A809 to Drymen, the B837 to Balmaha and the minor road towards Rowardennan. About 5½km from Balmaha the road passes Sallochy on the right and starts to rise up a hill, at which point a road into the forest leads off right (Map Ref 389 951). Park here and descend the hill to follow the West Highland Way, then the loch-side to the crag.

A large fallen block marks the left-hand side of the crag, in the centre is a prominent ridge and to the right a small steep wall toped by a roof, with a slab right of that.

Bite The Dust   45m   E4 6a   (1991)
Start below a thin quartz seam in the blank slab at the far right end. Ascend to a quartz pocket and a small crack, move left onto a quartz vein, then go up to the overlap. Now move right to a diagonal crack, go up to a small face, then continue up and left to another face.

The Bat Flake   45m   VS 4c   (1987)
Behind the large block and right of a smooth slab is a steep pocketed rib. Climb this and the best of the rock above

The Drag   45m   VS 4c   (1990)
Climb the layback flake right of The Bat Flake.

Sunset Ridge   40m   Severe 4a   (1987)
The central ridge. Start up and right of the wide crack, and traverse left to the
tree. The crack is HVS 5a from the ground.

Brimbles   40m   Very Difficult   (1991)
From a small chimney right of Sunset Ridge, climb up then right to a small ledge.
Follow a clean line until level with trees, then move left to belay. Go left and up
alongside the ridge through grass and brambles. A direct start takes the clean
slab to the right.

Twilight Slab   40m   VS 4c   (1987)
A prominent downward pointing flake can be seen on the small steep wall right
of Sunset Ridge. Climb up to this, traverse right below the small roof and follow
mossy slabs to the steep crack in the final wall. The initial wall can be taken in
various places at 4c/5a.

Sallochy Slab   40m   Very Difficult   (1987)
Right of the wall is a line of clean slanting slabs. Climb these to the top without
a lot of protection. Not a bad route.

ROSS POINT   *(Map Ref 374 955)*

This impressive wall of slate lies in a large cleft on the east shore of Loch Lomond
close to Glasgow University Research Station. The crag is probably natural, but
the amount of slate waste at its eastern end means that it has undoubtedly been
quarried at some time in the past.

   The crag is on the second headland south-west of the Sallochy Bay car park
(Map Ref 380 958), 6½km north-west of Balmaha (poor Forestry Commission
car park sign). Follow the West Highland Way west along the loch side to the
boat house below the research station. A path behind the boat house leads onto
a good track which is followed almost to the top of the second hill (approximately
630 metres from the boat house). Turn left into the wood, passing a conifered
hill and felled trees on the right, until the east end of the wall is met (approximately another 240 metres). Scramble through the cleft to its western end (15
minutes from the car park). The climbing is pleasant but limited and the midges
can be unbearable.

MAIN WALL
The routes lie on the wall opposite the massive cracked boulder.

Crystal Junction   10m   E4 6a **   (1986)
Climb the overhanging arete facing the cracked boulder, past three peg runners
(which may not always be in place).

One Way Trip   15m   E4 6a   (1987)
Start up Crystal Junction, traverse right and finish up Slug Death (peg runners removed).

Slug Death   10m   E2 5b   (1987)
Climb the right-hand corner past two peg runners.

To the right of the corner is an impressive long wall with an old bolt route and chipped holds. About halfway along is a ledge about 2m off the ground with a crack at its left and right ends.

Legover   4m   E2 5c   (1991)
Mantelshelf onto the ledge and continue up the left-hand crack.

Pullover   4m   E2 5b   (1991)
The right-hand crack.

THE BLOCK
Opposite the Main Wall is a massive boulder with an obvious forked crack.

Diagonal Chimney   8m   Severe 4a
The scary chimney on the right-hand side of the boulder.

Son of Cog   8m   E4 5c   (1991)
The right arete of the boulder, facing Crystal Junction, gives unprotected climbing with the crux at the top.

Forked Lightning   8m   VS 4b   (1989)
The left fork of the crack gives a pleasant route. The right fork is Severe.

Some routes have been done up the back of the block, including the obvious hand crack and the chimney. The pocketed wall also looks feasible if it were cleaned.

CREAGAN TOM DUBH   *(Map Ref 337 136)*

This mica schist crag lies about 1km south of Doune on the east side of Loch Lomond. The lower tier is the conspicuous wall seen from the A82 on the west side of Loch Lomond. Protection is sparse and difficult to arrange for both routes on the lower tier.

Approach either from the north on the West Highland Way from the Inverarnan Hotel (Map Ref 318 185), or from the south on the West Highland Way from the Inversnaid Hotel (Map Ref 337 089). None of these ways are short, requiring about 1½ hours.

LOWER TIER

Sequestrator   30m   E3 5b **   (1989)
Start 3 metres right of the central arete. Climb up and left to a small ledge on the
crest, where good holds lead up and right to the final wall, crux. An excellent but
serious route.

Mahabharata   25m   E2 5b   (1989)
Start 10 metres right of Sequestrator below a faint crack that runs up the lower
part of the wall. Climb past the crack, peg runner on the left, and make a difficult
move onto a horizontal break, crux. Bigger holds lead to the top.

UPPER TIER

Athena   30m   E1 5b   (1986)
Climb the main corner groove past two roofs. Steeper and harder than it looks.

Perfect Strangers   15m   E1 5a   (1986)
To the left of the previous route is a narrow slab giving unprotected climbing.

Crazy Cow   20m   E1 5b   (1986)
The slab about 20 metres left of Athena. Pull over the roof at the right end of the
slab and climb a short wall to a scoopy ledge. Traverse left a short distance and
climb the wall above to another ledge. Step right and finish straight up.

LEUM AN EIREANNAICH   *(Map Ref 516 245)*

From the Braes of Strathyre this is the impressive crag seen high on the hillside
above Balquhidder. Unfortunately, appearances can be deceptive and on closer
inspection the crag is rather broken and vegetated. Although the climbing is
pleasant and the location wild and beautiful, the crag is an hour's walk from the
road and off the climbers' beaten track. Consequently, it is rarely climbed on.
    Follow the A84 north from Callander and take a minor road west towards
Balquhidder. Park at the church (Rob Roy Macgregor is buried here) follow the
track beside the church into the forest, then up the Kirkton Glen. A path to Glen
Dochart continues through the forest to emerge on to open hillside below the
crag.
    Below the crag is a massive boulder, Rob Roy's Putting Stone, which has a
number of climbs and bouldering possibilities. **South Crack**, Difficult (1899),
takes the obvious crack and flake on the south side, while the well defined
slanting crack on the west side is **Bumper Crack**, Severe.

LEUM AN EIREANNAICH

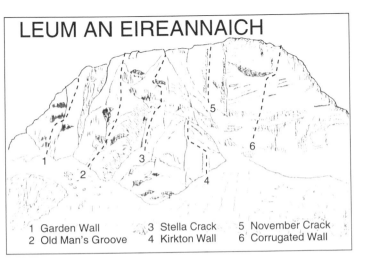

1 Garden Wall   3 Stella Crack   5 November Crack
2 Old Man's Groove   4 Kirkton Wall   6 Corrugated Wall

A nose-like feature dominates the centre of the crag, flanked on the left by steep walls and on the right by a grassy gully and slabbier rock.

1 Garden Wall   20m   Very Difficult
Start below the roofed recess at the left-hand side of the crag, about 100 metres up and left of the nose. Climb to grass then up to a ledge. Traverse right to avoid the roofs and follow the stepped ramp to the top.

2 Old Man's Groove   35m   Hard Severe
This takes the right-hand of the two impressive crack lines left of the nose. Climb a mossy slab to a crack and follow this to a ledge and broken walls. Follow ledges to the top.

3 Stella Crack   35m   VS
1. 15m   Follow the open corner right of the nose to a large grass ledge.
2. 20m   Climb the crack to a recess below a green slimy crack. Traverse left until it is possible to continue to the top.

4 Kirkton Wall   20m   VS
Start about 20 metres up the open gully to the right of the lowest part of the crag. A shallow groove leads to a ledge, followed by a left-rising traverse across the upper wall to its left edge.

5 November Crack   20m   Hard Severe
The central crack at the top of the open gully separating the central and right-hand sections of the crag is a bit loose at the start.

6   Corrugated Wall   20m   Severe
Start below the overhang on the right-hand section of the crag. Straight up to the right-hand end of the overhang, traverse right, then go directly up a steep wall.

BEN LEDI   *(Map Ref 562 098)*

The only recorded climbing on Ben Ledi is on the pinnacles and boulders in the upper part of the Stank Glen, on the north-east side of the hill at Map Ref 565 104. Many years ago these climbs, which have a fine mountain setting, were quite popular, but changing fashions among rock climbers and the rather long walk to the corrie (by present standards) has brought a decline in their popularity. The pinnacles, which are at a height of about 600m, can be seen as a serrated outline from the south end of Loch Lubnaig.

The approach from the car park 1 kilometre north-west of the Falls of Leny goes along the private road towards Stank and then west up the Stank Glen through the forest. Once clear of the forest turn left (south-west) and follow a path uphill. Just above the forest boundary fence the first boulder is reached. There are some easy climbs on it. Three other boulders lie slightly higher and to the west. The climbs on them are much harder.

The biggest pinnacle is directly uphill. It used to be known as the RIP Pinnacle, presumably by association with the nearby Lochan nan Corp (little loch of the corpses), but it is now known more prosaically as the Ben Ledi Pinnacle. It is not strictly speaking a pinnacle, but rather a group of boulders of which the largest is a tall pillar leaning against the hillside.

Ordinary Route   30m   Severe
At the foot of the pinnacle there is a narrow crack between the main wall and a slab at right-angles to it. Climb the slab, crawl upwards through a tunnel and move left onto a boulder whose narrow crest is climbed *à cheval*. Traverse right along an overhung ledge to the crest of the pinnacle and climb up a short slab to the top.

Cavern Route   30m   Severe
This is a variation of the previous route. From the top of the initial slab descend through a hole into a cavern and climb its back wall (usually wet and slimy) to join the previous route at the traverse. The cavern can also be reached through a narrow slit a short distance up the right-hand side of the pinnacle.

Direct Start   10m   Severe
Start just round the corner to the left of the initial slab of the Ordinary Route and climb directly up the wall on small holds.

The top of the pinnacle is very small and the drop on the uphill side is only 5m. A small rock spike just below the top safeguards the descent with a rope.

To the east of, and lower than, the Ben Ledi Pinnacle there is a smaller, isolated pinnacle which looks impressive from below. The ascent of its narrow north-east ridge is Severe. The south-west side of this pinnacle is a scramble.

MINOR CRAGS

ROB ROY'S CAVE   *(Map Ref 334 100)*

There is one 35m E2 5b called **Tree Creeper**, which climbs the obvious slab left of a holly bush, then goes left at an overlap and right to the top. Approach along the West Highland Way from the Inversnaid Hotel.

ABERFOYLE QUARRY   *(Map Ref 514 016)*

A couple of routes have been done in the 25m high quarry 400 metres north of Aberfoyle, which is easily seen from the road. They are described as "loose and not recommended" by the first ascentionists. **John's New Bike**, HVS 4b, takes the right-slanting diagonal crack and groove bounding the large black overhung slab. **Jackson's Hole**, E1 4c, climbs the obvious grey slab starting 3 metres left of the arete. Approach by walking west for 5 minutes from the David Marshall Lodge car park. Smaller natural crags further west might provide some interesting short problems, but the ground beneath them is very unpleasant for walking.

CREAG A'MHADAIDH   *(Map Ref 514 035)*

Heading towards Ben An on the A821 over the Duke's Pass there are a number of small mica schist buttresses on the left, a short distance after a house and about 3km north of Aberfoyle. Three routes have been done on consecutive buttresses up the hillside. They are: **Midged Off**, 15m Hard Severe 4a, on the Lower Wall; **Midget**, 5m Hard Severe 4a, on the Continuation Wall and **Midge Bite**, 5m VS 4b on the Top Wall.

Glasgow South and The Ayrshire Crags

South of the Clyde, the long established quarries of Court Knowe and Neilston give pleasant bouldering and some good short routes in the lower and middle grades. The natural crags of The Quadrocks and Loudoun Hill offer excellent short routes on natural rock in fabulous settings, while the more recently developed crags at Mauchline offer some adventurous climbs. Glen Afton provides a number of excellent routes which, unusually for this area, are on granite. The maps needed for the crags in this chapter are OS sheets 63 (The Quadrocks), 64 (Court Knowe and Neilston), 70 (Mauchline) and 71 (Loudoun Hill and Glen Afton).

COURT KNOWE QUARRY   *(Map Ref 588 600)*

Pleasant entertainment can be had in this tiny dolerite quarry on the wooded flank of Court Knowe, reputedly the hill from which Mary Queen of Scots watched the Battle of Langside. The rock is generally sound, although a bit lichenous and trees can prevent it drying for a while after rain. The routes are on steep walls and cracks and are usually soloed or top-roped. The crag faces an entrance to Linn Park, and lies within the public park system, so climbers should behave accordingly.

Access can be made by train from Glasgow to Cathcart, then take Merrylee Road to follow the north bank of the River Cart to Old Castle Road. This leads up the hill to Court Knowe on the left. Various buses serve the area. The routes are described from left to right.

THE LEFT WALL

The left wall has two chimney lines. The left-hand one below the tree is **Grotty Groove**, (4a); the right-hand off-width is **Chockstone Crack**, (5a). The wall between the two can be climbed at various points. The steep wall to the right of Chockstone Crack has been chipped, but not yet climbed.

THE MAIN WALL

Blue Tit's Nest Crack   5a *
Deceptively hard climbing up the cracked arete at the left end.

Wullie's Crack   5a
Start right of the previous route, make a hard balance move onto a hold and continue up a small corner

DF 118'S   6a
The wall and crack right of Wullie's Crack. Gain a hole and dyno for a sloping ledge, finish left.

Layback Crack   4c
The crack left of the central crack.

Coleptera Crack   3b
A botanical excursion up the obvious central crack.

Thin Finger's Crack   5c
Technical moves up the thin crack to the right.

Mountain Climber Route   4c
Start below the last route and climb the wall, trending up and right.

Last Route   4a
Follow the right edge of the Main Wall, starting left of the large tree and finishing by a left traverse.

THE SMALL WALL

Up and right of the tree is a small wall with various routes. **Andrew's Wall** (4c) follows the thin crack splitting the wall right of the tree; **Everest Corner** (3b) is the corner behind the tree; **Right Wall** (3b), not as fierce as its more famous namesake, takes the wall right of the corner; **Easy Arete** (3a) lies right of the corner; **The Long Reach** (4a) takes the wall and slab left of the muddy crack; **Mudcrack** (4b) is the crack, and **Consolation** (3a) climbs the right edge of the blank wall.

Ten Year Wall   6a *
The blank wall between Mudcrack and Consolation gives the most sustained and consistent route on this wall at any grade.

Girdle Traverse   5b
Start from Blue Tit's Nest Crack and finish at Consolation with a crux crossing the blank wall left of Consolation.

Snowy's Big Traverse   6b
A brief low-level traverse between Thin Fingers Crack and Coleptera Crack.

NEILSTON QUARRY   *(Map Ref 474 558)*

This small quartz-dolerite quarry is popular with beginners and its western aspect and lack of midges make it ideal for summer evenings. There are two main buttresses; a broken wall and slabs on the left and steep grooves and cracks on the right. It lies on the left-hand side of the back road to Dunlop, about 500 metres south-west of Neilston village. Parking is possible close by. There is a regular rail service from Glasgow Central to Neilston.

THE LEFT BUTTRESS

Descriptions for this broken and rather confused buttress are not definitive and climbers should follow the lines of least or most resistance as seems most appropriate. There are three small hawthorns at the base.

Right-Angled Corner   10m   Difficult
Climb the front of a small square buttress left of the first tree. Finish up grassy slabs.

Corner and Groove   10m   Difficult
Take the corner on the right and grassy slabs above.

Flake Route   10m   Very Difficult
The indefinite flake line between the first and second trees. Finish up walls and grooves.

Pinkerton's Corner   10m   Severe
Climb the wall just right of the second tree, past a break. Continue above from the recess.

Corner Arete   10m   Severe
Climb the broad arete on the right, followed by a line to the left.

Kristeen's Crack   10m   Very Difficult *
Climb cracks in the left wall of the deep Y-shaped recess, 7 metres right of the second tree.

Polish Direct   4m   Hard Severe
The short steep wall just left of the third tree.

THE RIGHT BUTTRESS

This part of the quarry starts with the Strawberry Tower, an obvious large block above a curving crack.

Juggy Crack   10m   Very Difficult
Climb the short crack on the left side of the tower.

Strawberry Crack   10m   Severe **
The fine curving crack below the tower.

Spiney Boulder   10m   Very Difficult
The indefinite crack in the wall of Strawberry Crack. Finish straight up.

Easy Gully   10m   Difficult
The grassy trough on the right, finishing right or left.

B.N.I.   10m   Severe
A small black-streaked wall left of the arete.

Broken Arete   10m   Very Difficult
Obvious!

Y-Crack   10m   Very Difficult
The short loose-looking crack.

Stephen Slab   10m   Hard Severe *
This is the short reddish wall.

Crack Corner   10m   Very Difficult *
Start about 8 metres right of Strawberry Crack where the main face begins. This
route climbs a right-slanting corner-groove, left of a stepped overhang.

Polish Hangover   10m   VS 4c *
Climb the steep arete and overhang to finish up Crack Corner.

Intrusion Line   10m   Very Difficult
This takes the left-curving groove and crack right of Polish Hangover.

Punk Rock   15m   HVS 5a *
Follow Intrusion Line until it is possible to move right to a crack with an old jammed
nut in it. Climb the wall above.

The wall between these two routes has been top-roped at 5c.

Curving Crack   15m   HVS 5a *
Climb the long left-curving crack, finishing up the wall just right of Punk Rock.

Willie's Route   15m   Severe **
Start at the broken crack line below and right of the tree stump. Finish right.
Variation: E2 6a
The slab can be climbed direct without touching neighbouring routes but with side
runners in them.

Fornication   15m   VS 4c
Round the corner from Willie's Route there is a white-speckled wall. Climb cracks
in the left side.

Grassy Crack   15m   Severe
Start 2 metres right of Fornication. Climb the mossy crack to an overhang, move
left and climb the broken crack in the speckled wall.

Jig-saw Jive   10m   Very Difficult
The mossy crack line passing the overhang of Grassy Crack on the right.

Grot Gully   10m   Moderate
Yuck.

Peg Leg   2m   HVS 5b
The short crack in the quarry's right wall was once pegged.

THE QUADROCKS   *(Map Ref 220 605)*

A superb outlook to the Firth of Clyde and the islands of Great Cumbrae, Bute and Arran, make a trip to The Quadrocks doubly satisfying. These west-facing crags of sound, rough basalt lie on the hillside about 1km north-east of Largs town centre and are visible from the town. The climbing isn't extensive, but enough to occupy a sunny afternoon or evening when the crags will be anything but the Cauld Rocks they're called on the Ordnance Survey 1:50000 map.

From Glasgow follow the A78 coast road. Just north of Largs town centre, turn into Burnside Road by following signs for the Inverclyde National Sports Training Centre. This leads in under 1km to a large car park outside the Centre. Walk onto the hillside behind the centre, avoiding a shooting range to the south; the crag is a stiff 15 minutes uphill.

LOW CRAG

1   Far Groove   6m   Very Difficult
Climb the open groove directly.

2   Far Wall   7m   Very Difficult
Follow a cracked wall to below an overhang, turn this on the left by a slabby shelf, or better, climb the overhang directly.

3   Boulder Rib   7m   Very Difficult
Go directly up the rib on good holds and gain a sloping shelf at the top. Pass a large boulder on the right.

4   Dank Chimney   7m   Difficult
The messy chimney immediately right of Boulder Rib.

5   Boulder Problem   7m   Very Difficult
Easy climbing leads to the boulder, whose stability is in some doubt, then make an awkward move to gain its top followed by a short steep wall.

6   Choc-Chimney   7m   Severe *
Strenuous climbing up the deep chimney-crack which contains a swinging chock-stone.

THE QUADROCKS – LOW CRAG

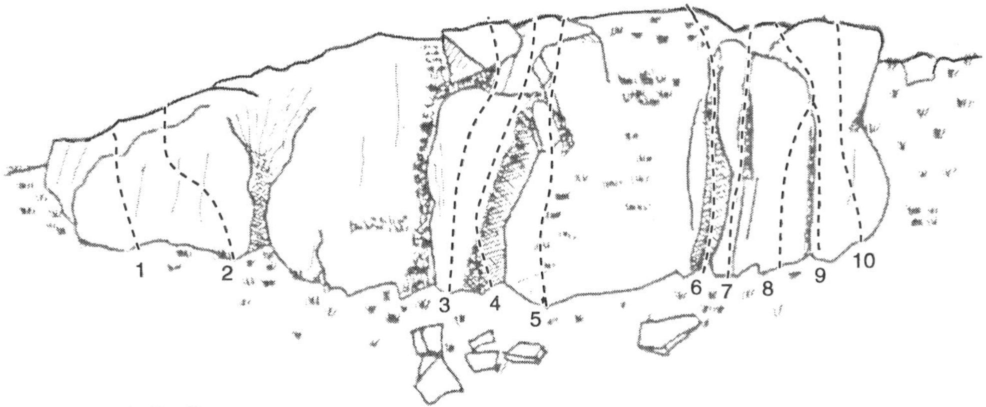

1 Far Groove
2 Far Wall
3 Boulder Rib
4 Dank Chimney

5 Boulder Problem
6 Choc-Chimney
7 Sentry-Box Crack

8 Fingers Wall
9 Curving Creek
10 Curving Crack Wall

7   Sentry-Box Crack   6m   Severe *
Climb easily to the sentry-box, then make a hard move to gain the ledge above.
Finish up a short wall.

8   Fingers Wall   6m   VS 4b
This brutal little wall problem joins Curving Crack at two-thirds height.

9   Curving Crack   6m   Very Difficult **
A good route which takes the crack direct.

10   Curving Crack Wall   6m   Very Difficult **
Climb straight up the attractive wall on good holds.

MAIN CRAG

This is the largest face. It has been girdled from left to right, finishing up The
Traverse.

11   Easy Face Groove   7m   VS 4a
The right edge of the easy face is followed by awkward moves directly up the
shallow groove.

12   Green Corner   10m   Very Difficult
At the left end is an obvious large corner which is climbed exiting directly or by
an easier shelf on the left.

13   Overhang Route   10m   VS 4b *
Step left from a convenient boulder then right to below a small roof. Climb the
roof by a slot high up for the right hand, strenuous. The first overhang can also
be climbed direct, raising the grade.

14   Flake Wall   10m   HVS 5a
This steep route climbs the tall narrow wall. Gain a foothold in the middle of the
wall, then make some hard moves up and left to better holds.

15   Vee Groove   12m   VS 4b
Climb the green groove, step right then left into a V-groove and climb this directly
to a hard finish. A variation finish is to step left to another groove on the upper
wall.

16   Big Corner   12m   Severe **
Climb directly up the very obvious corner running almost the full height of the
crag. It is possible to move left near the top and finish up an open groove.

17   The Arete   12m   E3 5b **
Protectionless climbing up the right bounding edge of Big Corner. Start in the
corner and as soon as possible make a hard move right onto the face and
continue up the arete.

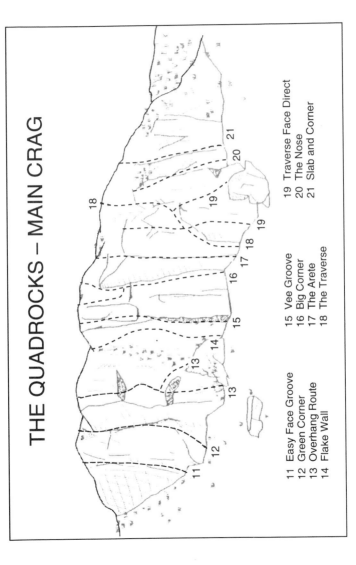

THE QUADROCKS – MAIN CRAG

11 Easy Face Groove
12 Green Corner
13 Overhang Route
14 Flake Wall

15 Vee Groove
16 Big Corner
17 The Arete
18 The Traverse

19 Traverse Face Direct
20 The Nose
21 Slab and Corner

18   The Traverse   12m   VS 4c ***
Probably the best route on the crag. Make a rising traverse across the steep face to a flake, gain its top and enter a bay above, exiting left or right.

19   Traverse Face Direct   10m   VS 4b **
Various starts lead to the middle of the traverse, from where it is possible to climb straight up very steep rock to a small niche and an easier finish.

20   The Nose   10m   VS 4a
Climb the edge forming the right-hand end of the traverse face, starting round the corner.

21   Slab and Corner   10m   Severe
Starting right of The Nose, follow a slab in the corner until the rock becomes vertical, then reach for holds high on the left.

22   Sunburst Red   10m   E3 5c **
The short wall at right end of crag, starting at a prominent hole in the rock.

HIGH CRAG
This is the outcrop well up and right of Low and Main Crags. The main line is quite long very pleasant and about Difficult in standard; it follows a direct line from the lowest rocks. Other short problems can be found.

LOUDOUN HILL   (Map Ref 609 379)

A prominent landmark for miles around, Loudoun Hill provides some excellent climbing on steep, rough and generally sound trachyte. Popularity is assured by a variety of quality routes at all grades, on walls, cracks and chimneys. The crags face south and dry quickly, but are quite lichenous, so care should be taken after rain. Alas, the expansion of the open cast quarry below the crag has marred an otherwise beautiful rural landscape.

   Two approaches are possible from Glasgow. Either follow the A77 and A726 via East Kilbride to Strathaven, then the A71 west to Darvel, or take the A77 and A719 to Galston then the A71 east to Darvel. A minor road below the hill (1.6km east of the Loudoun Inn or 4km west of Drumclog) leads in about 800 metres to the brow of a hill and parking. Go through the gate and follow the old wall on the right to the burn. The routes are described from left to right.

PULPIT ROCK
At the far left-hand end of the crag is a large isolated pinnacle, characterised on its left wall by the curving crack of Pulpit Crack and on the right the impressive Pulpit Arete. Although the face gives quality climbing, the rock is rather lichenous.

1   Pulpit Chimney   12m   Moderate   (1960s)
Climb cracks immediately left of Pulpit Rock to a ledge, then move right past
chockstones to the top.

2   Slings   12m   E3 5c **   (1978)
Sustained climbing with improving protection. The left face of Pulpit Rock has a
groove with an uninspiring, rusty, inverted and ancient knifeblade. Clip this, then
follow the groove to the top.

3   Lunge   15m   E3 6a ***   (1960s)
An excellent technical route requiring commitment and a cool head. The undercut nose leads past good runners to a small spike in the groove, poor nut runner.
Levitate into the groove and continue for some distance to protection. Finish up
the crack.

4   Pulpit Crack   20m   VS 4c **
The steep curving crack gives a classic climb, or a character building thrash,
depending on your skill with hand cracks. Finish up the arete. The wall to the
right can be climbed on small flake holds at 5c.

5   Pulpit Arete   20m   Severe 4a ***   (1930s)
Tremendous airy climbing up the arete dividing the two faces, but it's getting a
bit polished. From the gully on the right traverse left past a thin crack and climb
the arete direct to the top. A direct start coupled with the thin crack direct pushes
the grade to Hard Severe 4b.

   Cleaner rock can be found on the right face of Pulpit Rock. The steep slabby
wall rising from the gully gives an entertaining but rather artificial route; **Senile
Slab**, 5c (1978).

THE AMPHITHEATRE
Curving gently right from the Pulpit is The Amphitheatre. The left-hand side is
characterised by the small rectangular buttress taken by Mantelshelf Wall and
Cling, and the right-hand side by the flake crack of Epitaph Variation.

6   Amphitheatre Arete   15m   Difficult   (1960s)
Right of Pulpit Rock is a clean arete, which after a steep start leads to easier
climbing.

7   Gorse Route   10m   Difficult
Climb cracks on the left side of the small rectangular buttress.

8   Mantelshelf Wall   10m   VS 4b *   (1960s)
Technical climbing and no protection - a climb for the confident. The left edge
leads to a ledge, move right and go up with difficulty to finish on the right edge.

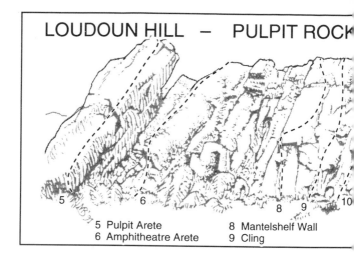

LOUDOUN HILL — PULPIT ROCK

5 Pulpit Arete
6 Amphitheatre Arete
8 Mantelshelf Wall
9 Cling

9   Cling   10m   E2 5c   (1960s)
Steep, technical moves up the right arete of the buttress lead to better holds, but
still no protection.

10   Shattered Corner   10m   Severe 4a   (1960s)
The corner forming the right-hand side of the small buttress.

11   Frustration Wall   10m   Hard Severe 4b **
To the right of Shattered Corner, climb twin cracks to a niche. Continue up the
groove, taking care with the rock to step left, then go up the wall above. Or, step
right and climb the steep crack (VS 5a). Popular and well worn.

12   Conclusion Wall   10m   Hard Severe 4b *   (1960s)
Just to the right, an inset groove gives easy climbing to steep bulging cracks at
the top.

   Mossy rock to the right can be climbed in various places at Moderate to Very
Difficult.

13   Epitaph   10m   VS 4c   (1960s)
Short but fun. Start below the obvious flake crack. Climb to the niche, take a deep
breath, then … delicately left.

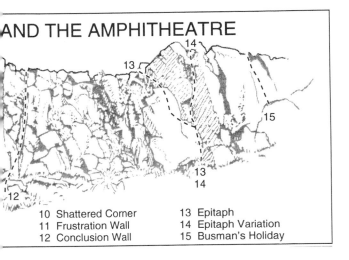

AND THE AMPHITHEATRE

10 Shattered Corner	13 Epitaph
11 Frustration Wall	14 Epitaph Variation
12 Conclusion Wall	15 Busman's Holiday

14   **Epitaph Variation**   10m   E2 5c **   (1960s/74)
Follow Epitaph to the niche, then power up the crack before the barn door opens.

Right of the flake crack is a green slot, **Coffin Chimney**, VS 4b (1960s), which is better than it looks.

15   **Busman's Holiday**   8m   VS 5a   (1993)
The cleaned crack right of Coffin Chimney gives a short, well protected problem.

THE WEST FACE
Below and right of The Amphitheatre is another long wall with a prominent hand crack and corners at its left-hand end, a steep wall with a small roof in the middle and the prominent chockstone-capped crack of Cave Crack at the right-hand end. The face has been girdled at E2 5b.

16   **Trench Direct**   12m   VS 4b   (1960s)
At the left end a short jamming crack gives pleasant climbing, but the gorse above and below is unforgiving. Finish up the crack on the right.

17   **Contortion Groove**   10m   VS 4c   (1960s)
Just to the right is a constricted, dirty V-groove with a mossy patch on the right wall. Grovel up the groove and finish up Trench Direct.

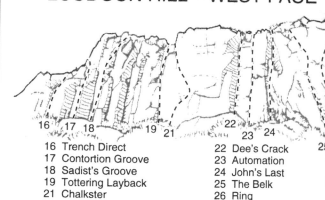

LOUDOUN HILL – WEST FACE

16 Trench Direct	22 Dee's Crack
17 Contortion Groove	23 Automation
18 Sadist's Groove	24 John's Last
19 Tottering Layback	25 The Belk
21 Chalkster	26 Ring

18 Sadist's Groove   10m   HVS 5a   (1960s)
This climbs the obvious corner leading to a prominent spike. Traverse right to a grass tuft and up.

19 Tottering Layback   8m   Hard Severe 4b   (1960s)
To the right is a green wall defined on its right by a flake crack overhung by a blocky roof. Layback the crack, move round the hollow roof with trepidation and dance through gorse bushes to the top.

20 Quick Skive   10m   HVS 5a **   (1993)
Exciting and surprisingly independent laybacking up the wall right of Tottering Layback.

21 Chalkster   12m   E2 5c **   (1981)
A fine crack and flake line cuts the left wall of the next steep buttress. Dangle right along the horizontal break to a runner (Rock 6), lunge for the flake and swing up the cracks. Great for gorillas.

22 Dee's Crack   10m   HVS 5a ***   (1960s)
Awkward climbing up the off-width and finger crack on the right side of the steep wall. A memorial to a certain Professor of Physics whose classes were skipped for the first ascent.

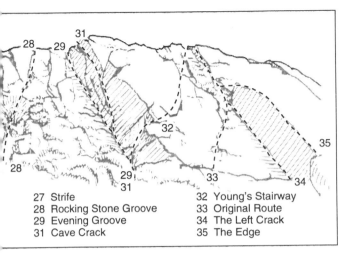

27 Strife
28 Rocking Stone Groove
29 Evening Groove
31 Cave Crack

32 Young's Stairway
33 Original Route
34 The Left Crack
35 The Edge

23   Automation   8m   E1 5b   (1960s)
Immediately right of Dee's Crack is a thin crack with an old peg. Independent
and hard at the start, but a bit artificial higher up. If you can avoid touching any
holds on other routes, the grade is E2 5c/6a.

24   John's Last   10m   HVS 5a
Loose rock and lichen mar the large overhung groove 2 metres right of Dee's
Crack.

25   The Belk   10m   E1 5b ***
Superb well protected climbing up the groove and crack line in the left-hand side
of the bulging wall right of John's Last. From the ledge below the top wall, climb
the crack, trending left to a block.

26   Ring   10m   HVS 5a   (1960s)
Poor protection and mossy rock characterise the shallow groove right of The
Belk. Finish right from the ledge below the top.

27   Strife   10m   Severe 4a *   (1960s)
This takes cracks up the right side of the bulging wall. Climb up to the large
semi-detached block on the right. From its top, step left and climb cracks on good
holds to the top.

28   Rocking Stone Groove   13m   Moderate
Behind the semi-detached block is a short grassy groove with two gorse bushes
at its base. This can be used as a descent, once you can find the top.

Further right, the West Face curves downwards to a wall with a prominent
hand crack topped by a chockstone.

29   Evening Groove   10m   Severe 4a   (1960s)
The wall left of the prominent crack is climbed to finish up the left-hand groove,
which is dirty.

30   Slab and Groove   13m   Hard Severe 4b   (1960s)
Start as for Evening Groove, but finish up the obvious slabby groove on the right.

31   Cave Crack   10m   VS 4c ***   (1960s)
Sustained and sometimes painful jamming leads to a spectacular finish over the
chockstone. Deduct points if you try to escape through the hole.

32   Young's Stairway   16m   Very Difficult
Start just right of Cave Crack, and follow the obvious traverse line up and right
across the face to above the pinnacle on the Central Wall. Finish by the easiest
line above. A direct start is possible at the same grade.

CENTRAL WALL

The upper part of this face is dominated by an impressive knife-edged pinnacle.
To its right is a steep wall taken by The Splits and right again are a series of
overhangs flanked on the right by the green groove of The Ramparts. A variety
of indifferent starts can be made up the broken mossy lower wall. The following
three routes can be gained by climbing the lower tier, or by a careful scramble
down grass from the base of Cave Crack. A high level girdle has been made at
VS 4c.

33   Original Route   45m   Difficult
Down and right of the old wall which crosses the path is a grassy area and then
a large mass of moss.
1. 30m   Climb the dirty wall left of the moss to the midway terrace. Ascend rock
and turf up the left side of the pinnacle to below the upper wall.
2. 15m   The right-slanting grass-filled diagonal fault is followed to a finish
behind the pinnacle.

34   The Left Crack   45m   Very Difficult   (1930s)
The wide chimney-crack between the left side of the pinnacle and the face gives
a good route.
1. 30m   Follow Original Route to below the upper wall.
2. 15m   The chimney-crack.

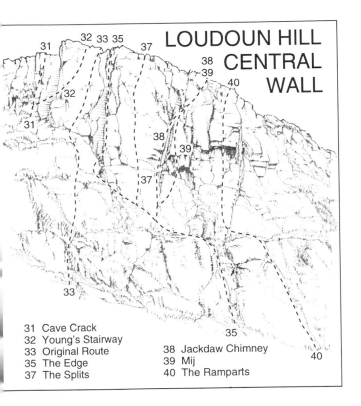

LOUDOUN HILL
CENTRAL
WALL

31 Cave Crack
32 Young's Stairway
33 Original Route
35 The Edge
37 The Splits

38 Jackdaw Chimney
39 Mij
40 The Ramparts

35   The Edge   45m   VS ***
A wild, wild route with a minimum of protection. The first pitch can be avoided by
an easy descent from Cave Crack.
1. 25m   Right of the mossy wall on the lower tier is a fairly clean open groove
with a large block on the right at the top. Ascend rock and turf up the left side of
the pinnacle to below the upper wall.
2. 20m 4b   Traverse right onto the arete and, with some trepidation, climb the
knife-edge to the top. A direct start has been made at 4c.

36   Foxglove Chimney   45m   Severe   (1930s)
The chimney-crack on the right-hand side of the pinnacle.
1. 25m   As for The Edge.
2. 20m 4a   Grunt up the crack, threading the chockstones as you go.

37   The Splits   45m   E1 **
Fingery climbing up the centre of the wall right of The Edge. The first pitch can
be avoided by a descent and traverse right from Cave Crack.
1. 25m   As for The Edge.
2. 20m 5b   Climb the thin crack in the wall to a small ledge, then move right and
up to the top.

38   Jackdaw Chimney   40m   Very Difficult   (1930s)
The groove forming the right edge of the wall gives pleasant but wandering
climbing.
1. 25m   As for The Edge.
2. 15m   Climb the corner crack to a ledge. Traverse right past loose flake, then
up to the top.

39   Mij   40m   Severe
Down and right of Jackdaw Chimney the line of overhangs are split by a wide
crack at their left-hand end.
1. 25m   As for The Edge.
2. 15m 4a   Follow the crack and wide groove to the traverse of Jackdaw
Chimney.

40   The Ramparts   40m   Severe *
Pleasant climbing leads to an exposed crux at the top of the shocking green
inverted V-groove, right of the overhangs.
1. 25m   Right of the mossy wall on the lower tier is a fairly clean open groove
with a large block on the right at the top. Climb the grassy groove right of and
below the block, then go up and right to belay below the groove.
2. 15m 4a   Climb the groove - lethal when damp - and make an energetic move
over the intimidating bulge on surprising holds. Continue by a choice of lines
above.

The cracks on the left wall of the crux of The Ramparts give a short and
artificial route – **Short Term Effect**, HVS 5a.

41   Staircase Crack   40m   Very Difficult
About 30 metres right of the old stone wall on the path is a clean rib. Climb the
left side of the rib, continue up the short wall above, then left and up corners,
grooves and short walls of good rock about 10 metres right of The Ramparts.

THE EASTERN BUTTRESS

A large roof characterises this buttress. The face gets less sun than the rest of the crag and the routes tend to be short, very lichenous and mossy. The best climbs take the ribs left and right of the roof. The face has been girdled at Severe.

42   The Hand Traverse   12m   HVS 5a

Down and left of the roof is an overhanging wall split by a horizontal crack. Traverse strenuously left to a ledge, then climb the shallow scoop above, or the blunt rib directly above the wall.

43   Nose Rib   15m   Severe 4a

A mossy and often wet rib bounds the left side of the large roof.

44   Suicide   25m   VS 4c

Start below the right side of the roof. Broken ground leads to a crack and a large flake. Stand on the flake and make a hard move up the crack to join Dusk Route.

45   Dusk Route   25m   Very Difficult **   (1930s)

Start at the lowest part of the crag below the roof. Climb a short wall to a slabby corner, which leads to ledges right of the large roof and below a small overhang. Climb the obvious left-trending flakes across the wall.

Further right the quality of the crag deteriorates. The grassy corner is climbed by **Spitfire**, Severe; **Wall and Groove**, Severe, takes the groove to the right and **The Blitz**, VS, the wall left of the overgrown zigzag crack right again. The wall right of the crack is **SCC Wall**, Severe. **Breakfast Route**, Very Difficult, climbs vegetated ground to the right.

MAUCHLINE GORGE   *(Map Ref 510 253)*

Adventure is the name of the game for anyone climbing on these red sandstone cliffs. The rock is generally solid, but a bit friable and the crags have a 'Lost World' atmosphere. Consequently, Mauchline is something of an acquired taste and certainly not for those of a nervous disposition. The crags lie on the banks of the River Ayr, a few miles south of Mauchline and close to the viaduct carrying the railway to Dumfries. The overhanging nature of River Buttress keeps it dry.

From Glasgow follow the A77 towards Kilmarnock, then the A76 to Mauchline. Follow the A76 south to make a hidden turn right, just before the sign for Bulloch-Myle Golf Club and the blue railings of the bridge carrying the road over the River Ayr. Follow the road to a parking place on the right. Cross the field and follow the path to the river, 5 minutes. The right side of the field has some fine examples of Stone Age cup and ring marks. The area is a Site of Special Scientific Interest and considerable care should be taken with the rock and the flora. The crags are described from left to right, going upstream from the prominent viaduct.

BOULDER CRAG

This is situated in the wood on the right of the approach path to the river. It has some bouldering, traverses and short routes.

BRIDGE BUTTRESS

This buttress lies below the viaduct and can only be reached when the river is very low, or by an abseil from under the viaduct.

Bushwhacker   20m   E1 5b   (1989)
Start below the viaduct at the right end of the crag. Climb up and past a tree root to a pocketed wall, then up and left to a ledge. Continue up a crack to a tree and a small slab.

RIVER BUTTRESS

About 100 metres upstream from the viaduct is an impressive buttress overhanging the river, with a prominent corner and roof in the centre. The routes are described from left to right.

Games of Chance and Sandancing   20m   E2 5b **   (1988)
The obvious steep crack line to the left of the prominent corner of Bridge Over Troubled Water gives a good route. Traverse right to finish at the same place as Ayrheid.

Bridge Over Troubled Water   25m   E4 5c **   (1988)
Well out there; some of the rock in the upper corner is thrillingly poor. Start in the centre of the buttress below and right of the corner. Climb a small corner and traverse left below roofs into the main corner line and follow this to a bay. Climb the overhanging corner above passing a peg runner. A very well hidden Rock 7 can be placed just before a step right to a resting place. Climb over two further roofs to a small ledge and runner. Traverse left and up to trees.

Ayrheid   25m   E2 *   (1988)
Generally good rock and very exciting climbing. Start in the centre of the buttress. 1. 10m 5b   Climb a small corner and traverse left below roofs into the main corner line. Follow this to a bay and belay.
2. 5m 5c   Traverse right and pull round the bulge to a good thread belay.
3. 10m 5a   Climb the wall above and move left to finish.

CHIMNEY CRAG

This is the large, wet and rather vegetated crag upstream from River Buttress.

The Chimney   20m   HVS 5a   (1970s)
Fight your way up the loose sandy fault and finish out left. It's a long time since it was climbed and it will probably stay that way!

THE MAIN QUARRY

This is situated in the woods above Chimney Crag. The crag is rather overgrown at the time of writing, but some good routes exist underneath for anyone prepared to do a bit of cleaning before they climb. There are also good belays for top-roping. The routes are described from left to right.

Bowman's Corner   10m   Severe 4a   (1986)
The dirty corner on the left.

Mossy Wall   15m   E2 5a   (1989)
The dirty wall right of the corner, finishing between the two trees.

Purism Personified   15m   E2 5a   (1986)
Start behind the puddle at a faint crack. Climb this and the steep wall above to finish left of the tree; unprotected.

Gardener's Corner   15m   VS 4b *   (1986)
Reasonable protection can be found for this shallow left-facing corner.

Board Walk   15m   E2 5b   (1987)
The clean wall between the two corners has been led with peg runners (not *in situ*).

Y Bother   12m   E3 5c   (1987)
Climb the left-hand crack of the Y-crack in the large square-cut corner. Hard to protect and climb.

Bye Eck   12m   E4 6a   (1987)
Unprotected climbing up the arete to the right of the corner. Tall and strongies should climb it direct, short and less strongies to the right (technical).

Green Machine   15m   VS 4b   (1987)
Climb the dirty wall between the two aretes, then the slab above.

Dredge Bog   15m   VS 4b   (1986)
The blunt arete to the right may be easier when clean!

Monstrously Horrible   15m   Very Dirty   (1986)
Slither up or down roots to the right. Several alternatives are possible, the best being to avoid it altogether!

Lightning Crack   6m   E2 6a   (1989)
The very far right end of the quarry is crossed by the path. This clean route lies on the small buttress forming the continuation of the quarry wall on the right, overlooking Table Rock, and is approached by a scramble down through bushes. Start with boulder problem moves up the left-hand crack, traverse right and finish up the crack.

SPHINX ROCK
Further upstream and beside the river is Table Rock, a large and very steep crag marred by its extremely soft lower section. Sphinx Rock lies to the left of Table Rock and has a large overhang on its left and a small slab on its right.

Corner Root   5m   Severe 4a   (1986)
Climb the corner to the right of the slab.

GLEN AFTON   *(Map Ref 629 054)*

A scattering of granite crags lie on the north-west spur of Craigbraneoch Rig, just north of Afton Reservoir. The most obvious feature is the 25m lower wall, known as Stayamrie. The rock is excellent, but seepage and the north-facing aspect mean three or four days are needed for the crag to dry. The crag is already quite popular with Ayr-based climbers, and the routes should improve with traffic.

From Glasgow follow the A77 to Kilmarnock, then the A76 to New Cumnock. Take the B747 to Dalmellington, but turn left after about 45 metres into Glen Afton. At the end of the public road the crag is easily seen on the left across the burn.

STAYAMRIE
This is the smooth steep buttress at the foot of the crag, identified by a prominent right-curving crack at its left end.

Magic Carpet   30m   VS 4c   (1992)
The wide crack at the extreme left end of the wall. Start 3 metres right of the crack and climb past an awkward ledge to a grass ledge at the start of the main crack. Exit left to finish.

Midnight Express   25m   E1 5b **   (1992)
Follow the thin crack in the wall left of the curving crack. A fine climb, but often wet.

Stone Circle   30m   E1 5b ***   (1992)
Exciting, sustained and unusual climbing up the prominent curving crack.

The Crack of Doon   30m   HVS 5a *   (1991)
When dry and clean this route gives excellent climbing up the obvious vertical crack leading to and joining the top of the conspicuous curving crack.

Hyacinth House   25m   E2 5b *   (1992)
Steep and uncompromising climbing right of the blank section of the wall. From a small niche, climb up and right into a large niche at 5m and continue, finishing up the wall to the left of the top grass ledge.

Sweet Liberty   25m   E3 5c *   (1992)
Thin and delicate climbing up the thin right-trending ramp right of Hyacinth
House and below an overhanging tree. A small corner leads to a ledge, then
move up the ramp right to finish.

Grass Roots   30m   VS 4c   (1977)
Start a few metres right of the smooth wall. Ascend a line of good holds trending
right to a perched block. Surmount this with care and follow awkward vegetated
ramp and rock steps. A direct start (E1 5b, 1990) climbs straight up to the right
end of the grass ledge.

Delirium   30m   E4 6a **   (1992)
A technical, sustained and quick-drying climb. Start at the foot of Grass Roots
and climb directly up the wall to an overlap and peg. Climb up to twin pegs and
move leftwards up the thin ramp line to finish.

The next two routes lie on the buttress up and right of Stayamrie.

Rehabilitation Route   40m   Very Difficult   (1977)
Start left of the vague central mossy groove and climb straight up on good holds,
by-passing the overhang on the right. Move left then up the edge to finish.

Two Plus Two   35m   Severe 4a   (1978)
Start a few metres right of the mossy groove and climb the rib to a perched block.
Turn bulging rock above by a corner on the right.

Deception Slab   30m   HVS 5a   (1978)
This route is on the narrow slab to the right of the previous routes and about 250
metres right of the Main Wall. The central line is sustained, but a bit dirty.

Raven Slab   25m   HVS 4c*   (1978)
The last route is on the large slab above and left of Stayamrie. Interesting but
unprotected climbing leads up a central line on the slab.

AYRSHIRE MINOR CRAGS

CRAIGS OF KYLE   *(Map Ref 428 155)*

This pleasant small crag gives entertaining bouldering. Leave the A713 (Dalmellington Road) east of Hollybush at the turning to Drongan, then continue to
an old quarry on the left, parking below it. Cross the gate on the right and walk
uphill into a small valley which leads to the crag in about 5 minutes.

BENBEOCH   *(Map Ref 495 083)*

This crag presents columns of rough south-facing basalt with short corner and crack climbs from Difficult to E2. The crags have been climbed on for many years, but no routes were recorded. Approach via the track leading to Benbain, which starts by bricked-up cottages below the crag; allow 20 minutes. Please ask permission at the farm. Well worth a look.

TAPPET HILL   *(Map Ref 533 128)*

This curious dolerite quarry, somewhat loose in parts, has magnificent views and two routes. **Tap Dance**, VS 4c, takes the prominent arete and **Cumnock Wall**, VS 4c, the wall to the left. From Dalmellington, follow the B741 towards New Cumnock for 10km to a left turning, signposted Cumnock. Continue for 5km, then turn left to Dalgig. Pass an open cast mine and park 200 metres later. A faint track leads to the quarry in 10 minutes.

The Galloway Hills

Tucked away in the south-west corner of Scotland lies this rounded and extensive range of hills. The area that is of interest to the rock climber is the chain of granite hills between the Merrick in the west and the Rhinns of Kells to the east. Relatively unfrequented and unspoiled, one of the attractions of this remote area is the large granite crags which await those prepared to step off the beaten track and risk a day's climbing. To date the best climbing has been found in two distinct groups: the first is the remote crags of the Dungeon of Buchan, and second, the friendly and accessible crags of Craignelder.

Since the publication of the previous edition of the guide, exploration at Dungeon of Buchan has produced a number of quality climbs and the new venue of Mullwharchar has been discovered.

The maps required for the crags in this chapter are OS sheets 77, 79 and 83.

MULLWHARCHAR   (Map Ref 460 872)

The granite cliffs on the north-east side of Mullwharchar give remote and idyllic climbing. Behind The Mask on the columnar rock of the Organ Pipes is worth a particular mention. The crags take about four summer days to dry.

The quickest approach for all the crags is from Loch Doon. Park at the south end of the loch and follow the forestry road south to its end. Cross the bridge about 140 metres to the right and follow the path on the left. For The Slock, leave the path after about 15 minutes and cut up right to the crags (1½ hours, 30 minutes with a mountain bike).

For the Giant's Stairway and the Organ Pipes, continue southwards along the valley for just over 2km. The crags are situated in the corrie under the summit of Mullwharchar and are visible from the path. The Giant's Stairway is immediately past the two burns in the corrie, with the Organ Pipes behind and higher (2 hours, or 1 hour with a mountain bike).

The approach from Loch Trool via Loch Enoch and Mullwharchar is 2½ hours, and from Craigencallie via Backhill of Bush 2½ hours (or 1½ hours with a mountain bike).

THE SLOCK   *(Map Ref 457 894)*

This is the large rambling cliff on the north-east end of Mullwharchar.

The Gullet   70m   Very Difficult   (1992)
Climb the right-hand of two vegetated parallel gullies, situated on the southern end of the cliff.

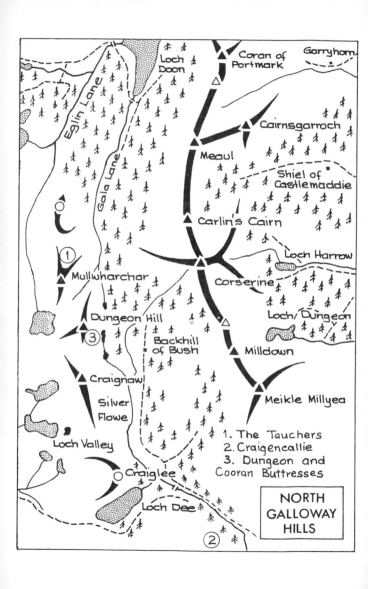

NORTH
GALLOWAY
HILLS

1. The Tauchers
2. Craigencallie
3. Dungeon and
   Cooran Buttresses

THE TAUCHERS   *(Map Ref 456 874)*

This is the north-east corrie of Mullwharchar, which contains the best climbing hereabouts.

THE GIANT'S STAIRCASE

A rather rambling cliff giving good mountain style routes - excellent rock separated by heather and scrambling. The main face looks north-east towards Loch Doon and is more continuous at its right end. The routes are described from right to left.

The Raiders   105m   HVS   (1992)
Towards the right side of the crag at about one-third height, and directly above the large tree in the burn, is a pale slabby wall. Scramble up to its foot. A superb first pitch.
1. 35m 5a   Climb steep parallel cracks to a ledge, then go two metres right and up and right to finish up a corner. Easier ground leads right to a block belay.
2. 35m 4b   Descend slightly right and follow a rib to finish up an awkward flared chimney. Two short walls lead to a belay in a grassy bay below a steep wall.
3. 35m 4a   Skirt the wall on the right and continue left via short walls to finish.

Bugle   125m   VS   (1992)
Good climbing on the first pitch and low in the grade. Slightly below and left of the pale slabby wall of The Raiders is a slab with a right-slanting corner in its middle section.
1. 40m 4b   Follow the main corner up then right to exit via a short and awkward corner. Climb the wall above and continue left to belay.
2. 40m 4b   A short wall leads to a large heather bay. Scramble up to a steep wall and follow the layback crack in its left corner. Climb another steep wall with two parallel cracks to an arete on the right and a belay.
3. 35m 4a   Follow a grassy ramp, then go up a short chimney to a small tree. Climb a small wall, then go left up the steep groove above.
4. 10m 4a   Scramble up easy rock to finish.

Solstice   25m   HVS 5b *   (1992)
Steep climbing up the obvious crack in the wall high on the left side of the crag.

Switchback   80m   Very Difficult   (1992)
At the left toe of the crag is a clean rib.
1. 45m   Climb a right-facing corner until it is possible to move onto an arete on the right. Follow this and the slab above, then go left up easier rock to belay below a short wall.
2. 20m   The short wall leads to a heather ledge below a steep wall. Walk right to below a right-facing corner.
3. 15m   Climb the corner and steep chimney-groove above to finish on slabs.

THE ORGAN PIPES
Up and left from the Giant's Staircase, this crag abounds with impressive corners and ribs.

The Dungeonmaster   75m   HVS *   (1992)
Good climbing. At the bottom right of the crag is a buttress with two steep corners.
1. 30m 5a   Climb the left corner to where it splits into three. Follow the leftmost corner to a belay ledge.
2. 10m 4a   Traverse left to a grassy ledge, then follow the ledge left to belay in a large corner.
3. 35m 4a   Follow the left-hand corner to finish up slabs and walls on the left.

Behind the Mask   45m   E1 5b **   (1992)
Climb the fine groove in the rib left of the huge corner on the left side of the crag.

GOAT ROCK
This two-tiered crag lies on the ridge on the left of the corrie and left of the Organ Pipes. The rock is good, but the climbing limited.

Kid's Stuff   25m   Severe 4a   (1992)
Climb the right-slanting slab on the right side of the upper tier.

The Nose   15m   Severe 4a   (1992)
Climb the nose on the upper tier by the easiest line.

CRAIGENCALLIE   *(Map Ref 500 783)*

A number of pleasant crags of easily accessible, clean rough epidiorite lie on this south-east facing hillside. The most impressive piece of rock is the steep Main Wall on the right-hand side, which provides one of the best lines on South-West granite in Delta of Venus. In addition, Flake Buttress on the right wall of the obvious gully splitting the left-hand area has a fine slab. Peregrines nest here and a voluntary ban should be observed from May to August.
    From Ayr follow the A713 through Dalmellington to a right turn to Glenlee just before the bridge south of the Earlstoun Loch dam (A762). Follow this past the power station to a right turn to Glenlee, which is taken to a left turn at a no-through road sign, on to a single track road over Maggot Hill. Turn right at the junction with the A712 and continue past Clatteringshaws Loch to a right turn to Craignell and Galloway Forest Park - Loch Dee. Follow the road to where it ends below the crag, which is 10 minutes up the hillside.

ARROW BUTTRESS
A grassy slope leads up and right to the Main Wall. About 80m down and left of this wall is a small steep buttress with trees at the top.

Decaffenator   12m   VS 4c   (1991)
Near the right-hand side of this buttress is a right-trending steep slab. Climb the
thin crack in the outer right side of the slab - worthwhile.

The Grey Man   20m   VS 4c   (1993)
Beneath the large oak tree in the centre of the crag is a large corner-crack. Climb
this for 7m, then go up the thin right-trending crack in the cleaned right wall to a
ledge. Continue up the walls above to another oak.

Across The Barricades   20m   E3 6a ***   (1992)
Excellent technical and sustained climbing. Start at the corner in the centre of
the steep white wall forming the left side of the buttress. Follow the corner to a
right-trending overhang and traverse below to the right edge of the buttress.
Move back left and cross the overhang at the break. Climb directly to a small
tree at the break and finish up the crack in the headwall.

Tree Sanctuary   15m   Hard Severe 4b *   (1993)
At the left end of the buttress is a cracked wall which leads past a small tree to
a steep cracked upper wall.

SLAB BUTTRESS
This is long slabby buttress which lies 30m up and right of Arrow Buttress, and
passed on the walk up to Main Wall.

Alligator   35m   Very Difficult   (1991)
Start near the left end of the buttress. Climb up to the left edge of the steeper
section, then traverse right for 3m and go up slabs to the top. A direct start is
possible at VS 4c.

The Scream   55m   HVS   (1984)
1. 35m 4b   Start in the middle of the buttress and climb up left to cross the
overlap and belay on the ledge above.
2. 20m 5a   The water-worn corner leads to a steep smooth slab and a finish
over steep blocks.

Walkabout   30m   Severe 4a   (1985)
Follow a line of good holds about 5 metres right of The Scream to finish on a
ledge.

MAIN WALL
Above and right is the steep Main Wall. The two routes recorded so far climb
lines on its left-hand side. The routes are described from left to right.

Deviator   40m   VS 4c   (1977)
A circuitous route. Gain a vegetated ledge from its right-hand end and traverse
it leftwards. Trend left up a vague rock ramp, surmounting a bulge to steepening

rock. Traverse horizontally right under bulging rock for about 5 metres until it is possible to break through overhangs on good holds.

Eliminator   35m   E1 5b *   (1977)
This climbs the crack just right of Deviator. Climb thin flake cracks up the mossy wall to the vegetated ledge. Follow the crack to a prominent triangular niche, then continue to gain an easier right-trending rock ramp. Go up the ramp to a horizontal flake runner, then pull left and break through overhangs. Good climbing, and worth a couple of stars if clean, but it's getting a bit dirty now.

Delta of Venus   30m   E4 6a ***   (1993)
Brilliant, sustained and technical climbing up the thin finger-searing crack 8 metres right of Eliminator. Start 3 metres right of the grass ledge of Deviator and climb past a small triangular niche to the start of the crack. The crux is reaching the first ledge, although the climbing above is sustained right to the top. Belay to the right on stakes on the grass ledge.

FLAKE BUTTRESS
This is the slabby wall forming the right side of the obvious short gully on the left-hand side of the hillside and identified by a large semi-detached flake on its right flank. The routes are described from right to left.

Cranium Edge   50m   VS 4c *   (1977)
Start about 5 metres left of the edge beneath an obvious wide crack. Climb the shattered crack, trending right to the edge. Surmount the cracked overhang (crux), then go up the groove to the top of a huge flake. Move left and up to the top of another flake. Climb short steep walls and the arete to finish.

Raven Seek Thy Brother   45m   VS **   (1985)
This takes the long crack up the full length of the wall. Start about 5m up the gully at a large spike.
1. 35m 4c   Climb the crack on the left side of the spike, pull over the bulge, move left onto the open slab and follow it until forced back into a crack. This leads to a ledge.
2. 10m 4c   Finish up the crack and wall.

Talk to the Wind   25m   HVS 5a   (1985)
About 15m up the gully is an open groove left of an obvious flake. Climb the groove to an ear-shaped flange of rock and continue up the slab above to the overhang. Move right then straight up (thin) to finish right of the final overlap.

Thumbs Up   25m   HVS 5a *   (1993)
Start about 20m up the gully and about 3 metres right of a triangular chimney, at an overlap and three thin cracks. Climb the central crack and surmount the bulge to gain a large flat hold below the overlap. Climb it direct and pull onto the upper slab (easier 2 metres to the right) and follow the crack to the top.

FAR SLAB BUTTRESS

The slab to the left of the gully has a number of routes, which are described from left to right.

The Cry   35m   Severe 4a   (1984)
Climb the left side of the slab to a hairline crack at 20m.

The Shout   35m   Severe 4a   (1984)
From the lowest point of the slab, follow the best rock to a suspect flake. Continue up the slab to a long thin crack.

Secret Garden   25m   Very Difficult   (1984)
Start 5 metres right of The Shout. Climb to a ramp and follow it up and left. Finishing via a steep wall increases the grade to Hard Severe.

DUNGEON OF BUCHAN   *(Map Ref 462 848)*

Three excellent south-east facing crags of sound clean granite lie in splendid isolation above the twin Lochs of the Dungeon. The arduousness of the approach is somewhat mitigated by the quality of the climbing and the wild beauty of the surroundings. Seepage can be a problem early in the season, while by late summer the crags take about a day to dry after rain. Scottish Natural Heritage have requested that no climbing takes place from 1st April to 31st July due to rare birds nesting.

From New Galloway, follow the A712 to Clatteringshaws Loch. Turn right past the loch and park at Craigencallie. From here follow the forestry road to Backhill of Bush bothy, an excellent base for this crag. Opposite the bothy, select an appropriate break in the forest to the edge of the marsh (a Site of Special Scientific Interest) which should be skirted to the north; 10½ km, 2½ hours from Craigencallie, although the approach can be eased to 1½ hours by using mountain bikes as far as the bothy.

DUNGEON BUTTRESS

This is the steep rectangular buttress on the left-hand side of the hill. A terrace splits the crag near the top and climbers with 45m ropes may wish to belay there, as many of the belays at the top of the crag are well back. The routes are described from left to right.

1   Galloway Grooves   35m   Very Difficult *   (1991)
Enjoyable climbing. Start in the gully at the left end of the crag and traverse right along a shelf. Swing round onto the face, move up to a right-slanting diagonal groove and follow this to a detached block. Gain the slab above and move rightwards to a short open chimney.

2   Battle Axe   35m   Hard Severe 4b   (1991)
Climb the crack just right of the edge of the gully to a wide crack and a grass ledge. Stretch up the groove behind to finish up the arete.

3   Carrick Corner   35m   VS 4c **   (1991)
The obvious corner on the left side of the crag leads to an awkward exit and the detached block of Galloway Grooves. The slab slightly left leads to an overhung niche and a thrutchy finish.

4   Bruce's Stone   35m   E1 5b *   (1991)
A fine route with a difficult start. Climb the right arete of the corner direct to a tiny ledge. Continue straight up the arete to a slab, move left and finish up the blunt arete between the finish of Carrick Corner and Galloway Grooves.

5   Scots Wha' Hae   35m   E1 5b **   (1991)
Excellent climbing. Right of the arete is a steep crack with several large jammed flakes. Climb the crack to the tiny ledge of Bruce's Stone. Make a hard move up and right to a shallow niche and pull left over the roof to regain the arete, which is followed to slabs. Trend right then left to finish.

6   Incy Wincy Spider   35m   E2 5b **   (1991)
A superb route, strenuous and intimidating. Climb the steep jamming crack 2 metres right of Scots Wha' Hae to a niche. Reach over the roof and hand traverse right to a reverberating pinnacle. Pull over leftwards using the pinnacle, step left and go up to a thread. Continue to the terrace, finishing up the corner right of the cracked arete.

7   Parcel of Rogues   35m   E3 **   (1991)
Superb strenuous and sustained climbing with good protection. Start below a crack leading to a huge overhung niche 10 metres right of Incy Wincy Spider.
1. 30m 6a   Climb up to the crack and follow it to a small ledge. Make a difficult jamming traverse left and climb the obvious undercut groove, exiting right at the top. A bold move leads to the terrace.
2. 5m 5b   Climb the prominent impending slanting crack in the narrow arete.

8   Free Land   35m   HVS 5b   (1991)
The first pitch gives a good jam session at the top end of the grade.
1. 30m 5b   Climb the left-hand crack in the wall 2 metres right of Parcel of Rogues to a small ledge. A short groove leads to a belay on a huge block.
2. 5m 5a   The cracks in the right side of the arete.

9   Bannockburn   35m   E1 5b *   (1991)
A good test of jamming technique. Climb the triple crack system in the centre of the wall to a ledge on the left - phew! Return to the cracks and make hard but well protected moves to gain the large heather ledge. Finish up the impending off-width at the back.

DUNGEON BUTTRESS

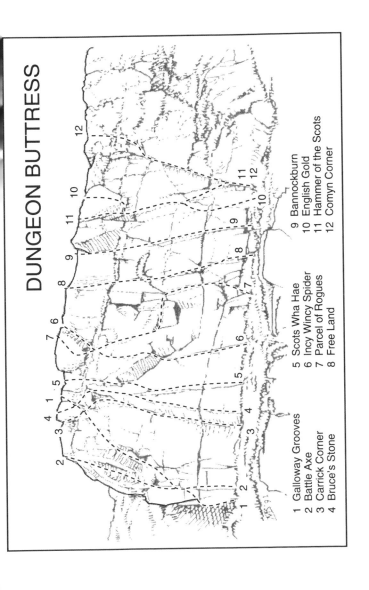

1 Galloway Grooves
2 Battle Axe
3 Carrick Corner
4 Bruce's Stone

5 Scots Wha Hae
6 Incy Wincy Spider
7 Parcel of Rogues
8 Free Land

9 Bannockburn
10 English Gold
11 Hammer of the Scots
12 Comyn Corner

10   English Gold   35m   E3   (1991)
A harder variation to Hammer of the Scots, starting 2 metres left of the right-slanting groove on the right side of the crag.
1. 25m 5b   Climb a crack and where it closes hand traverse diagonally right into
the crack of Hammer of the Scots, then go up this to belay in the niche.
2. 10m 5c   Traverse horizontally right under a hanging beak of rock and pull
over the roof to finish up twin cracks. A well protected but strenuous pitch.

11   Hammer of the Scots   35m   E1 5b   (1991)
A good route - when dry! Start at the base of the right-slanting groove on the right
side of the crag. An awkward crack leads to the huge niche which is surmounted
by difficult bridging.

12   Comyn Corner   35m   VS 4a   (1991)
Climb the right-slanting groove, or its right arete, finishing up the wall above. Low
in the grade.

COORAN BUTTRESS

This crag runs the full length of the hillside to the right of Dungeon Buttress and
has a number of good routes, split by heather ledges. The first route climbs the
broken ridge of clean rock that bounds the far left-hand side of the buttress.

13   Traitor's Gait   115m   VS   (1984)
Good climbing with escape possible to the left at most levels. Start at a crack
line at the lowest point of the left-hand toe of the buttress.
1. 30m 4a   Climb the crack to a ledge on the left after 8m, then continue up and
slightly rightwards to a large heather ledge.
2. 30m 3c   Move right to a slab, then climb to a ledge and thread belay on a
leaning block.
3. 20m 4a   Directly above and 4 metres left of the block is a short steep crack.
Follow this for 5m, then go left to a ledge and up the arete and slabs to the final
wall.
4. 35m 4c   Follow cracks and move left to a large ledge on the left edge of the
buttress. Climb the parallel cracks to the right of the arete to the top. The arete
can be climbed at 4b.

To the right are two grassy fault lines. **Cooran Buttress** (1955) and **Roriama**
(1978), both Very Difficult, meander in this area. Right again is a large clean
buttress flanked by an impressive corner.

14   The Highway Man   130m   HVS *   (1968)
The original hard route of the crag. Start 10 metres left of the corner, below
cracks.
1. 45m 5a   Climb a shallow groove to the central crack which is followed to the
slabs. After about 2m, traverse 3 metres right, then climb a groove to a large

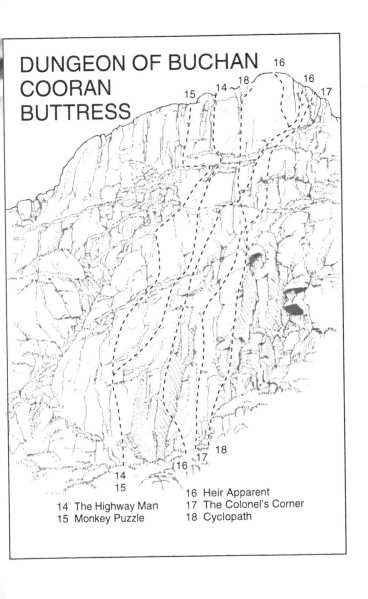

DUNGEON OF BUCHAN
COORAN
BUTTRESS

14 The Highway Man
15 Monkey Puzzle
16 Heir Apparent
17 The Colonel's Corner
18 Cyclopath

spike at its top. Move left and up onto an upper slab, climb a crack just left of the rib, then go left and over a bulge to a heather terrace. Belay at the right-hand end below a tiny roof.

2. 55m 4c   Climb directly up a crack just left of the roof to a narrow terrace (possible belay). Climb the crack in the short wall behind and scramble up heather to the final wall.

3. 30m 4a   Climb the crack-groove line a few metres up and left of the impressive central crack of Cyclopath.

15   Monkey Puzzle   130m   VS   (1991)
Pleasant climbing filling the gap left of The Highway Man and starting as for that route.

1. 45m 4c   Climb a shallow groove to the central crack which is followed to the slabs. Continue directly up the crack onto the upper slab and the terrace.

2. 25m 4c   Starting about 4 metres left of the tiny roof, climb a wide crack cutting through a bulge with difficulty. Follow it to a steepening, then take an obvious traverse right to a terrace.

3. 30m 4a   Start just right of a short wet chimney and take a right-slanting line up the short wall to heather. Scramble up the left-hand side to the final wall.

4. 30m 4b   Climb the fluted cracks to the left of the finish of The Highway Man to a perched block, then follow the cracks behind to the top.

16   Heir Apparent   130m   E1 **   (1991)
An excellent sustained way up the crag. Start at the foot of the corner on the right of the buttress.

1. 45m 5b   Climb steeply up the left wall to a good flake, then swing up left and make an awkward mantelshelf onto a small ledge. The groove above leads to an easier groove in the left arete of the corner, then go up and left to a large spike. Stand on this and swing back right into a corner which is followed to a belay under a tiny roof at the right-hand end of the terrace. A good pitch.

2. 55m 5a   Pass the roof on the right and continue, moving slightly right to an awkward move on to a sloping ledge. Easier climbing via a niche leads to a heather ledge (possible belay). Climb the short wall above and scramble to the final wall.

3. 30m 5b   Gain the long thin flake in the smooth wall with difficulty, then follow it past a small ledge until just below its top, where a step right onto a sloping foothold can be made. Swing right into the groove of The Colonel's Corner and climb the overhanging jam crack direct.

Direct Finish: E2 5b
Follow the long thin flake to its top. Swing up left to holds and stand on them, then go straight up the slight flake above to good handholds. Hand traverse left into a scoop and finish more easily. Superb, but committing.

17   The Colonel's Corner   130m   HVS **   (1991)

A tremendous outing starting up the huge corner on the right of the crag.

1. 45m 5a   Follow the corner to a steep finish and exit left by a poised flake. Above, cracks lead to two short V-grooves. Climb the right-hand one to the stance on Cyclopath.

2. 55m 4b   Climb up to and follow an easy right-slanting groove with a small bulge, which leads to a narrow ledge. Move up left to a square grass ledge, then go up to a higher ledge. Follow a wide crack on the right for a short distance before quitting it for the arete on the right. Climb this in a sensational position to a spike (possible belay). Scramble up to the final wall.

4. 30m 5a   On the right is an overhung groove with two poised blocks. Climb the groove with trepidation to the top of the second block. Either climb a jamming crack above (5b) or avoid it by traversing 2 metres right into a second groove and finish up this, moving right near the top.

18   Cyclopath   130m   E1 *   (1982)

Bold slab climbing on the first pitch puts this fine route into the Extreme grade. Start at the foot of the slabby right wall of The Colonel's Corner.

1. 45m 5a   Climb a groove in the slab, move left onto the wall and go up flakes to the start of a crack. Follow this widening crack to the right-hand of twin V-chimneys, which is followed to a belay on the right. An excellent pitch.

2. 55m 4c   Climb the wall behind the stance to a blunt spike in the right-slanting groove of The Colonel's Corner. Follow a thin crack through the bulge above to a possible belay on the terrace. Pick the best line up the short wall, then scramble to the obvious central crack in the final wall.

3. 30m 4c   Climb the crack to the top.

19   Cooran Chimney   135m   E1   (1993)

The obvious capped chimney high on the right side of the buttress proves to be a fine example of its type! Start in a grassy bay slightly down from and 20 metres right of The Colonel's Corner.

1. 50m 5b   Scramble across a slab and up grass to a notable rock fin. Climb this to a terrace, then traverse left to the buttress proper. Follow a long groove to the base of the chimney, then climb it with difficulty to a roof and a traverse left to a belay.

2. 25m 4b   Move back right above the roof and climb an easy groove to a shelf below a wall (junction with Colonel's Corner). Traverse right along the shelf, past where Colonel's Corner moves up, to a short corner. Climb this, pulling out left to easier ground.

3. 30m 4c   Traverse 5 metres right to a dirty V-groove splitting the arete. Climb this on excellent holds past a hollow flake, then follow slabs and grass to belay at the right end of the upper terrace.

4. 30m 4c   Climb the obvious rightmost groove in the headwall.

There are many small and broken outcrops on the hillside to the right of Cooran Buttress, but nothing has been recorded to date. However 300 metres down and to the right a route has been made up the clean terraced slabs.

20   Saddle Tramp   75m   E2 *   (1982)
A fine route at the lower limit of the grade. The major difficulties are concentrated in the final few moves of the excellent final pitch. Start below an obvious diagonal crack at 45m and a convex white slab just down and right from two perched blocks.
1. 40m 5a/b   Climb more or less directly up the middle of the slab, the technical grade depending on the directness of the line. Step right over grass and follow a crack in the second slab, through a bulge, to belay on a bilberry ledge below a right-slanting crack in the steep upper wall.
2. 35m 5b   Climb a groove left of the crack to a horizontal break, then follow this right to a large triangular niche. From the top of the niche, a crack leads to a large sloping ledge. Move left to a thin crack and finish boldly up this.

CRAIGNELDER   *(Map Ref 505 698)*

This northern outlier of Cairnsmore of Fleet exhibits lots of excellent granite, but few continuous faces and remarkably little climbing. The slabby crag overlooking the A712 New Galloway to Newton Stewart road and facing Murray's Monument is called Big Gairy (Map Ref 492 702) while Craig-an-Eilte (Map Ref 498 698) lies hidden behind, further to the south. Both crags require some effort to get to, despite their proximity to the road, but they offer the advantage of a southern aspect and solitude.

Park at the Talnotry Forest Trail car-park opposite Talnotry Camp Site (Map Ref 487 716). Walk through the site and follow the river downstream for a short way to a bridge. Cross and continue downstream until the first firebreak in the forest leads to Big Gairy (allow 1 hour).

BIG GAIRY

The vegetated terraces and slabs are split by a grassy gully.

Pale Face   65m   Mild VS   (1984)
This is a pleasant slab route, especially if the easier variations are avoided. Start immediately right of the gully.
1. 15m   From the right toe of a band of light-coloured slabs, climb easily to a ledge beneath a short crack.
2. 15m   Climb the wall above leftwards (crux) to a ledge and belay. A delicate pitch.
3. 5m   Twin cracks lead to a ledge.
4. 30m   Climb the slabs on the right to a bulge, move left and climb a short corner. Take a final slab and bulge direct to easier ground.

Cyclopath, Dungeon of Buchan (Climber, Joe Grinbergs)

CRAIG AN EILTE

Further south from Big Gairy is a hidden hillside with more vegetated slabs. However, high on the left-hand side is an impressive looking prominent tower with a number of routes. Alas, first appearances are often deceptive. The crag is about $1\frac{1}{2}$ hours from the road.

Gloom   25m   Severe 4a   (1984)
Atmospheric climbing. Start at the left edge of the tower, directly under the roof. Thrutch up the off-width to the roof, or, more elegantly, climb the rib on its left, and move up left to a large ledge. Traverse left again and finish up grassy corners.
Direct Finish: HVS 5a   (1992)
From the large ledge, mantelshelf onto a small ledge and move boldly up onto the wall. Toe traverse right to the arete and finish up this. A better finish.
Super Direct: E2 5c *   (1992)
From the large ledge, stride right onto a good foothold on the lip of the roof and follow the arete, mainly on the right. Good bold climbing.

The Original Route   20m   Severe 4b *   (1978)
An obscure gem. Start just right of Gloom at a narrow crack. Follow this and the prominent right-trending groove system to a steep finish up the impending crack.

The Flesh Market   25m   VS 4c   (1992)
Climb the steep wall just right of the Original Route on good holds to a ledge. Traverse right over a large flake, then go slightly downwards onto footholds on the wall. Move right and follow the jam crack to the top.

Elite Pinnacle Rib   25m   Difficult   (1992)
Right again, a short chimney with huge poised blocks leads to a ledge. Follow a second chimney on the left of a large pinnacle to a rib which is climbed mostly on the right on good holds.
Variation: Severe   (1991)
Step left from the top of the second chimney and follow a thin crack delicately up and left to a tricky airy step. Continue more easily to the top.

The next three routes lie on the tower above the previous climbs.

Guledig   20m   Severe 4c   (1992)
A useful finish for the lower routes. Start at an overhung groove in the arete on the right of the tower. Make a difficult move to good holds, then follow the arete above to the top.

Gwyr Y Gogledd, Craig an Eilte (Climbers, Adrian Moore and John Campbell)

Gwyr Y Gogledd   20m   E1 5b *   (1992)
The impressive north-facing wall overlooking the gully gives a fine sustained route. Start at the right-hand side of the wall and climb to a shallow V-niche in the centre of the face. Traverse right to footholds on the arete, then go up and left up cracks to the top.

No Hawkers or Campbells   20m   HVS 5a   (1992)
The left-hand side of the wall is harder than it looks. Climb strenuously up cracks to the large depression, then go up the left-hand crack to the top.

CLINTS OF DROMORE   *(Map Ref 542 641)*

Beautiful rock and beautiful scenery with pleasant but rather ill-defined climbing in the lower and middle grades. Many of the routes can be soloed or climbed in a variety of places, depending on the level of difficulty desired.

From Gatehouse of Fleet follow the B796, then go right on to a minor road and track to the viaduct across the Big Water of Fleet. Walk north along the old railway to the crags.

The two largest buttresses are found on the left-hand side of the hillside. The right wing of the right-hand buttress has a prominent black and white-streaked slab.

The Spanish Inquisition   60m   Mild VS   (1991)
Start at the left edge of the black and white-streaked slab.
1. 30m 4b   Climb up to an overlap at 15m, step right over it, then go rightwards up a slab to belay at the foot of a conspicuous right-trending overlap.
2. 30m 4b   Follow the line of the overlap up and right, then cross it near its top. Climb directly to a large ledge at the top of the main slab. Move right and follow subsidiary slabs to the top.

Central Buttress   40m   Very Difficult   (1978)
This route climbs the buttress, starting to the left of The Spanish Inquisition.
1. 10m   Climb easily to a ledge.
2. 30m   Climb the steep scoop above with difficulty. Slabs then lead to a crack in the crest of the buttress.

A number of routes at Difficult and Very Difficult are possible here and on the buttress to the left. None are described and climbers are left to savour the adventure of discovering their own lines.

GALLOWAY MINOR CRAGS

NORTH GAIRY TOP   *(Map Ref 522 869)*

A steep metamorphic cliff, probably unclimbed.

CRAIGDEWS   *(Map Ref 497 722)*

Terraced granite crags near the road with one Severe. They lie in a Goat Park and climbers are likely to get chased by a warden who's considerably more energetic than the goats.

CRAIGNAW   *(Map Ref 463 833)*

Two climbs have been found lies among the large and rambling cliffs of the east face. Approach from Glen Trool over the summit of Craignaw, or as for Dungeon of Buchan via Backhill of Bush bothy and a traverse south from the Round Loch of the Dungeon. **Drainpipe Gully** (100m, Very Difficult), climbs the central of three prominent narrow gullies. **Silver Flow** (Grade IV), takes the steepest of the three gullies, about 100 metres left of Drainpipe Gully. Climb a steep slab leftwards into a corner, then go up the gully to the left. Continue up chimneys on the left to finish out right.

SNIBE HILL   *(Map Ref 466 814)*

A couple of Difficults have been recorded. In addition, **The Arete** (VS 4c) follows the longest line possible on the crag in three pitches. Approach as for Craignaw.

MERRICK, BLACK GAIRY   *(Map Ref 420 855)*

This north-facing crag has seen some winter action from past generations of Ayr-based climbers. The main gully is **Black Gutter** (Grade III) and the buttress next to it has also been climbed at Grade III. **Interstellar Overdraft** (Grade V) takes the obvious icefall 200 metres right of Black Gutter. Start directly below the icefall in the centre of the steep wall, and climb mixed ground for 75m to a belay at its foot. Climb the 20m icefall directly, then traverse right for 30 metres. Continue on mixed ground for two pitches to the plateau. Other routes have been climbed but not recorded.

GLENWHARGEN CRAIG   *(Map Ref 763 031)*

An impressive mountain crag, but the rock isn't above suspicion. Half a dozen or so indifferent routes have been climbed, from Difficult to VS, but none have been properly recorded.

SWATTE FELL   *(Map Ref 123 130)*

There are two corries facing the Blackhope Glen which provide some easy winter routes. The left-hand corrie has a number of gully and buttress lines at grade I. The right-hand has a 150m central gully which gives a Grade II.

GREY MARE'S TAIL   *(Map Ref 183 149)*

This waterfall north of Moffat on the A708 has a variety of interesting winter routes at Grade III and IV. A prolonged low-level frost is needed to bring the ice into condition, when it becomes very popular. The ice forms quickly at the sides of the fall but, as the central cascade is so voluminous, it rarely freezes completely. Both sides are Grade III to IV, depending on the solidity of the ice. Above the initial steep section the fall continues in a series of steps which decrease in size as height is gained. There is also a shallow Grade III gully to the right, which comes into condition more quickly.

DOB'S LINN   *(Map Ref 196 158)*

A grade II has been made up frozen mixed ground to the left side of these waterfalls which lie just to the north-east of the Grey Mare's Tail.

CAIRNSMORE OF FLEET   *(Map Ref 501 671)*

The only recorded route climbs the obvious gully in the centre of the Spout of the Clints (Map Ref 509 668). **Lost Pilots' Gully** (160m, VS) climbs the gully in four pitches, the final pitch starting on the left wall, taking a groove back right into the gully, which is followed to an exit left. There were eight aircraft crashes hereabouts during the second world war, hence the name.

LOCH GRANNOCH CRAG   *(Map Ref 535 686)*

Two groups of slabs give a variety of short routes including **Goat Grooves** (45m Severe) taking a line left of the main slab in the right-hand area, and **Captain Madman** (25m VS 4b), which climbs a right-slanting crack on the upper slab in the left-hand area. Approach as for Clints of Dromore to the Big Water of Fleet viaduct and parking. Continue on the road, turn left and take a forestry road past Meikle Cullendoch. Then take the next left and left again to Loch Grannoch Lodge. The slab is reached in 1½ hours from the road.

The Dumfries Outcrops

Within 30km of Dumfries, there are a dozen crags that local climbers have investigated over the past fifteen years. Of these, Clifton is excellent, with good climbing, a nice outlook and sunshine. The Thirlstane is well worth a short visit, but the Lion's Head is worthwhile only if you're in the area. As these latter crags are close together and near the road, a trip round both of them is possible.

The other crags, though by no means worthless, are of more use to climbers based in the south-west. Most of the crags are quick drying: Sandy Hills has nature's idea of an indoor crag, a fact which can salvage a wet day.

LION'S HEAD *(Map Ref 822 581)*

This buttress of blocky mica schist stands clear of the trees above the A711 south of Palnackie. All save one of the routes are on the upper 15m tier. Although the scenery is splendid, the climbing is limited to a couple of good routes and the rock requires care.

From Dumfries, follow the A711 through Dalbeattie, heading for Palnackie. The crag is hard to see from the road, but it is up in the woods on the right, just before Kirkennan Cottage where trees give way to open fields. Parking is possible on an overgrown section of the verge on the right, about 20 metres before the cottage. The crag is clearly visible when approaching on the A711 from the south. Follow the path behind the lay-by, first left to the garden fence, then go diagonally right until a vegetated scramble leads up to the crag.

THE LOWER TIER

Snout Direct   30m   VS
Varied and interesting climbing, spoilt by a dirty first pitch. Start behind the large pinnacle.
1. 15m 4b   Climb the pinnacle by its right edge and step across to the groove which is followed to the terrace; tree belay.
2. 15m 4c   Traverse left to a small spike in the middle of the wall, go left of the tree and climb directly to a ledge. Either climb the cracked face on the right, or the flake crack above, past two ledges. From the left end of the second ledge, climb steeply to the top. An alternative second pitch starts on the right of the tree and takes the wall and layback crack above.

THE UPPER TIER

On the left, the steep loose side wall has two routes, both unsatisfactory. The front face has a large rock fall scar on the left and a corner on the right. The routes are described from left to right.

Catspaw   15m   HVS 5a
Climb the right wall of the corner past a sapling to the finishing groove; not bad.

Twinkletoe Wall   15m   HVS 5a *
Good climbing up the obvious corner; small wires needed.

Sheer Can   20m   HVS 5a
The right wall of the corner leads to a ledge. Traverse 4m right, move left up the groove to a large spike and finish up the wall above.

Claustrophobia   20m   E2 5b
The bold arete right of Sheer Can leads to the ledge on that route. Move right, follow a crack to a roof, make a hard move over it and finish up the groove above and left.

CLIFTON CRAG   *(Map Ref 909 571)*

Despite their brevity, these granite crags have an intensity, variety and quality that maintain their popularity. Facing south-west, they receive all the sun going and dry quickly, and the open prospect to the Solway Firth with the Lake District beyond, and the Galloway Hills to the north, makes for a most pleasurable climbing environment. The rock and the protection are generally excellent and the climbing steep and strenuous. However, bushwhacking through brambles to the bottom of some routes can be tiresome and painful!

Approach along the A710 Solway Coast road south from Dumfries. After the narrow bridge at Caulkerbush take the second turning on the right, signposted Nether Clifton, and follow the minor road for about 2km to Upper Clifton Farm, just after a cemetery on the left. The crags are up on the hillside on the right.

Walk into the farmyard and then right past barns, to a granite stile. It is best to cross the fields to the far left of the outcrop, from where a path leads up to the bottom of the other crags.

Permission to climb should be sought at the farm.

HOLLOWSTONES WALL
At the far left end of the crag is a yellow wall, flanked on the left by a hawthorn tree, and with a pleasant area of grass below.

Sideshoot   15m   VS 4b
Pleasant climbing up the undercut slab and small corner on the left side of the wall.

Sidekick   15m   Hard Severe 4a
The groove behind the hawthorn tree, finishing up the steep crack right of Sideshoot.

Aquiline   15m   E2 5c
Right of Sidekick is a steep arete. Start up the wide grassy crack, move directly up the left side of the arete to a crack and finish up the right side of the arete.

Jeune Ecole   15m   Severe 4a *
Follow the wide grassy crack right of the hawthorn to a steep crack above. After a few moves, holds lead left to the arete which is followed in an airy position to the top.

Overground   10m   Severe 4a *
A popular route taking the slabby wall right of the wide grassy crack of Jeune Ecole. Join that route and continue straight up the crack and corner to the top.

Outcast   5m   HVS 5a
This climbs the thin overhanging crack between the upper sections of Overground and Hollowstones Chimney, approached by either of those routes or Jeune Ecole.

Hollowstones Chimney   10m   Severe 4a   (1975)
The V-groove right of Overground leads to a chimney.

Outcast   10m   HVS 5a
Right of the V-groove, a wall leads to an overhanging crack, right of Overground's chimney.

DIRL CHIMNEY AREA
Up and right on the path is a bay behind an oak tree. The first route takes the twin cracked chimney on the left.

Dirl Chimney   13m   VS 4b ***
An entertaining, or exhausting, exercise in back and footing. Dirl is a Scots word used, among other things, to describe feeling when you tingle with emotion or pain, and the ringing vibrations of something when struck. Start up the left-hand crack, enter the chimney, tap the walls and scurry to the top. Low in the grade.

Lemur   13m   E3 6a *   (1979)
Strenuous and sensational climbing up the sharp arete and through the roof right of Dirl Chimney, finishing right then left.

Gibbon in Wonderland   13m   HVS 5a *
Start 3 metres right of Dirl Chimney. Traverse up and right across the slab to finish up the fist-sized crack.

Blazing Apostles   15m   E1 5b **
Good strenuous climbing up the twin cracks in the overhang below the slab of Gibbon In Wonderland. Finish up the overhanging groove right of Gibbon's crack. High in the grade.

Tour de Force   15m   VS 4c **
Quality climbing. Start as for Blazing Apostles, but traverse right below the overhang for 2m, then go over a bulge and up a small corner.

Owl Cave   15m   Difficult
A convenient descent (providing you can find it) down the corner in the scrub right of Tour de Force. Or crawl into the cave and exit above Lipstick. On the first ascent, the original occupant caused the leader to make a rapid retreat, aided by gravity.

JIGSAW BUTTRESS
Round on the path from Owl Cave is a steep undercut wall.

The Sucker   10m   E1 5a
The arete at the left end of the wall.

Lipstick   10m   Hard Severe 4b *
The crack to the right is hard to start; it is also possible to finish by moving right to a chimney.

Hotlips   10m   VS 4c **
Good climbing up the wall 3 metres right of Lipstick. Climb up right past a thread to a ledge, then go up past an undercling to finish by a thin crack.

Labrum   12m   E1 5b
An interesting route up the wall to the right, just before a step up in the path. Climb steeply to an obvious plate of rock and follow flakes to the top. A traverse left to the plate from the top of the step in the path reduces the grade to 5a.

THE MAIN AREA
A large beaked roof dominates this area which is defined by a steep corner on the left and a fine arete on the right.

Liplet   10m   Severe 4a **
A good but short route up the roofed corner left of the steep corner forming the left side of the wall.

Ratten's Rest   8m   HVS 5a *
The steep corner is short, but it shouldn't be under-estimated.

Wall Street   13m   E1 5b ***   (1977)
A truly superb route - strenuous, technical and well protected. Follow the crack right of Ratten's Rest, then finish up the awkward overhanging groove left of the roof.

The Groove   13m   VS 4c
The obvious V-groove right of the previous route can be a bit green and dirty.

Novice Crack   12m   VS 4b   (1976)
Start as for The Groove, but follow the grassy crack rightwards to the chimney. Low in the grade.

Kenny's Chimney   8m   Ungradeable
The nest-filled chimney left of the arete, the grade depending on your girth.

The next two routes start above the path, about 8m below and to the right of the Main Wall.

The Arete   15m   E2 5c ***   (1978)
Exciting climbing up the prominent arete. Start just left of Elder's Crack and climb up left of the arete until it is possible to traverse right to the arete and a spike, finishing by a short crack.

Elder's Crack   15m   VS 4b
This follows the prominent crack in the wall right of The Arete. Start as for that route, but move right to reach the crack.

The Esplanade   20m   Difficult
About 10 metres to the right is a gangway on which the previous two routes finish. A good descent route.

THE RED SLAB
This is bound by The Esplanade on the left and a leaning tower on the right.

Pegasus   20m   Hard Severe 4b
The wall right of The Esplanade is split high up by a left-slanting crack. Follow the crack to a ledge at the left end of an oak bush, and finish up a groove with jammed blocks.

Red Slab   13m   VS 4c
Climb left of the slab to battle through an oak tree, then climb the upper wall, traversing sharply right to finish.

D.I.Y.   15m   HVS 5a *
Unusual but satisfying climbing up the crack flanking the red slab on the right, followed by a hand traverse right to finish up an awkward break in the roof.

Toddamundo   15m   E4 6a ***   (1984)
Climb the blunt arete right of D.I.Y. to the break. A thought-provoking reach from a sharp fingerhold on the roof's lip gains a strenuous and exposed upper wall. A further hard move (crux) leads to a jug at the top. A Friend 4 is advisable. Finishing up D.I.Y from the break reduces the grade to E2 5b but gives a three-star climb.

Nebula   20m   E1 5b
Climb the corner right of Toddamundo, then follow a loose traverse right beneath the roof.

Crosswires   12m   E1 5b
Just right of Nebula is a thin groove in the left wall of the leaning tower. Finish up Nebula.

Fingerlust   12m   E3 6a **   (1979)
The thin crack in the leaning tower gives another tremendous route; short, but very strenuous and technical with excellent protection (providing you can hang in there and place it).

THE TWIN CRACKS AREA
About 100 metres right of The Red Slab is a buttress marked by a blasted tree in the centre near the top, with a large detached pinnacle below.

Horner Corner   8m   Very Difficult
The short crack on the left side of the buttress.

Crawl Wall   13m   VS 4c
Eliminate and rather pointless climbing up the wall left of the crack of Wiggle, to join that route.

Wiggle   15m   HVS 5a *
The right-hand curving crack gives good climbing, which starts and finishes with The Direct.

The Direct   15m   HVS 5a
Jam the straight meaty crack with minimal skin loss.

Crackshot   15m   HVS 5a *
Start just to the right of The Direct and climb the slender buttress to the ledge of Revolver, then go left to the top.

Revolver   15m   E2 5b *
To the right is an obvious flake. Climb this to the tree, make a hard reach left, then go right and direct to the top. Fine delicate climbing. The arete behind the tree can be climbed at E1.

Twin Cracks   15m   VS 4b **
Fine laybacking up the crack system behind the large pinnacle.

JUGULAR VEIN BUTTRESS
A short bushwhack down and to the right leads to a steep buttress with a large roof on the left.

Beyond the Terminator   15m   E3 5c **   (1984)
At the left side of the buttress is a slab topped by a crescent-shaped roof. Climb to a rest at the top of the slab, then swing out left to gain the obvious good hold. Continue directly to the top surmounting a small roof.

Moonshine   15m   E2 5c **
Follow the slab of Beyond The Terminator to the top. Move right to a junction with Jugular Vein at about mid-height and continue across this route for 3m to finish up a short crack right of the prominent crack of Jugular Vein. A meaty expedition.

The Slash   15m   HVS 5a
The obvious central crack.

Jugular Vein   15m   E1 5b ***   (1977)
Very fine and sustained climbing up the buttress round and to the right of The Slash. Climb the wall and the prominent crack near the top of the crag.

Loneliness of the Long Distance Runner   10m   E4 6a
A short but serious undertaking up the blunt arete forming the right side of the buttress.

Little Wall   15m   E1 5a
The cracked wall right of Loneliness of the Long Distance Runner is loose, vegetated and poorly protected.

THE SLAB
This lies another 200 metres to the right, flanked by flying buttresses. Both routes are rather dirty in their lower halves.

Crack-Up   15m   Hard Severe 4a
The obvious crack on the left is climbed via an awkward move.

Sunset   20m   VS 4c
Start in the middle of the slab at its lowest point. Climb to a horizontal break, then trend right with increasing difficulty.

THE THIRLSTANE   *(Map Ref 993 568)*

Rising straight from a shelly beach, this small outcrop of generally good quality sandstone lies on the shores of the Solway Firth, east of Southerness. The crag faces inland and gives a most entertaining afternoon or evening's bouldering with climbing in the lower and middle grades in a sheltered location, and a superb outlook to the Lake District. Sea action has bored a cave through the centre of the crag, producing two overhanging internal walls devoid of the weathered jugs common on the outer face. (Thirl is a Scots word with various meanings including a hole, or to thrill!).

From Dumfries follow the A710 Solway Coast road to a left turn signed to Southerness. Take the first left, signed to Arbigland - Paul Jones Cottage, and continue past a sharp left-hand bend. A short distance on, a turning on the right marked 'Powillimont' is followed to the sea; park on the left. The crag is a short walk eastwards along a shell-strewn beach.

THE OUTER WALL
The climbs are described from left to right, facing the crag.

Left Arete   10m   Very Difficult **
Climb the wall immediately right of the left edge of the crag. Steep and juggy, but with a rattly block at half-height.

Goodnight Irene   10m   E2 5c   (1981)
Start 2 metres left of the cave. Climb a short wall, pull over the small roof, then traverse left below the line of larger roofs to finish up a short groove.

Thank You Irene   10m   E5 6b   (1990)
A sensational eliminate on the previous route. Follow Goodnight Irene to the roof, then cross the widest part of the roof using a pinch for the left hand and a small hold on the lip.

Zigzag   12m   VS 4b
Bridge up the well-defined groove, right of the cave, into the recess. Either traverse the slab on the right and finish up the wide rippled groove, or traverse left via some doubtful rock to finish in a spectacular position. Low in the grade.

The Overhang   10m   HVS 5b
Climb the undercut blocky red roof on rattly holds from right to left to a ledge. Finish up the overhang above.

The Ramp   10m   Difficult
Further right is an obvious loose and vegetated left-slanting ramp.

Colourful and Carefree   8m   Severe 4b
Climb the wall to a prominent prow, swing left and climb the arete to finish. The slab below the prow can be climbed to the arete at 4c, and the small roof can be taken direct at HVS 5a (nasty, no gear, poor landing).

Rough Buttress   7m   Very Difficult
Start at a fence post and climb the buttress to the top.

To the right there is some vegetation, but the walls below the oak trees give excellent short routes and bouldering in a range of grades. The wall across the channel on the right gives some fun on big jugs, especially when the tide is in.

THIRL WALLS
The inner walls have always been considered extended boulder problems and so they are only given a technical grade. However they should not be under estimated. The climbs are described clockwise from the left, looking seaward. A number of other hard problems have been done, but not recorded.

Route 1   8m   5c
On the left wall of the cave, 2 metres inside, is a smooth groove formed by a series of sloping holds, Start with difficulty, balance, and finish with difficulty!

Route 1.5   8m   6c
Crank the smoothest bit of the left wall, starting by a rectangular slot.

Route 2   6m   5c
Near the sea entrance on the left is a small roof with a flake crack.

Route 6   6m   6a
Climb the right wall opposite Route 2 on poor pockets to a rounded finish.

Route 5   10m   5c
In the middle of the right wall inside the cave is a niche, left of a corner. Climb to the niche break out left and up the gradually steepening wall on dramatically improving holds. Strenuous and extended.

Route 4   10m   5c
As for Route 5, but exit right from the niche and follow the crack past the large chockstone.

Route 3   10m   5b
Climb the steep prominent corner on the right wall near the landward entrance past a protruding block to a large chockstone, then finish up the wall above.

About 65 metres east along the beach is a smaller crag with boulders at its foot rather than sand. The overhanging crack gives the main route.

Overhanging Crack   10m   E2 5c   (1984/5)
The obvious crack in the overhanging wall.

To the left is a Difficult crack and a 5a wall; to the right a wall with two Very Difficult cracks.

DUMFRIES MINOR CRAGS

SANDY HILLS BAY   *(Map Ref 892 553)*

East and west of the bay are numerous craggy outcrops on which bouldering and climbing is possible at low tide. West of the bay there are some particularly large crags in various states of decomposition. An E3 5c takes the crack in the inside face of the obvious arch, but it is very loose. Further east, the large crag at the spectacular Needle's Eye (Map Ref 916 562) is loose and vegetated.

GUTCHER'S ISLE   *(Map Ref 864 527)*

This tidal island has good longer boulder problems but needs at least two days to dry. It is found 1½km east of Rockcliff.

GEORGETOWN QUARRY   *(Map Ref 998 742)*

This sandstone quarry, 10m high and 30m long, has been used for dumping various bits of rubbish and manure. **Geronimo** (E2 5b) climbs the crack on the right and the central line on the wall has two *in situ* pegs and some tat. Three other routes have been done to the right, a rib at VS and a VS and HVS up shot holes. Although this is quality rock, it is an exceedingly crummy location. From Dumfries follow the A75 Carlisle road and take the second turning on the right after the turning to the A710 and A711 (Georgetown Road). Cross the railway and continue for about 2½km, through an estate and into more rural land. Take the first track on the right after the derelict Georgetown Hall and opposite a house called 'The Knowe'.

MAIDENBOWER CRAIGS   *(Map Ref 988 745)*

These 15m conglomerate crags overlook the Georgetown area of Dumfries. The prominent chimney at the left-hand end gives a Mild VS and there are a couple of Severes at the right-hand end. The rock needs careful handling.

SCREEL CRAG   *(Map Ref 785 552)*

The small granite outcrops here give some bouldering.

The South-West Sea-Cliffs

The south-west limit of the area covered by this guide is the coast of Kirkcud-bright and Galloway, an area blessed with better weather than areas further north. Since the previous edition, there has been considerable exploration which has produced not only good new climbs on established cliffs, but also on new crags. The climbing on some of these (especially on the granite crags of Laggantalluch Head and Crammag Head, and the on the greywacke of Por-tobello) rates with the best that this guide has to offer. Although it takes as long to get to these crags from Glasgow as it takes to get to many of the prime areas in the Highlands, or even the Lake District, the cliffs present good climbing in an uncrowded and unspoilt environment. The maps needed for this chapter are OS sheets 82 and 83.

MEIKLE ROSS *(Map Ref 652 433)*

The south-west's largest greywacke sea-cliff is something of an acquired taste, giving adventurous climbing in the middle grades rather than fine technical routes on perfect rock. Of course, there are a few of these, but a lack of traffic over the years has allowed loose holds to develop on some routes and at the top of the cliffs.

The crags are formed of distinct beds of yellow lichen-covered rock, and facing south-east, they get a lot of sun and can be quite sheltered. Only small sections of the cliffs are tidal. Nesting birds can be a problem on Limehouse Blues Cliff which should be avoided from May to late August, but the other crags are relatively bird free. Because of the salt air and state of the rock, climbers are advised to be cautious about the state or even presence of all the pitons mentioned in the text. Camping is possible at Brighouse Bay, immediately west of the cliffs.

From Glasgow follow the A713 to Kirkcudbright. From the town centre, turn right across the river (A755 Gatehouse of Fleet), then left to follow the B727 to Borgue. Turn left for Brighouse Bay and Ross Bay, then go left again to Ross Bay and follow the road and track to park at the far side of the bay. Follow the track to a barn. From there either skirt the beach on the left, then follow the fence to the top of Fox Craig, or head right over the hill to the crags surrounding Slack Heugh Bay (10 minutes).

FOX CRAIG

This is an impressive crag of steep cracks and corners formed by upturned beds in profile. Access to the cliff is best made by descending steep grass on the west side (facing Limehouse Blues Cliff) to ledges above a slabby wall. Descend the wall at its seaward end to the rock shelf above the sea. The routes are described from left to right.

1   Promontory Wall   15m   Severe 4a   (1975)
This climbs the stepped corners high on the right side of the descent wall. Start
5 metres left of the grotty chimney-corner and climb the wall to a ledge, then go
up the corner to finish directly.

The impressive overhanging wall to the right is characterised by a fine hanging
arete and is breached by one excellent route.

2   Corridor of Power   30m   E3 5c ***   (1984)
Strenuous and atmospheric climbing up the curving crack line and hanging
groove 5 metres right of the hanging arete and 4 metres left of the right edge of
the wall (Ken's Groove). The climbing is much better than it looks; take a good
selection of Friends. At the top of the crux hanging groove, move right to finish
up a groove on the left.

3   Ken's Groove   30m   Hard Severe 4b   (1976)
The right edge of the wall is marked by a shallow groove and corner. Follow the
groove to a ledge and finish up the corner on the left.

Right again is an area of upturned bedding planes, flanked on the left by a
slabby arrow-shaped wall with a distinctive crack on its right which leads to the
same ledge as Ken's Groove.

4   Crack and Corner   30m   VS 4c *   (1975)
Climb the crack to the ledge and finish up the corner on the left.

5   Dolphin Groove   20m   HVS 4c   (1976)
Start on the right of the distinctive crack. Climb to a ledge on the right, follow a
shallow groove on the left, then a steep groove on the right (peg runner) to a
ledge. Finish up an overhanging groove.

6   Curving Arete   15m   Severe 4a **   (1975)
The arete right of the upturned beds gives pleasant climbing.

Round the corner are two small walls, a higher one on the left and a long one
on the right. The easiest access is from the approach path.

7   Fats Waller   15m   HVS 5a   (1984/5)
On the higher wall, climb a crack for 7m, go slightly right, then go over the small
overhang.

8   Shark's Tooth   10m   Very Difficult   (1984/5)
Climb the cracks on the right of the longer wall.

9   Alligator Crawl   10m   VS 4c *   (1984/5)
Good slabby climbing up the middle of the right wall.

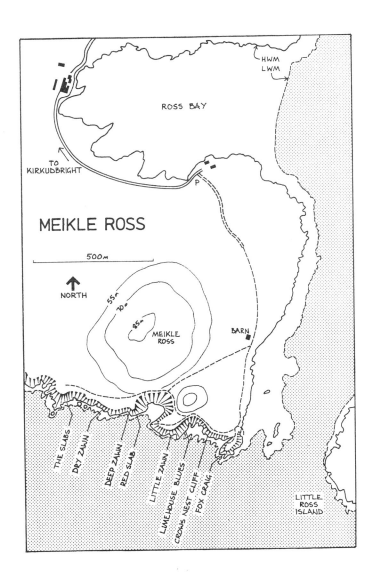

ROSS BAY

HWM
LWM

TO
KIRKUDBRIGHT

P

MEIKLE ROSS

500m

NORTH

55m
70m
95m

MEIKLE
ROSS

BARN

THE SLABS
DRY ZAWN
DEEP ZAWN
RED SLAB
LITTLE ZAWN
LIMEHOUSE BLUES
CROWS NEST CLIFF
FOX CRAIG

LITTLE
ROSS
ISLAND

CROW'S NEST CLIFF

West of Fox Craig is a hideous mass of twisted and decomposing beds of sandstone similar to but much less accommodating than the worst of South Stack, Gogarth. Left of the large cave a disgusting fault line crosses the cliff from bottom left to top right. Approach as for Fox Craig.

10   The Battle of Osfrontalis   45m   HVS   (1977)
A foul-looking route, most probably and quite justifiably unrepeated. Start left of the cave where a small promontory meets the cliff.
1. 20m 4c   Climb left of a chimney to a ledge. Make a precarious move up the wall and continue to a large bower, peg belay possibly still in situ.
2. 25m 4b   Move right to join the diagonal fault and follow this to a finish up short groove. Not for the nervous!

LITTLE ZAWN

These steep walls and corners of generally good rock are found to the left of the large and slabby Limehouse Blues Cliff which faces Fox Craig. Little Zawn is described first as it is the most usual approach to Limehouse Blues Cliff in anything but low tide. Continue down the hill behind Limehouse Blues Cliff to a flat area of grass above the crag. Descend the grassy bank to the west of the crag and make an exposed traverse above the sea onto the platform below the routes. The climbs are described from left to right.

11   Steve's Route   12m   VS 4b   (1979)
Start at a square recess where the airy traverse ends and about 4 metres left of the chimney. Make a long reach and continue direct.

12   Spectrum Wall   12m   HVS 5b
Start just left of Orange Chimney at an inverted-V recess. Climb through the recess then up the wall above; serious.

13   Orange Chimney   15m   Difficult *   (1975)
Climb the chimney, finishing either on the left or, better and harder, direct over the bulge.

14   Green Wall   15m   Hard Severe 4b *   (1976)
Good climbing. Follow the left-slanting crack 2 metres right of the chimney to a horizontal break. Move right and climb the right-leaning niche until a step left can be made. Finish up the wall.

15   Clockwork Orange   15m   Very Difficult   (1975)
Right again is a corner crack which is climbed on the left wall to a finish over loose blocks.

16   Pinking Sheer   20m   HVS 5a ***   (1977)
The arete right of Clockwork Orange gives an enjoyable route with surprisingly
good protection. Start just right of the corner, climb the first bulge and make a
move left to a ledge. Take the second bulge on the left, move right up a crack
and finish up the wall above on good holds.

17   Mellow Yellow   20m   VS 4c ***   (1975)
Classic climbing up the clean-cut crack splitting the yellow wall right of Pinking
Sheer.

18   Sunshine Superman   20m   E4 6a *   (1984)
A sustained eliminate gaining independence with height. Start just right of
Mellow Yellow and climb a short wall to the roof, move over this then make a
hard move up the wall to a small spike. Move right, then left to gain a crack above
the bulge, then go right again to the top. Runners in Mellow Yellow reduce the
grade to E3 6a.

19   Stepped Corner   20m   Hard Severe 4b   (1975)
Better climbing than expected up the corner bounding the Mellow Yellow wall.
Large nuts or Friends are required.

20   Bloody Crack   15m   E1 5b *   (1976)
A good strenuous effort taking the crack right of Stepped Corner.

21   Fil d'Or   15m   E3 6a ***   (1979)
Beside Bloody Crack is an alarmingly smooth corner with a peg runner at
half-height. A technical test-piece, high in the grade.

The left-hand and right-hand cracks at the back of the zawn are both Severe:
Left Corner (1975) and **Right Corner** (1976).

22   Amnesia   25m   VS 4c   (1975)
The right wall of the zawn has an obvious, long stepped corner which starts just
right of the green tongue of moss. It is disintegrating and dangerous.

23   Headcase   15m   VS 4c   (1975)
The steep corner right of Amnesia; swing right to finish.

24   A Walk on the Wild Side   50m   E1 **   (1979)
A girdle traverse starting as for Steve's Route.
1. 25m 5b   Follow the initial steep section of Steve's Route, then take a rising
line right, past Orange Chimney, until an overhanging arete blocks progress. A
hard move round the arete leads to Mellow Yellow. Continue in this line to a small
spike, then descend into Stepped Corner.

2. 20m 5b   Climb the pocketed rib on the right, then hand traverse right under a roof to Bloody Crack. Follow this, over its crux, to a ledge. Move right on excellent incuts, then go round a corner to a foot traverse which leads into Left Corner.

LIMEHOUSE BLUES CLIFF

From Little Zawn another exciting, though a little less airy, traverse leads right to Limehouse Blues Cliff. A number of enjoyable crack climbs can be found above the terrace on the main section of the slabby wall facing Fox Craig, but care should be taken with rock at the top. The crag is non-tidal, apart from the corners on either side of the arch below and right of the terrace. At low tide the crag can be approached from the beach below Crow's Nest Cliff, (access is also possible by abseil or by descending Exit Groove with great care). The climbs are described from left to right, with the first route taking the wall left of the obvious chimney and pinnacle forming the left end of Limehouse Blues Cliff.

25   Ancient Mariner   60m   E2 **   (1991)
The steep pillar left of the chimney gives varied climbing with a serious upper section. Start about 7 metres left of the chimney.
1. 4b 20m   Climb the grey wall to a prominent twin niche. Leave this on the left and follow easy ground right to belay in a large overhung niche.
2. 5b 40m   Move right out of the niche, then go up to twin overhung corners. Climb the left-hand corner to a large ledge, then go rightwards to a thin undercut slab, crux. Continue rightwards up easier slabs to exit at a small pinnacle.

26   Meikle Gorbachov   40m   VS 4c   (1988)
Start at the foot of the chimney. Climb a flake on the left wall of the chimney, then continue along this above the chimney. At its end (overlooking the pinnacle) climb the tower above.

27   Pigeon Chimney   20m   Difficult   (1975)
Climbs the chimney, going below a huge chockstone. Well guanoed later in the season.

28   Groovey   15m   Very Difficult   (1975/7)
Wander up the left edge of the pinnacle.

29   Compulsion   15m   E1 5b   (1980)
Follow the left-hand crack in the front face of the pinnacle for 8m, then move right on pockets to the top.

30   Zugsfang   15m   E2 5c *   (1981)
A good problem up the thin crack just right of Compulsion. Climb the wall at first on the right, then on the left of the crack, until forced right to a good pocket. Continue direct to the top. Harder for the short.

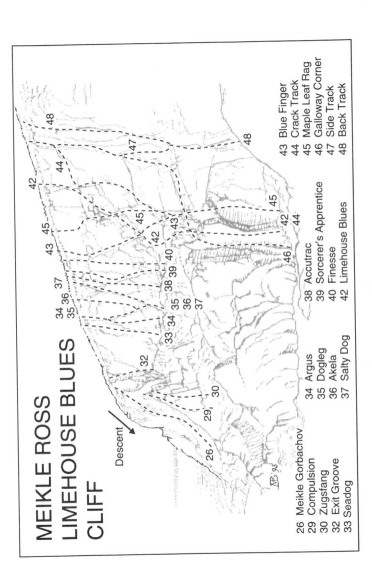

MEIKLE ROSS
LIMEHOUSE BLUES
CLIFF

Descent

26 Meikle Gorbachov
29 Compulsion
30 Zugsfang
32 Exit Groove
33 Seadog

34 Argus
35 Dogleg
36 Akela
37 Salty Dog

38 Accutrac
39 Sorcerer's Apprentice
40 Finesse
42 Limehouse Blues

43 Blue Finger
44 Crack Track
45 Maple Leaf Rag
46 Galloway Corner
47 Side Track
48 Back Track

NB '93

31   White Out   15m   Severe 4a   (1975/7)
The groove in the right-hand arete of the pinnacle.

32   Exit Groove   15m   Difficult   (1975)
Above the pinnacle at the left side of the main face is a groove; follow the left branch. This is a quick descent to the terrace, but make sure it's not too quick.

33   Seadog   25m   HVS 5a *   (1977)
Start at a thin crack below a shallow recess capped by a roof on the wall about 3m up and right of Exit Groove. Gain the crack and follow it and the wider continuation to a junction with Dogleg.

34   Argus   25m   E1 5b *   (1978/80)
A good route, starting just right of Seadog. Strenuous moves lead to a rectangular niche, then follow the continuation crack leftwards to a shallow recess. Climb the left edge of the recess, or better the finger crack in the recess to a roof.

To the right, two prominent crack lines meet at the top of the crag to form the letter A. The next three routes start at the crack forming the left side of the A.

35   Dogleg   25m   HVS 5a **   (1977)
Good steep crack climbing with the crux high on the crag. Start up the crack, but move immediately left and follow the left-slanting crack to the top.

36   Akela   25m   HVS 5a *   (1978/80)
Follow Dogleg for 3m, then step right to a good jug and follow the crack above.

37   Salty Dog   25m   HVS 4c *   (1975)
The left-hand crack of the "A" gives a fine strenuous route with the hardest moves in the first 4 metres.

38   Accutrac   25m   HVS 5a   (1978)
From a crack mid-way between the left and right cracks, climb directly to the apex of the "A".

39   Sorcerer's Apprentice   25m   VS 4b *   (1976)
Follow the right-hand crack to within a few metres of Salty Dog. Traverse right past a small ledge and climb direct to the top.

40   Finesse   30m   E1 5b **   (1978)
Bold balance climbing up a nice piece of rock. Start just right of the right-hand crack below a rectangle of light rock. Climb over a small overlap to a ledge, then move up past a hinged spike to an inverted-V overlap. Follow the fine wall above, moving right to an indefinite crack which leads to a ledge. Step left and follow a crack to the top.

At low tide Limehouse Blues Cliff can be approached from the beach below Crow's Nest Cliff. The following routes start from the beach at low tide, the right-hand end of the main terrace, or the large ledge further right above the rock arch and the sea.

41   Limpet Arete   20m   Very Difficult
The left edge of the slabby wall left of the rock arch and below the terrace has a pleasant arete. Climb to a ledge and continue above. The corner to the right gives a Hard Severe.

42   Limehouse Blues   60m   HVS *   (1972)
A bold airy finish enlivens the original route of the cliff. Start from sea-level, below the slabby wall left of the rock arch and right of a narrow chimney.
1. 20m 3b   Climb the middle of the slab to the belay on the terrace below a grassy flake crack. (The narrow chimney can be climbed at 4c and the right edge of the slab at 4a).
2. 20m 4b   Gain the obvious flake crack and follow it to the prominent large niche.
3. 20m 5a   Step down and climb the fine slab right round the edge to a short crack, then to a thin ledge. From the right-hand end of the ledge, climb a crack to gain a small ledge on the right (crux). The wall above leads to the top.

43   Blue Finger   30m   VS 4c   (1976)
Start at the belay at the right end of the terrace above the rock arch and below two obvious niches. Climb the steep wall on the right, left of a crack, to the left-hand niche. Follow a crack leftwards to a junction with Limehouse Blues. Move up and left to finish up the left-slanting crack. (If desired a start can be made from sea-level).

44   Crack Track   60m   HVS *   (1975)
Delicate climbing in a good situation. Start at sea-level as for Limehouse Blues.
1. 20m 3b   As for Limehouse Blues, but belay at the right end of the terrace, above the rock arch and below two obvious niches.
2. 20m 5a   Follow Blue Finger, but gain the right-hand niche. Traverse right to a crack and follow it past a small spike to a ledge and belay on the left.
3. 20m 5a   Traverse right to the base of an edge and follow this boldly to a junction with Galloway Corner. Move up, traverse 2 metres left and climb on good holds to the top.

45   Maple Leaf Rag   60m   HVS *   (1978)
A good route with a surprising last pitch. Start under the arch, just right of the left-hand slab.
1. 20m 4b   Climb the slab to the roof, move left across shaley rock, and climb a groove to belay at the right end of the terrace above the rock arch and below two obvious niches.

2. 20m 5a   The wall on the right has a steep crack. Climb steeply on the right of the crack to the right-hand of two niches. From the top of the niche, climb thinly up the slab to a good resting place. Step left and climb the front face of a large flake to belay in a large niche.
3. 20m 5a   Move left to reach a curving crack and a ledge with a horizontal crack, then climb the wall above.

46   Galloway Corner   60m   HVS *   (1975)
Start at sea-level at the long groove right of the arched slab. Good climbing on the second pitch. The first pitch can be avoided by traversing from the end of the terrace across the large ledge.
1. 20m 5a   Follow the groove until a traverse leads left to the large ledge above the arch and a belay below the leftmost corner.
2. 40m 5a   Layback up the left-hand stepped corner.

47   Side Track   60m   HVS **   (1975)
An interesting sustained route. Again, the first pitch can be avoided. Opinions are divided as to whether the top pitch is brilliant or disgusting!
1. 20m 5a   Start at sea-level, right of the cave recess. Move up a slab to the groove and follow it to a belay on the large ledge.
2. 40m 5a   Move 2 metres right and layback the groove until forced into Galloway Corner.

48   Back Track   60m   E1   (1977)
This takes the full length of the right-hand groove line. The top pitch is loose, vegetated, badly protected and extremely dangerous.
1. 20m 5a   Side Track, pitch 1.
2. 40m 5a   Regain the groove and follow it to the top. On second thoughts, don't bother.

49   Rhythm n'Blues   60m   HVS **
An enjoyable girdle with considerable atmosphere. Start 6m up the right branch of Exit Groove, at a ledge and thread belay.
1. 30m 5a   Traverse right, passing a small roof to a spike. Then, either climb a further 3m and descend Dogleg to a ledge, or harder, immediately descend a finger-crack then traverse right to the same point. Step down, and traverse right to a crack, then gain a traverse line leading to Salty Dog. Continue in this line to a ledge and horizontal crack.
2. 30m 5a   Move right to the ledge on Limehouse Blues, then follow Crack Track pitch three to Galloway Corner.

SLACK HEUGH BAY

The following routes are found on the headlands and inlets west of Slack Heugh Bay. They are best approached by taking the right-hand path after the barn. The cliffs are described as they would be approached along this path, moving westwards.

THE RED SLAB

The northern side of Slack Heugh Bay gives some enjoyable slab routes in the lower and middle grades. Access to the base of the crag is by carefully descending the grassy bank on the right. The climbs are described from right to left and the first two routes lie on the smoother right-hand section.

50   Scared to Dance   25m   HVS 5a **   (1979)
A satisfying slab route, adequately protected with small wires, but sometimes a bit dirty and then quite serious. Start just left of the corner forming the right-hand edge of the slab. Climb up for 15m, traverse left 4 metres, then go straight up to a break. Move up and left to finish.

51   Dolce Vita   25m   HVS 5a   (1979)
Start left of Scared to Dance, below a lyre-shaped mark in the rock. Climb up to the mark, move diagonally up and left for 5m, then continue direct to the top. Like Scared to Dance, harder when dirty.

52   Grand Central Couloir   35m   VS 4c   (1978/83)
The central depression immediately left of Dolce Vita gives good climbing in its first half, but the rest can be loose and dirty. Traversing left into Cairn's Cream gives a more pleasant finish at 4b.

53   Cairn's Cream   35m   VS 4c *   (1979)
Left of the couloir is an obvious tongue of rock. A crack leads to the right-hand side of the tongue which is followed until it becomes an overlap. Cross the overlap to a ledge and finish up the blocky rib on the left.

54   Bad Medicine Waltz   35m   HVS 5a *   (1981)
Climb a crack 3 metres right of Cairn's Cream to the left side of the tongue. Step right on to the tongue, then go boldly up its centre to a ledge, finishing up the twin cracks.

55   Mental Block   30m   VS 4c ***   (1979)
Good climbing taking in the projecting block high on the wall. Start at the long ledge higher up the crag. Take a direct line past a break to gain the block. Move left, go up 3m, and then climb right to finish up a corner.

56   Demolition Tango   30m   VS 4c **   (1983/4)
Hard moves up the slab 2 metres left of Mental Block lead to an overhang. Step left and climb the thin crack to a ledge, finishing on the right.

57   Tinman   30m   Severe 4a   (1976)
The large dirty crack right of the downward-pointing blade of yellow rock.

58   Coffin Crack   30m   Severe 4a   (1976)
Climb into and out of the coffin-shaped recess in the black wall 2 metres right of Tinman and continue through the overlap to the ridge.

59   Access Ridge   30m   Very Difficult   (1972)
The left edge of the slab gives a route of variable difficulty depending on the state
of the guano.

DEEP ZAWN
Left of Red Slab lies the area's only tidal cliff, Deep Zawn. It is characterised by
a gash on its right, The Rift (which almost runs the height of the crag), and a
prominent corner on the left. Though the angle is pleasantly slabby, the top 15m
steepen dramatically. Save for K9, the best approach, tide allowing, is by
descending the ramp forming the left edge of the crag, then traversing right to
ledges below the routes (Very Difficult). The climbs are described from right to
left.

60   K.9.   50m   HVS **   (1972)
The second pitch presents exciting and exposed situations. Abseil to the lowest
ledge, or better, traverse in left from Access Ridge (Moderate).
1. 20m 4b   Steeply past a large ledge until a traverse right can be made to
another ledge.
2. 30m 5a   Move left to a small groove bordering The Rift. Climb delicately up
this to a resting place, then continue in the same line, through the bulges, to the
top. An easier finish traverses right from below the final bulges and finishes up
a green slab.

61   Rift Route   50m   Severe 4a   (1972)
From ledges left of The Rift, traverse right to The Rift edge and follow it to the
top.

62   Eminence Grise   40m   Hard Severe 4b *   (1981)
Start for Rift Route, but climb right to a deep recess and at the top pull out right
to a ledge. Follow the thin crack in the slab above, pull over the overlap on the
left and thence to the top. Somewhat eliminate, but good climbing.

63   A Sop for Cerberus   40m   Hard Severe 4b   (1981)
From the ledges, move into the recess on the left and exit 2 metres left of the
previous route. Climb slabs, moving left, to a ledge below the roofs then go back
right across the overhanging wall on huge holds.

64   Yellow Dog   40m   HVS   (1973)
Start from the left end of the ledges.
1. 20m 4a   Climb the slab, trending left to a ledge and nut belay 3m below the
roofs.
2. 20m 4c   Go up right to the first overhang, then move left to a ledge. Continue
left and layback the second bulge, then go right and up grooves to the top. Stake
belay.

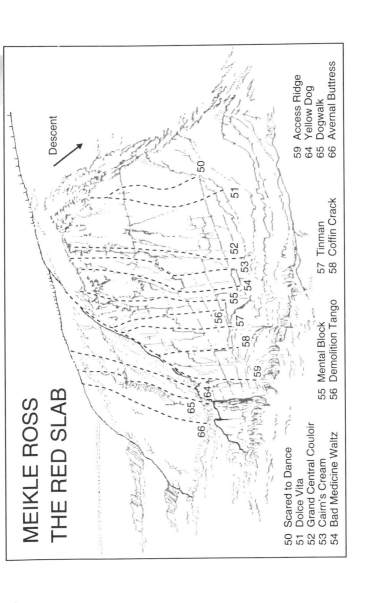

MEIKLE ROSS
THE RED SLAB

Descent

50 Scared to Dance
51 Dolce Vita
52 Grand Central Couloir
53 Cairn's Cream
54 Bad Medicine Waltz

55 Mental Block
56 Demolition Tango

57 Tinman
58 Coffin Crack

59 Access Ridge
64 Yellow Dog
65 Dogwalk
66 Avernal Buttress

65   Dogwalk   30m   Difficult   (1973)
Start at the same place as Yellow Dog. Well birded in the nesting season.
Traverse left to the prominent corner and climb it to a roof, exiting left to a ledge.
Continue to the top.

66   Avernal Buttress   30m   Very Difficult   (1981)
Follow the arete left of Dog Walk, just left of the edge.

DRY ZAWN
Descend the ramp at the left end of Deep Zawn to the sea, then traverse left to
the floor of the zawn. This cliff forms three sides of a rectangle and can be quite
sheltered from the wind. The following routes are on the left-hand wall facing
landwards.

67   Route One   25m   Severe 4a *   (1978)
Good climbing up cracks at the left-hand end of the cliff.

68   Route Two   15m   Mild VS 4b   (1983/4)
A worthwhile line up the wall in the centre of the cliff.

69   Route Three   10m   Very Difficult   (1981)
The right-hand corner with some turf at the top.

70   Pinko-Subversive   20m   Severe 4a   (1987)
The short steep corner on the right-hand side of the zawn.

About 3 metres left of Dry Zawn is a groove line.

71   Manic Nirvana   25m   HVS 5a *   (1991)
Steep technical climbing. Climb to the overhang, then traverse right and go up
the right-hand groove. Follow this back left and climb a short crack to a large
ledge and easier ground.

The next climbs can be found by following the cliff-top westward until a stake
is located at the top of a pointed headland. The cliff below is extensive but quite
loose. Access is by abseil, or via an entertaining traverse leftwards from Dry
Zawn ledge.

72   Bumper Dumper   30m   HVS 5b *   (1982)
Surprisingly good, well protected slab climbing. The smooth sound face at the
right-hand side of the cliff is split by two cracks. Climb the left-hand one to a
ledge, step right to a crack and follow it to the top.

73   The Moosetrap   30m   VS 4c   (1982)
Start 3 metres left of Bumper Dumper and climb the corner, which gets loose
towards the top.

74   Poison Ivy   30m   Difficult   (1982)
Left of The Moosetrap is a chimney whose left wall and upper section gives a
turfy escape, if you're lucky.

West from The Moosetrap is a large area of easy-angled but blank slab.
Immediately below the headland is the best slab, bounded on its right by a steep
wall and split by an easy-angled groove which provides the best access to the
next route. The climbs on this slab have become rather grassy.

75   Titan's Corner   40m   HVS 5a *   (1982)
Delicate and bold climbing up the right-hand corner, taking the overlap to finish.
Could do with a clean.

76   Marie Celeste   40m   Mild VS 4b   (1982)
Start midway between the descent groove and Titan's Corner. Follow the
prominent cracks up the slab, then continue through the overlap as for Titan's
Corner.

77   Blistering Barnacles   40m   Severe 4a   (1982)
Pleasant climbing up the middle of the slab left of the groove.

78   Barnacle Bill   40m   Severe 4a   (1982)
The arete left of Blistering Barnacles gives a mediocre climb.

Further west is a bay with a pinnacle. Access is best by abseil.

79   Grapeshot   15m   Hard Severe 4b   (1987)
Climb the overlapping slab.

80   Old Zawn   12m   HVS 4c   (1990)
Start on the same slab as Grapeshot, below the right-hand end of the overlap.
Follow thin cracks diagonally left to gain the left end of the overlap. Belay on the
abseil rope.

81   Evens   10m   VS 4c   (1990)
The left-hand of two thin cracks to the left of Old Zawn.

BURROW HEAD   *(Map Ref 458 340)*

One of the first areas to be developed, these crags have not aged well.
Looseness and abundant bird life put off all but the most dedicated climbers, and
though there are a number of gems in the dirt, Burrow Head remains the least
popular of the south-west sea-cliffs. However the sunny aspect and beautiful
surroundings are likely to make any visit a memorable experience. Particular
care should be taken with the rock at the top of some routes.

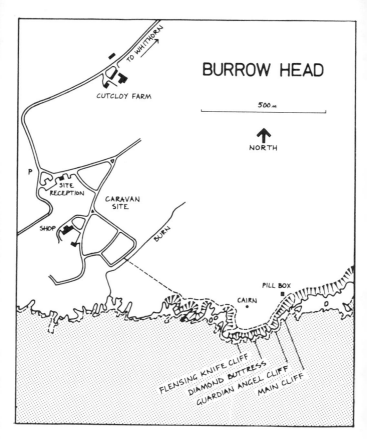

BURROW HEAD

500 m

NORTH

TO WHITHORN

CUTCLOY FARM

P

SITE RECEPTION

CARAVAN SITE

SHOP

BURN

PILL BOX

CAIRN

FLENSING KNIFE CLIFF

DIAMOND BUTTRESS

GUARDIAN ANGEL CLIFF

MAIN CLIFF

From Glasgow follow the A77 to Ayr. From Ayr, either follow the A713 to New Galloway, then the A712 to Newton Stewart and the A714, A746 and A750 to the Isle of Whithorn, or the A77 to Girvan and the A714 to Newton Stewart. In the village of Isle of Whithorn, follow the sign to Burrow Head caravan site, parking outside the main gate.

For the main crags walk to the coast and follow it east over some awkward fences to the first stakes, which are located where the path turns a sharp corner to the east (15 minutes from the caravan site and just past the cairn on the hill summit).

CAMP SITE WALLS
Various routes have been done in the vicinity of the caravan site.

The Fin   30m   HVS 4c   (1980)
The sea stack below the caravan site can be climbed to the left end of the flat narrow arete right of its summit.

The bay immediately east of The Fin contains a small tidal cliff with two routes. Approach by abseil from a large spike near the left end of the cliff. The most prominent feature is a left-trending crack in the middle.

Goblin's Eyes   25m   HVS 5a *   (1991)
Good steep climbing, starting about 8 metres left of the left-slanting crack. Climb up and through two niches, then go directly up, finishing to the left of the top of the slanting crack.

Killer on the Loose   25m   VS 4b   (1991)
Start below the left-slanting crack. Climb the twin crack lines and walls above slightly to the right. Low in the grade.

FLENSING KNIFE CLIFF
This cliff lies below the first stakes and is reached by scrambling down the grass and rock to the west and then traversing east to below the cliff. It is identified by a smooth wall, flanked on the right by a slim corner leading to the right-hand end of a quartz-flecked roof. The routes are described from left to right.

Run Rabbit Run   20m   Hard Severe 4b   (1980)
Start left of the smooth wall below a short groove which leads to a corner. A juggy but unprotected wall leads to the crux groove, which is difficult to protect. Move left to a longer easier groove and a good steep finish.

Lemming's Wall   20m   HVS 5a   (1981)
Immediately right of Run Rabbit Run is a wall which overlooks RRR in its top section. A party of seven made the first ascent, hence the name!

Watership Down   20m   VS 4b *   (1980)
An inviting wall climb needing some small wires low down. Start just right of Lemming's Wall below a crack high on the wall. Climb up past an undercling, move right to a ledge, then regain the original line at the crack.

Prometheus (on his crag)   20m   E1 5b *   (1980)
Good delicate climbing leads to a strenuous roof. Start 3 metres left of the prominent corner of Flensing Knife. Move left over quartz-flecked rock to gain a shallow scoop, then go up and right to a ledge. Climb the roof on the left by twin cracks.

Flensing Knife   20m   VS 4c   (1980)
Climb the corner to a bulge, then either layback left (strenuous) or bridge right
(technical) to gain a ledge. Follow a diagonal line of flake holds leftwards to
finish.

Yellow Crack   20m   Severe 4a   (1980)
The wall right of the corner has a good crack. Finish up a shallow scoop.

DIAMOND BUTTRESS
Further to the right is a yellow, lichen-covered, diamond-shaped face, streaked
with guano-like streaks of quartz. It has two good but hard climbs. The cliff is
marked at the top by a stake.

Naked Fun   35m   E2 5b ***   (1980)
Undoubtedly the best route in the area, sustained and well protected above the
difficult lower section. A grooved ramp left of the toe of the buttress leads right
to a foothold on the edge of the wall. Make a hard reach to a horizontal crack,
then traverse right to a jug. The ramp above leads delicately to a small ledge
(crux). Climb up left to a good jug, then traverse right until it is possible to go
directly up the wall to a ramp which leads to the finishing cracks.

Adventures in the Skin Trade   30m   E3 5c **   (1982)
Another excellent route, high in the grade and with a thin bold crux. Start at the
toe of the buttress and climb direct to the small foothold on Naked Fun. Move up
to the horizontal crack, step left and climb up (crux) to a line of good holds. Follow
these right until a flake line leads back left and up to a finishing crack.

Round the corner to the east, at a higher level, is a small triangular face. Right
of this are twin chimneys. The left-hand splits into two; the left-hand finish is
shaped like an upside down bottle (**Boozer's Chimney**, Very Difficult, 1981), the
better right-hand variant (**The Newt**, Very Difficult, 1981) gives good laybacking
to finish. The right-hand chimney is **The Python** (Severe, 1980). The wall
between the twin chimneys is a pleasant Severe (**The Changeling**, 1981).
Further east is a long 20m face seamed with grooves. **The Beastie** (E1 5b, 1981)
starts at the left-hand end of the cliff and climbs a crack through a small roof and
the groove above.

GUARDIAN ANGEL CLIFF
Hidden from above, this cliff lies about 75 metres east of the previous routes,
midway between Flensing Knife Cliff and the pillbox. A solitary stake marks the
top. Steep grass on the west leads down to the start of the climbs. A prominent
left-facing stepped corner identifies the cliff.

Naked Fun, Burrow Head (Climber, Bob Duncan)

Mephistopheles   20m   HVS 5a   (1980)
Climb a crack left of the stepped corner, with a hard move above the corner to
a ledge. Finish up and left to the top.

Wild Horses   20m   E1 5b   (1981)
Climb the stepped corner, with an excursion on the right-hand wall to gain a
crack at its top. Continue directly for 10m, stepping right to a ledge below the
final wall. Climb this using an edge on the left.

Guardian Angel   20m   HVS 5b *   (1980)
Well protected, with a sharp start and finish. Start immediately right of the
stepped corner. Make a strong pull up right to a ledge and climb the steep crack
above to a circular bulge, which forces the climber left then right to cross the slab
above to a ledge. Step left and climb the fingery wall to the top.

Devil's Daughter   20m   HVS 5a   (1980)
Start just right of Guardian Angel, below a steep finger crack. Climb the
right-slanting crack, step left then move up to a ledge. Climb the groove on the
left to its top, then go direct to the top.

THE MAIN CLIFF
The Main Cliff is located below the pillbox, 75 metres east of Guardian Angel
Cliff. An impressive cliff, it is unfortunately spoilt by loose rock, fish bones and
guano. The best descent is via a worn V-groove about 50 metres east of the
pillbox (not obvious), which leads to a grassy spur and the base of the cliff. The
routes are described from right to left.

Bright Eyes   30m   VS 4c   (1980)
Start at the obvious crack in the yellow wall left of the massive rock scar and
climb to a ledge. Finish up the twin finger cracks to the right of the upper
left-facing corner.

Waiting for Godot   30m   HVS 4c   (1981)
Start just right of the upturned beds of rock. Climb flakes to a ledge, then go up
the wall right of the upper right-facing corner. Exit onto 70 degree turf and shale.

Moving left, assorted rubble leads to another face flanked on the left by a
grim-looking vertical trench. The face is climbed by The Cutter.

The Cutter   45m   HVS   (1980)
1. 25m 5a   Start just right of the trench and climb flakes to a small stepped
corner and a ledge.
2. 20m 4b   Climb the slabby arete on the left.

Mussel Bound, Portobello (Climber, Jim Blyth)

The Cut   35m   Severe 4a   (1980)
The terminal trench.

Mirror, Mirror   45m   E3 *   (1981)
A serious climb up the centre of the fine wall. Steep fingery climbing on dubious
flakes but with reasonable protection leads to structurally unsound rock on a
grander scale. The start described here was previously described as a direct
variation, but the original first pitch seems to have lost vital holds and is no longer
possible at this grade. Start below the twin cracks.
1. 15m 5c   Climb the cracks gently and flop on to the ledge. The climbing would
be good but for the tendency of the flakes to shear off.
2. 10m 5b   Place gear behind the booming flake above the belay and jibber
upwards to a good Friend placement. Move right over a bulge and go up to a
ledge.
3. 20m 5a   Finish up the arete, as for Conquistador.
Variation to pitch 2:   25m 5b
From the ledge, traverse right and grovel up the crack past an *in situ* Friend to
the top - a bit safer.

Conquistador   45m   E2   (1980)
Start at the left end of the wall, below a right-slanting crack at half-height.
1. 30m 5b   Climb a distinct finger crack for 3m, move left and climb a deceptive
crack to the ledge. Above is an overhanging finger crack. Climb this rightwards
to a ledge and belay. A strenuous pitch.
2. 20m 5a   Climb the cleaned arete above.

MONREITH   *(Map Ref 370 393)*

South of Monreith the coast rises up to form a small headland of horizontally
bedded greywacke above a sandy beach. A few routes have been done here
and although the rock is lichen-free, sea-birds can be a problem for much of the
spring and summer and the base of the crag is tidal. Some areas are fanatically
patrolled by Scottish Natural Heritage volunteers. An usual excursion is the
girdle traverse of the coastline, which provides entertainment for 500 metres of
3a to 5b climbing.
   About 1km south of Monreith and 9km north of Whithorn, leave the A747
opposite the camp site and follow the road to St Medan's Golf Course and the
large car park beside the beach. At low tide the beach leads south east to the
crags.

THE MAIN CLIFF
This lies behind the prominent pinnacle which gives some bouldering. Right of
the pinnacle is a large slab with three grooves topped by overhangs.

The Big Dig   35m   HVS 4c *   (1987)
The central groove, or the arete just to its left, leads to the large groove running
down from the roof. Traverse right across the slab and climb an awkward crack
on the left of the large blocks to a stance. Continue right until a short slab and
arete lead to a grassy bay. The right-hand groove can be climbed direct to the
blocky crack at 5a.

THE PROMONTORY
Further east the crag becomes more vegetated, then a large gully is reached.
Right of the gully is a series of easy-angled slabs and east again is a small zawn
of sea-sculptured rock with quartz veins.

Hack Crack   15m   VS 4c   (1987)
The obvious crack in the back of the zawn, reached from the left corner by a
layback move.

Do Barnacles Bite?   15m   HVS 5b   (1987)
The slanting crack right of Hack Crack.

   Between the small zawn and the tip of the promontory lies a steep wall with
an obvious groove just left of centre. The next two routes lie between the small
zawn and the groove.

Stingray   15m   VS 4c   (1987)
From the centre of the wall, climb to the overlap above the previous route. Pull
over this to a large ledge and a variety of exits.

Fireball XL 1.5   15m   VS 4b   (1987)
Start as for Stingray and climb up and slightly rightwards to reach a right-facing
groove at half-height. Finish up the groove or to the left on big holds.

Soup Dragon   15m   Hard Severe 4b   (1987)
The barnacle-covered wall leads to the main groove, traversing off right at the
top. The groove can also be reached from the left.

Mobile-Bat   15m   VS 5a   (1987)
This climb takes a left then right-facing groove about 3 metres right of Soup
Dragon.

Mobile-Kack   15m   VS 4c   (1987)
Climb the easier-angled wall to the right.

CAVE 4
Round the corner are two caves. To their right is a grey wall with an impressive
hanging corner.

Satori   30m   E3 6a *   (1987)
Climb the grey wall into the central groove go up this to a good resting place above the overlap. A hard and sensational traverse out to the right gains a good jug at the bottom of the thin hanging groove which is climbed to the top.

Jelly Fish   15m   Severe 4a   (1987)
Climb obvious flakes up the seaward arete of the west-facing red wall, which is visible from the promontory.

GARHEUGH POINT   *(Map Ref 268 501)*

This is a small but steep and pleasantly situated slab of south-facing greywacke. The base of the crag is dramatically undercut and the boulders beautifully sculptured by the sea. There are no sea-birds and the crag is non-tidal.
   From Glasgow follow the A77 to Stranraer, followed by the A75 to Glenluce and the A747 to Port William. Park in the lay-by on the right, at the top of the hill before the B7005 turns off left to Wigtown (about 10½km north of Port William). Scramble down to the crag. The routes are described from left to right.

Battle of the Bulge   15m   E3 6a   (1987)
The thin crack towards the left side of the undercut slab. Make a difficult move over the bulge to a flat hold, then step right to the crack.

Secrets of the Coast   20m   Severe   (1987)
The left arete of the undercut slab, trending slightly right at the top.

Two Tyred   15m   E3 6a   (1985)
To the right is a thin right-hand crack in the undercut wall. An impressive route, difficult to protect and to climb!

Snailey-Whaley   15m   Severe   (1987)
Climb the left-trending crack in the right arete of the slab, then step right to finish at the top.

Flubb   15m   VS 4c   (1987)
Climb the corner at the right end of the crag.

Deathwish   15m   E1 5b   (1985)
The arete right of Flubb.

The E6 Process   15m   E1 5b   (1987)
Start about 5 metres right of the last route at a fin-like protrusion running from halfway up to the top of the crag. Climb up to the centre of the overhang and pull over using a large jug over the lip. Move left then back right to climb the groove on the left side of the fin.

About 100 metres to the north of the main slab is another smaller slab.

Smuggler's Grill   10m   Severe   (1987)
Climb the obvious wide central crack.

Landmark   10m   VS 4c   (1987)
Climb the centre of the slab past a peculiar wedged flake.

Cash n'Carry   8m   VS 4c   (1987)
Follow the right-hand side of the slab, trending left to finish by Landmark.

T Bone   12m   E1 5a
Follow the crack at the right side of the slab.

On the beach and around the road there is a lot of rock suitable for short routes and bouldering.

ROADSIDE CRAG   *(Map Ref 268 503)*

A number of climbs have been found off the A747 near the parking lay-by for Garheugh Point. From Glasgow, follow the A77 to Stranraer, followed by the A75 to Glenluce and the A747 to Port William. Park in the lay-by on the right, at the top of the hill before the B7005 turns off left to Wigtown (about 10½km north of Port William). The climbs are described from left to right.

Gorilla   8m   HVS 5c   (1985/6)
Starting from the left side of the first overhang, use an undercut to swing up and left. Gain the arete, move to its right, then continue to the top.

Jackdaw Crack   8m   VS 5a   (1985/6)
Take the overhang direct to a slab, then a thin crack to the top.

Wee Pig   10m   VS 4c   (1985/6)
About 50 metres to the right is a steep wall with yellow lichen. Climb the wall using a line of holds on its left.

Nay Sweat   10m   Severe 4b   (1985/6)
Starting at the cave, about 20 metres right of the yellow wall. Climb up on the right to a niche, then move up and right to the arete at the top.

Fine Line   8m   VS 5a   (1985/6)
This is on the slab at the far right of the crag. Climb either up and left using small pockets or straight up the thin crack.

PORTOBELLO   *(Map Ref 961 664)*

This is an interesting area, smaller and less impressive than Meikle Ross and Burrow Head, but thanks to the generally better rock and fewer sea-birds, well worth a visit. The rock is greywacke which gives sunny, easily accessible at all grade routes in a delightful location. It has the highest concentration of Extremes in the South-West, including a contender for the hardest route in this section of the guide. The protection is mostly good, but it is wise to take a generous supply of RPs and small wires. Some of the crags are tidal.

From Glasgow take the A77 to Stranraer, then go west on the A718 to Leswalt. Go straight through the village and continue on the same road to a T-junction with the coast road. Turn left, and after 800 metres turn right at a bend onto a minor road which leads down to Portobello (not signposted). The road dwindles to a track. Allow 2 hours from Glasgow.

AXLE BAY

About 90 metres from the end of the track, down the line of a small stream, is the main cliff. Immediately to the north is a small bay, characterised by vehicle debris. On the left (north) side is a steep south-facing pocketed wall.

Bootless   15m   VS 4c   (1992)
The left-trending line gives steep climbing.

SLAB BAY

About 180 metres north of the main cliff, just beyond a stone wall, is a small bay with a steep, slabby north-facing wall split by a zigzag crack with two pods.

Changeling   15m   E4 6a **   (1993)
An excellent sustained route. Climb the arete left of The Man from Del Monte with difficulty past two spaced *in situ* pegs, to reach the thin crack just right of the upper arete.

The Man from Del Monte   15m   E3 6a ***   (1987)
Excellent technical finger jamming up the crack.

Dances with Mackerel   15m   E2 5c   (1993)
Climb the cracks to the right of The Man from Del Monte.

THE MAIN CLIFF

This is the largest crag in the area. A deep sea-filled chimney divides the crag in two, with the routes on the left-hand section rising straight from the sea. The routes are described from east to west; they are easily viewed from the promontory which divides the bay.

Crawford's Crackers   20m   HVS 5a   (1987)
Start a few metres left of the old plaque and follow a left-slanting crack line to an overhang, which is climbed on good holds. Belay well back.

Underling   25m   E2 5c   (1993)
Bold and technical climbing up the groove in the undercut subsidiary buttress 5
metres left of Crawford's Crackers. Start up the groove at the left toe of the
buttress, then continue more easily up the left side of the main buttress.

Floating Voter   25m   HVS 5a   (1987)
Starting about 10 metres left of the previous route, follow a left-curving groove,
then go up and left until easier ground can be reached. Continue up and right to
finish.

The Crayfish Twins   25m   E2 5c **   (1993)
Good, well protected climbing up the improbable wall 3 metres left of Floating
Voter. Follow flakes and pockets, moving slightly left at 8m, then go back right
to cross the overlap.

Blockhead   15m   Severe 4a   (1987)
Climb the wide crack line in the slabby black wall left of Floating Voter.

Cockle Sucker   15m   Severe 3c   (1990)
Climb the wide crack at the junction of the main cliff and the chimney, directly
opposite the step across.

Shellfish Bastard   15m   Severe 3c   (1990)
Traverse left from the foot of the chimney and climb the corner.

Happy Man   15m   Hard Severe 4a *   (1987)
The conspicuous crack line in the buttress rising from the sea. Abseil to a good
nut belay at the base (crux!).

Soul Kitchen   15m   E1 5b *   (1992)
Climb the thin corner left of Happy Man.

Horse Latitudes   15m   E1 5a **   (1993)
Traverse left from the foot of Soul Kitchen to the arete, which gives fine climbing
with spaced protection.

Puffin Nuffin   15m   Severe 4a   (1989)
Left of Soul Kitchen and about 8 metres right of Surfin' Safari is a larger corner,
the line of this route. Abseil down Count Duckula to belay about 5 metres to its
left (very much the crux!).

Hanging Duck   12m   Hard Severe 4a   (1990)
Start as for Puffin Nuffin, but after 3 metres break out and climb the steep corner
which trends up left.

Count Duckula   10m   Very Difficult   (1990)
This is the shaley groove line about 5 metres left of the start of Puffin Nuffin.

Lost at Sea   10m   E2 5b/c   (1993)
Sustained edging, high on swimming potential. From the foot of Count Duckula, traverse 2 metres left into the middle of the wall and climb directly to the top, with a rightward diversion at half-height.

Surfin' Safari   12m   Severe 4a   (1989)
At the furthest left end of the crag is a wall with two thin, disjointed, right-trending cracks. Climb these, starting from a platform to the left.

Warsteiner   10m   Very Difficult   (1989)
Climb the left-hand arete of the cliff above a small platform.

SHARK FIN BAY

Walking south from the main cliff, this is the first bay, recognised by a pinnacle resembling a shark's fin. Scramble down an easy gully at the back; the crag is on the south-facing side of the bay. The crag comprises a larger vegetated section on the right and a smaller promontory to the left. The routes are described from right to left. All the routes, except the first, finish on a promontory from which it is necessary to scramble to the top via a ridge.

Silence of the Clams   25m   HVS 5a **   (1992)
This climbs the wall and roof below and right of the ridge that leads up from the promontory to the top of the crag. Start directly below the diagonal crack above the roof. Follow a dirty crack to a turf ledge, then go up directly to the roof. Move up and right to perched blocks, then go left to a diagonal crack in a fine position.

Basic Instinct   15m   HVS 5a *   (1992)
Further left is a steep wall with a prominent overhang and triangular niche. Start to the right at an undercut pillar, which is gained with difficulty. Continue boldly to finish at the right end of the promontory.

Cutty Shark   15m   Hard Severe 4b   (1990)
Start below the triangular niche and traverse left into it via flakes. Continue up right to a spike in the corner which is followed to the top.

Water Dance   15m   E1 5b *   (1993)
This gives excellent climbing up the arete left of Mussel Bound, reached by a left-trending undercut slab.

Mussel Bound   15m   HVS 5a **   (1990)
Climb the thin crack line left of the niche, surmount the overhang, then go directly above, via a jagged undercut flake.

Sanity Claus   15m   Severe 4a   (1989)
To the right is an undercut wall. Climb this and the prominent corner above.

Aqua Vitae   15m   Severe 4a   (1990)
Start as for Sanity Clause, but leave the main corner to follow a less obvious one
on the left.

Basking up the Wrong Tree   10m   Very Difficult   (1990)
The corner at the left-hand end of the promontory.

Speed Limpets   10m   Hard Severe 4b *   (1990)
Start at the foot of the corner of Basking and climb diagonal left-trending cracks.

Winklepicker   10m   Severe 4a   (1992)
The left-trending layback crack left of Speed Limpets is only visible at low tide.
The seaward face of the promontory has three small routes at Moderate to Very
Difficult.

THE U-BOAT PEN
This is the narrow tidal inlet between Shark Fin Bay and Cracked Block Bay. The
first two routes are on the slabbier right-hand buttress, the latter four are on the
steeper tidal buttress. The routes are described from east to west.

Feeling the Pinch   15m   VS 4b *   (1990)
Take the left-trending brown streak in the top half of the buttress, reached from
below by a crack.

The Water Margin   15m   E1 5b ***   (1991)
Start 2 metres left of the last route and follow pockets up the thin lower slab, then
climb the upper wall to the right of its left edge.

Dead Sea Strolls   15m   Severe 4a   (1990)
A conspicuous crack slopes diagonally leftwards across the seaward buttress.
Climb it for 8m, then take the corner above the coffin-shaped recess.

The Zombie   15m   Severe 4a   (1990)
Creep out of the coffin-shaped recess, then go leftwards up wall above, crossing
a small overhang near the top. Abseil descent.

Riverboat Gambler   15m   VS 4b *   (1989)
This takes the fine crack which springs from the bottom of the easy left-sloping
ramp at the left side of the crag. Climb the crack to its top, then traverse up and
right to a corner.

The Ducking Stool   20m   VS 4c *   (1991)
Start as for Dead Sea Strolls, then take the conspicuous, wide diagonal crack
slanting left across the buttress. Finish up Riverboat Gambler.

CRACKED BLOCK BAY

Walking south from U-Boat Pen, it is possible to scramble down mixed slopes on the north side of the next large bay. The first three routes are on a large block, set slightly back at the west end of the mainland south-facing crag.

Thunderbolt   15m   HVS 5a **   (1987)
Enjoyable climbing up the wide crack in the block. Gain the niche and follow the crack above.

St Elmo's Fire   15m   E3 5c ***   (1992)
Excellent climbing up the wall right of Thunderbolt. Follow the crack right of the Thunderbolt niche, move slightly right over a bulge with difficulty, then climb directly to the top.

Only Monsters   15m   E1 5a   (1987)
Climb the right-hand side of the wall on the block's seaward side.

The slabby wall facing The Block is climbed by three routes, from the left: **Mackerel**, Very Difficult, up slabs; **Herring**, Difficult, the left-hand of two cracks left of the deep chimney; **Goldfish**, Difficult, the thin crack in the rib right of the deep chimney.

Left of The Block and just right of the undercut sea-wall is a smaller wall, seamed with faint ripple cracks. This is taken by possibly the hardest climb in the south-west.

The Waster   10m   E5 6b ***   (1993)
A desperate and technical route. Climb the ripple cracks, using some holds on their left side. The crux is just below the small ledge at two-thirds height.

Another One Bites The Dust   10m   Mild VS 4b   (1993)
Climb the rather scrappy corner left of The Waster.

Left of the rather scrappy corner is a fine arete which bounds an impressive south-facing steep wall, undercut at its base.

Critical Mass   15m   E1 5b **   (1992)
Sustained climbing up the scooped arete forming the right edge of the steep sea-wall.

Sweaty Trembler   15m   E5 6b **   (1993)
Another contender for the hardest climb in Galloway, this superb steep climb has just adequate protection. Start 2 metres right of The Cruel Seaside, below and left of an *in situ* peg. Climb through the roof to the peg, then go right and up past the peg almost to the arete. Gain and follow a left-trending ripple to the top.

The Cruel Seaside   15m   E2 5c ***   (1991)
Forceful climbing up the steep crack line on the right side of the wall, a few
metres left of Critical Mass.

Acid Test   10m   E2 5c   (1992)
Climb cornflake rock 4 metres left of The Cruel Seaside. The climbing eases and
protection improves with height.

Pushed to the Limit   10m   E4 6a   (1992)
Bold and serious with a ground fall possible from the hard move at the top. On
the left side of the wall is a left-slanting ramp. Follow the left-trending crack
directly above the start of this ramp.

Ramplet   10m   VS 5b   (1992)
The left-slanting ramp is started with great difficulty and followed to its end.

   The small south-facing wall in the middle of the bay has three routes.

Betty Blue   10m   E3 5c   (1993)
Climb the middle of the wall left of Parallel Lines, with spaced holds and gear.

Parallel Lines   10m   VS 4b   (1990)
The parallel crack-chimneys in the face. Low in the grade.

Return of the Limpet   10m   Severe 4a   (1990)
Climb the face to the right, with an overhang at half-height.

Figgit's Rest   15m   HVS 5a   (1992)
Facing the latter two routes is a steep wall characterised by large ripple marks
and split by a vertical crack. Climb the crack and slab above.

JUPITER ROCK   *(Map Ref 960 649)*

On the coast south of Portobello is a large cove characterised by a striking 25m
pinnacle at its southern end and a large red fin in the middle. Please avoid the
pinnacle in the nesting season.
   Park as for Portobello, and follow the coast south for about 1½km. The routes
are on a north-facing wall at the north end of the cove, which is hidden from
above.

The Beauty of Flight   15m   E1 5b   (1993)
Climb the thin left-slanting crack.

Bridg it   10m   Severe 4a   (1993)
This takes the chimney between the left end of the wall and a neighbouring rock
fin.

KILN O' THE FUFFOCK   *(Map Ref 959 642)*

This curiously-named cliff of excellent greywacke rises straight from the sea and provides some of the most ferocious routes in Galloway, as well as some of a more amenable nature. The cliff forms the south-facing wall of a narrow inlet, at the landward end of which is an arch leading to a grassy depression. This natural blow-hole gives the crag its name, and is a useful identifying feature, avoiding confusion with the smaller inlets to the north. Access to most of the routes is by abseil, and it may be wise to leave the ropes in place. It is best to avoid the crag during the nesting season, and seepage can cause problems for a few days after wet weather.

Either park as for Portobello and follow the coast south for about 3km or, from Mains of Cairnbrook, continue on the B738 for about 2km before turning right up the track to High Mark Farm. Park just before the farm (please ask permission), then cut across fields to the coast and the crag (15 minutes).

The routes are described from left to right. At the left end of the cliff is the wide left-sloping ramp of Penguin Parade, beneath which lie the first three routes.

Seaside Buddies   7m   Mild Severe   (1993)
Directly beneath the top end of Penguin Parade is a shallow corner. This route takes the cracked wall 3 metres left of the corner.

Water Wings   7m   Very Difficult   (1993)
Climb the shallow corner.

Point Break   10m   E2 5c **   (1993)
A well protected test-piece. Start 3 metres right of Water Wings and climb the wall via cracks and pockets.

Penguin Parade   15m   Difficult   (1993)
The wide left-slanting crack at the left end of the crag is not as easy as it looks, but it is a useful escape route..

Directly above the lower part of Penguin Parade, at the top of the cliff, is a prominent corner which is a useful marker for the next 3 routes.

Body Swerve   12m   VS 4c   (1993)
Start on Penguin Parade, some 4 metres left of the corner. Climb a crack to thin left-trending ripples. Move right to the foot of the corner, then take the prominent left-trending crack to the top.

The Pincer   15m   VS 4c **   (1993)
A nice civilised route. Climb directly to the corner and follow it to the top.

Rock Lobster   20m   E1 5b *   (1993)
Steep, technical and unforgiving! Start at the lowest point of the ramp and 2 metres right of the corner. Climb a thin crack over a bulge, then continue up and left to gain the corner.

The next feature right of Penguin Parade is a roof with two distinctive down-pointing prongs.

Total Immersion   20m   E4 6a ***   (1993)
A magnificent route, delicate and sustained. Start just right of the bottom end of Penguin Parade. Climb up to and over the roof at the niche left of the left-hand prong. Very delicate climbing leads up the steep slab above to the top.

Echo Beach   20m   E3 6a **   (1993)
Another sustained and technical route. Protection is good but hard to place. Start 3 metres right of the bottom end of Penguin Parade. Take the very thin crack at the right end of the pronged roof, and once above the roof follow the crack slightly leftwards.

Right of the pronged roof is the lowest, central part of the cliff. The following two routes are immediately either side of this.

Abide With Me   20m   E4 6a **   (1993)
Sustained climbing with an appallingly delicate crux. Abseil just left of the central grassy low point to a hanging belay. Climb to a thin left-trending ledge beneath the widest part of the overhang. Traverse this delicately left to reach holds under the overhang, then move right to cross the overhang at its widest point. Continue slightly leftwards up cracks, then move right to finish.

Saturation Point   20m   E4 6a *   (1993)
A hard and serious route, particularly lower down. Start immediately below the lowest part of the cliff. Hanging belay on RPs. The line follows the slightly right-trending hairline crack which finishes just right of the central grassy low point. Climb the crack with difficulty over a bulge to a rest. Continue more easily up the better crack to the top.

Burning the Boats   20m   E3 6a *   (1993)
A technical but well protected route which takes the main challenge of the steepest part of the cliff. At the right end of the cliff are ledges at sea-level. Start at their left end, at the foot of a wide and prominent right-sloping crack. Access is either at low tide, or by abseil. Climb to the foot of the corner beneath roofs. Step left onto a desperate slab which leads to a prominent flat hold at a break in the roof (peg runner). Continue to the most prominent crack in the headwall, which succumbs with surprising ease.

Spirit Level   30m   HVS 5a **   (1993)
An excellent route in superb positions, somewhat reminiscent of the Carnivore traverse. Start in the centre of the sea-level ledges beneath a right-sloping crack. Climb the crack for 6m to a bulge, then move up and left to a good ledge at a niche (the mid-point of the prominent wide right-sloping crack). Traverse left and follow a superb, thin, left-trending ramp line which traverses the headwall and finishes just right of the central low point. The crux is at the top.

The Bends, The Bends   20m   E2 5c   (1993)
A strenuous climb. Start up Spirit Level, but follow a line below it to rejoin it at
the midway niche. Step left and climb the headwall directly to crux pinch moves
just below the top.

Arc of the Diver   20m   HVS 5a *   (1993)
A good route, steep but with huge holds. Start as for Spirit Level, but follow the
right-sloping crack over the bulge to ledges. Move 2 metres left and climb the
wide right-slanting prominent crack to the niche. Move up and left to gain and
follow a steep corner at the top.

    The small promontory to the north has small steep walls on its south-facing
side and two slabs on its north-facing side.

Breakaway   8m   Hard Severe 4b   (1993)
This is on the south-facing wall. Traversing in from the left, the first main feature
is a loose corner with left-trending cracks in its left wall. This route takes the steep
wall to the right, with a crack at its right end.

Dave's Slab   8m   Very Difficult   (1993)
This takes the seaward of the north-facing slabs.

Sea Fowl   10m   Mild Severe   (1993)
Climb the centre of the loose left-hand slab.

MONEY HEAD   (Map Ref 047 483)

A number of routes have been climbed on the coast around Money Head. The
crags are about 15m to 20m high, face south-west and are formed of clean,
good-quality metamorphosed greywacke with igneous intrusions. They are
mainly bird free, but seepage can be a problem in the central area.
    From Glasgow follow the A77 to Stranraer, followed by the A716/715 to
Sandhead. Just before Sandhead, take the B7042 (signposted Portpatrick) on
the right, then the first left after a sharp right-hand bend. At the cross roads at
Cairngarroch Farm, go straight over, down a dead-end road, to park about 100
metres after the first house. Follow the track on the left down to the house on the
beach.
    Skirt the coast to the south for about 10 minutes until a steep, slanting,
north-facing wall with a slabby south side is reached. Continue south-west for
about 10 minutes to the furthest point of the headland, and descend a slabby
platform sticking out into the sea. Ecu Wall is on the right (south), the central
Bear Pit Area on the left (north) and the Cioch Area left again. These crags cannot
be seen from above.

ECU WALL

All the routes are reached from the platform, save Insider Dealing, which is approached from the rib flanking Ecu Wall to the south.

Insider Dealing   40m   Severe 4a   (1992)
A left-rising traverse of the wall, starting just above the initial overhang.
1. 25m 3b   Steep ground and large holds lead left to easy slabs. Follow these left to descend a corner (Ecu Wall) to a cave belay below the large roof.
2. 15m 4a   A crack leads up and left beneath the roof. Cross the corner leftwards to a ledge from which an arete which leads to the top.

Ecu Wall   20m   Severe 4a   (1992)
Start below the cave beneath the large roof. Climb up and right via corners to a break in the roof, 5m up and right of the cave.

The Liquidator   20m   HVS 5a **   (1992)
Start about 8 metres right of the slot of Slot Machine where the crag is no longer undercut. Gain the short steep corner, then go right to the crack leaving the left side of the cave. Follow this for 4m, then limbo right across the undercut break in the roof for an exciting finish.

Slot Machine   20m   HVS 5a *   (1992)
A curious slot at 10m leads to good bridging up the corner, left of the large roof.

The Root of All Evil   20m   E3 5c *   (1992)
Follow Slot Machine to the slot, then traverse left onto the steep wall, peg runner. Move up and left to a spike on the arete, then go right to the ledge. Finish up Insider Dealing.

THE BEAR PIT

Corners on the right give way to an impressively compact central face. A flying buttress divides this area from easier rock to the left. Access can be difficult during high tide or rough sea.

Pay Day   6m   VS 5a   (1992)
Take the undercut corner left of the wide roof at the right-hand end of the crag.

Bolivars   10m   VS 4b   (1992)
The two left-trending corners just to the left of Pay Day. Low in the grade.

Free Enterprise   15m   E1 5b *   (1992)
The left-hand side of the steep central face culminates in an apex. Start right of and below a small, square, black wall. Climb up to the wall, then move leftwards to the apex and finish directly.

Tumbling Dice   20m   VS 4c *   (1992)
The stepped rib bounding the central face on the left gives varied climbing. Start
at the right end of the short wall, left of the central face. Climb an arete to a ledge.
Move left, then right up a steep hanging slab to a wide ledge. Continue up steps
and corners to finish right up slabs.

Cash Flow   20m   HVS 5a   (1992)
This climbs the corner line left of the stepped rib of Tumbling Dice. Start at the
left end of the wall, left of the central face and climb an overhung corner at sea
level, moving rightwards and up the steep corner above to an easier slab. Below
the steep top wall, move right up slabs to a steep finish just left of a protruding
beak of rock.

Tax Evasion   20m   Severe 4a   (1992)
The lichen-coloured flying buttress descending into the sea is only climbable at
low tide. Start as for Cash Flow and climb the short steep corner on the left to a
slab. Traverse left to a wide crack and finish up the crest of the buttress.

Filthy Lucre   20m   E1 5a   (1992)
Approach by descending slabs to the north, followed by a sea-level traverse for
about 100 metres. Climb the steep left-slanting corner in the bulging undercut
rib with difficulty, then finish out right.

THE CIOCH AREA
The northern section of the cliff is characterised by an overhanging beak of rock,
left of a sweep of slabs split in two by a corner. Both routes start at the bottom
left corner of the right wing of the slabs and are approached via easy slabs to
the south.

Pot of Gold   20m   HVS 5a *   (1992)
Move up right to the overlap, cross this at its left end, then traverse right along
the lip of the overhang to easier ground - good climbing.

Rainbow's End   20m   Severe 4a   (1992)
Climb directly for 10m, just right of the edge, before moving slightly right and then
finishing direct.

LAGGANTALLUCH   *(Map Ref 085 363)*

The granite sea-cliffs here give excellent climbing in pleasant surroundings on a
number of crags spread out along the headland. In general the higher grade
routes seem quite sustained and impressive. The quality of the rock is generally
very good and although the routes get a fair amount of sun, seepage can be a
problem. There are few sea-birds.
   From Glasgow take the A77 to Stranraer. Continue along the A77 towards
Portpatrick, then follow the A716 towards Drummore. Take a right turn about

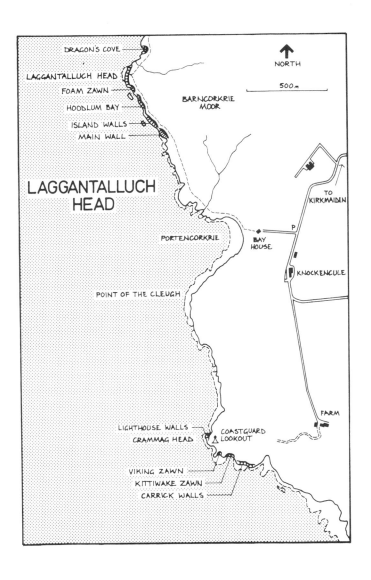

DRAGON'S COVE

LAGGANTALLUCH HEAD

FOAM ZAWN

HOODLUM BAY

ISLAND WALLS

MAIN WALL

BARNCORKRIE MOOR

NORTH

500 m

LAGGANTALLUCH
HEAD

PORTENCORKRIE

BAY
HOUSE

P

TO
KIRKMAIDEN

KNOCKENCULE

POINT OF THE CLEUGH

FARM

LIGHTHOUSE WALLS

CRAMMAG HEAD

COASTGUARD
LOOKOUT

VIKING ZAWN

KITTIWAKE ZAWN

CARRICK WALLS

1½km north of the village, at the 'Welcome to Drummore' sign, and veer left at the Y-junction. Drive through Kirkmaiden (B7065) and take the second turning on the right (the first is immediately after the telephone booth). Continue for 4km to Barncorkrie Farm, then park with due consideration in limited space after a further 500 metres. A track on the right leads down to a cottage overlooking Laggantalluch Bay. Allow 2½ hours from Glasgow.

Follow the track and go through a gate on the left, then go round the cottage to a stile and down to Portencorkie Bay. Follow the coast north until the Main Cliff is reached in about 20 minutes. Abseil ropes are useful for some of the descents.

CRAIG OF THE STONE DYKE AND THE ANCHORAGE
At the north end of Portencorkie Bay are two small bays after a stone wall. The first inlet has a few routes between Difficult and Severe up the slab and cracks. The next bay has a 10m south-facing wall with one Very Difficult which is poorer than it looks.

SMALL BAY
This bay lies just south of the main cliff. It has a steep north wall with an obvious corner facing the ribs and platforms of the main cliff. The rock is poorer than elsewhere.

Tormentil   15m   HVS 5a   (1987)
The corner. Descend the grassy rib on the right (facing out) and make a short abseil to a small ledge below the corner. Low tide or a calm sea is advisable.

Arete   10m   Difficult   (1987)
Take the wall on the seaward face, right of the corner.

THE MAIN CLIFF
This consists of a large cave to the south, a large slab hidden from above in the centre and to the north, and corners and fins above a rock platform. Easy access can be gained by abseiling down the fins to a large platform. The routes are described from left to right. The first seven routes lie on the steep ribs and corners to the left of the main slab.

Aqualung   15m   HVS 5b   (1991)
The steep wall at the extreme left end of the crag. Abseil down the corner immediately below Escape Route (low tide essential). Start up the corner left of Escape Route, until it is possible to move round left onto a steep fingery wall above the sea. Climb to a ledge, then go up a thin groove about 2 metres left of the buttress edge.

Stepped Corner   15m   Very Difficult   (1991)
Approach as for Aqualung, but continue up the corner left of Escape Route.

Escape Route   10m   Difficult
Left of the overhanging fin is a stepped corner. Step across a gap and climb the corner. This is a possible descent route, but it requires care.

Quick Seal   10m   E3 6a ***   (1992)
Excellent climbing up the obvious thin crack in the overhanging fin right of Escape Route.

Rogered Direct   12m   HVS 5a   (1991)
Climb directly up the corner system right of the overhanging fin. The initial difficult section can be avoided from the right (Severe).

Seventh Wave   20m   E1 5b *   (1987)
Start below and left of Laggantalluch Corner at a diagonal crack. Follow this into the base of the corner. Move up and across the left wall of the corner to a thin crack and spike on the arete, then climb the slab above. Eliminate, but good climbing.

Laggantalluch Corner   20m   HVS 5a ***   (1987)
The obvious corner gives fine climbing on good rock with good protection.

Ape Escape   20m   E2 6a **   (1987)
Spectacular and well protected climbing through the roof crack up and right of Laggantalluch Corner. Follow the main slab up past the corner until it is possible to step onto a steep yellow wall, which is followed to a ledge below the crack. Climb the crack to a good spike, make a long reach up and right to a good jug and continue with steep jamming to finish.

The next routes climb the main slab.

Irish Mist   40m   E1 5a   (1987)
Near the top of the large slab on the left side is a flake. Climb to the flake and from its right end climb the wall above, trending right. Minimal protection.

Freewheeling   40m   E2 5b **   (1987)
Quality in climbing, but not in gear! Follow the longest central black streak on the slab to a break on the right, runner. Continue up and left to a slight bulge, then trend up and left to finish. The best route on the slab, but a serious undertaking for the grade.

Dublin Packet   40m   E1 5a   (1987)
High on the right of the slab is a black streak leading to a small grassy ledge. Climb the slab to a break below the streak and follow this past the grass to the top.

Stingray   50m   Hard Severe 4b   (1987)
An enjoyable open traverse above the large roofs with the hardest moves at the
end. Traverse the lip of the overhangs until a groove and corner lead to a small
roof and the top.

Waiting for the Sun   12m   VS 4c   (1991)
About 120 metres north of the main slab is a steep green wall with an easier
right-trending, green lichen-covered upper slab. Finish up the slab, or scramble
down the crack to the left.

LUNCH BAY
To the north of the main cliff is a small bay characterised by a south-facing wall
with low overhangs and a small steep north-facing wall of fine granite.

Sciatic Nerve   15m   Severe 4a   (1987)
The stepped corners left of the overhangs. The arete to the left gives a Difficult.

Fish Fingers   15m   E2 5b   (1991)
The wall between Sciatic Nerve and the arete to its left.

Micro Niche   10m   HVS 5a   (1992)
The right side of this cliff is characterised by a long roof. Climb the overhung
break in the right side of the roof directly from below.

ISLAND WALLS
These relatively short and non-serious walls of immaculate granite lie opposite
the long low island. The first routes lie on the southern wall, approached by
descending a small gully opposite the northern tip of the island and traversing
left (facing out), to below the wall. The northern walls are approached from the
north down a sloping platform.
   The first route on the southern walls lies on the right (facing out) wall of the
gully. The other six routes lie opposite the island on the main wall to the left
(facing out). The routes are described from left to right.

Desert Island Discs   8m   VS 4c   (1991)
There are three cracks on the gully wall. Climb the right-hand crack with a
narrowing slab at the bottom. The left-hand two cracks are both Difficult.

A Plaice by the Sea   12m   VS 4b   (1991)
Start at the left-hand end of the main wall. Follow a thin crack to join Skating at
half-height, and finish up the steep corner crack above.

Skating   12m   Very Difficult   (1991)
To the right are stepped corners. Climb them, finishing to the right.

Bouillabaisse   10m   Severe 4a   (1991)
In the centre of the cliff is a corner. The rib to the left leads to a short corner at the top.

Little Feat   10m   VS 4c *   (1991)
Good climbing up the central corner, finishing just left of the top of Fish Ladder.

Fish Tales   10m   Hard Severe 4b   (1991)
A thin crack joining The Fish Ladder at two-thirds height.

The Fish Ladder   12m   Very Difficult   (1991)
The prominent left-slanting chimney crack on the right of the cliff.

The small northern wall is of excellent granite. The routes are described from right to left.

The Blind Man   7m   VS 4c   (1991)
Deceptively hard climbing up the stepped corners on the left side of the crag.

Good Morning Ladies   8m   Hard Severe 4b *   (1991)
An excellent route up the steep right-sloping crack about halfway along the platform.

HOODLUM BAY
Just to the north is a small bay with an impressive overhanging black wall in the centre. Scramble down slabby rock to the south. The routes are described from right to left.

The Foaming Hoodlum Traverse   Severe 4a *
The traverse of the Hoodlum Walls and Foam Zawn to Laggantalluch Head gives an exciting outing.

The Oyster Thief   20m   HVS 5a *   (1991)
Flanking the black wall on the left, a curving crack leads to a finish up the right-hand corner above.

The Clam Catcher   25m   VS 4c   (1991)
At the left end of the black wall, a white-streaked wall and crack lead to a small tower. Pull round and over this to finish. The stepped wall to the left is Severe.

To the north is a small island and an obvious squat pinnacle in the sea. This marks the southern end of Foam Zawn. The bay to the south has a prominent flat topped rib, easily identifiable from above.

Mourning Rib   25m   Very Difficult   (1991)
Climb the rib to the top.

White Sauce   15m   Severe 4a   (1991)
In the north corner of the bay and 10 metres south of the squat pinnacle in the
sea is a knife-edged arete, climbed on its left side.

FOAM ZAWN

This small zawn lies about 650 metres north of the main cliff, and is partially
hidden from above. Descend a rock and grass rib until the corner of Refusnik
becomes visible. Abseil towards the island and traverse ledges to the corner, or
descend the left-slanting corner right of Tunes of Glory (Difficult), but hard to see
from above. A calm sea is recommended. The zawn and abseil point can be
seen from the large platform of Laggantalluch Head to the north. Spongonema
can be reached by a traverse south from Laggantalluch Head (Mild Severe). The
routes are described from right to left.

The Shadow Line   20m   Difficult   (1991)
Climb the buttress immediately behind the island via a crack and stepped
corners. This can be reached by a traverse from Hoodlum Bay (Difficult).

Tunes of Glory   25m   VS 4b *   (1991)
At the right-hand end of the wall, facing the corner of Refusnik, is a prominent
steep crack to the right of the main overhangs. Climb it on good jugs, moving left
in the top half. Low in the grade.

Davy Jones's Locker   20m   E1 5b **   (1992)
Steep and strenuous climbing through the overhangs left of Tunes of Glory and
facing Refusnik. Follow the corner at the left end of the overhangs into and then
out of a niche to easier ground.

Refusnik   25m   E2 5c **   (1987)
A tremendous route with great exposure, but prone to seepage and bird nests.
The grade takes account of the seep at the bottom, but this tends to dry out in
afternoon sunshine. Climb the overhanging corner to a ledge, belay possible.
From the ledge climb poorer rock on the right to finish.

Pillar   25m   HVS 5a   (1987)
Descend the ramp below Refusnik and make a sea-level traverse round the
arete. Climb the wall above, moving right to the arete, and make a steep pull
onto a yellow slab (guano depending on the season). Continue up the slab and
easier rock to a large ledge, finishing up poorer rock on the right.

Spongonema   25m   E1 5b *   (1991)
The obvious hanging chimney line, round the corner from Pillar and conspicuous
from Laggantalluch Head. Technical and sustained, but with some poor rock to
finish.

LAGGANTALLUCH HEAD
This steep little crag of fine grey granite lies about 700 metres north of the main cliff. Hidden from above, it has a large rock platform at its base and a prominent line of overhangs at mid-height. The crag is best reached from the north by a scramble down and along the coast. The routes are described from left to right.

Obliteration   15m   E3 5c   (1992)
An intimidating route with nasty fall potential. The left side of the cliff drops directly into a fissure, at one point bridged by blocks. From the blocks move up left past a poor peg to a good hold. Continue up the steep crack with difficulty.

Seal Song   20m   E1 5b ***   (1987)
Enjoyable steep climbing. Start below the left end of the overhang where a line of holds lead out left to the lip of the roof. Traverse right across a small·wall and round a rib. Continue up and right to finish.

Back Burner   20m   E3 6a   (1987)
This breaches the line of overhangs via a steep chimney. Good technical climbing, but hard to protect as the runners fill the best holds.

First Touch   20m   E1 5b **   (1987)
Climb to the break at the right end of the overhang. Traverse left to a slim corner and climb this with difficulty to finish.

Wave Good-bye   20m   Hard Severe 4b   (1987)
Right of the above route is a cave-like recess. Enter it, then exit at the top and follow easy ground above.

DRAGON'S CAVE
Continuing north along the coast and just past a small burn is an obvious yellow slab of metamorphosed greywacke. The roaring sea cave below gives the crag a memorable atmosphere. At low tide descend the seaward slab (climbed by Darwin's Waiting Room) by abseiling from spikes at the top. The routes are described from right to left.

Heart of Darkness   35m   HVS 5a *   (1991)
The large yellow slab gives a superb atmospheric route, considerably better than it looks from above. Start near the right edge and follow a line of holds up and left to a conspicuous spike on the left edge of the slab. Move slightly right then directly up to the top.

Darwin's Waiting Room   35m   VS 4b   (1991)
Climb the corner in the seaward slabs until it eases, then climb steep cracks on the right wall of the corner. Worthwhile.

The Origin of Species   35m   VS 4c   (1991)
The steep left edge of the seaward slab, starting at the left end of a small platform. Move steeply up and left into a groove and climb to a large ledge. Slightly left is a hidden slab which is climbed to the upper arete of the seaward slab.

POINT OF THE CLEUGH   *(Map Ref 088 348)*

Midway between Portencorkrie Bay and Crammag Head, directly below a fence, is a slab of pink granite similar to a scaled-down version of the slab at Laggantalluch Head, but with bigger holds.

Approach in about 10 minutes by walking south from Portencorkrie Bay or north from Crammag Head (see access descriptions for Laggantalluch Head or Crammag Head).

The first route lies on an obvious block of pink granite with a steep landward wall, about 100 metres north of the Cleugh slab.

Comatose   12m   VS 5a   (1992)
Excellent climbing up the obvious incipient crack and over the small roof on the block's south-west face.

About halfway between the block and the Cleugh slab, at sea-level and facing northwards, is a chimney about 6m deep set into the cliff.

The Slot   13m   Very Difficult   (1992)
A traditional struggle!

The remaining routes lie on the Cleugh slab itself and are described from left to right.

The Chancer   15m   VS 4c   (1992)
Low in the grade. Step off a small grey boulder and climb the steep wall directly above to good holds on the slab. Continue up and left to brown water-streaked rock and finish straight up.

Cleugh Clamber   15m   Hard Severe 4b   (1992)
Start just right of the grey boulder and climb straight up the slab about 5 metres right of the previous route.

Just Friends   15m   Severe 4a   (1992)
Right of Cleugh Clamber is a clean slab with a small rock pool at its base. Climb the recess to the right of the slab until it is possible to swing onto the slab and follow a central line to a ledge and short wall.

CRAMMAG HEAD   *(Map Ref 089 340)*

A number of easily accessible climbs can be found in a beautiful situation on this west-facing headland. The granite is generally good quality and the routes are contained within a small area, with a less strenuous and a less serious feel than parts of the nearby Laggantalluch cliffs. The climbs are faster drying than Laggantalluch, although birds can be a greater problem during the nesting season.

   Approach as for the Laggantalluch cliffs. After passing the cottage in the bay, continue straight ahead for about 800 metres to Slockmill farm. The farmer is very sympathetic to climbers, but because of past vandalism to the lighthouse at the headland it is essential to get his permission before climbing. Follow the track from the farmyard to the crags (8 minutes). The crags are described southwards from the lighthouse.

LIGHTHOUSE WALLS

The walls beneath the lighthouse give good bouldering. The first three routes are located beneath the end of the concrete steps leading from the lighthouse. A black slab is flanked by a steep wall to its left.

Shining Path   7m   VS 4c   (1992)
The left arete of the steep wall.

Lighthouse Wall   8m   HVS 5a *   (1992)
Good climbing up discontinuous cracks and pockets in the centre of the wall.

Poisoned Ocean   10m   HVS 5a   (1992)
Climb the black slab, exiting through the break in the roof towards its left side.

Hourglass Slab   10m   Very Difficult **   (1992)
Round to the right and directly south of the lighthouse is a slab of pink granite. Climb it slightly left of centre. A wee gem.

Bully Beef   10m   Hard Severe 4b   (1993)
The corner right of the black streak on the slab. Delicate and poorly protected.

GABARUNNING ZAWN

South of the lighthouse is a lookout and directly below this is a bay containing a slanting overhanging south wall with a pinnacled crest.

Accommodations of Desire   25m   E2 5c **   (1992)
Steep and surprisingly good. Near the right end of the wall at half-height is a small triangular niche. Lean over to good handholds below the niche. Move up and left to a wide crack and go up to the ledge. From its right-hand side, follow the right-slanting crack to exit up the obvious corner.

VIKING ZAWN

The next inlet lies a little to the south of the lookout. It is identified from above by a rather broken wall with a conspicuous central pinnacle to the north and an impressive and compact buttress to the south. Both crags are accessible at low tide via a traverse south from Gabarunning Zawn. Access to the south buttress at high tide is by abseil.

Orabidoo   10m   VS 4c   (1992)
Left of the pinnacle on the northern wall is a chimney and left again is a buttress split by a wide sloping ramp. Climb the lower tier by a double chimney-jamming crack. On the upper tier a steep start leads to a layback flake and short groove.

Pillage   10m   Very Difficult   (1992)
The short chimney left of the pinnacle on the northern wall.

Fallen Star   25m   Hard Severe 4a   (1992)
Good climbing on large holds up the front face of the pinnacle, finishing up the corner behind.

Skol's Out   25m   Difficult   (1992)
Start at the outside edge of the narrow channel at the back of the zawn and climb the stepped wall to the left.

The Four Bees   35m   Hard Severe *   (1993)
A surprisingly enjoyable excursion up the obvious huge chimney left of Soft Parade. Traverse left at sea-level below Soft Parade for a few metres, step across the gap and climb up to an obvious handrail. Follow this to a good footledge, then bridge or back-and-foot up into the chimney on excellent rock. Exit left just below the top to finish up a steep corner.

Ragnarok   25m   HVS 5a *   (1992)
Varied and atmospheric climbing on the left side of the south buttress. Start as for Soft Parade to the foot of the square niche. Traverse left and climb the right-hand left-slanting ramp to easier ground. Break out left onto slab and cross the roofs at their widest part.

The Soft Parade   20m   E1 5b *   (1992)
Good climbing. Not very sustained, but quite high in the grade. Start at the left end of the buttress below a square niche. Gain the niche from the left and continue to an overlap. Cross the slab and follow the slab and crack to finish.

The Seven Seas   20m   E3 5c ***   (1993)
This takes the steep scooped slab left of Funeral Pyre. Move left from a conspicuous pocket, then go up via steep layaways to a good hold in the scoop. Stand on this (crux), then move up to the right end of the overlap. Pull over and follow the left side of the arete (bold).

Funeral Pyre   20m   E1 5b *   (1992)
This takes the slab in the centre of the wall to the right, via a small overlap, finishing up a flake-corner near the top.

Hagar the Horrible   20m   Severe   (1992)
The large right-slanting chimney-corner on the right side of the south buttress.

KITTIWAKE ZAWN
Some of the most impressive rock in the area can be found on the overhanging south-facing wall of this zawn. Unfortunately, the rock isn't above suspicion.

Sid Stingray   20m   VS 4b   (1993)
Left of the centre of the wall is an obvious open groove line. Climb the narrow groove on good juggy rock, then step left at the top and go up into the main upper groove. Climb a steep crack on the left wall of the groove(crux) and finish up a short loose corner.

Down Under   35m   E2 ***   (1993)
A superb atmospheric route up the obvious corner on the right side of the impressive overhanging south wall. Scramble down and traverse the wide ledge to the base of the corner.
1. 15m 5b   Climb the grey corner to a notch in the arete.
2. 20m 5c   Climb past a niche on the left, then move right above it to a spike. Continue to a recess, then traverse back left on good holds to finish direct.

Dormouse   20m   Very Difficult   (1992)
Follow the obvious, rather loose, slabby chimney near the right side of the slabby north-facing wall.

CARRICK WALLS
To the south again is a small off-shore island. The remaining routes lie on the walls to the north and south of the promontory pointing towards the island; they are some of the best in the area. Descend by abseil down west-facing grooves north of the promontory to reach the first four routes. The other routes are best approached by abseil down the south-facing slabby walls on the other side.

Freedom Fighter   15m   HVS 5b *   (1992)
The line follows the right edge of the short wall at the far left end of the Carrick Walls. A right-slanting crack leads to a ledge. Make an energetic move over the bulge and continue up the wall. Quite high in the grade.

Fresh Air   20m   E1 5b ***   (1993)
This impressive and intimidating climb is much easier than it appears. Climb the obvious chimney to its top. Place runners, then descend slightly to reach a prominent hole in the leaning left wall. Move onto the wall, trending left to the overhanging arete, and finish spectacularly on good holds.

Gorilla Warfare   20m   HVS 5a *   (1992)
Steep and intimidating, but on good holds. Start just right of Fresh Air and climb to a right-trending corner. Follow this to a ledge, then continue right to finish just right of the overhangs on dubious rock.

Kalashnikov   20m   VS 4b *   (1992)
Follow the prominent arete on the right, turning the overhang on the left. Continue to the upper level section of the arete. It is possible to cross the gully on the left and finish up the slabby red wall.

Molotov Cocktail   20m   E1 5b **   (1992)
Good climbing split by ledges. Left of the descent route and above a small sea-channel is a tower characterised by two crack lines. Follow the left-hand crack until it is possible to move left to a ledge. Climb the excellent twin cracks above, move right and finish up the crack in the upper wall.

Enfant Terrible   20m   HVS 5a   (1992)
The right-hand crack, avoiding any wet patches.

Yosemite Sam   20m   HVS 5b **   (1992)
Right of the descent is an overhanging crack above a pool. Bridge and jam the exciting crack, taking care of the rock inside the pod.

   To the right is a slabby wall, capped by a roof.

The Ship's Cat   20m   HVS 5a *   (1992)
Start just left of the central slanting crack, and follow easy slabby walls to below the roof. Spectacular and surprising climbing leads to easier ground.

The White Rabbit   20m   VS 4b   (1992)
Follow the central slanting crack on good holds. Low in the grade.

Mog   20m   E1 5b *   (1992)
The slim pillar to the right lacks independence, but gives good climbing. An awkward undercut start (avoidable on the left) leads to the pillar, which is short but unexpectedly fingery and sustained. Finish directly up the pillar (eliminate) or up the crack of The White Rabbit.

Anvil Chorus   25m   E1 5b   (1993)
Start as for Mog, then climb right up an undercut slab to the right-hand of twin grooves. At the top exit left via an obvious layback flake.

Fragile Edge   20m   HVS 5a   (1992)
Varied climbing, but with some doubtful rock. To the right is a pinnacle. Bridge up between this and the buttress and continue up the arete and crack.

WEST TARBET   *(Map Ref 140 308)*

While the rock at the Mull of Galloway is loose and unpleasant, there are a couple of worthwhile routes situated in the first inlet south of West Tarbet Bay.

From Glasgow take the A77 to Stranraer, followed by the A716 to Drummore. Go through Drummore and follow the B7041 signposted to the Mull of Galloway. Park off the road near to West Tarbet bay.

Bible Class   15m   Very Difficult   (1991)
The slabby black wall at the left end of the southern wall of the inlet.

Sundae School   10m   Hard Severe 4b   (1991)
Climb the twin buttress situated just north of the landward end of the inlet, via a steep crack and niche.

MINOR CRAGS

PORTPATRICK   *(Map Ref 000 542)*

The Witch Rock, the small sea stack about 500 metres north of the town, has been climbed by the obvious landward-facing groove system (15m Severe). There is an old peg just below the summit. Portpatrick Quarry is a greywacke quarry about 180 metres from the car park at the harbour. About 10 routes have been climbed from Difficult to HVS, the best of which is **Flight of the Falcon** (HVS 4c) which takes the steep curving band of white quartz.

MULL OF GALLOWAY   *(Map Ref 155 303)*

In general the rock appears loose and unfriendly, unlike the scenery. One 45m VS has been recorded up a clean sweep of rock about 800 metres from the lighthouse.

The Central Outcrops

This chapter returns to the Central Belt to describe the crags in the Stirling area. These provide some good climbing and training which is readily accessible from both Glasgow and Edinburgh. The maps required for this chapter are OS sheets 57 and 58.

NORTH THIRD   *(Map Ref 761 893)*

This is an extensive outcrop of dolerite, about 8km south-west of Stirling, in a beautiful setting overlooking North Third Reservoir. The climbing is characterised by long straight cracks which give some fine problems in jamming. After short periods of wet weather the cliff dries quickly. After longer periods of rain and during much of the winter the crag can take a long time to dry out.

Leave either the M80 or M9 at exit 9, and take the A872 towards Denny leaving it at the first turning on the right, under the motorway (zero your odometer). Turn left at the first junction (0.7 miles), then right (1.2) and then left towards Carron Bridge (1.5). Turn right at the fork (2.7) and park on the verge above the dam (4.6). Walk across the dam to the crags. The climbs are described from left to right.

Faulty Tower   12m   VS 4c
This lies on the buttress about 100 metres left of the Birds and Bees Buttress. Start from a cave on the right. Swing left out of the cave into a crack which is followed to the top.

BIRDS AND BEES BUTTRESS
This buttress lies directly above the dam, and is easily recognised by the huge bulbous nose right of centre.

Beeline   12m   HVS 5a
Climb the obvious groove on the right side of the buttress which lies 20 metres left of the nose. Swing right around the overhang at the top.

Cuckoo Crack   15m   VS 5a
This lies just below and left of the huge nose. Climb the crack to a glacis under a roof, traverse right into a groove and finish direct.

THE RED TOWER
This area lies about 400 metres right of Birds and Bees Buttress. The most obvious feature is a striking red tower set in a bay, round which the climbs are situated. The best descent is down the slope to the left.

The Flying Dragon   20m   E2 5c   (1982)
The crack in the left wall of the bay.

Jezebel   20m   E1 5b **   (1982)
The crack to the right of the Flying Dragon gives superb sustained jamming. Follow the crack through a strenuous bulge then continue up the groove above. Thread belay.

Jim's Chimney   20m   VS 4b
The hideous chimney to the right of Jezebel is followed to finish up its left wall.

Red Shift   25m   E5 6b *   (1982/84)
This route climbs the fine diagonal crack across the Red Tower. Climb a bulging vertical crack (crux) to gain the diagonal crack. Follow this, with particularly trying moves round the arete, to finish straight up.
Variation: 6a
It is slightly easier, but on poorer rock, to start up the vague groove left of the normal start.

Beemer   15m   E3 5c
This route takes the bulging chimney crack 15 metres further right.

Sma Gell   12m   E2 5c
Another 150 metres to the right is an obvious crack splitting a bulging nose. The climb gets increasingly harder and more difficult to protect as the crack gets wider.

CAMBUSBARRON QUARRY   *(Map Ref 772 923)*

This fine abandoned quarry bowl offers a good selection of high standard single pitch routes, mostly following prominent cracks or grooves. The routes are generally well protected and all but the last three are situated on the left-hand face at the back of the quarry. The quarry is very sheltered and the face catches the evening sun in the summer, though the routes are seldom dry in winter.

Since they were first cleaned and climbed, some of the routes have suffered from neglect and have become quite dirty. This is a shame, as most are quite good. A number of the climbs have been upgraded since the previous edition of the guide. The revised grades are for on sight leads; if you've dogged or top roped the route to death before leading, please don't moan about the upgrading, just award yourself the original number of E-points.

From the south leave the M90 at Junction 9 and head towards Bannockburn Heritage Centre. At the next roundabout (about 1km from the motorway) take the first exit, continuing towards the town centre. Now take the first left and, where the road curves back right after a few hundred metres, turn left onto the bridge over the motorway. On the far side, turn right towards Cambusbarron. Follow the main street through the village, and turn left at Quarry Road (about 200 metres after the centre of the village). The entrance to the quarry is at the top of the road, with limited parking on the right by a barrier.

Walk through the overgrown old quarry access track into the main amphitheatre. The climbs are described from left to right.

1   Power of Endurance   25m   E5 6b **   (1984)
A bit of a test piece, which requires a good selection of small wires and a very strong left arm. The wall near the left-hand end of the face is split by a thin crack line which leads to an obvious small pod. Follow a line of good but quite spaced holds which lead to a thin crack. Climb this until it is necessary to crank wildly to reach the pod (crux). Easier climbing now leads to below the final wall, which is best avoided by an awkward exit right.

2   Quantum Grunt   25m   E3 6a **   (1984)
A good climb with both strenuous and technical climbing. Start below the groove a few metres right of the previous route. Make difficult initial moves to gain the groove proper (large Friend useful). mantel into the niche using a doubtful-looking flake and continue up the groove above. A thin fingery crux leads to good holds, and an awkward pull out right to finish. An alternative finish continues up the undercuts on the left (harder).

3   Visions of Monaco   25m   E3 5c   (1984)
This takes the obvious groove and cracked arete to the right. Start at a prominent break. Climb up and right, passing a good resting ledge, to the foot of the crack. Climb this until forced to step left into the chimney at the top. It is possible, but very artificial, to continue directly up the crack to the top (6a).

4   Big Country Dreams   25m   E4 6a ***   (1983)
An excellent route tackling the striking S-shaped crack line. The grade is for an on-sight lead without weighting gear. Start just right of the main crack line. Climb onto a jutting block and pull up and left to follow a thin crack which leads to a good rest below the final crack. A short series of athletic moves leads to a pumpy finish. It helps to avoid filling the best finger locks with runners.

5   Grace Under Pressure   25m   E2 5b
The shallow flared chimney line just right of Big Country Dreams, starting just to its right. Gain the chimney line and follow it past a good undercut hold to an easier finish.

6   Formica Crack   25m   E3 6a **   (1984)
Further right is a fine buttress with a prominent shallow pod in the lower section on the left. Climb into the pod, then struggle up to better jams at its top. Continue past several interesting moves to the top.

7   The Purr-Blind Doomster   25m   E5 6a **   (1984)
An enjoyable well protected crack contrasting with a bold upper section on the upper arete. Start just right of Formica Crack. Climb the thin crack with difficulty to

Davy Jones's Locker, Laggantalluch Head
   (Climbers, Andrew Fraser and Robin McAllister)

an obvious vertical slot at its top. Move delicately right to the arete, take a deep breath, then move up on a series of sloping holds to the obvious jutting spike. Move back right round the arete to finish more easily.

8   Quasi Pulls Through   25m   E4 6a/b   (1984)
The secret to this one is visible from the quarry floor, but not while you're climbing. Start 5 metres right of The Purr-Blind Doomster, below a steep reddish groove capped by a bulging roof on its right. Climb the difficult groove to a slanting crack, then make a huge and strenuous reach up and left to a good hidden hold (crux) and resting spot. Step right under a small roof to finish up a groove.

The pile of blocks at the bottom just to the right are the remains of Oink Oink. Strangely, no-one has reported an ascent of the smooth chimney which now takes its place. Right of this is another fine buttress.

9   Both Ends Burning   25m   E5 6b ***   (1984)
Superb sustained, technical and varied climbing up the thin crack in the smooth wall. Steep initial moves lead to a good crack. Move up, then make a short series of hard moves to a resting foothold at half-height on the left. Step rather blindly back into the crack, then dash past the strenuous finishing moves.

10   Fuel for Thought   25m   E3 5c   (1984)
This climbs the slender groove in the arete right of Both Ends Burning, gained from the corner on its left. Climb the corner to a flake. Move up and across right to gain the groove. Climb this and go up right over a huge block to finish.

11   The Crowd   25m   E5 6a/b   (1985)
This takes a line between Fuel for Thought and Running on Methane; it has not become popular for obvious reasons. Climb the hanging groove past 3 poor peg runners to reach a ledge (crux). Continue boldly up the groove, with a hard move to finish (poor RP runners).

12   Running on Methane   25m   E4 6a
This fine-looking line has also been neglected, and is now rather loose and dirty. It would improve if some public-spirited individual would give it a thorough clean. Start below the right wall of the short arete about 5 metres right of The Crowd. Climb the arete (sustained, rather loose and poorly protected) to gain good holds and runners at the foot of the groove. Follow this past a bulge with difficulty to a stopping place. Step left, then move up right to the top.

13   Murray's Groove   25m   E2 5c   (1984)
The obvious corner at the right end of the face is now rather dirty with some loose holds. Finish on the left.

The Purr-Blind Doomster, Cambusbarron Quarry (Climber, Mark Garthwaite)

14   Adulterer's Repentance   25m   E3 5c   (1985)
The bold arete and wall left of Economy Drive; high in the grade. Climb the arete to a spike, step right onto the wall and climb the scoop to larger holds. Move left onto a block, then finish on good holds.

15   Economy Drive   25m   E3 6a **   (1985)
Climb the thin crack up the wall just left of the large corner to the right of Adulterer's Repentance.

The following two problems are located on the slabby face of the fallen block below Economy Drive. **LDV** (3m HVS 5c) takes the slabby right arete of the boulder. **Spanking the Monkey** (4m E5 6a, 1984) is the very bold left arete; an intimidating friction problem with an appalling landing.
The last three routes are on the right-hand side of the quarry's back wall, just left of the mound of earth at the foot of the obvious boulder problem finger crack.

16   Trail Blazer   25m   E2 5c   (1986)
A short distance left of the boulder problem finger crack is a right-facing corner crack. Climb this to a ledge on the left, then finish up the short leaning headwall.

17   Pathfinder   25m   E1 5b   (1986)
This takes a direct line immediately left of the finger crack to climb a left-facing corner crack. Start just right of Trail Blazer. Gain the foot of the ramp on which the finger crack finishes and climb the wide crack above, stepping up left to reach a good ledge. Climb the corner crack to the top of a pedestal, step up right then go back left to finish using a small tree.

18   Thug of War   10m   E4 6b   (1988)
The thin crack in the wall right of the boulder problem finger crack provides a hard challenge.

CAMBUSBARRON WEST QUARRY

This is the quarry around the back of the main quarry. Recently landscaped and with an expansive view towards the hills, it provides a pleasant environment with afternoon sunshine. It is also quick-drying, and year round climbing is possible. Although some of the rock is quite good, the climbs have only recently been produced, which means that much potentially loose material remains; take care. At the end of 1993 there was renewed interest in the quarry, and it is likely that there will be further developments (additions and deletions!) after this guide has gone to press.
Approach from the same parking place as for the main quarry. Go past the barrier and follow the track up and round to the left. The first climbs described are on the long left wall, starting from the left. The descent is down a small track through the trees, which comes down to the left of the left-hand wall. This is quite fiddly, so it is better to fix an abseil rope to the fence posts at the top for a rapid return.

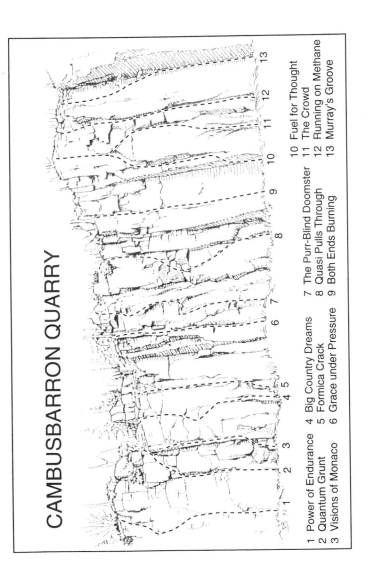

CAMBUSBARRON QUARRY

1 Power of Endurance
2 Quantum Grunt
3 Visions of Monaco
4 Big Country Dreams
5 Formica Crack
6 Grace under Pressure
7 The Purr-Blind Doomster
8 Quasi Pulls Through
9 Both Ends Burning
10 Fuel for Thought
11 The Crowd
12 Running on Methane
13 Murray's Groove

1   Ninety-Five   10m   E2 5c *   (1993)
This takes the obvious pillar on the left, as soon as one enters the quarry. Start on a small block, and using a convenient branch move right and foot traverse along the obvious fault. A couple of moves up gain better holds and protection. Move up again to another horizontal break, then make an awkward move right to the arete. Move back left to finish up the middle of the pillar.

2   Production Line   10m   E5 6b/c **   (1993)
The left-hand end of the wall is partially obscured by trees. This hard route takes a thin crack a few metres left of the start of the trees. Place gear up and right, before starting up the left arete. Climb to a break and two poor peg runners (there is also an RP placement between them). A series of hard moves leads up and left to a triangular hold. Climb the crack above on good slots (pre-placed runner advisable) to an *in situ* lowering point.

There is quite a lot of rock in this area which could provide some short climbs, but they would require extensive cleaning.

3   Cha   10m   Hard Severe *   (1993)
Climb the blocks on the small pillar left of Wind Up until it is possible to move right onto good holds. Climb to the horizontal break, then finish up the crack.

4   Wind Up   10m   VS 4c   (1991)
Climb the layback corner to the left of Force 8.

5   Force 8   10m   E1 5b   (1991)
About halfway along the left wall of the quarry is a cracked wall. Start directly below graffiti and a swastika. Climb the middle crack.

6   Optimist's Chimney   10m   VS 4c
About 40 metres right of Production Line an obvious pinnacle (if it's still there) leans against the face. Climb the chimney to its left without pushing too hard.

7   Chisel   10m   E4 6a **   (1993)
About 50 metres right of the pinnacle is a smooth wall with a prominent thin crack. This has been extensively sculptured to produce a flawed but enjoyable piece of climbing. Climb the crack past engineered finger locks to good holds at its top. Continue straight up the wall, past a peg runner, to a worrying last move on friable rock.

8   Gobi Roof   10m   E3 5c   (1990)
Start right of Chisel at a triangular recess. Climb up to a small roof, then pull over and follow the fault to the top.

Right again is a buttress, the most solid-looking part of the quarry, which has some good routes which follow a series of interconnected cracks.

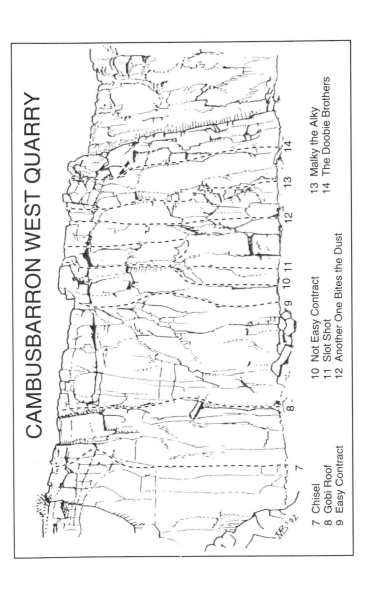

CAMBUSBARRON WEST QUARRY

7 Chisel
8 Gobi Roof
9 Easy Contract

10 Not Easy Contract
11 Slot Shot
12 Another One Bites the Dust

13 Malky the Alky
14 The Doobie Brothers

9   Easy Contract   10m   E1 5b *   (1985)
Climb the leftmost of the cracks by enjoyable jamming. Where it splits, take the
thinner right-hand option. Finish up the left arete of the buttress.

10   Not Easy Contract   10m   E1 5b **   (1980s)
Climb the wide crack just to the right to an awkward move onto a ledge at the
foot of a short groove. Climb this steeply, then finish straight up. Good climbing.

11   Slot Shot   10m   E3 5c   (1991)
Climb thin cracks up the wall right of the wide crack to the ledge at the foot of
the wee groove of Not Easy Contract (eliminate). Make a long bridge down and
right to the foot of a short crack. Climb this and continue straight up through a
small niche and another crack.

12   Another One Bites The Dust   10m   E1 5b *   (1980s)
Start at a large corner about 6 metres right of Easy Contract. Climb the corner
to a ledge at half-height, then continue up the fine jamming crack above.

13   Malky the Alky   10m   E1 5b *   (1980s)
Start just right of the obvious central corner of Another One Bites The Dust.
Climb up through a bulge to the large ledge, then continue up the corner above.

14   The Doobie Brothers   10m   HVS 5a **   (1991)
Starting 5 metres right of the central corner, just left of a really tottering pillar
which marks the right side of the buttress. Climb the obvious crack and avoid the
large loose-looking block near the top on the left.

A few metres further on the crag turns sharp right to present a rather unstable
collection of grooves, cracks and walls. Most appear too short-lived for climbing,
but a few routes have been done.

15   Scaresville   15m   E2 5c   (1991)
In the middle of the wall is a tapering slab, a sort of miniature Balance of Power.
Follow a flake until it is possible to mantel onto the hold on the arete (crux). Move
up and right, then back left to a large flake. Now climb slightly up and right, then
go back left to finish. Necky.
Variation: E2 5b
It is possible to start higher up the flakes, to step onto the hold on the arete.

About 20 metres further right lies a buttress with an impressive left arete.

16   The Ubiquitous Chip   15m   E4 6a   (1993)
The crack line starting just right of the arete is hard to start and has some difficult
jamming to gain a ledge at half-height. Above, the climb takes a short groove to

below a large roof, which is avoided on the right. The top section has some dangerously poised blocks.

17   Brat Attack   15m   E3 5c   (1991)
This route takes the thin cracks in the wall to the right of the wide crack just right of the left arete of the buttress. Climb to the top of a pinnacle, then follow a thin crack and holds to the top.

WOLFCRAG QUARRY   *(Map Ref 789 981)*

Tucked away on a residential estate in Bridge of Allan is a small greenstone quarry which provides good year-round climbing. It is a natural sun trap and due to its sheltered location and steepness, climbing is possible even during heavy rain. Although a dozen climbs are described many have unpleasant finishes, and the quarry's value is in its excellent boulder problems and low level traverses.

From the end of the M9 (junction 11) take the A9 to Bridge of Allan. Turn left immediately after crossing the Allan Water, into Blairforkie Drive, then turn right up Ferniebank Brae. The quarry is straight ahead behind the trees at the top of the Brae. The climbs are described from left to right.

The Arete   8m   HVS 5b
On entering the quarry the first obvious feature is a sharp arete. Either climb the arete or the wall on its right to an easy but loose finish.

The Second Arete   10m   Very Difficult
Some 12 metres to the right is another more blocky arete. Climb this to a loose and scary finish.

In Trance as Mission   15m   VS 4c
A poorly protected route through the roofs 12 metres right of the Second Arete. Start just left of an obvious short crack, at a 'giants staircase'. Follow this to the huge roof and traverse rightwards along ledges to escape.

The Outsider   10m   E2 5c   (1980s)
A bold climb up the arete just right of the previous route. A short crack leads to a ledge. A precarious mantel onto the arete leads to an easier but bold finish leftwards.

Up on the Catwalk   10m   E2 6a   (1980s)
A variation on the previous route. Protection, once found, is good. From the precarious mantel swing right and climb the overhanging wall.

A route has been established recently on the wall not far right of the arete, finishing up a thin crack (E5 6c).

Leonardo   10m   E2 5c **   (1980s)
Start 5 metres right of The Outsider, just left of a thin crack. Follow a line of
chipped holds up the wall passing a bolt and a peg. Since it's good climbing wall
stuff, lower off and do it again.

Tribal Look   12m   E4 6a **   (1980s)
A good sustained route. Climb the thin crack just right of Leonardo to a horizontal
niche, move right then athletically crank up to a good break. Traverse right to a
flake, move up and go boldly through the overlap to gain a line of hidden jugs
leading right to the top (bolt on the left).

Lock-it   10m   E4 6a   (1980s)
A direct start to Tribal Look. Climb a thin left-slanting crack to gain Tribal Look
at the horizontal niche.

Experiments in Incest   20m   E1 5c   (1980s)
Climb the open groove to the right of Lock-it, then traverse the break leftwards
to the big ledge of The Outsider. Finish here or go up the arete.

Ian's Wa'   10m   E1 5c *   (1980s)
Some 15 metres right of the previous route is a wall with an overlap at half-height.
Climb to the overlap, go over this rightwards and continue straight up on big
chipped holds to the top.

Waterfront   10m   E2 6a   (1980s)
Gain a standing position on the low break at the right side of Ian's Wa' without
using the arete. Surmount the overlap via a precarious layback then make a long
reach left to bigger holds and a finish up Ian's Wa'.

Kalahari   10m   E1 5a   (1992)
Start 3 metres right of Waterfront. Climb the arete to a thin crack (peg runner),
move right, then go up and left up a crack to another peg. Abseil off.

Thirty Frames a Second   12m   E2 5c   (1980s)
A further 5 metres right of Waterfront is a groove line. This route takes the wall
to its right. Start up a rib 3 metres right of the groove to gain a ledge on the left.
Leave this by a thin crack then climb a flake on the right. At the roofs, swing right
across the wall to gain ledges on the arete and a bolt belay.

DOLLAR QUARRY   *(Map Ref 964 991)*

This scruffy dolerite quarry is set on the southern slopes of the Ochils above the
town of Dollar. Facing south-west, the quarry dries quickly except during the
winter, when seepage is a problem. It is split into two tiers but all the climbing
takes place on the larger, graffiti daubed, upper tier. In common with many other
dolerite quarries the finishes of the routes are unpleasantly loose.

From the main road (the A91) in the centre of Dollar turn up East Burnside then follow the signs for Castle Campbell. Park at a picnic area on the right and walk up the road taking the second track on the right into the quarry. The climbs are described from right to left and the best descent for all routes is the earthy gully between God Nose and Modern Dance.

God Nose   15m   Very Difficult
Start just left of the lowest point of the cliff and pull strenuously over an overhang. Climb slabs to a tree then make a rising traverse right, then go back left to finish.

Modern Dance   12m   VS 4c
About 15 metres left of God Nose is a V-gully. This route takes its slabby left wall. Climb to a tiny ledge, move right, then go up a right-slanting groove. Avoid the loose finish by traversing off right.
Direct Start: 6a/b
Climb the smooth slab right of the normal start.

Double Indemnity   15m   VS 4b
Start as for Modern Dance but move up and left to the base of a corner. Swing round the rib on the left and finish up a slabby groove.
Direct Finish: E1 5b
The obvious smooth corner provides a bold finish.

D.A. Groove   15m   Severe
Climb the slabby right-slanting groove starting 10 metres left of Modern Dance.

Everyone Loves Strawberries   6m   E2 5c
A nasty little problem. Start from a pile of boulders well up and left of D.A. Groove. Step off the top boulder and climb the short wall above, finishing up easier rock on the right.

Applause from the Gallery   15m   E1 5b *
Start at a blunt arete below some overhangs. Gain the arete from the left and climb to a big block forming the lowest overhang. Move left either below or on top of the block (it seems to be well jammed in place, but appearances can be deceptive!) and climb the wall above trending right to the top.

Energy Transfer   15m   E3 5c *
Bold climbing up the fine left-slanting groove. Start up Applause from the Gallery then make a series of hard moves up the groove to gain a loose ramp leading back right to the top.

Who Dares Wins   20m   E3 5c
A serious finish to Energy Transfer. From the top of the groove move left into a scoop and exit leftwards to gain a horizontal crack. Follow this to a ledge and climb straight up with a huge reach past a peg to finishing jugs.

Tent Roof   15m   VS 4b
Start in the centre of the slab at the top right-hand corner of the quarry. Climb a corner to a ledge, traverse left to the cracked arete and follow this to an exit rightwards. There are easier variations on the right.

Electric Edge   15m   E1 5a
This route climbs the left edge of the slab. Make a tricky mantelshelf onto the arete, which rapidly eases with height.

CRAIG ROSSIE   *(Map Ref 985 122)*

Although the cliffs on Craig Rossie are fairly loose and vegetated they are the best the Ochils have to offer. The poor quality of the climbing is offset by the pleasant, easily accessible mountain environment and succulent bilberries. Facing north-east at an altitude of 400m, the crags take a couple of summer days to dry out after rain.

Turn off the A9 onto the B8062 and when about 3km west of Dunning, directly below the crags, take a forestry road as far as a locked gate. The climbs are located on the upper of two bands of crags, about 20 minutes walk from the gate. The first two routes need a belay line from the summit fence.

Bristler   30m   E1 5b   (1984)
This climb is situated on the largest buttress, just below the summit. Follow the big right-facing chimney-groove, exiting on alarmingly loose flakes.

Blazer   30m   E2 5c   (1984)
Some 100 metres to the left is an open corner with a pale bulge guarding its base. Climb over the bulge and move up the corner, swinging blindly out onto the face at the top. Finish up a mixture of tombstones and oatmeal.

Fizzler   10m   E1 5c   (1984)
On the last short buttress is a series of vertical cracks. Climb the central one.

CENTRAL REGION MINOR CRAGS

WALLACE MONUMENT CLIFFS AND QUARRY
(Map Ref 810 953)

There are some good climbs on the cliffs below the Wallace Monument near Stirling, however a strictly enforced ban on climbing exists and no attempt has been made to describe routes here.

At the right hand end of the cliffs, behind the Acre Wood Nursery, is an old quarry. As this is in a less conspicuous position climbing may be possible, although as far as is known there are only two routes. **Zeig Heil**, E2 5c, climbs the obvious arete at the back of the quarry and **Sandinista**, E3 5b, takes the unprotected wall 20 metres to the right.

DUMYAT   *(Map Ref 836 977)*

At the western end of the Ochils is a hill called Dumyat. There are numerous crags scattered over its southern flank which from a distance look quite promising. Unfortunately, closer inspection reveals that the rock is not of the best quality. However quite a number of routes have been recorded, including the ubiquitous **Raeburn's Gully**. The climbs do not merit detailed description but a pleasant day could be spent exploring the various cliffs and gullies, if approached in the appropriate spirit! Access is best made from the village of Blairlogie just off the A91. Apart from Raeburn's Gully most of the existing routes were first climbed by J.H.B.Bell.

The Edinburgh Outcrops

This chapter covers the crags within a few kilometres (sometimes a few metres!) of the centre of Edinburgh. Since the previous guide, several crags have been lost and others are under threat. Not a happy situation, but the promise of at least partial legal access to Salisbury Crags is at least some compensation. The maps required for this chapter are OS sheets 65 and 66.

RATHO QUARRY   *(Map Ref 128 709)*

This fine dolerite quarry offers the best range of extreme climbs close to Edinburgh. It is very sheltered, catches the sun and most routes dry quickly after rain in both summer and winter. The quarry floor is rapidly being overwhelmed by trees and bushes which can make identification of climbs difficult, and although the rock is sound on most routes some of the finishes require care. (Note: the extension to the M8 motorway is being constructed just north of the quarry and blasting may have affected the stability of some routes).

The village of Ratho is situated just off the A8 on the west side of Edinburgh. Park in the vicinity of the Bridge Inn and follow a good path westwards along the north side of the Union Canal. After about 1km a track heads off into the trees on the right, this leads into the quarry. There is a regular bus service between Ratho and the St. Andrews Square bus station in Edinburgh.

The routes are described from left to right. Descents can be made at the left end of the West Wall and between the East Wall and the East Bay.

THE WEST WALL

This is the long steep wall which appears on the left as the quarry is entered. Towards the left-hand end is a huge open corner, the line of Godzilla. Further right, the wall becomes more broken until, near the centre, it rears up into a series of steep grooves and aretes before finishing in a very impressive smooth wall on the right.

1   Terminal Street   12m   VS 4c   (1975)
The stepped groove at the left-hand end of the West Wall. Take a machete to cut through the bush at the top.

2   Terminal Case   15m   HVS 5a   (1975)
Start at a groove in the arete left of Godzilla. Climb the groove, then traverse up and left to finish as for Terminal Case. Don't forget the machete.
Alternative Finish: 5c/6a
The bush can be avoided to the right, finishing at the same place as The Blob.

RATHO QUARRY – THE WEST WALL

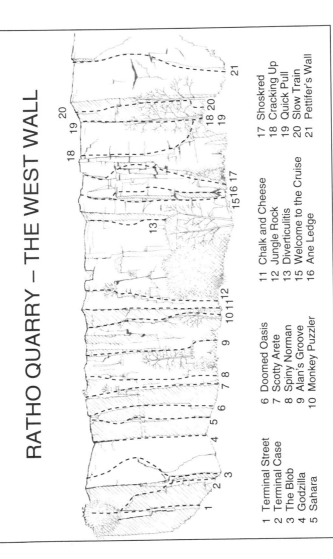

1 Terminal Street
2 Terminal Case
3 The Blob
4 Godzilla
5 Sahara

6 Doomed Oasis
7 Scotty Arete
8 Spiny Norman
9 Alan's Groove
10 Monkey Puzzler

11 Chalk and Cheese
12 Jungle Rock
13 Diverticulitis
15 Welcome to the Cruise
16 Ane Ledge

17 Shoskred
18 Cracking Up
19 Quick Pull
20 Slow Train
21 Pettifer's Wall

3   The Blob   20m   E4 6a **   (1985)
The big wall left of Godzilla. The original route started up the left arete to gain a
right-slanting groove. It is also possible to reach this direct. Climb the groove into
the middle of the wall (good protection), then make a series of hard moves up
and left to the top.

4   Godzilla   20m   E2 5c *   (1975)
The monstrous corner. Good climbing, but the last section tends to be dirty.

5   Sahara   20m   E5 6b **   (1981)
A scorcher, taking the thin crack line up the wall 3 metres right of Godzilla. Climb
to a ledge below and right of a shallow right-facing groove (small RPs). A couple
of desperate moves lead to better holds and a good runner. Continue to the
obvious niche. Pull out left and finish strenuously up the wall above on good but
well spaced holds.

6   Doomed Oasis   20m   E3 5c **   (1980)
Fine steep climbing straight up the crack line right of Sahara. The crux is at 8m.
Variation: E1 5b *
Climb Scotty Arete for 10m, then traverse into the crack line above the crux. This
gives access to the fine easier upper section.

7   Scotty Arete   20m   Severe *   (1976)
The right arete of the Godzilla corner.

8   Spiny Norman   20m   Severe   (1976)
Gain a grass ledge 3m up, just right of Scotty Arete, and follow a chossy line of
corners and bushes to the top.

9   Alan's Groove   20m   HVS 5a
Gain a ledge and a big tree 8 metres right of Scotty Arete, then climb the long
left-hand groove above.

10   Monkey Puzzler   20m   Severe
Start at a tree immediately left of a sharp arete. Climb a wall, then a left-trending
groove and grass to the top.

11   Chalk and Cheese   20m   E2 5a *   (1992)
Climb directly up the sharp arete 15 metres right of Scotty Arete. Poorly
protected but good.

12   Jungle Rock   20m   Very Severely Vegetated
An arboreal adventure up the wall and corner right of Chalk and Cheese.

13   Diverticulitis   15m   E3 6a **   (1980)
Halfway along the west wall there is a prominent left-facing corner, starting from a platform 7m above the quarry floor. This gives a superb sustained route. Climb it direct except for a few moves on the left wall at 12m.

14   Alopecia   20m   E4 6a *   (1993)
Although escapable, this route has good situations on the final leaning prow. Climb the arete between Diverticulitis and Welcome to the Cruise, passing two peg runners.

15   Welcome to the Cruise   25m   E1 5b **   (1983)
A justly popular route up the series of grooves right of a big leaning arete. Start at some large boulders and climb the grooves direct, moving left into the final steep corner which provides the crux.

16   Ane Ledge   25m   E3 5c *   (1983)
This is the sharp arete which ends 15m up the cliff. Start immediately right of the previous route. Climb the arete and a thin crack on its right to a tiny ledge. Step left and layback boldly up the top part of the arete to a larger ledge. Finish up either Welcome to the Cruise or Shoskred.

17   Shoskred   25m   HVS 5a *   (1976)
The grooves just right of Ane Ledge. There is a choice of lines in the central section.

18   Cracking Up   25m   HVS 5a *
Scramble up vegetated ground past a tree towards a corner. Move left to gain and climb the wide crack near the arete.

19   Quick Pull   25m   HVS 5a
Scramble up as for the previous route and climb the deep corner.

20   Slow Strain   25m   E2 6a *   (1982)
The prominent arete right of Quick Pull, with good safe crux moves but unconvincing protection elsewhere. Scramble to a ledge 4m up on the left. Start up the arete then move left and up to a thin crack. Climb this (crux) to a ledge. Continue up the final crumbly wall, trending slightly leftwards.
Variation: E1 5b *
Avoid the crux by moving round the arete and up a crack to gain the ledge.

21   Pettifer's Wall   25m   E4 6a **   (1980)
A fine serious route up the impressive face at the right end of the west wall. Start 4 metres right of Slow Strain. Climb an open black groove to a small triangular overhang (peg runner). Move rightwards over this and continue up a shallow groove to the top.

THE BACK WALL

The left-hand side of the back wall is loose and grassy but to the right is a tall square buttress with a prominent left arete.

22   Sedge Warbler   20m   E2 5b **   (1981)
Scramble up to the left-hand side of the arete. Step up and swing round the arete to gain a narrow ramp. Climb this rather precariously, then follow the cracks above to a large ledge. Climb the cracked wall above to finish.

23   Time's Last Gift   20m   E2 5c **   (1983)
Start below an obvious groove 5 metres right of the arete. Climb the groove until a move right can be made onto a ledge, move up to a higher ledge and continue up the groove on the left to a large ledge. Finish up the steep crack in the final wall (crux).

24   Up the Creek   12m   E1 5b   (1981)
The repulsive wide crack 5 metres left of Artho.

25   Pete's Wall   10m   E1 5b   (1981)
Start up in the corner as for Artho. Step left and climb a shallow left-facing groove and the short wall above. Often wet.

26   Artho   10m   E4 6a/b *   (1983)
This short but action packed climb takes the black-streaked corner in the angle between the back wall and the east wall. Start in the corner but move left and up as for Pete's Wall to a small roof under a block. Step right and climb the corner to the top.

THE EAST WALL

This is the long wall stretching rightwards from the back of the quarry. It starts off quite tall but reduces in height above a huge pile of boulders, where there is an arete and corner daubed with graffiti. To the right of this there is a long series of broken walls, corners and ribs ending at a descent path.

27   Ouroborus Eliminate   20m   E3 5c   (1981)
Start 4 metres right of Artho. Climb a thin crack to a ledge and continue up a short ramp on the right (peg runner). Climb the wall above, trending right to the arete, then finish up a groove on the right. Very necky in the upper section.
Variation: E3 5c *
After climbing the initial thin crack, escape leftwards up Ouroborus.

28   Ouroborus   25m   HVS 5b **   (1976)
Start at the lowest point about 10 metres right of Artho. Climb up to a small tree, then follow a flake away up to the left to the top of Artho. A good route with a perplexing crux.

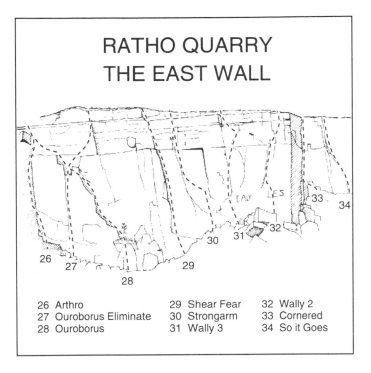

RATHO QUARRY
THE EAST WALL

26 Arthro
27 Ouroborus Eliminate
28 Ouroborus

29 Shear Fear
30 Strongarm
31 Wally 3

32 Wally 2
33 Cornered
34 So it Goes

29 Shear Fear   20m   E2 5c **   (1976)
The fearsome flake crack 6 metres right of the start of Ouroborus and just left of
the pile of boulders.

30 Strongarm   15m   E3 6a *   (1992)
Right of Shear Fear are two thinner flake cracks. The left fades away at the
bottom and the right ends in an overlap. Move up and place a high runner in the
right-hand crack, then make a difficult move to the left-hand crack. Climb this to
a ledge and go through a bush to the top.

31 Wally 3   15m   E4 6a *   (1983)
Start from the huge pile of boulders 6 metres left of the arete. Climb some flakes
to reach a shallow groove, then follow this, exiting right at the top. Traverse left
and finish up a small corner.

32   Wally 2   15m   E4 5c *   (1983)
Not quite as hard as its neighbour but a more serious lead. Start just left of the arete. Climb the wall, moving left to a shallow groove. Climb this to a large hold, then move right to finish up the wall just left of the arete.

33   Cornered   10m   E1 5c
The smooth, short corner right of the arete. Peg runner at 3m.

34   So it Goes   10m   E2 5c   (1989)
Climb the crack line right of Cornered.

35   Fledge   8m   VS 5a   (1993)
Climb the corner crack 10 metres right of Cornered.

About 20 metres to the right are two obvious grooves left of a rusty wall.

36   5000 Christmas Trees   10m   E2 5c *   (1991)
The left-hand groove gives good strenuous back and footing.

37   Business as Usual   10m   E3 6a   (1991)
The right-hand groove yields to crotch splitting bridging.

38   Danger No Entry   10m   VS 4c   (1991)
Start at the foot of Business as Usual. Pull out right round the arete onto a ledge and finish up over blocks.

Towards the right end of the east wall there is a pea-pod groove starting from a ledge a few metres up. The following four routes take lines up the wall left of this.

39   Fairy Feat   12m   VS 4c
The unpleasant corner line which slants slightly leftwards, about 8 metres left of the pod-shaped groove.

40   Mon   12m   VS 4c
Start just right of Fairy Feat and climb a right-trending line up the wall.

40a   Zam Zam   12m   E2 6a
Climb the thin straight crack which cuts directly through Mon.

41   Pull the Other One   12m   E1 5b/c   (1990)
The crack 3 metres left of Beanpud, joining Mon near the top.

42   Beanpud   12m   E1 5b **   (1976)
The pea-pod shaped groove gives an excellent and interesting problem.

43   Election Sickness   12m   VS 4c   (1992)
The crack line between Beanpud and Rock-a-Boogie.

44   Rock-a-Boogie   12m   VS 4c *
Start 4 metres right of Beanpud and climb the straight crack at the back of a
V-groove.

45   Rebel Without Claws   12m   E2 5c **   (1983)
A good short route which climbs the smooth curving groove just right of Rock-a-
Boogie. Gain the groove and climb it using the right arete.

THE EAST BAY
This is the shady bay in the south-east corner of the quarry. It contains three very
fine routes on excellent rock.

46   This Septic Heil   20m   E5 6b ***   (1983)
The overhanging wall on the left-hand side of the bay gives a brilliant test piece.
Gain a series of steps which are followed up and right to a resting place (2 peg
runners). Traverse right, move up, then continue up the wall to a ledge (peg
runner). Finish up to the right. Low in the grade.

47   Gruel Brittania   15m   E3 6a ***   (1982)
A great little route taking the sharp arete in the left wall of the east bay. Make a
few hard moves up a thin crack just right of the arete and swing up left onto a
ledge. Regain the crack and follow it to a flat hold. Finish by making some
interesting moves up the arete. (It is also possible to finish up the crack).

48   Jumping Jack Splat   15m   E3 6a
Gain the stepped groove in the wall right of Gruel Brittania (peg runner) and
follow it to a grassy ledge. Go left and up to finish. Necky.

49   The Lone Groover   20m   E3 6a *   (1983)
The clean-cut groove at the back of the bay leads to a grass ledge and an
unpleasant finish. Much harder than it looks.
Alternative finish: E3 6a *   (1988)
Hard, but it avoids the unpleasant finish. From the grass ledge move up and right
into a groove, then step right to climb a thin crack just left of Wally 1.

50   Wally 1   20m   E2 5c ***   (1983)
Fine technical climbing. Start 2 metres right of the Lone Groover. Climb a thin
flake to a small ledge then continue up the cracked wall above.

51   Blue Rinse   20m   E1 5b *
Climb up past a tree, just right of Wally 1, and continue up the groove and flake
crack to the top.

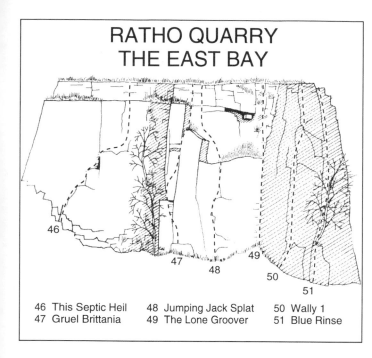

RATHO QUARRY
THE EAST BAY

46 This Septic Heil   48 Jumping Jack Splat   50 Wally 1
47 Gruel Brittania   49 The Lone Groover   51 Blue Rinse

RATHO QUARRY NO.2

This small quarry lies hidden amongst the gorse bushes about 200 metres north of Ratho Quarry. There is a repulsive pool at its foot (seek medical help in event of falling in). The first two routes lead to a clean rock platform at the top. (Note: access to and even the existence of this quarry is under threat due to the construction of the M8 extension).

Right Under   10m   E3 6a *   (1985)
Traverse in from the right and belay on a small ledge. Climb the obvious thin crack above a small square overhang.

Left Over   10m   E2 5c   (1985)
The corner immediately left of Right Under, starting from the same belay.

In a Prickle   10m   VS 5b   (1992)
The corner left of Left Over, behind a tree.

Thorn in my Side   10m   E1 5c   (1992)
The corner further left, right of a pile of blocks.

DALMAHOY HILL   *(Map Ref 136 671)*

The cliffs on the northern side of Dalmahoy Hill provide some good climbing in
the lower and middle grades. However, a huge new quarry is being worked just
to the east and the associated plant and machinery has been built immediately
below the crags, spoiling the once pleasant outlook. The Mines and Quarries Act
forbids access but discreet climbers are not likely to be turned away.

The climbing is located on the largest and cleanest section of cliff towards the
east end of the hillside. The rock is columnar dolerite giving rise to a uniform
series of grooves and ribs, and unfortunately is rather green and lichenous.
However the routes are often better than they appear and would benefit from an
increase in traffic to keep the vegetation down.

Take the A70 out of Edinburgh to about 1km beyond Balerno. Park in a lay-by
just before emerging from trees to more open ground. Walk northwards through
a field, keeping right to avoid boggy ground, onto the eastern end of the hill. The
top of the crag lies just beyond a fence, directly above the main quarry buildings.
Scramble down at the east end of the crag or descend The Arete.

The climbs are described from left to right.

1   The Arete   8m   Difficult
The short arete above a rowan tree at the left-hand end of the crag. A useful
descent route once identified.

2   Professor Groove   8m   Mild Severe
The mossy groove in the slab right of The Arete.

3   The Corner   8m   Severe
The grassy corner right of Professor Groove.

4   Ivy Tower   10m   Severe
The rib right of The Corner.

5   Lightning Groove   15m   VS 4b *
The first long groove on the left-hand side of the crag. It is split by an overlap at
half-height.

6   Munich Climb   15m   VS 4b *
The obvious corner right of Lightning Groove. Go up a broken groove to below
diamond-shaped overlaps, move left and climb the corner to the top.

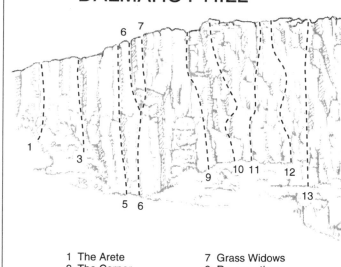

DALMAHOY HILL

1 The Arete	7 Grass Widows
2 The Corner	9 Resurrection
5 Lightning Groove	10 Midgy Gem
6 Munich Climb	11 Elation

7   Grass Widows   15m   HVS 5a *
A short technical problem taking the double overlap to the right of Munich Climb.
Follow Munich Climb to the overlap, then gain the slabby groove above. Climb
this to finish.

8   Curving Groove   15m   VS 4c
Follow Munich Climb to the overlaps, then move right round the bulges to finish
up the rib on the left.

9   Resurrection   15m   VS 4b *
Climb the groove right of a vegetated bay, then go up the wall above into an
upper slabby groove. Move left to small ledges and finish up the groove above.

10   Midgy Gem   15m   VS 4c *   (1991)
Start 3 metres right of Resurrection at the left end of some clean slabs. Climb

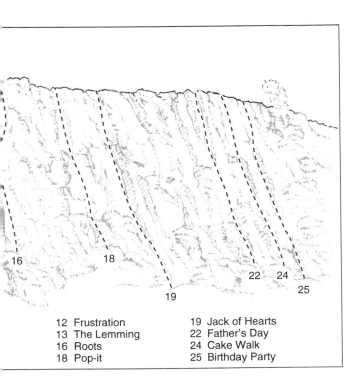

12 Frustration	19 Jack of Hearts
13 The Lemming	22 Father's Day
16 Roots	24 Cake Walk
18 Pop-it	25 Birthday Party

the slab, passing left of an obvious triangular overlap, to the big overlaps at 7m. Traverse 2 metres right and follow left-slanting grooves and ribs to the top.

11   Elation   15m   HVS 5a *   (1991)
Start up a left-facing groove about 3 metres right of Midgy Gem. Use a loose-looking block to pull through a break in the overhangs, then follow the groove above until forced right onto a rib. Finish up the groove above. A good route, high in its grade.

12   Frustration   20m   Mild VS 4b *
Start at the right end of the clean slabs, 4 metres right of Elation. Climb an easy groove to an obvious diamond-shaped overlap at 4m. Move left then up until forced right by the overhangs. Continue up a pleasant open groove to the top. A harder direct finish is possible.

13   The Lemming   20m   HVS 4c *   (1992)
Follow the open slabby groove, midway between Frustration and Cleaned Sweep, to a steepening finish. Exit by Cleaned Sweep (or directly through the bulge, 5b).

14   Cleaned Sweep   20m   VS 4c   (1991)
This takes the prominent left-facing hanging corner 4 metres right of Frustration. Follow a scrappy groove to an overlap. Move up and right into the corner, and follow it to a choice of hard or easy exits.

15   Triad   20m   HVS 4c
Dangerously loose. Start in a large overhung niche just left of Roots. Pull over the overhang onto a slab and surmount a further steepening to reach a small ledge. Continue up the groove above to the top.

16   Roots   20m   Very Difficult
This route starts at an obvious narrow rib near the centre of the crag. Climb the rib and the mossy wall above via a twisting groove, to finish up a short slab.

17   Insertion   20m   VS 4b
Just right of Roots are a series of slabs leading to a wall with a down-pointing flake. Climb the slabs to the base of the wall. Climb this to footholds on the flake, then move diagonally left to join Roots.

18   Pop-it   20m   HVS 5a
This route climbs through the overlap to the left of Jack of Hearts. Scramble up slabby grooves to a steep wall. Gain the upper groove with difficulty, then continue to the top.

19   Jack of Hearts   25m   VS 4c **
This fine route climbs the prominent long clean groove towards the right end of the cliff. Climb the groove to two overlaps. Surmount these directly, then continue up the slab above.
Variation:
Slant left after the first overlap and climb diagonally right to the upper slab.

20   Fine Escape   25m   Hard Severe
The groove immediately right of Jack of Hearts. Climb to an overhang and walk right to a break in the wall above. Climb up a twisting groove to slabs which lead leftwards to the top.

21   Draconian   20m   Very Difficult
The groove left of Father's Day.

22   Father's Day   20m   Very Difficult
Start at a tree below a triangular overhang. Go up through a notch right of the overhang and follow the groove above to the top.

23 Rearguard 20m Severe
Some 4 metres right of Father's Day is a rib. Climb this to a mantelshelf move left at 7m, then follow an open-sided groove to the top.

24 Cake Walk 20m Severe *
A good route taking the square-cut groove and prominent hanging rib near the right end of the crag. Climb the groove and a slab, then the rib over two bulges.

25 Birthday Party 20m VS 4c *
The obvious groove and right-facing corner in the upper slab at the right end of the crag. Climb the long groove over a steepening and mantelshelf on to a broad ledge below the final corner. Climb the corner to finish.

26 Scree Surfing 70m E1 (1987)
A high-level left to right girdle traverse, starting at The Arete. Three pitches were climbed (4c,5b,4b) but details are lacking and the route length would suggest that the traverse was not completed.

BLACKFORD HILL *(Map Ref 255 706)*

Blackford Hill is situated within the city boundary on the south side of Edinburgh. Rock climbing has taken place here for many years but has become unpopular due to the discovery of better venues elsewhere. Two areas are of interest, Blackford Quarry and Corbie's Craig.

Follow Blackford Glen Road off Liberton Brae to its far end (car parking) then carry on in the same direction towards The Hermitage. After about 300 metres a small crag is seen on the right, Agassiz Rock, which gives good bouldering. A few metres further on the path forks. Take the right fork for Blackford Quarry. For Corbie's Craig take the left fork and, when a wooden bridge is reached, turn right and the crag appears on the right after 150 metres. Both crags can also be reached by following paths south from the car park at the Royal Observatory.

BLACKFORD QUARRY

The main west-facing wall is often used to introduce novices to climbing and abseiling, and can be climbed pleasantly anywhere, increasing in difficulty from Difficult on the right to HVS on the left. Protection is sparse but there are bolt belays in place at the top. At the quarry entrance is a pinnacle with one recommended route.

Quarry Pinnacle 10m Difficult * (1896)
The west-facing crack. There are belay stakes at the top.

Komik Kuts 10m Difficult (1950s)
Facing the pinnacle, to the west, is a miniature buttress. This route takes the corner left of the nose.

Elsewhere in the quarry there is plenty scope for short routes and bouldering.

CORBIE'S CRAIG

This is a pleasant sunny crag which has lots of good incut holds. However, the climbs tend to be quite serious due to the lack of cracks for protection and the loose nature of the harder routes. It is also well defended by gorse bushes; not the place for shorts or lycra. The routes are described from left to right.

Slab and Tower   12m   Difficult *   (1950s)
Start below a green slab at the extreme left end of the cliff. Climb the right corner of the slab then traverse right on sloping holds under an overhang to finish up the steep final tower.

Moderate Route   15m   Moderate   (1950s)
Take an indefinite line up the left flank of Retromingent Ridge.

Retromingent Ridge   30m   Moderate **   (1950s)
The ridge forming the left edge of the front face of the cliff. Climb straight up to a large block at 10m, then trend right and finally back left near the top. Good climbing, but with little protection and no belay at the top.

Sunny Scoop   30m   Difficult   (1950s)
The gorse-filled groove right of Retromingent Ridge can be climbed avoiding most of the gorse, with care! There are a choice of finishes.

Queasy Slab   30m   HVS 4c   (1950s)
Right of Sunny Scoop is a big undercut slab. Climb the right edge of the slab round an overhang. Move right past a small gorse, then go straight up to finish up the open groove above. A good start but loose higher up.

Whinchat   35m   VS 4b *
From the elm tree at the foot of the crag climb up and left under overhangs (peg runner) and over a large gorse to a hanging slab. Move right across this to the arete and finish directly.

Burning Bush   35m   HVS 4c
Start just right of the elm tree. Climb an orange slab for 3m, then climb the obvious left-trending line to a small pinnacle. Finish easily up a corner.

La Folie   30m   HVS 4c
Climb a black slab 2 metres right of Burning Bush to a gorse bay. Stand on a block on the right and step onto the slab above. From the top of the slab make a scary swing right onto the arete, where Fast and Loose is joined at the peg.

Fast and Loose   25m   Very Difficult   (1950s)
At the right side of the crag, where it starts to turn uphill, are two 2m walls one above the other. Climb these, then ascend diagonally left to reach an arete (peg runner). Finish up the obvious groove above.

The Trap   20m   Very Difficult
From midway along the diagonal traverse of Fast and Loose pull out right at an ivy and continue by slabs and grooves to finish trapped in gorse bushes.

HOLYROOD PARK   *(Map Ref 274 732)*

The cliffs in Holyrood Park have attracted the attention of rock climbers for over a century. This is hardly surprising as the park is near the centre of Edinburgh and the cliffs are both accessible and enticing. Although there are areas of loose rock there are also many good routes in pleasant sunny situations on rough solid basalt. BUT, and this is a big but, at present climbing on any cliff in the park is illegal and anyone caught doing so is likely to be prosecuted. The routes are described purely for their historical interest and no right to climb is to be inferred from their inclusion here. There is a glimmer of hope, however, as negotiations are underway to allow climbing in certain parts of the Park. For the latest information, call the Park Constabulary on 031 566 3407.

To find Holyrood Park just head for Arthur's Seat, the prominent hill visible for miles around. Cars are best left near the Royal Commonwealth Pool to the south-west. From here, a short walk leads into the park. All the cliffs are easy to reach, and by using the layout map their whereabouts should be obvious.

THE SALISBURY CRAGS

This is the long line of imposing cliffs which dominates much of the Edinburgh skyline, often referred to as simply 'the crags'. Parts of the cliff face have been quarried and these sections now have the soundest rock and best climbing. The chief attraction for most is the excellent bouldering in and around the South Quarry. For the more adventurous, some of the longer routes give very good climbing in exposed situations. The climbs are described from right to left.

PINNACLE QUARRY

This is the deep bay at the right-hand end of the crags and just left of The Hawse, (the gap between Arthur's Seat and the crags). On the left and rear walls are many short routes; the pinnacle itself is the obvious buttress on the right.

1   Pinnacle Corner   10m   Very Difficult   (1944)
The right side of the pinnacle. Turn an overhang on the right and climb up left of some gorse bushes. A prickly route.
Variation: Severe
Turn the overhang on the left.

2   Pinnacle Face   12m   Very Difficult *   (1946)
The front face of the pinnacle 10 metres right of Falseface. Start up the middle of the obvious slab, then climb its right-hand side until a small projecting overhang is reached. Move left around this and go up to easy ground.

3   Falseface   12m   Severe
Start at the left side of the pinnacle and gain a sloping ledge above a bore mark. Make a rising traverse right and pull over a black bulge into a slabby recess. Finish out left.

4   The Conflict with Temptation   12m   Severe   (1946)
Start as for the previous route, but after a few moves up the rising traverse climb to a smooth mottled slab. Move right and climb a corner to finish at the same point as Falseface.

MIDDLE QUARRY
This is the less well defined bay, some 100 metres left of Pinnacle Quarry.

5   Centre Slab   15m   Moderate *
Start 2 metres left of a prominent slab of white rock. Climb a groove, then a red slab rightwards to finish past some white rocks.

6   The Slant   20m   Difficult
The obvious left-slanting line starting 5 metres left of the white slab.

7   Tournez en Face a ma Gauche   20m   Severe   (1946)
Start in the centre of the quarry and climb to a block overhang halfway up the face. Pull over, then traverse left and finish straight up.

8   Toujours Tout Droit   15m   VS 4c   (1946)
Start just right of Butterfly. Climb a groove and at 6m turn a projection by a delicate move left. Finish up a groove on the left.

9   Butterfly   15m   Severe
Look for two black block overhangs forming the shape of a butterfly. Climb up to and over the blocks to finish rightwards on poor rock.

EASTERN BUTTRESS
The projecting section of crag between middle and south quarries, easily identified by the huge boulder leaning against the face at the right-hand end. The rock is loose above half-height but there are some excellent boulder problems and low-level traverses.

10   Eastern Buttress Face Route   20m   Very Difficult   (1897)
Left of centre is a thin rib projecting into the grass. Climb the rib, then trend right up to a grassy ledge. A friable wall leads to the top.

11   Black Chimney Buttress   20m   Very Difficult *
The left edge of the buttress provides a good line but is loose in the upper half. Climb the smooth wall right of the arete to a large block on the left. Step right (peg runner), then continue up the exposed but broken arete to the top.

SOUTH QUARRY

Previously known as Little Quarry, this is the most deeply recessed section of the crags. Over the past 100 years it has always been the most popular cliff in the park. It provides many good short routes on solid rock, as well as the best bouldering in the area. The climbs tend to be fairly serious due to a general lack of protection and scarcity of belay points at the top. Many variations to the routes have been climbed.

To the right of Black Chimney, towards the arete, is a steep black wall. The traverse is a very polished 6b, and to climb straight up left of some old bolts is 6a.

12   Black Chimney   15m   Severe *
The open groove in the right-hand corner of the quarry. Climb the steepening groove until it is possible to pull into a short steep corner. Finish left of a large projection at the top.

13   Roofer Madness   15m   HVS 5a
A somewhat loose climb through the roofs about 6 metres left of Black Chimney. Start just left of a low overhang. Go up until it is possible to step right into a groove. Climb this and pull through the roofs at their narrowest point to gain the top.

14   Hanging Slab   15m   Severe *   (1946)
Start 8 metres left of Black Chimney, above a large boulder. Climb up onto a hanging slab, then move up and left to a small triangular niche. Continue up to the overhang and pass it on the left.

15   Sentry Box   12m   Severe *   (1935)
Some 12 metres left of Black Chimney is a slab with a sentry box recess just below its top. Start to the left of an overhang directly below the sentry box. Climb a shallow groove, moving right to gain the recess. Finish direct.

16   Rib and Mantelshelf   12m   Severe   (1946)
Start immediately left of Sentry Box. Climb directly up a narrow steepening rib. At the top mantelshelf onto a large hold and finish more easily.

17   Graham's Route   12m   Severe *   (1946)
Climb the left side of the smooth red slab, just right of Recess Climb, finishing rightwards.

18   Recess Climb   12m   Severe *
Start at some boulders where three grooves slant up the cliff, the left one being less well defined. Climb the right-hand groove.
Variation: VS 4c
It is possible to climb directly up the right edge of Recess Climb, keeping left of Graham's Route.

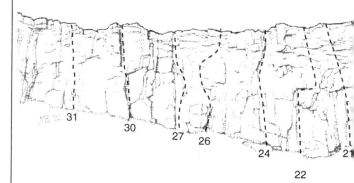

HOLYROOD PARK

31
30
27
26
24
22
21

12 Black Chimney	17 Graham's Route
13 Roofer Madness	18 Recess Climb
14 Hanging Slab	20 Spike Fright
15 Sentry Box	21 Idle Gossip

19   Notch Climb   12m   Severe
Climb the central square-cut groove.

20   Spike Fright   12m   HVS 5a *
In the centre of the quarry is an overhang with a large square-cut recess in it.
Climb to a hanging block right of the recess. Pull up to its right, stand on it, then
find a way up the slab above. (Sometimes called Great North Road).

21   Idle Gossip   12m   E3 5c *   (1992)
Left of the square-cut recess is an overhang with a cluster of down-pointing red
spikes below it. Climb a groove to the spikes, pull through the overhang using a
flake hold and continue through the overhangs above on good holds.

22   Black Slab   12m   Severe **
An enjoyable climb, possibly the best in the South Quarry. Start 7 metres left of
Spike Fright below a series of black overhangs. Climb to a block at the left side
of the lowest overhang, pull up and hand traverse right, surmount the bulge
above and finish up an exposed wall.

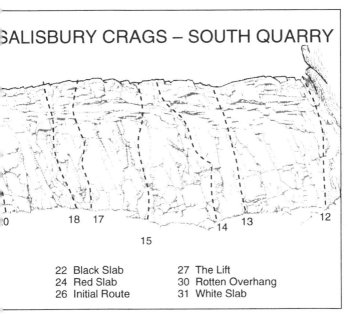

0   18 17   14 13   12

15

22	Black Slab	
24	Red Slab	
26	Initial Route	
27	The Lift	
30	Rotten Overhang	
31	White Slab	

23   Hyphen route   12m   HVS 5a *   (1944)
Start 2 metres left of Black Slab and climb a straight crack to a slab and bore
hole. Step right and pull over a bulge to finish up the black wall above.

24   Red Slab   12m   Difficult *
The groove left of the previous route leads to the left side of a red slab. The black
groove above then leads to the top.

25   Horrible Hook   12m   VS 4c
Climb a black corner crack below a small quartz mark, then pull up left by
pinching a hooked block. Continue directly to the top.

26   Initial Route   10m   VS 5b *   (1936)
Start at a 2m long boulder in the grass. Climb a short smooth corner, moving out
left at the top (crux). Go up and traverse right to a prominent projection, then
finish up the wall above.

27   The Lift   10m   Moderate *
The obvious right-facing corner line some 15 metres from the left-hand corner of
the quarry provides a good descent route and a worthwhile climb in its own right.
Climb the corner to gain some ledges on the right. Move up and left back into
the corner, then follow it to the top.

28   The Lift Arete   10m   Very Difficult   (1945)
The arete immediately left of The Lift.

29   The Splits   10m   Severe
Climb the corner 2 metres left of the Lift, and 8 metres right of White Slab.

30   Rotten Overhang   10m   HVS 4b
Climb the corner left of The Splits past a great rotten overhang at half-height (if
it's still there).

31   White Slab   8m   Very Difficult
Near the left end of the rear wall is a white-flecked slab. Climb this at the left-hand
flecks.

32   The Long Stride   8m   Moderate *
Start at the twin corners left of White Slab. Climb the left corner for 3m, then
stride left to a small ledge. Finish up the easy wall above.
Variation: VS 5a *
A short crack provides an interesting direct start.

33   Athlete's Arete   8m   HVS 5a   (1945)
Climb the bold arete between the Long Stride and Original Route as directly as
possible.

34   Original Route   8m   Moderate
Gain a shelf left of an orange slab with a bore hole, step up then traverse right
across a bulge until it is possible to gain the easy wall above.
Variations:
No less than five variations to this climb were recorded in the 1940s, at grades
up to VS 4c. Take your pick.

35   Wicked Lady   10m   VS 4c **   (1946)
Left of Original Route is a sloping shelf under a black overhang. Climb easily to
the left end of the shelf, then traverse awkwardly right past the bulging overhang
until it is possible to get established above. Continue to the top on good holds.
So named because "She tries to cause your downfall just as you're getting round
her". Beware!

Shear Fear, Ratho Quarry (Climber, Austin Harley)

36   Archie's Slab   12m   HVS 5a *   (1945)
Start as for Wicked Lady, then traverse left passing the base of two corners to a
scooped slab. Climb this with difficulty. (The corners have also been climbed).

37   Harrison's Climb   15m   Severe **   (1945)
A steep route with some unusual moves. Start just left of a square cave. Climb
the rib for 7m, then step right onto a small ledge. Pull up to a higher ledge and
finish up the exposed wall above.

38   Doubledecker   20m   Severe   (1947)
Starting from the boulders at the left side of the quarry, climb slabs leftwards
towards the arete then directly to the top, keeping just right of the edge.
Variation: Very Difficult   (1952)
Start from the right end of The Platform (see below). Climb slabs rightwards to
join the normal route at the arete.

WESTERN BUTTRESS
This is immediately left of South Quarry. A broad level ledge, The Platform, runs
across the base, and a broken ledge, The Terrace, runs the length of the face
just below the top.

39   Slab and Wedge Route   25m   Very Difficult
Below the right-hand end of The Platform is a short steep corner. Start up this,
then climb the left side of the slab above. At its top go left, then back right to easy
ground and the top.

   Several lines are possible between Slab and Wedge Route and Wall Route.

40   Wall Route   20m   Severe   (1937)
Start at the left end of The Platform at a steep corner. Climb the corner with a
wide excursion to the right to pass a black overhang.

41   Groove Route   20m   VS 4c
Start as for Wall Route, but where that route moves right continue up the groove,
turning the overhang on the left.

42   Black Corner   25m   HVS 5a *   (1960/91)
Climb the prominent black corner to the left of The Platform past two triangular
shelving overhangs. Previously aided.

43   Horne's Slab   20m   VS 5a   (1945)
Some 8 metres left of The Platform is a red slab with a groove on its left which
leads to a large ledge at 12m. Climb the slab to a layback hold, step up then
move left and climb the groove. Scramble to the top.

Gruel Brittania, Ratho Quarry (Climber, Grahame Nicoll)

44   Hewit's Groove   20m   VS 4c   (1933)
Round the rib to the left of Horne's Slab is a short twisting groove. Climb this to
the ledge at 12m, then scramble to the top.

To the left of Western Buttress the cliff rears up into a series of steep loose
bays and buttresses. The leftmost of these, about 80 metres from Western
Buttress, is called Great Buttress. Beyond this the cliff steps sharply back into
the Great Quarry. Two very loose routes have been done up the right side of
Great Buttress and are not described.

45   Great Buttress   35m   Very Difficult **   (1902)
A classic route in a magnificent situation. The rock requires care. Start slightly
right of centre at a broad pillar. Climb the pillar to a terrace at 4m, follow this up
and right then traverse left along a ledge round a nose. At its end climb a short
corner (crux), then follow another ledge to the left. Mantelshelf and climb a
'staircase' to a wide recess and the top. A more direct line can be taken at little
increase in grade.

THE GREAT QUARRY
This is the long section of cliff set back from the path to the left of Great Buttress.
In the centre is a terrace at three-quarters height. Below the left end of the terrace
is a deep right-facing groove (Steeplejack's Staircase), with two bolts obvious
on the wall to the left.

46   Walk On By   30m   E2 5a   (1991)
Start just right of the only tree at the foot of the cliff. Climb up to a groove and
follow this to exit right onto a ledge. Continue up leftwards via loose ledges to
the top. The name gives good advice.

The following nine routes finish on the terrace from whence a loose scramble
leads to the top.

47   Ped Xing   20m   E1 5b *   (1992)
Good climbing marred by a worrying poised block. Start below the right end of
the terrace, under some blocky quartz overhangs. Climb a rib to a niche left of
the overhangs. Swing right round the arete of a block and pull through the
overhang above. Finish left or right.

48   Second Offence   20m   E3 5c   (1991)
Start as for Ped Xing but step left to climb a vertical crack through black rock. A
hand-placed peg was used for protection behind a flake at the crux.

49   The Blackdance   20m   E2 5c **   (1983)
Start 6 metres right of Steeplejack's Staircase below a triangular overhang.
Climb past the overhang and go up a groove (peg runner) to a sloping foothold
on the right. Move up the groove then out right (peg runner) and continue up the
wall to finish.

HOLYROOD PARK, SALISBURY CRAGS

GREAT QUARRY

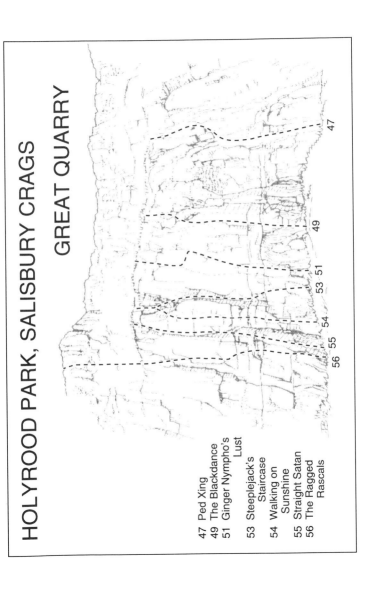

47 Ped Xing
49 The Blackdance
51 Ginger Nympho's
   Lust
53 Steeplejack's
   Staircase
54 Walking on
   Sunshine
55 Straight Satan
56 The Ragged
   Rascals

50   After the Axe   20m   E2 5b/c *   (1983)
Climb The Blackdance to the first peg. Traverse left across the wall and go round the arete to the base of a shallow groove. Climb this to finish.

51   Ginger Nympho's Lust   20m   E2 6a *   (1982)
From the right-hand end of the ledge below Steeplejack's Staircase climb a crack rightwards (peg runner) to gain a shallow groove. Climb this (peg runner), then traverse left to the base of a smooth groove. This provides a technical finish past 2 peg runners.

52   Election Special   20m   E2 5c   (1987)
Climb the left-hand crack directly to the third peg on Ginger Nympho's Lust, clip the top peg as well, then move left and go up to finish.

53   Steeplejack's Staircase   20m   E2 5b *   (1946)
The deep groove gives a classic climb, bold and technical for its time.

54   Walking on Sunshine   20m   E3 6a ***   (1983)
The smooth wall left of Steeplejack's Staircase provides one of the best climbs in the area. Climb the wall (2 bolt runners) to gain a standing position on a long narrow hold. Move up and right to finish in an easy groove.

55   Straight Satan   20m   E2 5c **   (1982)
This takes the vertical quartz crack left of the previous route. Climb the rib to the left of the crack until it is possible to step into the crack just below a peg runner. Continue up the crack to the terrace (peg runner).

56   The Ragged Rascals   30m   E3 5c   (1991)
Start just left of Straight Satan and climb pleasantly up a black groove to a ledge left of the terrace. Climb the final wall (crux, skyhook runner) to the top. Then, presumably, run round and round the Radical Road.

57   Transatlantic Trip   30m   E3 5c   (1983)
The obvious right-facing white corner 50 metres left of Straight Satan. The route finishes on a ledge about 6m below the top; the final wall is fairly easy but extremely loose.

The next important feature is the Cat Nick, an obvious deep gully about 80 metres left of the Great Quarry.

58   Cat Nick Buttress   30m   Very Difficult   (1900)
The loose buttress immediately right of the gully. Climb over easy ledges to gain a chimney, then climb this to the top of a prominent block. Cross slabs on the left to a right-angled corner, then move up this (crux) to reach a shallow chimney in the far wall. Follow the chimney to the top.

59　The Cat Nick　30m　Moderate ** **
The superbly positioned gully in the centre of the crags. A vintage route, which even in 1897 was "well worn and polished by the hands, feet, and knees of generations of youthful climbers". In winter it gives the finest snow climb in the park. In 1947 the cornice was some six feet thick, with an overhang of ten feet, and lasted for many weeks, despite much tunnelling.

60　Cat Nick Arete　30m　Difficult
Start up the rib left of the Cat Nick then trend right up the left wall of the Cat Nick to the top. Crumbly rock.

The crags to the north of the Cat Nick are dangerously loose and only seven routes, dating back to the 1890s, have been recorded here. However, perhaps fortunately, most of the lines can't now be identified. Historians wishing details can find them in the SMCJ Vol. IV (1897) p335.

Opposite Holyrood Palace, near the north end of the crags is the pinnacle of Pic Robbieson. Like the Inaccessible Pinnacle on Skye it has a short side (Moderate) and a long side (Difficult). Both are very exposed.
The Great Electrocardiogram Traverse gives a 1km VS 5a excursion across the crags, first explored in 1946. Start just beyond Pic Robbieson and continue across Great, South, Middle and Pinnacle Quarries to the Hause, if daylight permits!

MINOR CRAGS IN HOLYROOD PARK

HAGGIS KNOWE
The isolated hillock north of The Long Row has a crag which is not high, but the rock is solid and there is good bouldering.
　There are larger crags to the east, near St. Anthony's Chapel, which are both loose and vegetated. No climbs have been recorded.

THE LONG ROW
This is the long line of cliffs overlooking Hunter's Bog, the deep depression behind the Salisbury Crags. The rock is good and there are many worthwhile climbs other than those described.

Fallen Column Climb　10m　Severe *　　　　　　　　(1897)
The 'column' is a conspicuous feature near the left-hand end of the cliff. Climb its outside face and continue up the wall above.

Waverley Crack　10m　Difficult　　　　　　　　　　(1946)
The crack in the wall to the right of the previous climb.

Stomach Layback   10m   Severe *   (1946)
A further 7 metres right of the column is a corner crack. Climb the corner, which curls right around an overhang.

Editor's Crack   7m   Difficult   (1947)
Some 50 metres right of the column, right of some easy slabs, is a buttress with two adjacent cracks. Climb the left-hand crack.

Reporter's Crack   7m   Very Difficult
Climb the right-hand crack.

THE DASSIES
These are the three small outcrops in front of The Long Row. The left and right-hand Dassies provide some short routes and problems on poor rock, the central Dassie contains the following problems on much better rock.

Question Mark Crack   6m   Very Difficult   (1945)
Climb the obvious crack 3 metres left of a green recessed slab.

Black Heart   6m   VS 4c *
The thin bulging crack splitting the left side of the central buttress.

Vague Arete   6m   E3 6a *   (1987)
The blunt arete 2 metres right of Black Heart. The crux is near the start but there is no protection and a bad landing.

Black Edge   6m   E2 5c *
Start on the left side of the arete immediately left of Raeburn's Crack. Make a few bold moves up and right to better holds near the arete. Climb this to the top. Unprotected.

Raeburn's Crack   7m   Severe *
The wide corner crack to the right of the central buttress.

Cracked Slab Crack   7m   Difficult   (1946)
The crack-chimney immediately left of Cracked Slab.

Cracked Slab   7m   Very Difficult   (1946)
Climb the slab on the right side of the central Dassie via two short cracks. Finish directly above.

DUNSAPIE BUTTRESS
This is the small crag overlooking Dunsapie Loch. No doubt routes have been climbed but no records can be traced.

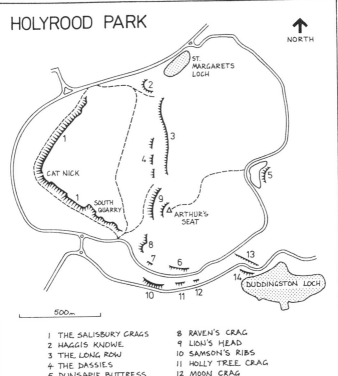

HOLYROOD PARK

NORTH

ST. MARGARETS LOCH

CAT NICK

SOUTH QUARRY

ARTHUR'S SEAT

DUDDINGSTON LOCH

500m

1 THE SALISBURY CRAGS
2 HAGGIS KNOWE
3 THE LONG ROW
4 THE DASSIES
5 DUNSAPIE BUTTRESS
6 RED CRAIG
7 HAWORTH'S CRAG

8 RAVEN'S CRAG
9 LION'S HEAD
10 SAMSON'S RIBS
11 HOLLY TREE CRAG
12 MOON CRAG
13 LOCH CRAIG
14 GIRNAL CRAIG

RED CRAIG

This is the line of crags about 40m above the road with a clean red wall at the left end and a red buttress with a prominent overhang at the right end.

Eureka   20m   Hard Severe *   (1946)
This takes the centre of the right-hand buttress. Start at the lowest point and zigzag up between two bulges to finish above the prominent overhang.

Red Buttress   20m   VS 4c   (1945)
Climb the left edge of the buttress via large steps overlooking a gorse and ivy chimney (Ivy Cleft). Finish at the same point as Eureka.

Pentland Slab   20m   Very Difficult
At the extreme left end of the crag is a slab with a steep red wall above and to its right. Climb the slab, keeping as close in under the wall as possible.

HAWORTH'S CRAG

A tiny outcrop of red and black rock and with ivy at the top, halfway between Red Craig and Raven's Crag.

Wee Chokestone Crack   8m   Severe   (1947)
The prominent right-facing corner crack at the left end.

RAVEN'S CRAG

The large crag to the right of the Gutted Haddie (the big earthy gully) has an impressive bulging black buttress on the right, which unfortunately consists of equally impressive loose rock. However, a low level traverse gives good training.

The Gutter   40m   VS 4b
The long left-facing corner on the left side of the crag. Horrific! (Sometimes called Vertical Sand).

Bacchus' Buttress Route   30m   Very Difficult   (1946)
The first buttress left of the Gutter. Start just right of the foot of the buttress. Climb up 6m, then traverse left onto a good ledge. Continue to another ledge, then go directly to the top.

LION'S HEAD

This is the sprawling crag on the north-west flank of Arthur's Seat, and includes the short tier of rock immediately under the summit. Most of the longer routes are appalling and best forgotten about, however the upper tier has three reasonable climbs.

Hanging Over Gladys   10m   Very Difficult   (1946)
At the right end of the tier of rock just below the summit, not far left of the top of the Gutted Haddie, are three black ribs. This route takes the right-hand rib, which has an awkward overhang at the start.

Gladys' Rib   10m   Difficult   (1946)
The central rib.

No Love Rib   10m   Difficult   (1946)
The left-hand rib.

SAMSON'S RIBS
The finest cliff in the park. The unmistakable ribs of red basalt would provide superb climbing, however the conspicuous position of any climber would result in certain arrest, justifiably so, because of the danger of rocks falling onto the road.

Left Ribs   45m   Scottish VS **   (1956)
Near the top left corner of the line of red ribs is a large overhang formed by the hexagonal sections of broken ribs. Find a way up to the overhang, escape left, come back right over the top of the overhang and finish straight up. A fine-looking route.

Grand Finale Route   60m   Hard Severe *   (1947)
Left of a bulging black wall (Evil Wall) is an isolated gorse bush. Climb up on vegetated rock, passing left of the bush, to a terrace. Continue up and right to another grassy terrace below some ribs with overhanging tops. Belay. Traverse up left, crossing the base of seven ribs, to reach a grass ledge. Ascend the rib above until it becomes broken near the top, then move left to a belay on the adjacent rib. Scramble to the top.

Scuttle   60m   Scottish VS   (1960)
Right of the centre of the bulging black Evil Wall is a small grass ledge at 10m. Climb to this, then go up and right on rotten rock to escape onto easy ground. Belay. Find a way through the tangle of ribs above.

HOLLY TREE CRAG
Right of Samson's Ribs, above a roadside bench, is a large crag with a weather-beaten holly at the top.

Holly Tree Slab   45m   Very Difficult
Start right of a black wall at the right edge of the crag. Climb to a ledge, then take a wall leftwards to reach easy ground above a recess. Continue in this direction over slabs to finish at the holly tree.

MOON CRAG

About 100 metres right of Holly Tree Crag is a small black crag with overhangs on its left side and a slabby wall on the right. The crag is apparently named after a certain Doctor Moon, but why, and who, what or when he was remains obscure.

Overhanging Route No.2   15m   Severe   (1946)
The big bulge on the left-hand side of the crag is split by a crack. Climb to the bulge and pull through a bush to gain the crack. Follow this to the top.

Zigzag Route   30m   Difficult
Climb the obvious pillar to a ledge, then traverse 8 metres left below the bulge and pull over to a slab. Climb this diagonally right to the top.

Overhanging Route No.1   15m   Hard Severe *   (1945)
Climb the pillar as for the previous route and continue up the steep right-facing corner above, passing a prominent overhang.

Short Slab Climb   10m   Severe
Climb the left wall of a right-angled corner near the right end of the crag.

LOCH CRAIG

The long crag stretching diagonally from the low road to the high road above Duddingston Loch is broken at its left end and rarely exceeds 8m in height. Not worth the bother.

Moonlight Traverse   200m   Hard Severe   (1946)
A complete traverse of the crag from right to left. Loose rock and death by gorse bushes.

GIRNAL CRAIG

This is the secluded crag below the road, which forms a promontory into Duddingston Loch. On the left-hand side of the cliff a buttress, above some large boulders, abuts the main face. The following routes start from the top of this buttress; no doubt others have been done.

Barbed Wire Route   15m   Very Difficult   (1946)
Starting from the highest point of the buttress, move to the left of a small overhang then climb to the top.

Red Slab   15m   Hard Severe
Some 5 metres right of Barbed Wire Route is a prominent red slab. Gain this from the left and climb it to the top.

ROSLIN GLEN   *(Map Ref 280 632)*

Between Penicuik and Loanhead, only 10 km from the centre of Edinburgh, the River North Esk winds its way through picturesque Roslin Glen. Hidden among the trees on either side of the glen are several natural sandstone outcrops which provide a large number of mostly short hard routes.

The rock varies from solid, knobbly and pocketed to frighteningly friable and sandy. The main drawback however is the dense undergrowth. Locating routes and even crags can be a problem and the thick foliage, especially in summer, results in a humid oppressive atmosphere, not to mention midges. Better conditions are often found in the winter months. At present, access to Hanging Rock and Lover's Leap Cliff is not permitted by the landowner. The routes are described in the hope that access will be allowed sometime in the future.

The cliffs on the west side of the glen can be approached easily from Roslin Chapel. However, the river has to be negotiated to reach the cliffs on the east side. This can be done via a fallen tree spanning the river near the Gorge Cliff (if it's still there). Shorter alternative approaches to the east side cliffs can be made from the roadway near Rosewell (over private land). These are described in the introductions to these cliffs. (See map).

To reach the river using the chapel approach, turn off the A701 5km north of Penicuik to reach the village of Roslin, then follow the signs to Roslin Chapel where there is ample parking. Continue along the track and, just after passing under some telegraph wires, branch off right down a muddy path. Follow this through a line of yew trees then take the zigzag path down to the river. Wallace's Cave can be seen on the opposite bank while descending.

The cliffs are described working northwards along the west bank (Chapel side) then southwards along the east bank. The routes are described from left to right when facing the cliffs.

THE GORGE CLIFF

Walk down to the river from the chapel, turn upstream, and after 100 metres the crag appears just above the path.

1   Absentee Landlord   15m   HVS 5a *   (1991)
The tallest part of the cliff is capped by a 6m long roof. Scramble over subsiding sods and brambles to the left side of a projecting wall below the roof. Climb up on pockets, then go over ledges trending left to pull over the final roof at its left end.

2   The Slater's Revenge   15m   Severe *   (1985)
Start 4 metres right of Absentee Landlord at the right side of the projecting wall. Climb up on pockets to an overhang, step left and continue up to surmount the final roof at the right-hand side.

JUMBO'S BUM CLIFF

Walk down to the river from the chapel and follow the path downstream to two red buttresses beside the path. The cliff is named after the right-hand buttress for obvious reasons. The grotty corners at either end of the left-hand buttress have been climbed at Severe, and the small buttress above has a couple of short problems.

THE LEFT-HAND BUTTRESS

3   Rock All Over Me   10m   E4 6a   (1985)
Climb the arete near the left end of the buttress to three large pockets. Pull up and make awkward moves round the left side of the bulge above to reach good holds.

4   Bum Fun   10m   E4 6a   (1988)
Climb the wall just left of Centre Line and, using a large pocket, climb into a runnel and finish out left. Serious.

5   Centre Line   10m   HVS 5a *   (1976)
Follow a line of holds in the centre of the buttress to a crack splitting the final bulge.

6   The Forty-Twa   10m   E4 5c **   (1985)
Start just right of Centre Line. Climb 3m to reach a smooth scoop and continue with difficulty to a recess right of a projecting flange. Either finish directly or traverse right and climb a groove in the arete. Low in the grade.

7   Monodoigtism   10m   E2 6b   (1988)
Climb the hanging pillar immediately right of The Forty-Twa using a one finger pocket and a pebble on the right wall. Finish more easily up the wall on the right. Escapable.

8   Dangleberries   15m   E4 6a   (1988)
A girdle of the left-hand buttress. Gain the ledge above the crux of Monodoigtism from the right, move up and left under the bulge of Centre Line and continue left to finish up the crux of Rock All Over Me.

THE RIGHT-HAND BUTTRESS

9   Jumbo's Proctoscopy   10m   E3 5c   (1992)
Climb the central corner to below the overhang. Move left to get established above the bulge and finish up the short crack capped by a tree. A sandy route suitable for beach bums.

10   Turn the Other Cheek   10m   E3 5c   (1992)
Climb the left side of the right arete (buttock) to ledges, then pull through the centre of the bulge and finish leftwards at a crack.

ROSLIN GLEN – JUMBO'S BUM CLIFF

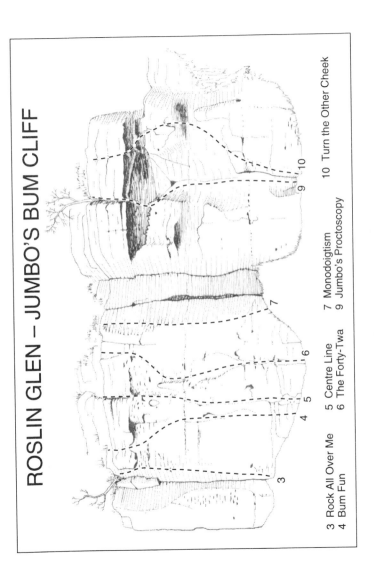

3 Rock All Over Me
4 Bum Fun

5 Centre Line
6 The Forty-Twa

7 Monodoigtism
9 Jumbo's Proctoscopy

10 Turn the Other Cheek

THE RED CLIFF

Not far beyond the Jumbo's Bum the path rises above a long line of red cliffs on a bend in the river. Although the cliff is large and reasonably solid, the rock unfortunately has a very sandy surface. Most of the routes can be approached by either bushwhacking along the river bank or by abseiling from any convenient tree about 20 metres before reaching a fence and stile. However, the first three routes start from a grassy ledge high up at the left end of the cliff. Abseil from a tree below a small rock outcrop with a rounded black recess, 40 metres before the fence, and belay on the ropes.

11   Red Face   10m   E2 5b/c   (1985)
Gain and climb a short right-facing corner crack 3m above the ledge, then trend left to the top.

12   Gruesome Gamboge   10m   E4 5c   (1985)
Start 3 metres right of Red Face. Climb 3m to a small pocket, reach a jug above, pull up and traverse right to a ledge. Step back left to gain a thin curving rib and use this precariously to reach the ledge above and the top.

13   Pinky and Perky   10m   E2 5c   (1985)
From the start of Gruesome Gamboge follow a line of holds up and right to sloping ledges. Climb the thin rib above to a ledge and pull onto grass above.

14   Incarnadine   15m   HVS 5a   (1991)
Right of the previous three routes is an unpleasant corner. Climb this moving right near the top to finish as for Panama Red.

15   Panama Red   20m   E3 6a *   (1985)
This route takes the obvious wide crack through the overhang just right of the corner. Climb a green groove and mantelshelf onto a ledge on the left. Struggle up the wide crack above, then head to the infirmary for a skin graft.

16   Brown Sugar   20m   E3 5c   (1985)
About 5 metres right of Panama Red is a flake. Climb the crack on its left until it is possible to step onto the steep wall on the left. Make an awkward move to reasonable holds, pull over a bulge on the left to reach a ledge and continue more easily to the top.

17   Red Ringer   20m   E2 5b   (1985)
Climb the thin groove 3 metres left of Old Red Eye to the top of a large flake and mantelshelf onto a ledge above. Pull up and right, then step left and pull onto a ledge. Climb more easily to the top.

18   Old Red Eye   20m   E2 5c   (1985)
The obvious left-facing corner with a tiny beech tree at the start.

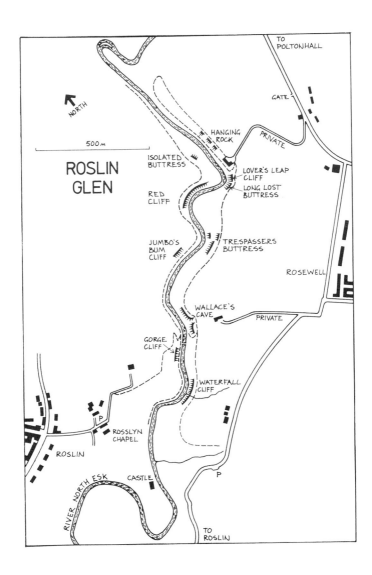

NORTH

500 m

ROSLIN
GLEN

TO
POLTONHALL

GATE

PRIVATE

HANGING
ROCK

ISOLATED
BUTTRESS

LOVER'S LEAP
CLIFF

LONG LOST
BUTTRESS

RED
CLIFF

JUMBO'S
BUM
CLIFF

TRESPASSERS
BUTTRESS

ROSEWELL

WALLACE'S
CAVE

PRIVATE

GORGE
CLIFF

WATERFALL
CLIFF

P

ROSSLYN
CHAPEL

ROSLIN

P

CASTLE

RIVER NORTH ESK

TO
ROSLIN

19   Red Wedge   20m   E3 6a   (1985)
Climb the slim groove 10 metres right of Old Red Eye to a ledge. Traverse right and move up to a corner, which is followed to a larger ledge. Easy to the top.

20   Dusty Road   20m   E4 6b *   (1985)
At the right end of the cliff are a series of corners. Approach by walking down from the path and upstream along the river bank. This route takes a short wide corner below and slightly right of a large fir tree which overhangs the cliff. Climb to a ledge on the right, then the groove above.

The short tier above The Red Cliff sports two micro routes. The central slabby arete with a break at one third-height is **Veg-hog** (E2 5b), and the rightmost arete is **Time Waster** (VS 5a).

ISOLATED BUTTRESS

Continue along the path beyond the Red Cliff until a buttress is glimpsed down to the right. It has a prominent overhanging nose.

21   Faustus Entor   12m   HVS 5a *   (1985)
This takes the wall left of the overhanging nose. Climb up left until the right wall can be gained. Continue up and right, passing a ledge with a spike, to the top.

22   Ham Jam   6m   VS 4c   (1980)
The obvious short jam crack right of the overhanging nose.

HANGING ROCK

This is actually three separate buttresses located on the east bank of the river near Hawthornden Castle. The best climbing in the glen is to be found here, however the crags are on private property and the landowner does not permit climbing. It is hoped that this situation will improve. The easiest approach is across fields from the road between Poltonhall and Rosewell, starting at two metal gates. Alternatively, follow the approach to Tresspasser's Buttress, then continue along the path passing below the castle.

THE LEFT-HAND BUTTRESS

23   Rock Lobster   15m   VS 4c   (1991)
The zigzag line of wide cracks on the left-hand side.

24   Hanging Rock   20m   E4 5c ***   (1985)
Bold climbing up the gobsmacking arete. Climb the left wall of the arete to the first break. Above, the arete forms a flat frontal face. Climb the left edge until it is possible to pull onto the front and go up to a second break. Climb up and right (crux) to gain and climb a wide crack. Finish more easily.

25   Give 'em Enough Rope   20m   E5/6 6b **   (1992)
This takes the middle of the steep right hand wall of the buttress. Climb a hollow
flake to the break. Move left to a wedged block before climbing the shallow runnel
above. Move back right and go up to a better hold, then make a long reach to
join Deep in Diana.

26   Deep in Diana   15m   HVS 5b *   (1988)
Start well up right of the arete and climb a dirty groove to a bush. Now make a
spectacular hand traverse using a monster juggy flake on the left wall, to finish
up an awkward wide black crack.

THE CENTRAL BUTTRESS
There is good all weather bouldering here.

27   No Picnic   12m   E2 6a *   (1985)
On the left side of the buttress is a wrinkled wall. Climb a shallow groove on the
left to a small roof, pull over to a recess and continue to a ledge. Finish up a thin
crack.

28   Plunging Neckline   15m   E3 5b **   (1985)
Climb the right edge of the wrinkled wall for 6m to reach a poor spike (Friend
runners on the right). Step right onto the front face, move up, step right again
and boldly climb a steep slab to a tree. The crux is just below the top.

29   Beyond Traprain   20m   E4 6b **   (1980)
The prominent crack splitting the big roof in the centre of the buttress provides
Roslin's answer to Separate Reality. A groove leads to the roof and gymnastic
climbing leads out and around the lip into the groove above.

30   The Cue   15m   E2 5c/6a *   (1985)
Gain and climb the right edge of the short wall below the big roof. Reach right
and pull over into a peapod groove. From the horizontal break above, move left
and finish up a steep slab.

31   Enzyme   12m   VS 5a   (1985)
The short overhung chimney on the right leads to a corner crack and a dirty
finish.

THE RIGHT-HAND BUTTRESS

32   Roslin Roulette   20m   E6 6b ***   (1988)
An audacious route up the left wall of the buttress. Start at a square recess and
climb to a ledge at 5m. Move left and climb the right-trending arete until a step
right can be made onto a steep ribbed scoop. Climb up (possible runners in
Gaping Gab) and pull out left onto the steep slabby headwall using a good
hidden flake. Make hard moves up then left to finish at a welcome branch.
Excellent bold climbing.

33   Gaping Gab   20m   E2 5c ***   (1980)
Continuously interesting crack climbing. Start as for Roslin Roulette and climb
5m to a ledge and recess left of a large roof. Climb a crack up and right to a small
ledge above the roof, then continue up until a move left can be made into another
crack on the crest of the buttress. Follow this to the top.

34   Eddie the Eejit   20m   E3 6a *   (1988)
This is the big roof overhanging the path. Place runners in Gaping Gab, then
traverse right under the roof. Make some powerful moves out and over the roof,
then climb a short crozzly wall to the small ledge of Gaping Gab. Move right up
a slab to finish at the same point as Voice in the Dark.

35   The Golden Apple of Eternal Desire   20m   E4 6b *   (1991)
The widest part of the roof right of Eddie provides a hard problem. Climb to a
hidden thread under the roof then make a huge reach to the lip, cut loose and
power up and over. Finish up Eddie or go straight up the arete above. (A skyhook
runner was placed on the jug above the right end of the overhang on the first
ascent). So named because it goes way over the top!

36   Voice in the Dark   15m   E3 5c *   (1987)
The obvious slabby corner and chimney right of the nose of the buttress gives a
strenuous but well protected struggle.

37   Under Pressure   15m   E3 6a   (1986)
High on the right is a smooth corner. Climb past a holly bush to enter and climb
the corner, exiting left at the top.

38   Life in the Bus Lane   12m   E3 5c   (1988)
Climb the arete at the right edge of the buttress, with an excursion left to place
runners at the holly bush.

LOVER'S LEAP CLIFF

This is the big cliff overhanging the river just south of Hawthornden Castle. There
is a metal fence at the top. Approach as for Hanging Rock. The landowner does
not permit climbing. On the right side of the cliff is a large rock ledge with a
smaller vegetated ledge below it, the vegetation being mostly peppermint!

39   Always the Sun   30m   E5 6b *   (1992)
Abseil to Peppermint Ledge and belay. The route awaits a first pitch! Move left
off the ledge onto a narrow red ledge. Climb an open green groove and step right
to gain the large rock ledge. Step left onto a rib and climb this (poor rock) to a
thin crack (runners). Go up this then move left on wrinkled rock where a hard
move gains an awkward rest below the big overhang. Use a large hold on the lip
to gain the vicious finger crack in the back of the bottomless corner above and
left. Wriggle up this to a small ledge and finish up the fine jam crack above.

LONG LOST BUTTRESS

This is the cliff 50 metres upstream from Lover's Leap Cliff. There is a metal fence at the top.

The Chocolate Orgasm   15m   E1 5a *   (1993)
Abseil from a fir tree to a vegetated ledge below a wrinkled wall on the right side of the buttress; belay on the abseil rope. Climb a scoop on the left side of the wrinkled wall (bold) until it is possible to pull left onto a slab. Climb the crack above and pull onto another slab, and so to the top.

TRESPASSER'S BUTTRESS

Halfway between Jumbo's Bum and the Red Cliff, on the other side of the river, are a number of crags known collectively as Trespasser's Buttress. There are two ways to approach the cliff. Either descend from the chapel, cross the river, walk up past Wallace's Cave and follow the high path until the crag is glimpsed down to the left. Or park in a lay-by on a bend in the road between Roslin and Rosewell (see map), walk a short distance towards Rosewell, then go through a field to a faint path in the trees. This leads past Waterfall Cliff to a better path above Wallace's Cave. Continue until the crag is glimpsed down to the left. Descend at the far end, about 15 metres before a stile.

Just below the path is a short wall giving a number of extended boulder problems. The first of these is **Feel Free** (HVS 5a), the crack at the left-hand end. The twin cracks 3 metres to the right are taken by **Precious Groan** (VS 5a); the crux is the bulging start. Another 5 metres right again is **Lazy Diamond** (VS 5a). The obvious open corner is **Stem Gem** (E2 6a *), again with the crux at the start, and immediately right is **Cruel Jewel** (E2 5c). The groove with a rounded recess is **Diamond Punters** (VS 5a) and the wide crack is **Welly Boot Crack** (VS 5a).

About 10 metres below and right is the start of a much larger wall with a gnarly tree overhanging a gloomy recess in the centre.

40   Shinbones Field   12m   E1 5c   (1986)
Start at the left side of the wall, well left of the tree. Climb a thin crack to a ledge, step right, gain a second ledge and climb a short wall to reach a crack which leads to the top.

41   The Shouting Man   20m   E5 6b *   (1990)
This takes the smooth wall left of the gnarly tree. Starting from a holly bush, hand traverse right and pull over an overhang. Climb up and right, then using flakes and a pocket gain the break. Finish straight up.

42   Strange Apparatus   10m   VS 4c   (1991)
Start just right of the gloomy recess. Gain the obvious flake crack from the left and climb it, passing a small cave.

43   Two Tier Crack   10m   E1 5c *   (1986)
This route lies on the small buttress below Stem Gem. Climb the obvious layback crack, step left and climb a similar crack to the top.

WALLACE'S CAVE

This cliff is in two sections separated by a muddy overgrown gully. The right-hand cliff contains the cave (used as a hideout during the War of Independence in 1338 by Sir Alexander Ramsay and 65 soldiers!). Approach as for Trespasser's Buttress. From the cave entrance continue left and cross the unpleasant gully to reach the left-hand cliff.

THE LEFT-HAND CLIFF

44   Scotch Corner   7m   E2 6a *   (1992)
About 10 metres left of a shallow cave at the left end of the cliff is a clean open groove. Climb this on small edges and undercuts.

45   Cave Crack   8m   HVS 5a   (1985)
Near the left end of the cliff is a shallow cave. Climb the crack springing from the roof and transfer into the left-hand crack above.

46   Basil Brush   6m   VS 5a   (1991)
The short mossy open corner 7 metres left of Rampo has a few moves on rock.

47   Gadaffi's Ear   8m   E2 5b   (1992)
Just down and left of Rampo is a curving flake crack. Climb this to a grass ledge. Step up and right and make a 'cosmic rockover' to finish as for Rampo.

48   Rampo   8m   E2 5b *   (1985)
Climb the obvious left-trending scooped groove, stepping left near the top.

49   The Thin Crack   8m   E1 5c   (1985)
The thin crack immediately right of Rampo. Often dirty.

50   Claymore Crack   10m   E1 5c   (1991)
Climb the crack behind a tree to a ledge on the right and fight through bushes to finish. The grade is reduced to VS 4c if the tree is used.

51   The Wrinklies   10m   E3 5c **   (1985)
Boldly climb the wrinkled wall right of the tree to a ledge on the right. Gain a larger ledge on the left and finish up a short wall. Superb.

52   Robin Hood   10m   VS 4c *
The obvious chimney above a sandy terrace.

ROSLIN GLEN – WALLACE'S CAVE
LEFT-HAND CLIFF

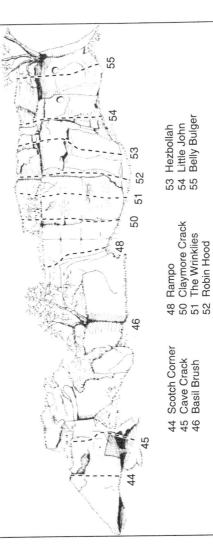

44 Scotch Corner
45 Cave Crack
46 Basil Brush

48 Rampo
50 Claymore Crack
51 The Wrinklies
52 Robin Hood

53 Hezbollah
54 Little John
55 Belly Bulger

53   Hezbollah   10m   E6 6b **   (1989)
Climb the open groove and overhang 3 metres right of the obvious chimney with increasing difficulty. Good but unprotected climbing.

54   Little John   8m   VS 5a
The shorter wider chimney 5 metres right of Robin Hood.

The facet of rock left of Little John has been climbed at 6b with runners and easy escape into that route.

55   Belly Bulger   10m   HVS 5b   (1986)
Near the right end of the cliff is a large bulge high up. Surmount this on the right, protected by a runner on an obvious branch.

THE RIGHT-HAND CLIFF

56   The Climbist   6m   VS 5a   (1985)
Pull over a roof at the extreme left end and continue to the top.

57   Ruggosities   8m   HVS 5b   (1986)
Start at an obvious oval hole. Pull over a bulge, climb a steep pocketed slab and surmount an overhang using a tree.

58   Dougie's Route   10m   HVS 5b *
Climb the shallow groove 3 metres right of the oval hole to reach an overhang. Pull out right and climb a wide crack to the top.

59   Day of the Jockal   8m   E2 6a *   (1985)
Climb directly up the wrinkly wall just right of Dougie's Route.

60   Gorton Crack   12m   Very Difficult *
Climb the corner crack which trends right then left to finish at a big pine tree.

61   Robert the Moose   12m   E4 6a *   (1985)
Start up Gorton Crack and climb to an obvious hole on the wall above. Pull out onto the front face and climb boldly to the top. Low in the grade.

62   Duncrankin   20m   E4 6a **   (1986)
Start at the entrance to Wallace's Cave and climb 10m to a ledge. Excellent thin face climbing up the wall left of the wide crack leads to the top. Easier for the tall.

63   Harry Dodder's Crack   15m   E1 5b *   (1985)
Start 4 metres right of the cave. Follow a flake crack to the ledge, then climb the short crack and wall above.
Variation: HVS 5a   (1989)
Climb to the ledge then finish up the wide crack on the left.

ROSLIN GLEN – WALLACE'S CAVE RIGHT-HAND CLIFF

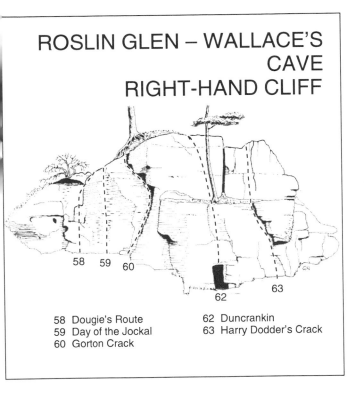

58 Dougie's Route
59 Day of the Jockal
60 Gorton Crack

62 Duncrankin
63 Harry Dodder's Crack

---

64 Scots Wha Hae   15m   E3 5c   (1985)
This is the right arete of the buttress. Climb an orange pillar above a roof for 2m to reach holds on the front face. Continue up the arete (crux) until good holds can be reached on the left. Easier climbing leads back to the arete to finish.

65 Hoppy's Least Favorite   8m   Hard Severe   (1991)
The chimney right of Scots Wha Hae, finishing direct.

WATERFALL CLIFF

This atmospheric cliff lies about 350 metres upstream from Wallace's Cave and is in several sections with the waterfall obvious in the centre. Descend from the chapel and cross the tree. Wearing wellies, walk up the river and scramble up to the waterfall. The river can sometimes be crossed without wellies just upstream from Gorge Cliff. Approach can also be made from the bend in the road between Roslin and Rosewell (see map) but the cliff is difficult to locate from there.

66   Rufus   6m   E2 6a   (1985)
Some 80 metres left of the waterfall is a long low roof. Start below two obvious pockets near the right end. Gain the lip, move right and mantelshelf onto the ledge above. Scramble up to a belay.

67   Praying mantel   12m   E2 5a/b   (1986)
Climb to an obvious circular recess above the right end of the long roof. Step right and climb up left to an awkward mantelshelf onto a ledge. Pull over a bulge to the top. Often dirty.

68   Last Slap   6m   HVS 5a   (1986)
Gain the shelf 3 metres left of Aficionado, then traverse left and pull onto the next shelf. Finish by climbing onto the big tree on the left.

69   Aficionado   12m   HVS 5a *   (1991)
The cliff stretching left from the waterfall has a prominent left-facing prow and corner. Climb the corner and traverse right to the prow. Finish straight up.

The next four routes take the grossly overhanging cliff right of the waterfall. The finishes to these climbs tend to become dirty and will probably require cleaning before an ascent.

70   Edge of Darkness   15m   E3 6a *   (1985)
In the gloom immediately right of the waterfall is an overhanging crack, gained by traversing left along a shelf. Much better than it appears.

71   Walk On By   15m   E6/7 6c **   (1992)
Rather steep. Start on the shelf as for Edge of Darkness and climb up to where Survival of the Fattest moves right. Undercut left and make very powerful moves on tiny holds (passing an *in situ* nut) to gain a break. Move up and right onto the slab to finish up easier ground.

72   Survival of the Fattest   15m   E5 6a **   (1992)
Equally steep but on larger holds. Start on the shelf as for Edge of Darkness. Climb to the start of a flake handrail leading right, then move along it until moves can be made straight up (via a letter box handhold) to join Piano Player. Finish up this.

73   Piano Player   20m   E5 6a **   (1985)

A wild traverse across the most overhanging part of the cliff. Climb a short corner at the right-hand side to a tree, then follow a line of small holds on the left to large breaks and the arete. Have a breather then set off on a horizontal traverse, exiting with difficulty onto the ledge at the far end.

74   Syzygy   6m   HVS 5b   (1991)

Thirty metres right of the waterfall is a damp overhung bay. Climb the stepped groove at its left-hand side, then escape out left at the top.

75   The Flying Start   10m   VS 4c *   (1991)

Gain the upper part of Syzygy by hand traversing from halfway up Mein Sumph.

76   Mein Sumph   8m   HVS 5a   (1985)

Climb the left-trending overhanging corner in the centre of the bay.

77   Ruff Stuff   6m   E3 6a   (1985)

Pull over the bulge right of Mein Sumph to gain and climb a tiny crack on the left. Make an awkward move to exit.

LOTHIAN MINOR CRAGS

BEECRAIGS   *(Map Ref 008 739)*

There is a small cliff, part quarry, part man-made located within Beecraigs Country Park, near Linlithgow. The crag is about 8m high, faces east and is often damp. It is useful only for abseiling or self-rescue techniques, and is amply provided with solid belays. Permission, upon payment of a small charge, MUST be obtained from: Beecraigs Country Park, Nr Linlithgow, West Lothian. Tel 0506 844516.

BINNY CRAIG   *(Map Ref 043 735)*

This is the west-facing crag on the prominent little hill between Broxburn and Linlithgow. Drive to Oatridge Farm, turn right and park beside the crag. The main face is rather loose and grassy but there are a few fairly good VS routes down to the left, on and around a big slab above a pond.

CAERKETTON HILL   *(Map Ref 237 663)*

This is the hill in the Pentlands with the Hillend Ski Slope on it. The climbing is found high up, to the west of the ski slope. The routes are rather discontinuous, vegetated and of an easy nature, however the situation is highly attractive. Some of the great names in Scottish mountaineering have climbed here, so it is hoped that would-be explorers will bring a suitably reverent approach.

EDINBURGH CASTLE ROCK   *(Map Ref 252 735)*

Climbing on this rather conspicuous piece of rock is strictly illegal and anyone caught doing so, which is almost certain, is likely to be prosecuted. However two routes have been recorded. **The Closet Climb**, severe, takes the Princes Street Face and was done by R.Smith and A.Frazer in May 1958. **Breach of the Peace**, Grade III, takes the smear of ice which forms down the Princes Street Face once in a blue moon. It was climbed on 16th Jan 1987 (at 10.00pm) by G.Taylor and J.McKeever, who were charged.

CARLOPS ROCK   *(Map Ref 162 557)*

The village of Carlops is 25km south of Edinburgh on the A702. The rock is a prominent feature in the centre of the village. It is often used for abseil practice and, although the rock is fairly loose, it also has a few climbs. The best of these is the obvious line up the front face, **Pentland Squire E2 5b.**

LOTHIAN CLIMBING WALLS

Most climbers nowadays make use of man-made walls for training. These can be divided into two categories: those built specifically for climbing, and those built for some other purpose (bridges, buildings, boundary walls, etc.) which just happen, through their construction and location, to be suitable for climbing, or 'buildering'. Unfortunately, both British Transport Police and Edinburgh District Council have informed the SMC that these unintended training facilities should not be described in this book. Given the risks of legal action, the following list is limited to purpose-built climbing walls.

HERIOT WATT CLIMBING WALL

Heriot Watt University Sports Centre, Riccarton, Edinburgh. Tel. 031 449 5111. It is open to community members (annual fee £14), but it is often booked by clubs and other groups on winter evenings.

MEADOWBANK CLIMBING WALL

Meadowbank Sports Centre, London Road, Edinburgh. Tel. 031 661 5351. This was a state-of-the-art wall when it was built in 1970 but is rather dated now. Access is difficult. At the time of writing there are public sessions on Monday and Thursday evenings (except in the summer) which are very popular and expensive. There is a user's card system which allows access for experienced climbers when the wall is not booked by clubs or other groups.

ALIEN ROCK

Old St Andrew's Church, 8 Pier Place, Newhaven, Edinburgh. Tel. 031 552 7211. This excellent new climbing wall complex provides leading, top-roping and bouldering facilities, and is open 7 days a week.

Fife

North of the Forth there are a variety of quarries and natural crags which provide some good climbing. The Hawkcraig at Aberdour is, of course, an old favourite. Unfortunately, the only limestone climbing in the whole of the central and southern Scotland region (at Limekilns) is currently out of bounds.

NORTH QUEENSFERRY QUARRY   *(Map Ref 133 807)*

Shrouded in trees behind North Queensferry is a small dolerite quarry which has a few good, well sheltered routes. The rock is of good quality only in the two areas where the climbs are located, and even here it should be handled with care towards the top of the routes.

Park in the vicinity of the Ferrybridge Hotel. Walk uphill, turning right opposite the war memorial, and follow a track under the Forth Rail Bridge to an open level area. A path leads from a brick shelter into the quarry. The worst of the undergrowth can be avoided by following the base of the crag starting at right hand end, and routes are described in this direction.

The first three climbs are situated in a tree-shaded bay where the rock is daubed with graffiti.

The Boat   12m   E1 5b *   (1985)
The wide curving crack at the right side of the bay. Strenuous.

Dive Dive Dive   12m   E3 6a *   (1986)
The thin crack in the wall 2 metres left of The Boat. Climb to the second break and gain holds up on the right wall. Move back into the crack and finish more easily.

The Vital Spark   12m   VS 4c   (1991)
The right-facing corner crack at the left-hand side of the bay. Finish up ledges on the right.

About 20 metres to the left is another open shaded area. Behind a large tree is the obvious central corner of Scharnhorst.

Nearly an Angel   20m   E3 6a *   (1991)
Some 7 metres right of Scharnhorst is a large black overhang. Reach this via a tiny corner, pull over and move up to a horizontal break (rest). Climb a finger crack on the left (crux) to another break. Move right and use large detached blocks to gain a left-trending groove which leads to easier ground.

Fleet Air Arm   20m   E4 6a   (1989)
Climb the thin wall crack 4 metres right of Scharnhorst with difficulty and only
adequate protection to a ledge. Easier and looser climbing leads to the top.

Scharnhorst   20m   E1 5b **   (1985)
The mighty corner, with the crux at the start. Large friends or hexes are useful
higher up.

Edge of Time   20m   E4 6a *   (1987)
The arete left of Scharnhorst. Start at the arete and climb to a crack on the right
wall. Use this to gain horizontal cracks and a rest. Continue up using holds on
the arete and the left wall to reach a platform. Easy but loose climbing leads to
the top.
Variation: E3 5c   (1987)
Gain the horizontal cracks from a thin crack and flake on the left. Make one move
up the arete, then pull left into a corner to rejoin the arete at the platform.

Bismark   20m   E3 6a   (1989)
The big corner 5 metres left of Scharnhorst. Move right at 12m and climb a
layback crack and a loose wall to finish.

ROSYTH QUARRY   *(Map Ref 125 834)*

This dolerite quarry lies only a stone's throw from the M90 about 3km north of
the Forth Road Bridge. It gets plenty of sunshine and the rock dries very quickly
after rain. However, climbing here is not an aesthetic experience. The walls are
daubed with graffiti, there is constant traffic noise and it is frequented by local
youths with air guns. But, if you don't mind these distractions there are some
worthwhile climbs and good bouldering.
    Some areas of the quarry are appallingly loose and only the more solid routes
are described. Natural belays at the top are scarce so there are stakes in place,
sometimes hard to find. Descent can be made at either end of the quarry and by
easy down climbing at several points; look for well worn paths disappearing over
the edge!
    The quarry lies south-east of the M90-A921 junction. Turn off the motorway
at Junction 1 (the second turn off north of the Forth Road Bridge) and turn into
Rosyth. Take the first right, and go right again and park in Admiralty Road. Walk
back under the motorway and follow a small path up through bushes into the
quarry.
    The routes are described from left to right. The first major feature is a corner
starting as a blackened recess and ending at a big tree overhanging the crag.
There are a number of short routes to the left of this which finish on vertical dirt
and impenetrable gorse; they are best forgotten. However there are some
worthwhile boulder problems, particularly the sharp arete 10 metres left of the
corner (5c), and the bulge and thin crack (5b) just left of the corner.

1   Route to Root   10m   VS 4c   (1972)
Climb the obvious corner overhung by a big tree. Finish on horrendous dirt either left or right of the tree, or better, climb back down again.

2   Grot Corner   10m   Severe   (1975)
Climb the slim groove trending slightly leftwards in the right wall of Route to Root. Well named.

3   Skinny Lizzie   10m   HVS 5a   (1990)
This is the sharp arete right of Grot Corner, with runners and the occasional hold in that route.

4   Chemical Warfare   10m   Severe *   (1972)
Climb onto a block 4 metres right of Route to Root, then go up the deep groove between two aretes.

5   Sickle   10m   Very Difficult *   (1972)
This route follows the open corner with a prominent crack in its left wall, 6 metres right of Route to Root.

6   Wireworm   7m   Moderate   (1972)
Trend right up a stepped depression, finishing at some gorse bushes visible at the top. Often used in descent.

7   Smith's Dilemma   6m   Difficult *   (1972)
Climb the prominent curving groove, which widens as it rises.

8   Jack's Route   6m   Very Difficult   (1972)
Climb the line which goes directly through an area of quartz-faced rock.

9   Legover Groove   6m   Very Difficult   (1972)
Climb the bulging depression just right of the quartz-faced wall to easy ground above.

10   Andy's Route   7m   Very Difficult   (1974)
Start at a right-facing wide crack 3 metres right of the quartz-faced wall. Climb the crack and steps leading left to the top.

11   Drizzle   8m   Severe   (1974)
The steep groove immediately left of a smooth wall.

12   Philistine   8m   E2 6a   (1974)
The smooth wall seamed with shallow cracks can be climbed using old peg pockets. Trend slightly left to a good hold in a deeper crack, then finish more easily.

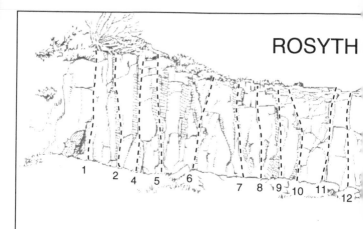

ROSYTH

1 Route to Root
2 Grot Corner
4 Chemical Warfare
5 Sickle
6 Wireworm
7 Smith's Dilemma
8 Jack's Route
9 Legover Groove
10 Andy's Route
11 Drizzle

13   The Waullie   10m   HVS 5b *   (1975)
Right of the smooth wall is a recess at ground level. Climb the thin right-facing
crack above the recess to a wider horizontal break, step left and go up the crack
above.

14   C.N.D.   10m   Severe *   (1974)
Climb the wall just right of The Waullie, finishing up a large slabby recess.

15   Hands Off   10m   VS 4c   (1975)
Start just left of some loose blocky overhangs. Climb a steep blunt rib and bulge
on poor rock to a slabby ledge. Finish up a crack on the left, immediately right
of the slabby recess of C.N.D.

16   Iconoclast   15m   HVS 5a *   (1973)
Start 6 metres right of Hands Off at the left side of the painted slogan TACK.
Climb the straight crack past an awkward bulge and the short headwall above.

There is a tall blocky buttress, daubed JACK and HEATHY, behind a hawthorn
tree about 60 metres from the left end of the quarry. The next four climbs are
found here.

QUARRY

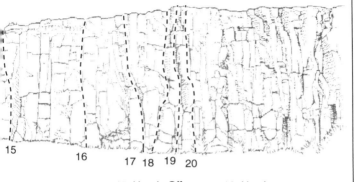

15
16
17 18 19 20

17 Grenville 15m VS 4b (1973)
Start just left of Heathy and climb a left-trending line of cracks and grooves.

18 Heathy 15m VS 4c ** (1972)
Climb a corner crack to the left end of a roomy ledge at 3m. Continue up the fine right-angled corner to the top.

19 Cathy 15m VS 4c ** (1972)
A slightly harder sister route to Heathy. Climb cracks to the right end of the ledge at 3m and the deep V-groove above. Large Friends or hexes are useful.

20 Broken Pillar 15m HVS 5a * (1972)
Start in a corner just round to the right of Cathy. Climb cracks to a ledge on the left and continue up the awkward off-width crack above. Finish more easily.

21 Corpuscle 15m E3 5c (1975)
Some 12 metres right of Broken Pillar is a V-groove capped by a triangular roof at 4m. Bridge up the groove, exiting left at the roof. Using poor sidepulls move right to the arete and climb this until the left wall can be regained where the angle starts to ease. Unfortunately the rock in the cracks is poor.

To find the next two climbs, go to the back of the quarry, well right of the previous routes, and look for a pointed pillar with a bore hole slanting up into it.

22   Ram Jam Corner   6m   HVS 5a   (1975)
The stepped groove left of the pillar.

23   Pogo Groove   6m   VS 4c   (1974)
The wall and groove right of the pillar.

24   Flakeoff   6m   VS 4c   (1975)
Another 12 metres right of Pogo Groove, behind some bushes, is a smooth wall seamed with cracks. Climb the left-hand crack line, using a prominent niche on the right.

25   Changeling   6m   VS 4c   (1975)
Climb the crack 2 metres right of Flakeoff, passing a ledge at 4m.

The next routes can be found in the most dense group of trees at the back right-hand side of the quarry, near a tombstone-like rock standing at the base of the cliff.

26   The Beauty   6m   HVS 5a *   (1976)
Climb the stepped arete just left of the tombstone. The second step proves troublesome until a 'secret' sidepull can be found.

27   The Beast   6m   VS 5a   (1975)
Behind the tombstone is a steep corner. Climb this to a ledge on the right, then go up the corner above.

28   The Grinder   6m   HVS 4c   (1975)
The obvious layback crack 4 metres right of the tombstone.

At the right hand side of the quarry is a deep V-groove (Gold Foil) with two projecting square-cut buttresses to its right.

29   Gift Horse   7m   VS 4b   (1975)
Climb the left-slanting layback crack 3 metres left of Gold Foil.

30   Plod   7m   HVS 5a   (1986)
Climb the cracked wall just right of Gift Horse, to finish up the wide crack on the left.

31   Gold Foil   7m   VS 4c **   (1972)
The prominent deep V-groove.

Jaws of the Law, North Berwick Law (Climber, Duncan McCallum)

32   The Flying Bink   7m   VS 4c   (1976)
Immediately right of Gold Foil is a slimmer groove formed by the right side of a
pinnacle. Climb the groove and attain a standing position on the pinnacle. Make
a hard move up to finish.

33   If Pigs Could Fly   8m   E2 5c **   (1977)
The impending crack line in the square-cut buttress 4 metres right of Gold Foil
is strenuous and sustained.

34   The Stinking Swordsman   8m   E4 6b *   (1973)
The steep cracks in the centre of the right-hand square-cut buttress prove to be
very strenuous and sustained.

35   Fat Sam   7m   VS 4c   (1974)
The groove at the right end of the buttress, 2 metres right of The Stinking
Swordsman.

36   The Rust Bucket   7m   E2 6a   (1992)
Climb the right-hand side wall of the Stinking Swordsman buttress, without using
the rock rib on the right or the tree on the left.

The last group of routes are about 25 metres from the right end of the quarry,
at a tall semi-detached flake pinnacle, not easily distinguishable. Look for the
slogan FREE LOVE; they are just right of this.

37   Late Night Final   8m   Difficult   (1975)
Climb the left-hand side of the flake, to finish at a small tree.

38   Jagdhond   10m   HVS 5a   (1985)
This route takes the face of the flake. Climb to a niche just left of a small roof,
then move up and right to the top.

39   Serendipity   10m   VS 4c *   (1974)
Climb the crack forming the right-hand side of the flake.

40   Tiger Pad   10m   HVS 5a *   (1975)
Climb the tiers of small steep slabs just right of Serendipity, using the crack of
Serendipity for protection only.

41   Inspiration   10m   E1 5b   (1975)
Climb the groove 3 metres right of Serendipity. Step right at a prominent
undercut, then continue directly to the top. Well protected by small wires.

Squid Vicious, The Souter (Climber, Owen Hayward)

THE HAWKCRAIG   *(Map Ref 200 849)*

The sea-cliff at Hawkcraig Point, Aberdour, has an excellent collection of middle grade climbs in a very pleasant sunny location on the Firth of Forth. As a result the cliff is quite popular, particularly on warm summer evenings.

At low tide the cliff is easily accessible. However, at high tide only the routes at the west end are unaffected; to reach the others an abseil approach or a traverse will be necessary. The rock is a form of quartz dolerite and is sound at the base, but nearer the top it requires careful handling, particularly between Gaucho and Guano.

The A921 runs through Aberdour. Once in the town follow the signs to the Silver Sands, turning off the main road opposite the Drift Inn. Follow this road and park either in the huge car park on the right or at the very end of the road. From here, paths lead to the cliff top.

To reach the base of the cliff at low tide, either scramble down at the east end (left facing out), or climb down Moderate rock at the west end above the boundary between a hotel garden and the boulder beach. At high tide the second option must be taken, or an abseil is necessary. The climbs are described from left to right when facing the cliff.

The obvious corner within the hotel grounds is **Cut Glass Corner** (Severe). The arete just to its left is **Crystal Arete** (E2 5b) and further left again are **Porcelain** (E1 5a) and **Crockery** (VS 4c). **Doo'cot Wall** (Very Difficult) takes the smooth wall right of Cut Glass Corner. These routes are worthwhile, but are perhaps best avoided to preserve good relations with the hotel.

The western end of the cliff, just right of the hotel grounds, is split by a terrace at half-height. Below the terrace is an obvious overhung recess.

1   Fish Head Arete   20m   Very Difficult *   (1965)
This is the left arete of the slabby wall which forms the left side of the recess. Climb the arete to the terrace and a tree stump belay. Continue up the crack line above the stump.

2   Fish Head Wall   10m   Very Difficult   (1965)
Start 2 metres right of the arete. Climb the wall trending up and left to join the arete. Finish on the terrace.
Direct Finish: Severe
A slightly harder alternative is to mantleshelf onto an obvious ledge and finish directly.

3   Ugh!   8m   Hard Severe *   (1965)
Climb the obvious crack in the slabby left wall of the recess.

4   Sacrilege   8m   VS 5a   (1965)
Climb straight up the bulge between Ugh and Eech to finish up the quartz corner right of them both.

5   Eech!   8m   VS 4c   (1965)
At the back of the recess there is a quartz-filled corner crack. Climb the corner until forced left under an overhang, then finish up Ugh.

6   Squirrel Slab   12m   VS 5a *   (1965)
Start on the terrace, just right of the tree stump belay of Fish Head Arete. Climb a slab with 'Ken' scratched on it, and the bulging wall above to easier ground.

7   Weasel Wall   12m   E2 5c   (1975)
Start on the terrace below a white corner 3 metres right of Squirrel Slab. Bridge up to below a small overhang, then move over it slightly leftwards to climb the tricky wall above via its left edge.

8   Cranium Crack   20m   VS 4c **   (1965)
This good strenuous route starts just right Eech. Climb the obvious fault at the back of the recess and belay on the terrace. Continue up the corner with a white left wall.

9   Conquistador Crack   7m   VS 5a *   (1965)
The overhanging crack in the right wall of the recess is short but sharp.

10   The Groper   7m   VS 5a
Climb the rounded arete to the right of the recess, without using the crack on the right at the start. Finish up the left-hand side of the capstone.

11   Stomach Ache   7m   Severe *   (1965)
An easier version of The Groper. Start just right of the arete and climb to join The Groper at 4m. Finish boldly up the right-hand side of the capstone.

12   The Beast   7m   Hard Severe 4c *
The obvious crack just right of Stomach Ache gives a short but awkward struggle.

13   Gismo   20m   VS 4c   (1965)
Climb the chimney 3 metres right of The Groper. Move right at the top, then go up to the right-hand end of the terrace. Finish up the broken black groove above, taking care with some loose blocks.
Variation: HVS 5a *
Climb the obvious short jamming crack above the chimney.

14   Pain Pillar   25m   VS 4c ***   (1965)
The local classic, giving exposed and well protected climbing. Start 5 metres right of The Groper and climb the tall narrow pillar, following the easiest line.
Variation: VS 5a
A slightly more difficult climb can be had by keeping to the left edge of the pillar.

15   Gaucho   25m   HVS 5a **   (1965)
A good climb up the deep groove to the right of Pain Pillar. Climb the groove to a black overhang at 15m, turn this on the right (peg runner), then move back left and continue up the groove and bulge above. An easier finish (4c) is to move left onto Pain Pillar above the overhang.
Variation: HVS 5a
Climb the narrow chimney below the overhang, then pull directly over it.

16   Psylocibie   25m   E2 5a   (1990)
A loose and poorly protected eliminate. Climb the crack in the pillar right of Gaucho to a ledge. Continue up the blunt black rib and loose wall above to reach a finger slot over a shaky flake. Use this with trepidation to surmount a bulge, then finish straight up.

17   Rebel's Groove   25m   VS 4c   (1965)
Start 5 metres right of Pain Pillar. Climb an obvious twisting groove to a ledge on the left, continue up the steep cracked wall above and finish up a right-facing corner formed by unstable blocks.

18   Saki   25m   VS 4c *   (1965)
Start 8 metres right of Pain Pillar. Climb a straight groove which slants slightly left to a ledge on the left (poor protection). Continue up the black wall above to a choice of finishes. A good start but loose higher up.

To the right of Saki there is a 6m high flake at the base of the cliff. At high tide this can be gained by abseil. It provides a useful starting point for the routes on this part of the cliff.

19   Slack Alice   20m   Hard Severe
This is the obvious wide groove starting from the left side of the flake and with tufts of grass visible higher up. Well named.

20   Brutus   20m   Hard Severe   (1965)
Climb the flake then the rib above, passing left of an overhang.

21   Torment   20m   Hard Severe   (1965)
From the top of the flake, step right, then climb a narrow rib and a wall right of an overhang to a loose and scary finish.

22   The Dwarf   20m   HVS 5a
Starting about 3 metres left of Guano, climb a series of shallow corners past an obvious small projecting nose.

THE HAWKCRAIG, ABERDOUR

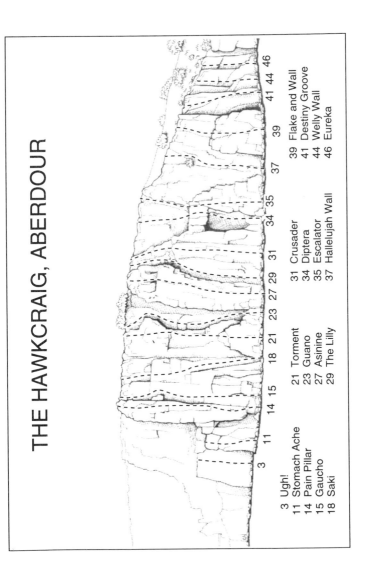

3 Ugh!
11 Stomach Ache
14 Pain Pillar
15 Gaucho
18 Saki

21 Torment
23 Guano
27 Asinine
29 The Lilly

31 Crusader
34 Diptera
35 Escalator
37 Hallelujah Wall

39 Flake and Wall
41 Destiny Groove
44 Welly Wall
46 Eureka

23   Guano   20m   HVS 5a **   (1965)
An excellent sustained route. Start 4 metres left of The Chimney at an obvious overhung curving groove. Climb the groove to a peg runner at 12m. Move right, then continue up the groove passing a bush to finish.
Variation: E2 5b   (1975)
From just below the peg, step left and climb boldly up the wall above.

24   Ganja   20m   Very Difficult   (1965)
Follow the vague groove midway between Guano and The Chimney, to join the latter two-thirds of the way up.

25   The Chimney   20m   Very Difficult   (1965)
Climb the obvious deep cleft in the centre of the cliff, moving left at a bulge to finish up a wide groove.
Direct Finish: Severe
Climb the overhanging crack at the bulge.

26   Chimney Arete   20m   Very Difficult   (1965)
Climb the right arete of The Chimney on poor rock.

27   Asinine   20m   VS 5a **   (1970)
A good exposed route. Start 2 metres right of Chimney Arete and climb directly to an obvious jutting nose. Finish by pulling through a groove splitting the nose.

28   The Arete   20m   E1 5b *   (1975)
The undercut arete right of Asinine. Start at the same point as The Lilly but climb a tiny corner to reach the arete. Now follow the arete, always keeping to the right of Asinine, to finish right of the jutting nose.

29   The Lilly   20m   Severe **   (1965)
Climb the obvious right-facing groove, 6 metres right of The Chimney, to a rounded recess. Step right and finish up easier ground.

30   Gunga Din   20m   Severe *   (1965)
Climb the narrow groove 3 metres right of The Lilly, to join that route at the rounded recess.

31   Crusader   20m   Hard Severe   (1965)
Follow the rib between Gunga Din and Saracen.

32   Saracen   20m   VS 4c *   (1965)
Climb steeply up the obvious rusty groove, to finish up easier ground above.

33   Toerag's Wall   15m   Severe *   (1965)
Left of a deep overhung recess is a fine wall. Gain the wall from the recess and climb it to the left end of a large balcony. Finish easily on the left.
Variation: VS 5a *
A direct start is possible.

34   Diptera   15m   VS 4c   (1965)
Climb a crack in the right corner of the deep overhung recess, pulling over the overhang directly to gain the balcony. Finish up a shallow groove in the centre of the wall behind.

35   Escalator   15m   Very Difficult *   (1965)
Climb the wall immediately right of the deep recess and finish up the groove above the right end of the balcony.

36   Tink   15m   Severe   (1965)
Follow the ragged crack up left behind blocks towards the right end of the balcony. Finish up right on poor rock.

37   Hallelujah Wall   15m   Hard Severe *   (1965)
Climb a crack running directly up to a gorse bush, pass this on the right and continue to the top. Some poor rock but worthwhile.

38   The Whang   12m   Very Difficult *   (1965)
Start at a chimney marking the left side of a huge flake. Gain and climb a flaky crack in the wall above, moving left to finish.

39   Flake and Wall   12m   Severe *   (1965)
About 15 metres from the right end of the cliff is a 5m high flake. Climb the face of the flake and continue up the short crack in the wall above.
Variation: Severe
From the top of the flake, climb the harder thin crack on the right.

40   Shadow Corner   10m   Severe   (1965)
The obvious three step corner to the right of the flake.

41   Destiny Groove   10m   Severe *   (1965)
Follow the thin left-slanting groove to finish at the top of Shadow Corner.

42   Urmi   10m   VS 4c *   (1965)
Between Destiny Groove and Maureen is a crack starting halfway up the wall. Gain the crack directly and follow it to the top.

43   Maureen   10m   Severe   (1965)
Climb directly up the groove 4 metres right of Shadow Corner.

44   Welly Wall   10m   Very Difficult
Climb to an obvious sloping shelf, then finish up the groove above.

45   Serendipity   10m   HVS 5a   (1983)
Climb boldly up the centre of the pillar between Welly Wall and Eureka.

46   Eureka   10m   VS 5a *   (1965)
Climb the strenuous but well protected right-facing corner 4 metres from the end
of the cliff, passing an awkward overhang.

47   Where Were You?   10m   E2 5b   (1990)
Without using holds on Eureka or Termination, climb the wall to a good undercling at a small overlap. Pull over using sidepulls and finish directly.

48   Termination   10m   VS 4c   (1965)
Climb the crack at the extreme right end of the cliff, without using the bulges
behind on the right. The top is loose.

49   The High Girdle   70m   HVS *   (1965)
Most of this journey is straightforward, but the crux is strenuous and exposed.
Take care to protect the second! Start on the terrace at the left end of the cliff.
1. 10m 4b   Traverse round Pain Pillar to a small ledge on Gaucho.
2. 20m 4b   Follow the ledge system down and right, belaying just before The
Chimney.
3. 20m 5b   Move across The Chimney into Asinine. Follow this, then make an
exposed step out right round the arete to below a small roof. Swing down rather
wildly to join The Lilly, and continue to a belay on the balcony.
4. 20m 4b   Continue at half-height, moving slightly down to the top of the flake
of Flake and Wall. Climb this to finish.

50   The Low Girdle   80m   VS 4c *   (1965)
Follow the line of least resistance along the foot of the cliff, solo and at high tide
for maximum enjoyment.

BENARTY HILL   *(Map Ref 154 979)*

This is the hill to the south of Loch Leven. There is a discontinuous line of dolerite
cliffs running around the rim of the hill, but all the routes described are on the
largest cliff, just below the summit. As the crag faces north at an altitude of 300m
it can be rather cold and slow to dry, and the rock is not of the best quality.
However, there are some worthwhile climbs especially for those who enjoy the
masochism of wide jamming cracks or thrutchy chimneys.
   Turn off the M90 at junction 5 and follow the B9097 eastwards to park on the
verge opposite the crag. Walk along the edge of fields then make a lung bursting
ascent up the steep hillside. The routes are described from left to right.

   Near the centre of the cliff is a gully slanting up left with a large rock jammed
across it. This provides an easy descent, and is directly above a pile of boulders
at the base of the cliff.

A Fist Job   20m   E1 5c *   (1983)
The bay to the left of the gully has a chimney on the right and an obvious crack on the left. Enter the crack from the right and climb it to a roof. Pull over and layback to the top.

Treasure Seeker   25m   Severe   (1991)
This route climbs the left bounding ridge of the gully via a rattly chimney crack, gained from the right.

Dolly Parton   15m   E3 6a   (1983)
This is the straight wide crack between two tall smooth bulges, just right of the entrance to the gully. Descend by abseil.

Hot Potato   15m   HVS 5a *   (1991)
Climb the obvious jamming crack in the narrow slab up and right of Dolly Parton. High in the grade.

Cubism   20m   E3 5c   (1982)
To the right of Dolly Parton is a long, narrow square-cut buttress which provides good but slightly contrived climbing. Start 4m up on the left side of the buttress. Climb a crack to a ledge on the right side. Step left and go up to a horizontal break. Climb up and right to a ledge, then follow a crack until it is possible to step left into the centre of the buttress. Climb up the right-hand side (crux) to the top.

Ram   12m   E4 6a   (1983)
Towards the right-hand side of the cliff is a short steep wall. Scramble up rough ground to its foot. Climb a crack on the right to an undercut flake. Traverse left to a thin crack, then climb it until it is possible to step right and move up to the top. Sustained.

   The end of the cliff, well right of Ram, is split into two tiers. At the right end of the lower tier is a knobbly prow of good rock.

Demerara   12m   Severe   (1991)
The thrutchy chimney left of the prow leads to a roof, which is turned on the right.

Goblin   10m   Hard Severe 4c   (1991)
Climb the wide fault in the right-hand side of the prow.

Oat Flake   10m   VS 4b   (1991)
This is the right-hand chimney line in the upper tier, above the previous two routes.

LIMEKILNS   *(Map Ref 070 837)*

Unfortunately, the landowner does not allow climbing on the two blocks of excellent limestone near the village of Limekilns. In addition to the strictly enforced ban there is a high fence around the blocks and the holds up to a height of about 2m have been smeared with grease. The climbs are described in the hope that access will be permitted sometime in the future.

The western block is called The Sentinel and is smaller than the eastern block, The Gellet Block, which has a flagpole on top. The rock is most unusual and provides some superb climbs in very pleasant surroundings.

The blocks are located on the wooded hill overlooking the Firth of Forth between Limekilns and Charleston. The approach is through private ground from the Post Office in Charleston. The Sentinel is reached first, and The Gellet Block is about 150 metres further on. The climbs are described rightwards around the blocks.

THE SENTINEL

Descent is by abseil from any convenient tree.

THE SOUTH FACE

Pickwick   12m   VS 4b
Climb the left arete of the slabby south face delicately and with no protection.

Hunter and the Hunted   12m   E1 5b   (1983)
A fragile and bold eliminate. Start 3 metres right of Pickwick at a bulge. Climb straight up with minimal holds and no protection.

Humbug   12m   VS 4c *   (1981)
The obvious crack in the centre of the face.

Kiln Dance with Me   12m   E1 5a
Climb the vague crack line just right of Humbug.

Empires and Dance   10m   HVS 5a
Start 2 metres left of the right arete and climb straight up the wall.

Dingley Dell   10m   Severe   (1983)
Start as for Empires and Dance but move rightwards to climb the arete on large but friable holds.

THE EAST FACE

The Struggler   12m   E3 6a **   (1984)
Start just left of Cruel Summer. Boulder up the wall until forced into Cruel
Summer. Move back left to a peg runner and climb the steep crack to the top.

Cruel Summer   12m   E2 5c ***   (1983)
The obvious corner gives a good, well protected climb. Make some hard moves
into the corner and follow it to exit left.

Colours Fly   12m   E1 5c *   (1983)
Start just right of Cruel Summer. Climb up to a tiny ledge, then go rightwards
passing a tree stump to gain a left-slanting ramp. Follow this and finish straight
up.

On the Blocks   12m   E3 6a *   (1986)
Climb directly up the wall between Colours Fly and Marley's Ghost to reach the
tree stump. Step left and finish up a thin crack.

Marley's Ghost   12m   E2 5c *   (1983)
Climb the right arete boldly to the ledge, move left up the ramp, then go back
right to finish up the arete.

THE NORTH FACE

Velvet Glove   15m   E4 6a ***   (1984)
This route takes the left-hand of the two magnificent cracks on the north face.
Gain the corner crack and follow it to a horizontal break. Move right to the base
of a parallel crack and follow it to the top.
The Satin Finish: E4 6a *   (1986)
Instead of moving right continue straight up, pulling left to a break at the very top
to reach a tiny sapling to finish.

The Iron Fist   15m   E4 6a ***   (1984)
The right-hand crack.

THE WEST FACE

Methods of Dance   12m   E3 6a **   (1983)
The fine left arete is an excellent climb. Climb up past a tiny groove to a hanging
block. Move left to the arete and climb it on good but widely spaced holds.
Right-Hand Finish: E3 6a *
Finish up the right-hand side of the arete.

New Gold Dream   12m   E1 5b *
The left-facing corner line.

THE GELLET BLOCK

Descent is by the stone staircase down the north face.

THE WEST FACE

Slots   10m   HVS 5b   (1985)
Climb the thin crack at the left end of the wall via finger slots to a ledge, then finish up the tiny corner.

Sunsetter   10m   HVS 5a *   (1985)
Climb the disjointed cracks right of Slots to step left and finish up either of two short wider cracks.

Forbidden Colours   10m   HVS 5a **   (1985)
Climb directly up the wall right of Sunsetter, move left and finish up a wide crack to the highest point of the wall.
Direct Finish: E1 5c *
Continue straight up the thin crack where the ordinary route moves left.

DT's   10m   VS 4c **   (1985)
Climb the short crack in the centre of the face to a ledge at 4m and finish up the obvious twin cracks above on the right.

D-Day   10m   HVS 5a *   (1985)
Climb the thin crack and wall left of White Ensign to pull up into the crack just left of that route's niche.

White Ensign   10m   VS 4c **   (1985)
The obvious wide crack 4 metres from the right arete.

VE Day   10m   E1 5b *   (1985)
Follow the thin cracks up the wall right of White Ensign.

Neutral Gear   10m   VS 4c *   (1985)
Climb the right arete, staying on the left-hand side.

THE SOUTH FACE

Lion Rampant   10m   VS 4b *
Climb the left arete, staying on the right-hand side.

Wall Straight   10m   E1 5b *
Climb straight up the wall 2 metres right of the arete.

Protectless   12m   E1 5a   (1985)
Climb the shallow groove and wall just left of Red Flag, moving right near the top
to finish as for that route.

Red Flag   12m   VS 4c *   (1985)
The obvious corner crack, stepping out left at the top.

Grasp the Nettle   15m   E2 5b *   (1985)
Climb the thin crack in the wall right of Red Flag to reach a peg on the left. Move
up to another peg, then climb up and right to the top.

Edge of Fear   15m   E2 5c   (1985)
The arete right of Grasp the Nettle. On the first ascent the arete was apparently
gained by a traverse at quarter-height from Red Flag.

Through the Motions   15m   E3 6a **   (1985)
Start just left of Dead Ringer. Step up to pull over the right end of the roof and
climb the crack to a break. Make a move up to a good hold where Dead Ringer
traverses in, then move left and climb the crack directly, passing a loose block,
to just below the top. Move left to finish on the arete.

Dead Ringer   15m   E1 5b *   (1985)
Climb the left-hand corner of the amphitheatre to a ledge, move left and follow
the thin crack past two iron rings.

Two Ringer   15m   VS 4c   (1985)
Follow the left-hand corner all the way to the top.

One Ringer   15m   VS 4c   (1985)
The right-hand corner of the amphitheatre.

Link Rib   15m   Severe   (1985)
The stepped rib, starting on the left-hand side.

A few short problems exist either side of the right arete to gain the first ledge
of the rib, the best being up the left wall without using the arete (HVS 5c).

THE EAST FACE

The Charleston   15m   E4 6b **   (1985)
This follows the hairline cracks right of the arete. Climb up to a thin crack, step
left then go up to the break. Step up and move across to gain flanges on the right,
then climb the thin crack to another break. Move up the wall above to the arete
and climb its right side to the top.

The Ivy League   15m   E4 6a ***   (1985)
Climb the obvious groove and crack right of The Charleston to gain the top break.
Move left to pull over a small roof by flake holds and continue to the top. Low in
the grade.

Yuppie   15m   E4 6a   (1985)
A serious route with some suspect holds. Climb the wall just right of The Ivy
League and move up slightly left past a thin crack to gain ledges. Go up to a
block and hand traverse the break to finish as for The Ivy League.

Elgin's Crack   15m   E2 5c ***   (1984)
The obvious crack provides the original and best route on the Gellet Block.

The Sting   15m   E2 5b   (1985)
Climb up to a ledge right of Elgin's Crack and follow the thin crack to a steep
ramp which trends right to the top.

Rock Around the Block   75m   E3   (1985)
A girdle traverse from left to right, starting across the West Face.
1. 5a   Belay on the left edge on a platform. Move up and right until a step down
gains the ledge system. Follow this across the face, move round the arete and
belay in the crack of Red Flag.
2. 5c   Move up and across to clip the top peg on Grasp the Nettle. Climb back
down until the lower peg can be clipped and make hard moves up and right onto
the arete. Step down to a block and traverse over to Dead Ringer. Move up to
clip the lower ring, then move into the corner. Descend to a ledge and belay.
Great care should be taken in extending runners and protecting the second on
this pitch.
3. 5c   Move up and across to the arete. A high runner can be placed in the top
break. Step back down and follow the obvious foot ledge across the East Face.

FIFE MINOR CRAGS

DUMFERMLINE CLIMBING WALL

There is an excellent climbing wall in the Carnegie Leisure Centre, Pilmuir
Street, Dunfermline. It opened in October 1992 and is available to the public 7
days a week from 9am to 10pm. Telephone 0383 723211.

WEST LOMOND AND BISHOP HILL

These two hills lie side by side to the east of Loch Leven. They form a high
plateau around which are a series of dolerite cliffs in a fairly advanced state of
decay. There are also a few outcrops of white sandstone, this too is very friable

but cleaner than the dolerite. The cliffs are described below working from north to south.

CRAIGENGAW (Map Ref 200 071) lies north east of the summit of West Lomond and is split by a wide gully. Several routes have been recorded including the longest in the area, **The Split Nose** (40m VS), to the right of the gully. J.H.B.Bell who pioneered most of the climbs recommended crampons for dealing with the rotten and vegetated rock.

GLENVALE (Map Ref 189 058) separates West Lomond and Bishop Hill and has a few routes on the largest white sandstone outcrop on the north side of the glen.

CARLIN MAGGIE (Map Ref 183 044) is a pinnacle due west of the summit of Bishop Hill and is the main attraction of the area, approach from near Glenlomond Village. The first recorded ascent was made in 1951 by I.Oliver, I.Brown and A.Grieve up the short side at Very Difficult with a point of aid, now free at VS 5a. The 15m long side, was first climbed with aid by N.MacNiven, but now goes free at E1 5b courtesy of J.Andrew and D.Kirk (30.10.93). About 20 climbs have been done on the cliff behind the pinnacle.

WHITE CRAIGS (Map Ref 183 033) stands directly above Kinnesswood. There are a few routes, including an E2 6a up the thin peg-scarred crack on the highest section of rock.

KINNESTON CRAIGS (Map Ref 194 023) face south above Scotlandwell and have lots of extended boulder problems and short routes of all grades up to 6b.

CRAIGLUG   *(Map Ref 404 183)*

This is an excellent little crag located near the village of Dairsie (near Cupar). There are about twenty routes of all grades up to HVS and good bouldering at the steep right-hand end. If only the crag was a bit bigger! To reach it take the road northwards at the west end of the village, the crag is visible straight ahead. Take care not to leave cars obstructing the road or gates. The first recorded ascents were by J.Baines and T.Wilkinson in the late 1950s.

DALACHY QUARRY   *(Map Ref 209 863)*

At the back of this dank sandstone quarry is a remarkable square-cut hole of huge proportions. It used to provide the only aid climbing in the region but sadly, holds were chipped, bolts placed and half a dozen routes from F6c to F7b+ were manufactured. The lines are obvious but at the time of writing the hangers have been removed from the bolts. Anyone wanting to brush up their aid technique before that visit to Yosemite can still do so, but a bit of ingenuity is required to make progress on the bolt heads. The quarry is located 1km east of Aberdour. Park at an obvious tree stump and take the left-hand track, turning off right, just before a house, onto a path leading to the quarry.

BELL ROCK   *(Map Ref 191 847)*

This is the large sandstone tor on the coastline beside the first green of Aberdour golf course. There are almost a dozen routes of up to 10m in height on the seaward face. The contorted rock gives interesting climbing but unfortunately a band of poor yellow coloured rock has to be overcome to reach the much better black rock above. There are also two smaller tors immediately to the west which give a few short routes and problems.

INVERKEITHING QUARRY   *(Map Ref 137 824)*

This is the large quarry, partly filled with water, on the north side of Inverkeithing Bay. The aficionado of loose dolerite will find plenty of scope for new routes. Only one, well cleaned, climb has been recorded so far, **Vidi, Vici, Veni** E3 6b takes a line up the slabby wall at the left side behind the pool. (R.Campbell, P.Thorburn 1990).

THE ISLE OF MAY

Some climbing has been recorded on the Isle of May in the Firth of Forth, 10km off Anstruther. The best and cleanest rock is to be found at Pilgrims' Haven in the south-west corner of the island, and a number of routes have been done here. However the chief attraction is a 25m sea-stack, the first ascent of which was made by a StAUMC party in May 1935, by the seaward ridge. Access is problematic and there are restrictions as the island is a nature reserve.

THE ST. ANDREWS COASTLINE

The coastline stretching eastwards from St. Andrews is fairly rocky and provides a few routes and some bouldering. There are three areas of particular interest. **MAIDEN ROCK** (Map Ref 527 158) is a sandstone tower about 1km along the shore from the east sands. More than a dozen routes have been recorded varying in length from 7m to 14m. Many of the harder routes were pioneered by Harold Raeburn during a visit to St. Andrews in 1901. **ROCK AND SPINDLE** (Map Ref 538 157) lies 1km further east. It is a seriously loose 10m pinnacle which becomes a sea-stack at extremely high tides. There is a Severe route up the west side. **BUDDO ROCK** (Map Ref 563 150) is an isolated lump of sandstone 5km from St. Andrews. It has a strange semi-detached pillar on the south side and has numerous routes and boulder problems, although the rock is very sandy. To reach it go through Boarhills, take the left fork at a dovecot and about 200 metres before the end of the track cross fields to the shore.

East Lothian

The contrast between the two crags in this chapter could not be greater! Good old-fashioned traditional Traprain contrasted with good modern sporty Berwick. Both provide lots of fun in their different ways.

TRAPRAIN LAW   *(Map Ref 582 745)*

Traprain Law is the prominent isolated hill 6km east of Haddington. It is well known both for its rock climbs and its archaeological importance; ancient settlements and Roman silver have been discovered here. The best climbing is found on two high-angled slabs, Overhang Wall and Lammer Wall, on the south side of the hill. There is a large loose quarry on the north side.

The sunny aspect, pleasant rural situation and good climbing particularly in the lower and middle grades, combine to make this an attractive venue. The rock is trachyte, a fine-grained volcanic rock which is generally very solid. However, the popularity of the cliff has resulted in the rock becoming extremely polished and care must be taken to avoid sudden unexpected slips.

Turn off the A1 about 25km from Edinburgh and drive through Haddington, taking the left fork at the church. After crossing Victoria Bridge and about 2km out of town, take a right turn signposted to Garvald and Stenton, and after another 3km turn left at a cross-roads. Park just beyond a sharp right bend and walk through a field to the cliff. Take great care not to damage crops.

The climbs are described from left to right.

Away to the left above a hedge between two fields there is a rather grassy cliff which gives several routes of an easy nature. Above this is a short steep wall which provides a few problems.

OVERHANG WALL
This is the left-hand of the two main faces. It has a band of overhangs at mid-height and some large flakes leaning against the face at the left end. Descent is best made on the right-hand side of the cliff.

1   Flake 1   6m   Severe
The front face of the left-hand flake. Pull over a bulge above a recessed black boulder, then climb up and right to the top.

2   Flake 2   6m   Difficult
Climb the left side of the front face of the second flake.

3   The Right Edge   6m   VS 4c
Climb the right edge of the second flake.

4   Steptoe   15m   Severe *
Climb the prominent narrow strip of clean rock right of Flake 2.

5   Moss Groove   15m   Very Difficult
Climb the left-facing groove starting 2 metres right of Steptoe.

6   The Shield   15m   HVS 4c *
Start below the right arete of Moss Groove. Climb up and right into a scoop, then go up this until it is possible to pull out left onto a ledge to finish. Bold.

7   Down my Street   15m   E1 5b
A nasty route up the mossy rib right of The Shield.

8   Flake Wall   15m   Difficult
A poor climb taking the wall above Flake 3.

9   Flake 3   6m   Difficult
The slabby face of the third flake. Follow a slim right-facing groove.

10   Flake 4   5m   Severe
The triangular front face of the right-hand flake.

11   Torque   15m   HVS 5a *
The soaring corner above Flake 3. Move out right at the top.

12   Swingin'   15m   VS 5a
Follow Torque to a ledge on the right wall. Swing right round the arete to gain a sloping ledge, then follow the arete to the top.

13   Left Edge   20m   Severe **
A fine route. Start just right of Flake 4 and climb up until it is possible to move left onto a sloping ledge at 10m. Continue up the obvious crack to the top.

14   Via MacNiven   20m   VS 5a *
Start 4 metres right of Flake 4. Climb a short wall to a small ledge, then go straight up the long slim groove which slants slightly rightwards to the top.
Variation: VS 4c *
From the small ledge, bridge up and move left to below a black bulge. Pull over this and climb directly to the top.

15   Wobble   20m   VS 5a *
Follow Via MacNiven to the small ledge, or better, gain it from the right. Step right and go diagonally right to a small black overlap. Climb over this, then go up and right to a sloping ledge. Pull over a bulge to another ledge, then finish more easily.

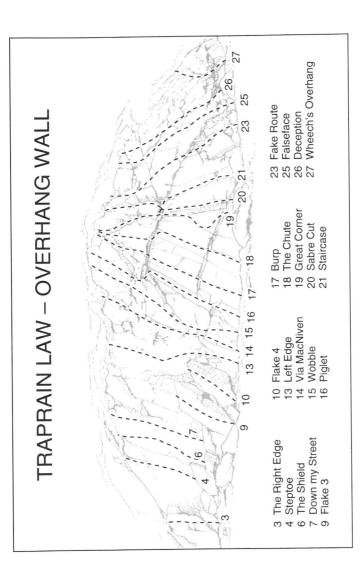

TRAPRAIN LAW – OVERHANG WALL

3 The Right Edge
4 Steptoe
6 The Shield
7 Down my Street
9 Flake 3

10 Flake 4
13 Left Edge
14 Via MacNiven
15 Wobble
16 Piglet

17 Burp
18 The Chute
19 Great Corner
20 Sabre Cut
21 Staircase

23 Fake Route
25 Falseface
26 Deception
27 Wheech's Overhang

16   Piglet   20m   HVS 5b **
A fine strenuous route, sadly becoming very polished. Climb the leftmost groove below the band of overhangs, then step left onto a glossy rib and pull up left over the bulge to finish up easy slabs.

17   Burp   20m   HVS 5a *
Climb the next groove right of Piglet. At the overhang step onto the rib on the right, which has as much friction as a bar of soap, and make one hard move to surmount the overhang. Finish up an easy groove.

18   The Chute   20m   E1 5b *
Climb the first groove left of Great Corner to the band of overhangs. Step left and make a hard and committing move to get established on the slab above. Finish easily.

19   Great Corner   20m   Severe **
The obvious left-facing corner gives an excellent but highly polished climb. Gain the corner from a slanting shelf on the left and follow it up to a ledge on the right. Climb a groove until it is possible to regain the corner, which is then followed to the top.
Direct Start: Hard Severe 4c
It is possible to start directly up the corner.

20   Sabre Cut   20m   VS 5a *
Climb the arete right of Great Corner to a ledge at 10m. Finish up the short groove left of a clean nose of rock.

21   Staircase   20m   Very Difficult
Start 3 metres right of Great Corner. Climb a crack until it is possible to move onto the slab on the right. Climb this on good holds to the ledge at 10m, then finish up Great Corner.

22   Slab and Tickle   20m   HVS 5b
A contrived route but with some interesting moves. Climb the slab right of Staircase, moving right at the top. Go back left to below a clean nose of rock. Pull over this and finish straight up.

23   Fake Route   15m   Severe *
The left-slanting crack line starting below some ivy. Follow the crack over an overlap to a steep flake crack. Go up and left to gain a rib on the left and finish straight up.

24   Cat's Paw   15m   HVS 5b
Basically a variation start to Falseface. From the slab below the ivy pull right-wards over the overhang and continue up the slabs.

25   Falseface   15m   Severe
The overlapping slabs left of the twin cracks of Deception.

26   Deception   15m   Very Difficult *
The obvious twin cracks, passing left of a large flake.

Between Deception and Wheech's Overhang there are some short interesting problems.

27   Wheech's Overhang   5m   VS 5a
The large overhang low down at the right end of Overhang Wall. The initial footholds are polished to a smooth sheen.

28   The Western Girdle   60m   VS *
A traverse of Overhang Wall from left to right. It gives some good climbing but is best avoided when the crag is busy.
1. 20m 5a   From Flake 3, climb up and right as for Swingin' then go horizontally right to a stance on the sloping ledge of Wobble.
2. 20m 4c   Continue right below the band of overhangs to belay on the ledge at the top of the arete of Sabre Cut.
3. 20m 4a   Continue rightwards to the end of the crag.

Between Overhang Wall and Lammer Wall there are some slabby ribs. Two are worth climbing.

29   Ripple Rib   15m   Severe
Climb the clean rib, skirting the small black overhang on the left.
Variation: VS 4c
Climb the small black overhang direct.

30   Via Dolorosa   15m   Hard Severe
Climb the clean strip of rock in the mossy face about 10 metres left of the deep chimney bounding Lammer Wall on the left.

LAMMER WALL
This is the right-hand of the two main crags. Although it is small there are many climbs crammed onto its slabby face. Descent is by a deep chimney on the left or by some large ledges on the right, just left of Queue Corner.

31   Retard Arete   12m   VS 5a
This is the right arete of the deep chimney. The initial blunt nose can be climbed from several directions, the easiest being from the left. Continue up the groove above to the top.

32   The Direttissima   12m   VS 4c
Below and right of Retard Arete is a smooth wall. Climb a short black crack in the left side to the left-hand of two black niches. Pull out left, then step right and go up to join Tiger Wall.

33   Tiger Wall   12m   HVS 5b *
Make some hard moves up the middle of the smooth wall below and right of Retard Arete to gain the triangular niche above. Pull over the overhang and finish straight up.

34   The Vertical Ladder   15m   Very Difficult *
To the right of Tiger Wall is a wide fault jammed with blocks. Climb this and exit either left or straight up.

35   Double Stretch   15m   Severe *
Start at a shallow left-facing groove just right of the Vertical Ladder. Climb the slab to the top of the groove and continue up to a wide crack. Follow this to the top.
The Keystone Variation: Hard Severe
Left of the wide crack is a projecting rock rib. Gain it direct and climb it to the top.

36   The M.S. Route   15m   Hard Severe **
An excellent route, giving sustained and delicate climbing. Start immediately right of Double Stretch. Climb a bulging slab for 6m and gain a small ledge on the left (crux). Continue up the slab above to the top.

37   Pinch   15m   Hard Severe *
Near the centre of the face is a shallow left-facing groove leading to three small overhangs side by side. Climb the groove, turn the overhangs on the left, then trend up and right to the top.
Variation: VS 5a
Climb the overhangs.

38   Brute   15m   Severe
Start just right of Pinch. Climb up until it is possible to move right onto a ledge at 7m. Continue up the crack and groove to the top.

39   Pedestrian   15m   Hard Severe
Start 3 metres right of Pinch at some tiny black grooves. Climb up, keeping left of black rock, to the ledge at 7m. Finish directly up the slabs on the left.

40   Spider Route 1   15m   Severe
About 4 metres right of Pinch two hairline cracks, one metre apart, run up the crag. High up they are separated by a mottled rib. Start just to the right and climb up and left to finish up the rib.

TRAPRAIN LAW – LAMMER WALL

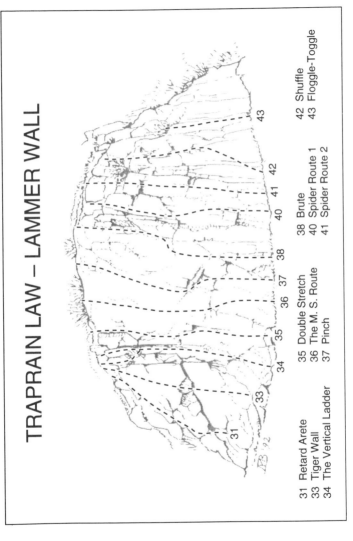

31 Retard Arete
33 Tiger Wall
34 The Vertical Ladder

35 Double Stretch
36 The M. S. Route
37 Pinch

38 Brute
40 Spider Route 1
41 Spider Route 2

42 Shuffle
43 Floggle-Toggle

41   Spider Route 2   12m   Severe
Climb smooth slabs and a small capping overhang obvious at the top.

42   Shuffle   12m   Very Difficult
Start just right of Spider Route 2 and climb diagonally right then back left to a niche. Continue up to a large ledge beside a broom bush.

43   Floggle-Toggle   7m   Very Difficult
Climb directly to a broom bush at the right-hand end of the crag.

44   Parabola   35m   Severe
This is a left to right girdle of Lammer Wall. Start by traversing the diagonal fault across Tiger Wall. Cross the Vertical Ladder and traverse open slabs above the Pinch overhang, descending slightly to the end of the crag.

45   Queue Corner   12m   Severe *
This is the fine right-facing corner starting from some bushes above the right-hand end of the crag.

46   Turf Trundle   25m   VS 4b
To the right of Queue Corner is an expanse of mossy slabs. Pick the cleanest line and climb it.

About 20 metres right of Lammer Wall is a large cracked slab bounded on the right by a series of overhangs arching up to the right.

47   Hexagon Wall   25m   Very Difficult *
Start just right of a long boulder leaning against the face. Climb the slab by the line of least resistance. Descend well to the left, facing out.

48   Dangle   20m   HVS 5a
Start below the left end of the overhangs on a black and sometimes wet slab. Go up the slab and gain a clean-cut right-facing corner. Climb this and pull over its capping overlap to join Hexagon Wall.

49   Tipp   10m   E2 6a
Scramble up below the overhangs for about 12m to take a belay under two steep thin cracks. Climb the left-hand crack, with a runner in the right-hand one.

50   Beatle Crack   10m   E1 5c *
Pull into the right-hand crack from the right and climb it, passing a peg runner, to easier ground.

51   Hanging Crack   10m   HVS 5a
Start up and right of Beatle Crack where a rib abuts the underside of the overhangs. Climb the right-hand side of the rib and pull over the overhang to finish up a groove.

52   Utang   8m   Very Difficult
Climb the obvious clean-cut corner 3 metres right of Hanging Crack.

53   Pip's Pillar   VS 4b
Below the band of overhangs there is an expanse of vegetated slabs. Right of centre are two huge flakes, one above the other. Climb the face of the lower flake, step across the gap and climb the face of the upper flake.

The cliffs further right and at the top of the hill have been climbed on, and give short routes mostly at Severe.

NORTH BERWICK LAW QUARRY   *(Map Ref 554 839)*

This is a tiny quarry at the base of the law, comprising two clean faces at right-angles to each other. An old aid route on the slabby right wall has been freed and eight routes have been created on the steep left-hand wall. The climbing is good, the crag quick drying and sunny, and there are bolts for protection. Buoux comes to East Lothian! The grades are quite stiff compared to those at the Angus Quarries.
Head for North Berwick Law, the big pointed hill behind the town. At the north-west side opposite Law Primary School a narrow road leads to a car park. From here walk south around the base of the hill until the quarry comes into view on your left. The routes are described from left to right.

Necktie   10m   E3 5c   (1989)
This is the left arete of the steep wall. Gain the arete and layaway up the right-hand side. Necky and neglected.

Fogtown   10m   F6c **   (1989)
The left-hand bolt line, exiting left at the third bolt and finishing up the ramp.
Alternative Finish: F6c+ *
Continue up and right from the third bolt to join Law of Gravity.

Eliminate Law   10m   F7c   (1992)
Climb the narrow strip of rock between Fogtown and Law of Gravity, protected by the bolts on these routes. Contrived.

Law of Gravity   10m   F6c **   (1989)
The line of four bolts, starting at a short corner. Weaklings can escape left near the top. Not the most technical route on the wall, but very sustained.

Jaws of the Law   10m   F6b+ **   (1989)
The left-hand of three routes, starting from a ledge 3m up, has some reachy initial moves. Three bolts.

Law of the Flies   10m   F6c **   (1989)
A tough route for those less than six foot tall. Three bolts and a lower off bolt at the top.

Law and Disorder   10m   F6a *   (1989)
The line of three bolts passing a niche, at the right-hand end of the wall. Again, a dyno to start for those of a lesser stature.

Law of the Rings   25m   F6c *
A left to right girdle. Start up Necktie, then take the obvious traverse line clipping the second bolts of the routes as far as Law of the Flies. Climb this to its third bolt, then finish up Law and Disorder.

Igneous Intruder   12m   F6c   (1993)
This is the left-hand of the two bolt routes on the red slab on the right. Climb up passing the first bolt on the left and the second bolt on the right, then run it out up the slab.

Old Lawbreaker   12m   F6b **   (1989)
Follow the right-hand line of bolts. An interesting move where the angle eases provides the crux.

DUNBAR CRAG   *(Map Ref 675 793)*

There is a horrendously steep crag of rather sandy sandstone on the coast about 500 metres west of the harbour at Dunbar. There are two bolt lines at the left end of the crag, the right-hand of which is an E5 6b (F7b) called **Celebration Day** (first ascent G.Latter 1991). The left-hand line is as yet unclimbed.

The Fast Castle Sea-Cliffs

On the Berwickshire coast between Cockburnspath and St Abbs Head lie a series of greywacke cliffs offering good climbing in an atmospheric setting. All the characteristics that give sea-cliff climbing its unique adventurous appeal can be found here: bald wave-washed slabs, faces overhanging the sea and the centrepiece of the area, a 25m sea-stack. Sheltered from the prevailing winds, it is possible to climb here throughout the winter months. The nature of the cliffs help in this respect, as fins of rock jut into the sea at right-angles to the coast to form havens of shelter on blustery days.

Climbing activity has increased noticeably since publication of the previous guide and many of the cleaner harder routes have become popular. It would be fair to say, however, that climbers venturing onto the less frequented routes can expect to find a certain amount of dubious rock. Any dangerous climbs are highlighted as such, but caution should be exercised as a matter of course, particularly with routes given the Scottish VS grade. Climbs without stars vary from being merely uninteresting to treacherous. However, it is possible that a gem has been overlooked.

Descents to and from some crags rely on *in situ* pegs or slings. These should be checked and replaced as necessary. Peg runners should also be treated with caution, although with modern protection many are no longer needed. Any public-spirited climber replacing old ironmongery should try to use stainless steel pegs as these are more durable.

A final word of warning; beware of the tide! Although not a problem on most cliffs, there are certain areas where it is possible to be stranded. These are not always obvious, so if the tide is coming in, stay alert and make sure there is an escape route.

The climbing is located in four separate areas, Midden Craig, Fast Castle Head, The Souter and The Brander. From Edinburgh take the A1 for 60km until about 1km past Cockburnspath. Turn left onto the A1107 signposted for Coldingham and Eyemouth, and follow this for 5km to a single track road on the left, signposted Dowlaw. For Midden Craig, follow this for almost 1km and park on the right at a small quarry and aerial. For the other areas continue for another 2km and park on the left just before Dowlaw Farm.

From Newcastle take the A1 to Burnmouth, 9km north of Berwick upon Tweed. Turn right onto the A1107 signposted Eyemouth and Coldingham. Follow this for 17km to the single track road on the right signposted Dowlaw.

St. Abbs Head is a designated Bird Sanctuary so climbing there is strictly forbidden. Although outside the sanctuary, Fast Castle has its own rich supply of sea-birds. Of particular concern to climbers is the influx of birds during the nesting season. Climbing cannot be recommended at this time due to the commotion, noise and smell, not to mention guano raining from the sky. Most nesting birds have some protection in law and the proximity to the sanctuary means there is a fair chance of encountering bird watchers at any time. If conflict can be avoided then the peaceful coexistence of birds and climbers will continue. Therefore, as a guideline climbing should not take place between April 1st and July 31st.

MIDDEN CRAIG   *(Map Ref 838 702)*

From the quarry, cross the road and go into the field. Head north-north-east into another field, aiming for a concrete post in the corner of the field nearest the sea. Cross the fence, then turn right (east) and descend steep bracken to the bay. The crag is at the bottom of the slope on the left. It is characterised by a band of jagged overhangs at one quarter height, which gives most routes a strenuous start. At the seaward end is a small sea-stack, Midden Stack. The first routes start from the scree slope at the left end of the crag.

Constant Hunger   25m   E4 6a **   (1993)
This sustained route starts between the left end of the crag and a right-slanting crack. Climb the wall, pull right over the bulge, then go up and left through the overhangs to gain a left-slanting crack. Move left and up to reach a thin resting ledge below the overlap. Move up to the overlap via a plaque, then pull through and follow a right-slanting crack. Near the end of the crack, move left and climb the wall to finish.

Welcome to the Midden   25m   E3 5c *   (1993)
Start 6 metres right of Constant Hunger, on the wall right of the crack. Climb the wall to the break below the overhang, then pull up and right through the break to gain a right-sloping ledge. Climb the wall moving slightly right, then go up and slightly left to the niche. Finish up and right.

Inferno   25m   E3 5c   (1993)
An airy climb up the cracked wall between the two wide chossy grooves. Climb loose ledges to below the overhangs, then pull right through them to gain a wide right-slanting crack. Stand in the crack, then move up and left to reach another right-slanting crack. Where this crack divides, follow the feint left branch which forms a short slim groove (crux). Finish up and right.

The next routes are on the right section of crag. The most striking feature of the wall is a large inverted V-shaped overhanging alcove.

Curve of the Earth   20m   E2 5c *   (1992)
This follows the slim clean-cut groove right of the large chossy groove. Climb the wall rightwards to the left side of the alcove. Move left through the overhangs to a crack, then follow the groove to the top.

A hard route has been established between Curve of the Earth and Enigma;
Brucellosis E4 6b.

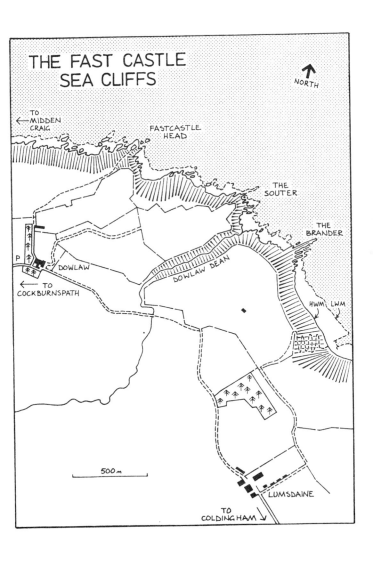

THE FAST CASTLE
SEA CLIFFS

NORTH

← TO MIDDEN CRAIG

FASTCASTLE HEAD

THE SOUTER

THE BRANDER

P

DOWLAW

← TO COCKBURNSPATH

DOWLAW DEAN

HWM LWM

500 m

LUMSDAINE

TO COLDINGHAM ↓

Enigma   20m   E2 5b/c *   (1993)
Start right of the alcove at a small bay. Climb the wall to a smaller alcove. Pull over the overhang using large pinch-grips, then move right and up to a left-slanting crack. Follow this for a short distance, then climb the wall above and a small overlap near the top.

Mea Culpa   15m   E3 6a *   (1993)
Start right of Enigma. Climb up and left to a spike below a wide crack. Gain the crack above (crux) and follow it for a short distance, then traverse right to a thin crack and follow this to the top.

THE MIDDEN STACK
The next routes lie on the small stack. In the middle of the south-east face there is a distinctive square-cut groove, capped by an overhang. The climbs are described from the right side of this face, moving left (clockwise) around the stack. Descent is by abseil from blocks and *in situ* pegs.

Starboard Bow   15m   E2 5c *   (1993)
Start right of the square-cut groove. Climb the wall to the break below the overhang on the right of the start of the groove. Pull straight over the overhang onto the wall, then move up and right to the right edge of the wall. Finish up the arete.

Turning in-tide-out   20m   E2 5c **   (1993)
This takes the corner formed by the left side of the square-cut groove. Near the top, move out left to a ledge, then step up and right to climb a thin crack on the right to finish.

Lunar Pull   20m   E3 5c **   (1993)
A superb route up the pillar forming the left side of the square-cut groove. Climb the double overhangs left of the corner, then go up the wall to the ledge and finish direct.

Port Bow   20m   E1 5b *   (1993)
The left arete. Pull over the bulge (crux) to reach a jammed flake in the V-shaped groove. Climb the groove to the overhang, then move round the edge to finish up a wide crack.

Unnamed   20m   E1 5a
A serious route up the green slabby wall on the south-west face. Climb a groove near the left corner of the face. Move left to a ledge on the left arete, then move right onto the upper slab and climb to the top.

The north-west face of the stack is generally scrappy, but the short cracks on the summit block have been climbed (E1). It is possible to reach the summit by a bold scramble on the north side. Starting on the right, go up and traverse left to a blocky groove near the left edge (Very Difficult).

TOD'S LOUP FIN

About 100 metres west of Midden Craig and its stack is another fin or stack with a fine north face. This consists of two slabs separated by an obvious corner. Descend by scrambling down the chossy south face, or abseil. The routes are described from left to right and are accessible except at high tide.

Tidal Race   20m   Moderate   (1993)
The green corner line on the left side of the face.

Ranald's Rant   20m   Very Difficult   (1993)
The arete just right of Tidal Race, finishing direct up a crack.

The next three routes start from a large block which is submerged at high tide.

Whitebait Can't Jump   15m   Very Difficult   (1993)
Climb cracks up the centre of the main slab. The direct start is 5a.

Flounder Member   15m   Severe   (1993)
Climb the big left-facing corner.

Pirrett's Progress   20m   VS 4c *   (1993)
Climb the previous route for 3m, then traverse right to the arete using the obvious handholds. Continue the traverse to a clean-cut crack which splits the slab above, and climb this to finish.

Further west still, a slab and a small buttress provide pleasant routes from Very Difficult to VS.

FAST CASTLE HEAD   *(Map Ref 862 711)*

From the parking place cross the cattle grid and turn left down a track, passing the end of a row of cottages. Go through two gates then turn right and follow a path to the headland. To the south-east the top of a sea-stack is visible, this is The Souter. Iron railings protect the bad step across to the headland and the gully dropping from here to the right is Abseil Gully.
   To reach the foot of the cliffs there are several possibilities:
1. Abseil from the railings down, you've guessed it, Abseil Gully.
2. Abseil from a huge block at the top edge of the cliff near a big hollow in the ruins. This takes the line of Atlanta.
4. Routes 8,9 and 10 are reached by abseiling from the outermost tip of land beyond the ruins.
3. Scramble down steep grassy slopes to the south-east.
   The routes are described from left to right when facing the cliff.

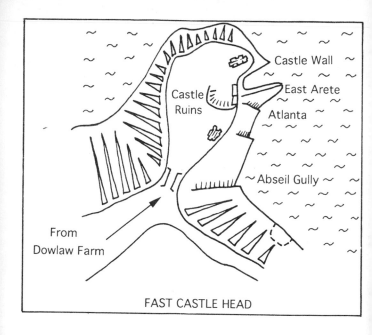

FAST CASTLE HEAD

1   Cyclops   100m   Scottish VS/A2   (1974)
A horrific-looking route. It lies on the high east-facing wall, well left of the main
slab mass and Abseil Gully. Start at the right-hand side of a large cave, below a
diagonal overhanging crack.
1. 15m   Climb the crack using pegs, pull into a shallow groove and free climb
to a stance and belay.
2. 15m   Continue up the corner to an overhang (peg runner), go over this using
a peg for aid, and climb the corner above moving out right to the arete. Use two
pegs to move up to a big stance on the left.
3. 30m   Climb the black corner above, then follow the arete breaking left to the
foot of a big grassy groove. Follow the shaley slab to the right until it steepens.
Stance and peg belay.
4. 15m   Traverse left towards a steep solid wall and climb this to a stance and
block belay on the right side of a right-slanting grassy rake.
5. 25m   Climb steep loose rocks above the belay, trending left until overhangs
force a traverse to the right. Climb straight up to finish and belay to the fence.

True Finish of East Arete, Fast Castle Head (Climber, Jamie Andrew)

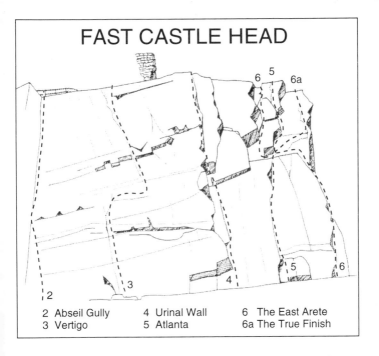

FAST CASTLE HEAD

2 Abseil Gully	4 Urinal Wall	6 The East Arete
3 Vertigo	5 Atlanta	6a The True Finish

2 Abseil Gully 60m Very Difficult (1965)
A chossy route. Climb the wall to the right of the chimney for 10m, then continue up the right-angled groove, using many bridging moves, all the way to the railings at the top.

3 Vertigo 60m HVS * (1965)
An interesting climb which would benefit from an increase in traffic as it is loose in places. It takes the middle of the slab right of Abseil Gully and below the castle ruins, following the obvious line of weakness.
1. 20m 4c Climb the slab to the foot of a crack. Climb the crack and continue to a small ledge.
2. 40m 4b Continue directly up over three slight bulges to the top. An enjoyable pitch.

The Souter

4   Urinal Wall   55m   Scottish VS   (1965)
A fine line, but overgrown and loose. Start at the very foot of the corner bounding the slab mass on the right.
1. 40m   Climb the wall and groove to a ledge and peg belay.
2. 15m   Continue up the corner for 10m, then go left onto loose blocks on the arete, and so to the top.

5   Atlanta   45m   VS *   (1965)
A continuously interesting route. Start 5 metres from the right end of the face, on a block strewn ledge at the foot of an apparently holdless corner.
1. 30m 4c   Climb the corner (poor peg runner) to a ledge and thread belay.
2. 15m 4a   Continue up the corner for 6m, then go left onto the arete (loose) and finish up a thin crack.
Direct Finish: Hard Severe 4b   (1992)
Climb the upper corner directly. Not as good as the original route.

6   The East Arete   45m   Severe   (1965)
Another good line, but it is loose in places.
1. 30m   Climb the slab and arete at the east end of the crag for 20m, then trend left to a ledge and thread belay in the Atlanta corner.
2. 15m   Move left round the arete and into a corner. Follow this to finish up a wide broken crack on the right.
The True Finish: E2 5a *   (1991)
From the thread belay, move up and right onto the edge of the slab and follow a slim groove to a steepening finish. This can also be used as an alternative finish to Atlanta.

7   Gannet Groove   75m   Scottish VS   (1966)
Too appalling to contemplate! This route follows the obvious crack up the bands on the east face of the crag. As soon as the route is started one is over the sea.
1. 15m   Step from the pinnacle at the left-hand corner into a groove. Move slightly down and to the right. Cross the wall, then move up to a pointed stance in the groove. Climb the groove (crux) with the right leg hanging over the wall and the left jammed in the groove. Continue up the wall above into another groove which leads to a stance and peg belay.
2. 25m   Continue up the groove and go round the overhang at the top to a large stance.
3. 35m   Traverse round a corner on the left and continue up a small gangway for 10m. Traverse right onto more solid rock and then go straight up to the top.

The next three routes are found to the right, behind the main slab mass, beyond a cave and a 12m strip of water. Abseil in from the outermost tip of land.

8   Rapunzel   40m   E1 5a *   (1992)
Start 3 metres left of Castle Wall and climb straight up the unprotected slab to join that route at half-height.

9   Castle Wall   40m   VS 4b *   (1966)
After a good start, this climb becomes a bit loose near the top. Climb the crack in the right side of the face, then traverse left towards a groove. Finish by an upward traverse to the right.

10   The Folly   35m   VS 4b   (1991)
Traverse right from the bottom of Castle Wall, just above sea level, until the second right leaning groove from the left is reached (or abseil in directly). Rounded spike belay.
1. 10m   Climb the groove and traverse left to belay on a shelf.
2. 25m   Continue left around the edge and follow the right edge of the face to the top. Poorly protected.

THE SOUTER   *(Map Ref 869 709)*

This is the impressive sea-stack nearly 1½km east of Fast Castle Head. It is surrounded by a complex series of rock fins jutting out into the sea which give the best climbing in the area.
    From the parking place walk right around the farm, then follow a track towards the sea, passing through two gates. When it fades, trend left and go through a drystone wall. Now head seawards down fields to the coast opposite The Souter. Away to the right a big slabby promontory can be seen, The Brander.
    The routes are described working from west to east, fin by fin, and from the landward to the seaward end of each fin in turn. Descend steep grassy slopes opposite the sea-stack. On the right is the boulder-filled inlet containing the stack and to the left is a small inlet, beyond which is a fin with a prominent crack running up its seaward prow. This is Second Sight Fin.

SECOND SIGHT FIN

1   Gull Talk   10m   Very Difficult
Climb the corner and slab at the back left-hand end of the fin. Walk right to descend a chimney.

2   The Fish Business   10m   E2 5c   (1982)
To the right of Gull Talk are three short corners. Climb a thin crack, just to the right of the corners, to gain an easy slab.

3   A Drop in the Ocean   12m   E2 5b *   (1982)
The left arete of the prow. Start below the wide crack of Second Sight. Move left to the arete and climb the wall just right of the arete on good holds. Swing round left into a small niche, pull out and continue more easily to the top.
Direct Start: E1 5b
When the tide is out, climb a line of cracks just left of the arete to join the original route.

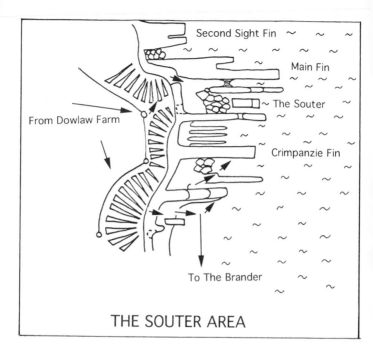

THE SOUTER AREA

4 Second Sight 12m HVS 5b ** (1982)
The prominent crack running up the prow of the fin gives an excellent climb.

5 Bloodbath 10m HVS 5a (1982)
The short arete just right of Second Sight.

THE MAIN FIN
This large fin runs out into the sea from the bottom of the steep grassy approach slope. The south-east side faces The Souter and is the most popular face in the area. The north-west side is more sombre but has superb rock. It is reached by descending a steep gully beside the face.

6 Stiff Bunnies 10m E1 5b * (1982)
This climb follows the thin crack up the prow of the small fin which lies to the left as the gully is descended.

The North-West Face
Do not be put off by the nest-strewn ledge as this does not affect the climbing.

7   Souterrain   20m   E3 5c **   (1982)
Climb the deep chimney near the right-hand side of the face and exit right to a ledge. Move up with difficulty to a recess and pull out left to the top.
Direct Start: E3 6a **   (1982)
Climb the crack to the right of the chimney.

8   Fast Bleeder   20m   E3 6a ***   (1982)
The obvious central crack provides one of the finest routes in the area. Climb into and up a narrow sentry box. Thrutch out right to good holds on the halfway ledge, then climb the crack above, pulling over a bulge (crux) to finish.

The South-East Face

9   Walli   4m   VS 5a   (1982)
The short crack at the left-hand end of the face.

10   Wallow   6m   E3 6a *   (1982)
Just right of Walli are two fierce thin cracks that converge near the top. Follow the left-hand crack. Desperate!

11   Wallette   8m   E2 5c/6a **   (1982)
The right-hand crack, gained from the right is not quite as hard.

12   Zigzag   12m   HVS 5b *   (1979)
Start below a thin crack 6 metres left of an obvious diagonal fault. Climb the crack, then hand traverse right to gain the fault. Finish up this.
Direct Start: E1 5c *
Start midway between the thin crack and the diagonal fault. Fingery moves lead to a jug and a hard move to gain the traverse line.
Direct Finish: E2 5c
From the start of the traverse, move up and left to climb a thin crack.

13   Mingy Metro   10m   E3 6a *   (1982)
Immediately right of the diagonal fault is an undercut bulge. Surmount the bulge to gain an undercling below a block and thin crack. A long reach (crux) gains a wider crack and a resting place below the easier final wall.

14   Fraud Escort   10m   E3 5c **   (1982)
From the undercling on the previous route, continue undercutting right on down-pointing flakes to a stopping place right of a crack. Move up into the crack, then follow it to the top.

15   Fated Panda   10m   E3 5c *   (1990)
Start 2 metres right of Fraud Escort. Climb over an obvious block and follow a thin crack to the top.

16   J.P.S.   8m   HVS 5a   (1982)
Climb the slim corner above the col between the Main Fin and Limpet Fin.

17   Plain Sailing   15m   E1 5b ***   (1982)
Start at the bottom of the deep cleft at the seaward end of the fin. Climb the superb crack line which starts at the right-hand side of a large block. The crux is at the top.

18   Drunk and Disorderly   15m   E3 5c   (1983)
Worthwhile variations on Wallnut. Climb parallel cracks to reach and pull over the overlap as for Wallnut. Step left and finish up a thin crack.

19   Wallnut   15m   E3 5c ***   (1982)
Excellent wall climbing. Start midway between Plain Sailing and the end of the fin. Climb a thin crack into the middle of the wall. Move right and up to the overlap, then go left through the overlap at a good sidepull. Continue up the wall above to the top.

20   Porker's Wall   15m   E4 5c   (1982)
A rather contrived and serious route. Start up the wall right of Wallnut then go up and right, passing a large pocket, to the arete. Move up and left to cross a bulge and continue to ledges and the top.

21   Coming up Roses   15m   HVS 4c *   (1992)
At the end of the Main Fin is a long green slab bounded by aretes on either side. The left-hand arete gives a good but serious climb.

22   Merlin and Wendy's Day Out   15m   VS 5a *   (1992)
Climb the right-hand arete; one hard move leads to pleasant easier climbing up cracks.

23   Return to Sender   50m   E3 *   (1982)
The girdle traverse of the Main Fin is an exciting excursion, especially at high tide with a stormy sea. Start below J.P.S.
1. 25m 5a   Follow the obvious traverse line across the wall and round the arete to belay on a ledge at the start of the north-west face.
2. 25m 5c   The return trip. Traverse the ledge to Souterrain, move up to the recess, then finish up a groove on the right.

LIMPET FIN
Between the Main Fin and The Souter is a small narrow fin. All the routes are on the south-east side facing the stack, except the first one, Orgasmatron.

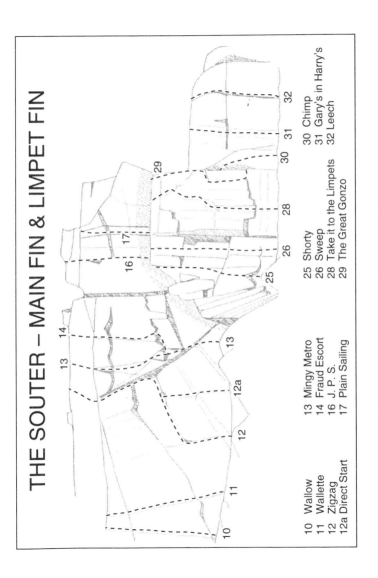

THE SOUTER – MAIN FIN & LIMPET FIN

10 Wallow
11 Wallette
12 Zigzag
12a Direct Start

13 Mingy Metro
14 Fraud Escort
16 J. P. S.
17 Plain Sailing

25 Shorty
26 Sweep
28 Take it to the Limpets
29 The Great Gonzo

30 Chimp
31 Gary's in Harry's
32 Leech

24   Orgasmatron   8m   E2 5c *   (1982)
Directly opposite Plain Sailing are twin thin cracks. Gain them from the right and
follow them with a tricky move near the top.

25   Shorty   8m   Severe *   (1982)
Climb the crack and arete at the left end of the south-east face.

26   Sweep   8m   VS 4c *   (1982)
Climb the cracks right of Shorty.

27   Sooty   8m   VS 5a *   (1982)
Follow the obvious short chimney and crack.

28   Take it to the Limpets   10m   E3 5c **   (1983)
A good bold face climb up the grey wall opposite the stack. Climb the left-hand
of two cracks to a jug in the centre of the wall. Move up and right to follow a vague
crack line to the top.
Variation: E2 5c
From the jug, go left to the arete. Move up and right under a small roof before
pulling onto the slab.

29   The Great Gonzo   10m   E2 5c *   (1982)
This route takes the crack in the arete to the right of the previous climb, gained
from the chimney on the right.

30   Chimp   10m   VS 4c   (1982)
Continue up the chimney from the start of The Great Gonzo.

31   Gary's in Harry's   7m   HVS 5b *   (1991)
Climb the left-hand (wrinkled) of two short cracks right of Chimp.

32   Leech   6m   HVS 5b *

(1982)
Climb the right-hand of two short cracks to the right of Chimp.

THE SOUTER
The next four routes tackle the sea-stack. Descent is made by abseil down the
landward face from *in situ* pegs and slings. These should be treated with caution
and replaced if necessary.

33   Landward Side   25m   Scottish VS   (1965)
The original route up the stack is now ridden with nests and guano and cannot
be recommended. Start in the middle of the face. Climb to a ledge at 7m and
traverse 3m right on to the south-east face. Move up to a ledge, then traverse
left to gain the top slab. Climb this to the top turning an overhang on the right.

Direct Variant: Scottish VS   (1970)
From the ledge at 7m, climb a smooth corner for 3m, break right and climb an
overhanging wall to a ledge left of a small wall. Cross the wall and climb a sharp
crack to join the original route at the top slab. It is also possible to finish over the
overhang. A nut and peg were used for aid on the first ascent.

34   Squid Vicious   25m   E5 6a ***   (1983)
The impressive crack line on the north-west face gives a classic hard route.
Climb the crack to a small roof at 8m. Traverse right and climb to two obvious
pockets in the wall (peg runner up and right). Return to the crack and climb to
the roof. Pull over on the right and climb to another roof. Go over this on the left
and climb up and right across a wall to reach a V-groove; block belay on the left.

35   Ordinary Route   25m   HVS 5a **   (1970)
This takes the seaward face starting from a raised platform. At high tide gain the
platform by making an awkward traverse across the base of the south-east face.
Climb the groove above the platform with difficulty to a ledge. Move up and right
(peg runner) to a V-groove. Go left up this, then climb a diagonal crack and the
wall above to the top.
Variation: Scottish VS   (1970)
Traverse left from the ledge above the initial groove, then go round the arete and
traverse a narrow ledge to join the landward route.

36   Seal of Approval   25m   HVS 5a   (1990)
This is on the south-east face of The Souter. Start above the bad step at the
south arete, next to a rusty peg.
1. 15m 5a   Step up to a sloping ledge and climb an obvious crack over a bulge
and small ledge to a continuation crack leading to the left side of a large ledge.
2. 10m 5a   Pull over a bulge and continue up the crack on sharp holds to join
the Landward Side near the top.

BLOCKBUSTER BUTTRESS
Opposite the landward face of The Souter is an impressive undercut buttress.
When reaching the top it is advisable to pull a rope up and belay to the fence.
The first route takes the zigzag crack on the right wall, left of an impressive
unclimbed groove.

37   Lightning Crack   15m   HVS 5a   (1982)
Climb the crack right of the undercut arete to the break. Traverse left to the edge
and follow a ramp to the top.

38   Moving Like a Slug   15m   E2 5b   (1982)
From below Lightning Crack, follow a traverse line left to the arete. Climb boldly
up the arete and finish up the ramp above.

39   Blockbuster   20m   E1 5b   (1982)
Round on the seaward face is a break in the roof. Climb through this using a
block of dubious stability, then continue up the crack and loose wall above.

40   Pigeon Shit   6m   E3 6a *   (1982)
Down and left of Blockbuster is a deep cave. Start just left of the entrance and
climb the fierce crack up the wall.

41   Graddled   6m   E5 6a *   (1983)
Boldly climb the wall immediately left of Pigeon Shit.

CRIMPANZIE FIN

This is the second fin to the south-east of The Souter. The climbs are concentrated at the seaward end of the south-east face and are only accessible at low
tide. Access can be made through an obvious gap in the fin opposite the stack,
or by descending grassy slopes to the south and working back northwards
crossing two minor fins.
    The face is broken by a guano splattered ledge at half-height. Below this a
short but steep wall offers superb climbing on compact grey rock. The routes
finish on the ledge. There are *in situ* pegs at the top of the fin for belaying and
abseiling. Beware of quickly rising tides.

42   Kylie   6m   E1 5b   (1990)
The first crack line left of the central groove.

43   Crimpanzie   8m   E5 6b **   (1990)
Blind, bold and fingery climbing up the wall left of the central groove line. Climb
to an undercut flake. Move up and right past a hammered nut, then move right
to a good hold under the roof. Move left and finish up the open groove.

44   Not the HVS   8m   E2 5c **   (1990)
The central groove line.

45   First of Four   8m   E4 5c **   (1990)
The weakness right of the central groove. Climb the wall to an undercut flake.
Move left and follow the scoop to the roof (good nut). Continue straight up to
finish.

46   The Undercut Kid   8m   E4 6a *   (1990)
An eliminate straight up the shield right of the previous route to reach the juggy
spike on Tied up at Work.

47   Tied up at Work   8m   E3 6a **   (1990)
Climb to the first of two undercut flakes near the right end of the face. Break
diagonally left up the wall to a juggy spike, then pull easily over the roof to finish.

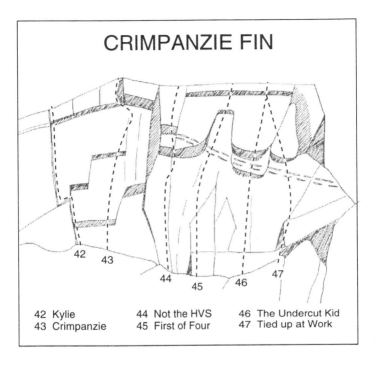

CRIMPANZIE FIN

42 Kylie
43 Crimpanzie

44 Not the HVS
45 First of Four

46 The Undercut Kid
47 Tied up at Work

---

48   Psittacosis   20m   E5 6b *   (1990)
This is a left to right girdle which follows the weakness under the roof all the way to Tied up at Work. Stork-like manoeuvres are optional.

THE WEDGE

Where the series of fins end and a wide pebble bay starts there is an isolated, thin triangular pinnacle. The north-west face provides an excellent boulder problem traverse.

49   Edge of the Wedge   15m   E2 5a   (1992)
Climb the seaward edge through several bulges.

50   Fuzzy Stone   15m   E3 5b   (1992)
The south-east face of The Wedge. Pull through the overhang in the centre and traverse right along a narrow ramp. Climb the wall above, using holds on the right arete.

THE BRANDER AREA   *(Map Ref 873 706)*

This area can be divided into two sections. The Brander Slab is the long green promontory running out into the sea, and East Brander Bay is the shorter fins between The Brander Slab and the big pebble bay to the south.

THE BRANDER SLAB

The climbing is located on the north-west face, to the left of a small low promontory in front of the main slab. Access has to be made from above. There are two options:

1. From the field opposite The Souter descend a wide grassy bowl to the south to a pinnacle (The Wedge), and cross the pebble bay. The small low promontory has a ledge running out to its tip from here. This is an excellent point from which to view the climbs. A steep grass and scree gully leads up to a narrow col connecting The Brander promontory to the mainland. From the col traverse the narrow ridge down to ledges and large blocks overlooking a cave at the landward end of the slabs. It is possible to continue descending the whole promontory to the sea, doubling back along the base of the slabs, but many parties abseil from the blocks (near the top of Spring Shower) to a ledge above sea-level at the mouth of the cave. In rough seas some massive waves can swamp the cave, and spray has been known to reach the roof – beware!

2. From Dowlaw Farm, head east on a track along the edge of a field to a burn. This is at the head of a gorge called Dowlaw Dean. Cross the burn and follow the fence on the south side of the gorge, which turns right and rises steeply at the sea. A faint path goes diagonally left up the slope. When it relents, trend left and cross the fence. Find a steep grassy ridge running down to the col at the top of the Brander promontory, then continue as described in the first approach above.

The routes are described from right to left.

1   Up-helly-aa   35m   E3 5c **   (1991)
This route gains and climbs the right bounding corner of the slab at the mouth of the cave; an impressive line with some serious climbing. Start on the ledge directly below the crack of Bouma Sequence. Follow a line of holds up and right to a niche in a thin crack. Step out right, then go straight up (crux) to a ledge. Enter the corner and at its top move up and left to finish as for Bouma Sequence.

2   Bouma Sequence   35m   E1 5a **   (1991)
A superb bold climb up the crack left of Up-helly-aa. Gain the crack directly up the slab (crux), moving right through the small overlap, then go back left.

3   The Ancient Mariner   35m   E2 5b **   (1991)
Start midway between the cracks of Bouma Sequence and Spring Shower. Climb direct to the right end of a ledge. Traverse this left and go up towards a crack in the overlap. Climb through this and follow a diagonal crack right to another ledge. Moves up and left lead to a crack and a loose finish.

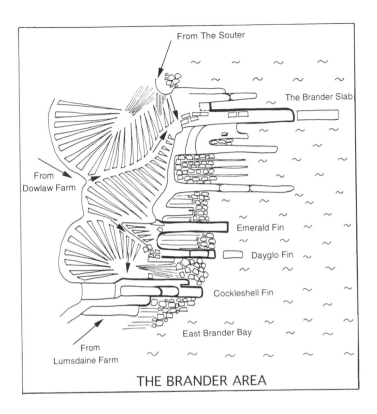

From The Souter

The Brander Slab

From
Dowlaw Farm

Emerald Fin

Dayglo Fin

Cockleshell Fin

East Brander Bay

From
Lumsdaine Farm

THE BRANDER AREA

4   Spring Shower   35m   VS 4c **   (1981)
This is the obvious continuous crack right of the centre of the slab, started from
the lower ledge. A traditional classic in an exciting position, low in its grade.

5   Jonathan Livingstone Shitehawk   35m   VS 4c   (1981)
Start on the lower ledge about 6 metres left of Spring Shower. Climb up directly
into the right bounding corner of a huge shield of rock. Surmount an overlap then
move diagonally left to reach a thin crack line which leads to the top.

6   Blue Moves   40m   E1 5a *   (1981)
At low tide, start from a hanging stance under the sea-level bulge directly below
the centre of the huge shield in the middle of the slab. Make bold moves up and

diagonally right to reach the lower ledge. Move up a shallow overlapped groove to reach the middle ledge. Climb through the overlap at the apex and go up the shield, passing some shallow pockets. Poorly protected.

7   Sea Sprite   40m   HVS 5a **   (1981)
Good climbing up the thin disjointed crack line in the left side of the shield. Start as for Blue Moves and climb directly up the lower slab to the halfway ledge. Climb through the overlap and continue up cracks to the top.

8   What Have The Vikings Ever Done For Us?   40m   HVS 4c   (1981)
Start just left of Blue Moves directly below the left bounding corner of the shield. Move up the slab to the corner and climb this to pull out right at the top.

9   Rufus the Red   35m   E1 5a *   (1981)
Start at the base of a ramp and follow cracks to the halfway ledge, then move up into the apex of the overlap near the top. Unprotected.

10   Sea Ahoy   35m   Hard Severe   (1981)
Climb the crack line left of Rufus the Red, bearing left at the top.

THE SEAWARD SLAB

This is the fine slab out at the tip of the Brander. The upper half of the slab is overlaid by a shield of perfect rough rock. There are about five routes on 'go anywhere' rock with grades varying between 4a and 4c.

EAST BRANDER BAY

This is the series of fins at the northern end of a big pebble bay, immediately behind the Brander Slab. There are three access routes.
1. Approximately 80m above the col connecting the Brander Slab to the mainland, a steep, grassy, rocky slope leads down into a gully between Lucky Day Wall and Dayglo Fin.
2. It is possible to scramble down the rubble slope immediately south-east of the Spring Shower abseil point. Work south with some interesting route finding to the climbs, encountering the smooth overhanging north face of Emerald Fin first. Care should be taken in this area to avoid being cut off by the tide.
3. A more obscure but pleasant approach is to walk in from Lumsdaine Farm instead of Dowlaw. Turn off the A1107 1km north of Coldingham and drive along a single track road for 3km to the farm. Walk north-east on a track past some ruined cottages to a gate. Turn left and follow the fence to the far end of a wood. Turn right and go to the top of a wide overgrown gully dropping to the sea. An old smugglers path winds down the wide slope just north of the gully to the shore. Head north to reach the Cockle Shell Fin.

The climbs are described when going from south to north, as they are approached from the bay (access route 3). The first route is to the left of the Cockle Shell Fin.

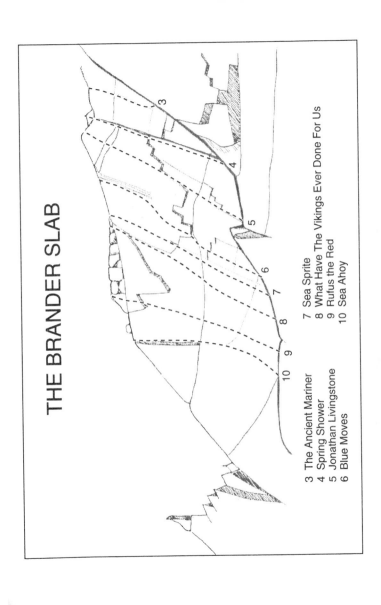

THE BRANDER SLAB

3 The Ancient Mariner
4 Spring Shower
5 Jonathan Livingstone
6 Blue Moves

7 Sea Sprite
8 What Have The Vikings Ever Done For Us
9 Rufus the Red
10 Sea Ahoy

11   The Skate   90m   Severe   (1970)
Climb a vegetated ramp until broken ground is reached. Follow this and trend right to the upper tier of rock. Finish up a chimney.

THE COCKLE SHELL FIN
This is the main fin, which has a distinctive nest-infested forked crack in its south face (Cockle Shell Cracks). The rock is much poorer in this area and although all the routes are described, some are repulsive and probably best avoided. These will be obvious! A few routes do have good climbing and would be greatly improved with more traffic. Descent is by a grassy gully to the north of the fin.

12   The Bat Crack   25m   Severe *   (1989)
Well up and left of Cockle Shell Cracks is a short wall with a left-slanting crack in its left side and a narrower parallel crack to the right. Scramble up grass and loose rock to the base of the wall. Climb the wide left-slanting crack.

13   The Buoy Wonder   25m   E1 5b *   (1989)
The thin crack 3 metres right of the Bat Crack can be reached via a short wall and a right-facing corner.

14   Carapus   60m   E1 4c   (1970)
A horror show! Climb the obvious chimney line right of the Skate; wellies and a gas mask might help.
Variation:
Climb the crack left of Carapus until progress is barred by an overhang. Move right and continue up the Carapus chimney.

15   Guano Corner   60m   E1 4c   (1981)
A wet suit might be useful for this one. Climb the slimy corner at the left end of the main wall. Avoid during periods of seismic activity.

The best descent from the next three routes is to traverse an exciting narrow ledge on the north face to the grassy gully.

16   The Twilight Hour   40m   E5 6a   (1989)
The impressive wall between Guano Corner and Cockle Shell Cracks gives some good climbing but is poorly protected and on dubious rock. Start from the boulder at the foot of Guano Corner. Climb straight up to a peg runner, move right and up to a large porthole, then go up to another peg and a couple of small but good wire placements. Go up and left through the bulge, then move up and diagonally left for 5m to a large flat hold. Continue up, keeping just left of loose cracks, to a 'thank God' ledge. Move right to finish up easier ground.

17   Cockle Shell Cracks   40m   Scottish VS   (1970)
Start in the middle of the wall and follow the crack system to where it splits. Take the left branch and climb past loose blocks to a ledge and easier ground.

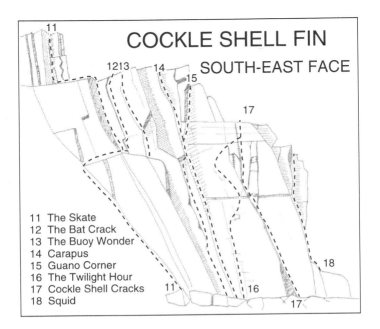

COCKLE SHELL FIN

SOUTH-EAST FACE

11 The Skate
12 The Bat Crack
13 The Buoy Wonder
14 Carapus
15 Guano Corner
16 The Twilight Hour
17 Cockle Shell Cracks
18 Squid

18 Squid 50m HVS 5a *   (1970)
A good route up the obvious corner on the seaward edge of the fin. Climb straight up the corner passing a large bulge (peg runner, crux) and ascend a chimney to reach the top.

LUCKY DAY WALL
The north face of Cockle Shell Fin is an impending black wall, split with crack lines and a long right-trending ramp. The climbs traverse off rightwards along the ledge that splits the face starting at two-thirds height, and which peters out at the grassy gully.

19 Sperm 20m Severe   (1970)
Another slime monster. Climb the chimney at the left end of the north face, if you must!

20 Seize the Day 20m E1 5b **   (1992)
The first crack line on the wall right of Sperm. Climb blocky cracks, taking the shorter left-hand finish to a ledge on the left. Finish up Sperm.

21   Lucky Day   30m   E3 5b   (1981)
A very serious route taking the right-trending diagonal ramp. Climb the ramp
(poor peg runner) and pull onto an obvious block with difficulty. Traverse right
on an overhung ledge, then climb a short ramp to a niche and the ledge above.
Traverse off.

22   Drop the Pilot   20m   E4 6a **   (1992)
Start up the slope from Lucky Day, below a large boulder. Climb the thin crack
line to an overlap. Move over this (crux) to the upper crack, then go left onto the
short ramp of Lucky Day and finish up this.

DAYGLO FIN
This is the small fin opposite Lucky Day Wall. The next three climbs are on the
south face.

23   Dayglo   20m   HVS 5b **   (1970)
Climb the superb long crack running diagonally leftwards up the face. A short
traverse left at mid-height leads to another crack and a groove leading to the top.

24   The Left-Hand Crack   15m   HVS 5a
Climb the cleaned crack right of Dayglo, finishing up the crest of the fin.

25   The Right-Hand Crack   12m   HVS 5a
Climb the shorter crack just to the right, to gain the crest.

26   Quasi's Back   12m   E3 6a **   (1983)
Climb the zigzag crack in the middle of the north face to a ledge. Follow the crest
to the top.

EMERALD FIN
The next fin to the north has a green and chossy south face and an impressively
blank overhanging north face.

27   Purve   50m   Scottish VS   (1970)
Take a confident partner, an ice axe and some valium then set off up the thin
seaward arete of the fin. If you reach the top, belay to a block at the end of the
crest or go up the slope to a peg and flake on the right.

28   The Voyage of the Mad Manxman   45m   E2 5c **   (1992)
This takes a thin crack line up the blank wall at the left end of the south face.
Start 2 metres right of the left-bounding corner. Climb up to a left-slanting break.
Move left and up to a thin left-trending crack, then go left and follow the main
crack line up the wall. At two-thirds height, make moves left to the crack
branching left. Follow this to good flake holds, then move left to a short thin crack
leading past a small niche to the top.

TEVIOTDALE

FATLIPS CRAG   *(Map Ref 581 207)*

This 30m sandstone crag is in beautifully wooded surroundings, prominently situated to the west of the A698 Hawick to Jedburgh road. The rock is fairly sound, and protection is adequate, but lichen can be a problem. The rock is rather broken except for a steep tower near its left end, and there are many groove lines of between Severe and VS which have been climbed but not recorded.

This crag can be found on OS sheet 73. Turn west at Denholm, cross the river Teviot, and turn immediately right along a minor road that passes under the crag. Follow this road past a small gate lodge, and 100 metres further on turn left onto a forest track with a wooden gate. Park here and follow a good path to Fatlips Castle. From the Castle, walk a few metres towards the river and descend a hidden stone staircase to reach paths which lead to a derelict wooden pavilion at the top of the crag. A gully on the right makes an easy descent.

Fatlips Corner   30m   VS   (1993)
This is the main corner immediately left of the steep tower, entered direct. An easier alternative traverses in from the groove on the left at 5m.

Who youse callin' Fatlips   30m   E1 5b   (1993)
A good sustained climb which takes the tower direct. The impending wall at the foot of the tower is broken on its right side by a short wide crack. Climb the crack with difficulty, then step up and left to a small ledge. Follow the obvious line above, moving slightly right, until awkward moves up and left surmount the final bulge. Follow the easy groove to the top, passing a large block with care.

List of First Ascents

The following list includes the information that we have been able to unearth from incomplete records. In some instances the details given are the first known ascent of routes which may have been climbed before. Further information for inclusion in the next edition of the guide is invited.

DUMBARTON

1571	1 Apr	The Beike	Thomas Crawford of Jordanhill and party
1963		Boulevard	N.MacNiven
1963		Frendo	B.Shields
1963		Stonefall Crack	N.MacNiven
1963		Stonefall Crack Direct	N.MacNiven, B.Shields
1963		Monsoon Gully	B.Shields, M.Connolly
1964		The Big Zipper	B.Shields, A.Baillie (aid)

FFA M.Hamilton. Direct Start freed by G.Latter, 1983

1964		The Neilweg	B.Shields, M.Connolly
1964		Angel's Pavement	N.MacNiven
1964		Chemin de Fer	N.MacNiven, B.Shields (aid)

FFA D.Cuthbertson, 1980

1964		Ganglion Grooves	K.Haggerty, B.Shields
1964		Grey Slab	B.Shields, M.Connolly
1964	2 Feb	Longbow	B.Shields, J.R.Houston (some aid)

FFA S.Belk, J.Dalrymple

1964		Nameless Crack	N.MacNiven
1964		Poison Ivy	B.Shields
1964	19 Feb	Windjammer Crack	B.Shields, J.R.Houston
1965		Old Socks	B.Shields
1965		Requiem	B.Shields, M.Connolly (aid)

FFA D.Cuthbertson, climbed over several weeks in summer 1983

1965		West Face Gully	B.Shields and others
1965		Route Three	B.Shields, K.Haggerty
1960s		Alleyway	N.MacNiven
		Hailstone Climb	M.Connolly
		Left Edge Route	I.Nicolson
		Plunge	L.Mitchell
		West Face Girdle	B.Shields, M.Connolly
1974	Mar	Cyclops	B.Shields, K.Haggerty (aid)

FFA D.Cuthbertson, 1981

1970s		Banana Rib	I.Fulton
		Banana Groove	I.Nicolson, R.McFarlane
		Left Edge Route	I.Nicolson
		Bobtail	S.Belk, J.Dalrymple
		Rag	I.Nicolson

1970s		Sunset Groove	I.Fulton, I.Nicolson
		Tag	I.Nicolson, R.McFarlane
		Desperado	B.Shields
		Ciamar a tha Sibh	A.Kelso
		Snowwhite	A.Kelso (some aid). FFA W.Todd
		Fever Pitch	N.Colton
		Rough Sea	K.Johnstone
		Gaucho	W.Todd
		Slainte	K.Johnstone
		Drizzle	K.Johnstone
		Antigrav	K.Johnstone (2PA). FFA W.Todd
1980		Woops	D.Cuthbertson
1980		Datura	R.Kerr
1981		Big Ears	G.Latter, T.Prentice
1983	1 Mar	Requiem Direct Start	B.Masterton, A.Wren
1983	20 Mar	Rock of Ages	G.Latter
1983		Grey Wall	G.Latter
1984		Rising Power	G.Latter
1984		Samora	G.Latter
1988	May	Supple as a Brick	T.Prentice, R.Everett, S.Richardson
1993		Omerta	A.Gallagher
1993		Appliance of Violence	B.McLaughlan
1993		Bad Attitude	A.Gallagher
1993		Half Breed	C.Phair
1993		Unforgiven	A.Gallagher

DUNGLAS

1975	6 May	Skirmish	J.Mackenzie, B.Clarke
1975	11 May	Downfall	J.Mackenzie, C.Garthwaite
1975	11 May	Dunglas Corner	J.Mackenzie, C.Garthwaite
1975	11 May	Joker's Groove	C.Garthwaite, J.Mackenzie
1975	15 May	Curioser and Curioser	J.Mackenzie, C.Garthwaite
1975	7 Jun	The Ramp	J.Mackenzie
1975	13 Jul	The Cross	J.Mackenzie, M.Astbury, G.Rooney
		Top-roped and cleaned some weeks before	
1975	14 Sep	Little Gripper	J.Mackenzie
1976	15 Apr	Pullover	J.Mackenzie, D.Nicholson
1976	24 Apr	The Gentle Touch	J.Mackenzie, B.Clarke
1976	3 May	A Dream of Brown Trousers	J.Kerry, J.Mackenzie (both solo)
1976	3 May	Last Grasp	J.Mackenzie (solo)
1976	Summer	North-East Arete	J Mackenzie
		Top-roped in 1975 before being led	
1976	7 Jun	Moss Flop	J.Mackenzie
1976	3 Jul	The Nightmare	J.Mackenzie (solo with back rope)

| 1976 | 12 Jul | A Feet of Arms | J.Mackenzie, N.Tennent |
| 1977 | 13 Jul | Wall of Horrors | J.Mackenzie, C.Garthwaite |

Top-roped three days before being led

1977	6 Aug	Ribbish	J.Mackenzie (solo)
1977	6 Aug	Rubbish	J.Mackenzie (solo)
1982	21 Jan	Overlord	G.Little, A.Savage (1PA)

FFA P.Linning, G.Little, 7 Jul 1983

1987	10 Aug	Deviant	S.Richardson, T.Prentice
1987	10 Aug	Bite them Bequerels	T.Prentice, S.Richardson
1989	2 Jul	The Beef Monster	B.Kerr, G.McIntyre
1991	Jun	Steel Finger	G.Dudley
1992	Aug	Negotiations with Isaac	A.Gallagher
1992	Aug	Political Legacy	A.Gallagher
1992	Aug	Airhead	C.Phair

THE WHANGIE

The first ascent details of most of the routes here have been lost in the mists of time. However, the perpetrators of one modern route have owned up:

| 1985 | 30 Jul | Sudden Death | S.Richardson, M.Fowler |

A free ascent of Slim Crack.

SLACKDHU

Pre-1939		Pinnacle Arete, Jenny's Lum Arete
1992	Spring	Tendons
1992	Spring	Blocker
1992	Spring	Moss Kills
1992	Spring	Classic Crack

All the routes recorded in 1992 were climbed by A.Coon and D.Adams, although it is almost certain that they had been climbed previously.

AUCHINSTARRY QUARRY

1975		Mascarade	K.Johnsone, D.Benn
1975	Nov	Gold Rush	J.F.Kerry, S.N.Smith
1976	Jun	Promontory Direct	J.F.Kerry, H.P.Reader
1976	Sep	Spirogyra	J.F.Kerry, D.McCallum
1976	Oct	Whiplash	J.F.Kerry, H.P.Reader, P.Greenwell
1976	Oct	Kelvin Way	H.P.Reader, J.F.Kerry, P.Greenwell
1976	Oct	Short Reach	P.Greenwell, H.P.Reader
1976	Oct	Fool's Gold	J.F.Kerry, D.McCallum, P.Greenwell
1976	Nov	Urea	H.P.Reader, J.F.Kerry
1976		Tar	C.Ogilvie, H.P.Reader
1976		Maypole	K.Johnsone, D.Benn

The direct was added in 1978 by R.Kerr

1976		Christmas Corner	K.Johnstone, B.Swan
1977	Feb	Lion	J.F.Kerry, H.P.Reader

Reclimbed after partial demolition by R.Everett, D.Gaffney 25 Sept 1993

1977	Mar	Talisman	J.F.Kerry, H.P.Reader
1977	Mar	Lion Cub	D.Sanderson
1977	Mar	Pigeon Hole	J.F.Kerry, R.Kerr
1977	Apr	Separated Edge	J.F.Kerry, C.Macadam
1977	Jul	White Slab	K.McKluskie
1977	Jul	Trundle	K.Johnstone, B.Swan
1977	Sep	Red Lead	J.F.Kerry, F.Yeoman
1977	Sep	Cracked Arete	J.F.Kerry, P.Greenwell
1977	Oct	Scream	R.Kerr, A.Campbell
1977	Oct	Discord	J.F.Kerry, R.Kerr
1977	Oct	Knock Back	J.F.Kerry, N.Macfadyen
1977	Oct	After the Gold Rush	W.Todd
1977	Nov	Caftan, Bazaar	J.F.Kerry, H.P.Reader
1977		Slinky Lizard	D.Benn, D.McCallum
1978	Jun	Newcastle Brown	J.F.Kerry, R.Kerr
1978		Soft Machine	R.Kerr
1979	Sep	Power Play	R.Kerr, A.Colville
1980		Green Onion, Mr. Men	R.Kerr
1980		I Spy	N.Morrison, A.Kay
1980		Think of England	W.Todd, K.Johnstone
1980		Walk on the Wild Side	R.Kerr
1980		Midas Touch	M.Putnam
1981	Aug	BC's Return	S.Taylor, R.Kerr
1981		Southern Man	R.Kerr, S.Taylor
1982		Nijinski	D.Cuthbertson

Climbed previously with side runners by W.Todd

1983	Feb	Dream Machine	J.Handren, J.Melrose
1980s		Blade Runner	J.Handren
1980s		Death is the Hunter	J.Handren, D.McCallum
1980s		Carouselambra	G.Latter
1980s		Surface Tension	D.McCallum

The top part was straightened out by C.Gilchrist in 1986

1980s		High Dive	C.Dale
1986	May	Shot in the Dark	T.Prentice, J.Christie
1986	May	Band Aid	T.Prentice, P.McAra
1986	May	Race Against Time	J.Christie, T.Prentice
1986	Jun	Both Toes Burning	T.Prentice, R.Everett
1986	Jun	The Color Purple	T.Prentice, P.McAra
1986	Jul	Red Snapper	J.Christie, T.Prentice
1988	26 Sep	The Gold Bug	I.Taylor, J.Nairn
1989	1 Apr	Promontory Runner	R.Anderson, K.Spence
1990	24 May	Harry Goes West	G.MacIntyre, T.Gould, J.Sime

1990	27 May	Hopelessly Treading Water	G.MacIntyre
1990	31 Jul	Spanking the Rustbucket	G.MacIntyre
1992	May	The Surf Shack	A.Gallagher
1992	28 May	The Seven Year Plan	I.Taylor, S.Munro
1992	Jun	Twilight Zone	A.Gallagher
1993	May	In Through the Out Door	G.Harrison, J.Thompson
1993	25 Sep	Glass	R.Everett, D.Gaffney

Probably climbed before.

COWDEN HILL QUARRY

1976	28 Feb	Ladybird	J.Kerry, K.Johnstone
1976	Oct	Lorraine	J.Kerry, P.Greenwell
1976	16 Oct	D-Day	J.Kerry, P.Greenwell
1976	17 Oct	Hole in the Wall	K.Johnstone
1976		Newton Blues	J.Kerry, H.Reader (AL)
1977	29 Jan	Ostrich	P.Greenwell, J.Kerry
1986		Narita	G.Latter
1992	18 Aug	Earth Summit	M.Garthwaite, A.Wren

CASHEL QUARRY

| 1989 | Sep | Polly | J.Taylor, A.Coon |
| 1991 | 16 May | Heel Hooker | J.Nairn (solo after top-rope) |

CREAGAN AN AMAIR GHLAIS

| 1991 | Jun | Sarsaparilla | G.Dudley |
| 1992 | May | Root Beer | G.Dudley, C.Dudley |

ACHRAY WALL

| 1983 | 25 Jun | The Bow | G.Little |
| 1983 | 14 Aug | The Arrow | G.Little, P Linning |

BEN AN

1896	21 May	Left-Hand Gully	G.Thomson, H.C.Boyd, Rev A.Boyd
1898	1 Jan	Right-Hand Gully	W.W.Naismith, W.Douglas, J.Maclay
1898	22 Jan	Oblique Crack	H.Raeburn, J.Napier
1930		Ash Wall	W.White
1930		The Last Eighty	J.B.Nimlin
1934		The Rent	J.B.Nimlin
1937		Birch Wall	J.B.Nimlin
1970		Coriander	K.V.Crocket, K.Simpson

1985   31 Jul   Tricky Vicky   G.Suzca, J.Parker

CARN NA MUICE

1987   22 Jul   Sallochy Slab   K.Black, N.Milton
1987   22 Jul   Sunset Ridge   N.Milton, K.Black
1987   2 Sep   Twilight Slab   N.Milton, S.Richardson
       K.Black and N.Milton climbed the top section, 22 July 1987
1987   2 Sep   The Bat Flake   S.Richardson, N.Milton
1990   Mar   The Drag   J.Taylor
1991   1 Jun   Bite The Dust   J.Taylor
1991   7 Jun   Brimbles   A.Coon, J.Taylor

ROSS POINT

1986   May   Crystal Junction   J.Christie, A.Kirk
1987   May   One Way Trip   J.Christie, A.Leary
1987   May   Slug Death   J.Christie, A.Leary
1989   Jul   Forked Lightning   S.Robinson, K.Lawson
1991   16 May   Son of Cog   I.Taylor, J.Nairn
1991   Pullover   J.Taylor, A.Coon
1991   Legover   J.Taylor, A.Benson, P.Benson

LEUM AN EIREANNAICH

1899   27 Feb   South Crack   W.Inglis Clark, J.Gall Inglis
       All other routes by T.Low of the Ochils Mountaineering Club.

CREAGAN TOM DUBH

1986   4 Oct   Athena   S.Yates, F.Mains, D.Gardner
1986   4 Oct   Perfect Strangers   S.Yates
1986   4 Oct   Crazy Cow   S.Yates, F.Mains
1989   30 Apr   Sequestrator   S.Richardson, R.Reid
1989   7 May   Mahabharata   R.Reid, S.Richardson

LOUDOUN HILL

1930s   Pulpit Arete, Left Crack   R.Anderson, D.Scott
1930s   Jackdaw Chimney   R.Anderson, D.Scott
1930s   Foxglove Chimney   R.Anderson, D.Scott
1930s   Dusk Route   R.Anderson, D.Scott
1960s   Pulpit Chimney   J.R.Jackson, D.W.Young
1060s   Lunge, Cling   J.R.Jackson
1960s   Amphitheatre Arete   J.R.Jackson
1960s   Mantelshelf Wall   J.R.Jackson
1960s   Conclusion Wall   J.R.Jackson, J.Clelland

1960s		Shattered Corner	J.R.Jackson, D.W.Young
1960s		Epitaph	D.W.Young
1960s		Epitaph Variation	J.R.Jackson, D.W.Young
		FFA: 1974 R.Sandilands, D.Pratt	
1960s		Coffin Chimney, Ring	J.R.Jackson
1960s		Trench Direct	D.W.Young
1960s		Contortion Groove	J.R.Jackson
1960s		Sadist's Groove	J.R.Jackson, B.Dale
1960s		Tottering Layback	J.R.Jackson
1960s		Dee's Crack	J.R.Jackson, K.Bryan
1960s		Strife	J.R.Jackson, D.W.Young
1960s		Evening Groove	J.R.Jackson, B.Dale
1960s		Slab and Groove	J.R.Jackson, B.Dale
1960s		Cave Crack	J.R.Jackson, D.W.Young
1978		Slings	K.McClusky, R.Sandilands (FFA)
1978		Senile Slab	K.McClusky, R.Sandilands
1981		Chalkster	A.Taylor, K.McClusky
1993	19 May	Quick Skive	T.Prentice
1993	24 May	Busman's Holiday	T.Prentice

MAUCHLINE

1979/80		The Chimney	A.Watson, J.Wilson
1986		Purism Personified	S.Lampard (solo)
1986		Bowman's Corner	S.Lampard (solo)
1986		Gardener's Corner	S.Lampard, J.Lampard
1986		Dredge Boy	S.Lampard (solo)
1986		Monsterously Horrible	S.Lampard, J.Freeman, I.Rooney
1986		Corner Root	S.Lampard (solo)
1986		The Arete	S.Lampard (solo)
1987		Board Walk	S.Lampard (solo)
1987		Y Bother	S.Lampard (solo)
1987		Bye Eck	S.Lampard (solo)
1987		Green Machine	S.Lampard (solo)
1988		Bridge Over Troubled Water	S.Lampard
1988	Jun	Ayrheid	T.Prentice, Bish McAra
1988	Jun	Games of Chance and Sandancing	T.Prentice, R.Everett
1989		Bushwhacker	S.Lampard, C.Stenhouse
1989		Lightning Crack	S.Lampard, M.Reed

GLEN AFTON

1977	Grass Roots	G.Little
	Direct start,1990, S.Lampard (solo)	

1977		Rehabilitation Route	G.Little
1978		Two Plus Two	G.Little
1978		Deception Slab	G.Little
1978		Raven Slab	G.Little
1991	31 Jul	The Crack of Doon	S.Lampard, A.Fraser
1992	24 Jun	Midnight Express	R.McAllister, A.Fraser, D.McGimpsey
1992	7 Jul	Stone Circle	R.McAllister, D.McGimpsey
1992	10 Jul	Hyacinth House	R.McAllister, D.McGimpsey
1992	19 Jul	Magic Carpet	A.Fraser, R.McAllister
1992	21 Jul	Sweet Liberty	R.McAllister
1992	24 Aug	Delirium	R.McAllister, D.McGimpsey

One poor nut placed on abseil and removed after the ascent.
Direct Start, R.McAllister 17 Sept 1992

MULLWHARCHAR

1992	4 Mar	The Gullet	D.McGimpsey, S.Ravey
1992	14 Jun	The Raiders	A.Fraser, D.McGimpsey
1992	17 Jun	Bugle	D.McGimpsey, W.Cartner
1992	17 Jun	Switchback	D.McGimpsey, W.Cartner
1992	21 Jun	Solstice	S.Lampard, G.Scott
1992	21 Jun	The Dungeonmaster	A.Fraser, J.Dickson
1992	21 Jun	Behind the Mask	R.McAllister, D.McGimpsey
1992	21 Jun	Kid's Stuff	J.Dickson, A.Fraser
1992	21 Jun	The Nose	S.Lampard (solo)

CRAIGENCALLIE

1977	9 Aug	Cranium Edge	G.Little
1977	9 Aug	Deviator	G.Little
1977	18 Aug	Eliminator	G.Little
1984		The Cry	A.Plumb
1984		The Shout, The Scream	A.Plumb, S.Aird
1984		Secret Garden	A.Plumb, S.Aird
1985		Talk To The Wind	S.Aird, A.Plumb
1985		Walkabout	A.Plumb, S.Aird
1985		Raven Seek thy Brother	A.Plumb, S.Aird
1991	16 Apr	Alligator	A.Fraser, R.McAllister.

Direct start D.McGimpsey, G.Gerrard 8 Aug 1992

1991	16 Apr	Decaffenator	R.McAllister (solo)
1992	18 Oct	Across the Barricades	A.Fraser, D.McGimpsey, R.McAllister
1993	Apr	Thumbs up	A.Scougall, A.Plumb
1993	8 Jun	Tree Sanctuary	M.Reed, A.Fraser, J.Freeman, R.McAllister
1993	8 Jun	The Grey Man	A.Fraser, D.Gibson, R.McAllister
1993	Jun	Delta of Venus	D.Gibson, R.McAllister, M.Reed

DUNGEON HILL

1955	Sept	Cooran Buttress	J.Simpson, Miss J.Ratcliffe
1968	12 Apr	Highway Man	G.Little, J.Dykes.

The route was climbed but unrecorded and unnamed. Named by J.Fotheringham and P.Whillance on second ascent in 1982. Various other shorter routes in the area were done by G.Little.

1978	May	Roriama	A.Fraser, W.Todd, M.Burgess, D.Walker
1982	Jul	Cyclopath	J.Fotheringham, P.Whillance
1982	Jul	Saddle Tramp	J.Fotheringham, P.Whillance
1984	10 Jun	Traitor's Gait	A.Fraser (solo)
1991	24 Apr	Galloway Grooves	S.Reid, J.Grinbergs
1991	24 Apr	Carrick Corner	S.Reid, J.Grinbergs
1991	24 Apr	Scots Wha' Hae	S.Reid, J.Grinbergs
1991	24 Apr	Battle Axe	J.Grinbergs, S.Reid
1991	5 May	The Colonel's Corner	S.Reid, J.Grinbergs (AL)
1991	12 May	Bruce's Stone	S.Reid, J.Grinbergs
1991	12 May	Comyn Corner	J.Grinbergs, S.Reid
1991	17 Jul	Heir Apparent	S.Reid, J.Grinbergs (AL)

Direct Finish climbed on same day. Top-roped before leading.

1991	20 Aug	Incy Wincy Spider	S.Reid, J.Grinbergs

Named after interesting ropework on early attempts.

1991	20 Aug	Bannockburn	J.Grinbergs, S.Reid
1991	20 Aug	Hammer of the Scots	S.Reid, J.Grinbergs
1991	29 Aug	Monkey Puzzle	D.Wilson, S.Reid (AL)
1991	3 Sep	English Gold	S.Reid, D.Wilson (AL), W.O'Connor
1991	3 Sep	Parcel of Rogues	D.Wilson, W.O'Connor, S.Reid
1991	10 Sep	Free Land	S.Reid, W.Freeland (AL)
1993	9 Jun	Cooran Chimney	S.Reid, D,Scott

CRAIGNELDER AND THE GALLOWAY HILLS

1978	Apr	The Original Route	A.Fraser, M.Burgess, W.Todd
1984	18 Jun	Gloom	A.Fraser, D.Walker

Direct and Super Direct finishes by J.Campbell, A.Moore and S.Reid, May 19 1992

1984	18 Jun	Pale Face	A.Fraser, D.Walker
1991	Sep	Kerb Crawler	J.Biggar, L.Biggar
1992	14 May	The Flesh Market	S.Reid, J.Campbell
1992	14 May	Elite Pinnacle Rib	S.Reid (solo)
1992	14 May	Guledig	S.Reid, J.Campbell
1992	14 May	Gwry Y Gogledd	S.Reid, J.Campbell
1992	14 May	No Hawkers or Campbells	S.Reid, J.Campbell
1993	31 Dec	Interstellar Overdraft	R.McAllister, S.Mearns

| 1994 | 16 Jan | Silver Flow | S.Lampard, J.Thompson |

CLINTS OF DROMORE

| 1978 | May | Central Buttress | A.Fraser, K.Donaldson, A.Carmichael |
| 1991 | 25 Aug | The Spanish Inquisition | A.Fraser, R.McAllister |

CLIFTON

1975		Hollowstones Chimney	D.Gibson, A.Fraser
1976		Novice Crack	C.Macadam, D.Gibson, A.Fraser
1977		Jugular Vein	C.Macadam, G.Macadam
1977		Wall Street	C.Macadam, G.Macadam
1978		The Arete	C.Macadam
1979		Lemur	C.Macadam
1979		Fingerlust	C.Macadam
1984		Toddamundo	C.Macadam
1984		Beyond The Terminator	D.Austin

THIRLSTANE

Most of the routes inside the cave were done by C.Macadam 1976-85. The outer routes are all quite old.

1981	Jul	Goodnight Irene	C.Macadam (solo)
1984/85		Overhanging Crack	D.Gibson
1990		Thank You Irene	D.Gibson (solo)

MEIKLE ROSS

1972	22 Apr	Rift Route	W.Cheverst, R.Scoltock, C.Dickinson
1972	22 Apr	Limehouse Blues	W.Cheverst, C.Dickinson
1972	22 Apr	Access Ridge	W.Cheverst, R.Scoltock, C.Dickinson
1972	28 May	K.9.	W.Cheverst, J.Cottingham, C.Dickinson
1973	23 Apr	Yellow Dog	C.Dickinson, W.Cheverst (AL)
1973	23 Apr	Dogwalk	C.Dickinson, R.Scoltock
1975		Clockwork Orange	J.Kerry (probably)
1975		Crack and Corner	J.Kerry (probably)
1975		Curving Arete	J.Kerry (probably)
1975		Exit Groove	J.Kerry (probably)
1975		Orange Chimney	J.Kerry (probably)
1975		Pigeon Chimney	J.Kerry (probably)
1975		Promontory Wall	J.Kerry (probably)
1975	31 Mar	Mellow Yellow	J.Kerry, F.Craddock
1975	31 Mar	Stepped Corner	F.Craddock, J.Kerry
1975	31 Mar	Salty Dog	J.Kerry, F.Craddock
1975	6 Apr	Amnesia	B.Shields, G.Hamilton, J.Kerry

1975	6 Apr	Left Corner	B.Shields, G.Hamilton, J.Kerry
1975	26 Apr	Galloway Corner	J.Kerry, J.Mackenzie
1975	26 Sep	Crack Track	J.Kerry, K.Johnstone
1975	6 Dec	Side Track	J.Kerry, G.Todd
1975	7 Dec	Headcase	J.Kerry, G.Todd
1975/77		White Out	J.Kerry (probably)
1975/77		Groovey	J.Kerry (probably)
1976		Sorcerer's Apprentice	K.Johnstone, D.Benn
1976	Jan	Right Corner	J.Kerry, G.Todd
1976	Jan	Bloody Crack	J.Kerry, G.Todd
1976	Jan	Green Wall	J.Kerry, G.Todd
1976	17 Jan	Ken's Groove	K.Johnstone, D.Benn
1976	31 Jan	Tinman	D.Mullen, H.Reader
1976	Feb	Blue Finger	K.Johnstone, D.McCallum.

Originally included what is now the first pitch of Maple Leaf Rag, climbed by J.Kerry and C.Macadam in Sept 1977.

1976	1 Feb	Coffin Crack	J.Kerry, G.Todd
1976	1 Feb	Dolphin Groove	J.Kerry, G.Todd
1977		The Battle of Osfrontalis	C.Macadam, G.Macadam
1977		Pinking Sheer	C.Macadam, G.Macadam
1977		Seadog	J.Kerry, H.Reader
1977		Dogleg	C.Macadam, G.Macadam
1977	17 May	Back Track	J.Kerry, H.Reader
1978		Grand Central Couloir. Bottom section, climbers unknown.

Upper section, W.Todd, C.Macadam 1983/84

1978	Sep	Route One	W.Todd, G.Macadam
1978	Oct	Maple Leaf Rag	C.Macadam, N.MacFadyen (2nd pitch only)
1978	Oct	Finesse	C.Macadam, R.Souter, N.Cockburn
1978	17 Dec	Accutrac	C.Macadam, E.Todd
1978-80		Akela	C.Macadam
1978-80		Argus	C.Macadam
1979	Aug	Steve's Route	S.Bartlett (solo)
1979	Aug	A Walk on the Wild Side	C.Macadam, S.Bartlett
1979	Aug	Dolce Vita	C.Macadam, D.Lampard
1979	Aug	Scared to Dance	C.Macadam, S.Bartlett
1979		Cairn's Cream	C.Macadam, J.Gerrard
1979	30 Sep	Mental Block	C.Macadam, A.Fraser, W.Todd
1979	30 Sep	Fil d'Or	C.Macadam
1980	6 Sep	Compulsion	C.Macadam, A.Fraser
1981	29 Mar	Zugsfang	C.Macadam, D.Austin
1981	23 Jun	Bad Medicine Waltz	C.Macadam, A.Fraser, E.Kellar
1981	6 Sep	A Sop for Cerberus	C.Macadam, G.Macadam
1981	6 Sep	Route Three	A.Fraser, W.Todd
1981	6 Sep	Eminence Grise	C.Macadam, G.Macadam
1981	6 Sep	Avernal Buttress	C.Macadam (solo)

1982	6 Apr	Blistering Barnacles	A.Fraser, E.Kellor, D.Gibson
1982	11 Apr	Marie Celeste	A.Fraser, G.Macadam
1982	20 May	Titan's Corner	A.Fraser, M.Whitford
1982	20 Jun	Poison Ivy	A.Fraser, W.Todd (solo)
1982	20 Jun	Barnacle Bill	A.Fraser, W.Todd
1982	15 Sep	Bumper Dumper	D.Austin, A.Fraser, D.Gibson, W.Todd
1982	18 Sep	The Moosetrap	A.Fraser, R.Webb
1983/84		Route Two	C.Macadam (solo)
1983/84		Demolition Tango	C.Macadam, W.Todd
1984		Corridor of Power	D.Austin, C.Macadam
1984		Sunshine Superman	C.Macadam
1984/85		Shark's Tooth	C.Macadam, S.Steer, D.Gibson
1984/85		Fats Waller	C.Macadam, S.Steer, D.Gibson
1984/85		Alligator Crawl	C.Macadam, S.Steer, D.Gibson
1987	11 Apr	Pinko-Subversive	A.Fraser, C.Robb
1987	27 Sep	Grapeshot	A.Wilson, S.Jackson
1988	4 Apr	Meikle Gorbachov	A.Fraser, G.Robb
1990	1 Apr	Old Zawn	A.Caren, I.Taylor
1990	1 Apr	Evens	A.Caren, I.Taylor
1991	21 Aug	Manic Nirvana	R.McAllister, A.Fraser
1991	25 Aug	Ancient Mariner	R.McAllister, A.Fraser

BURROW HEAD

1980	Jan	Conquistador	C.Macadam, D.Lampard
1980	Jan	Bright Eyes	C.Macadam, D.Lampard
1980	26 Jul	Watership Down	C.Macadam, A.Fraser
1980	15 Aug	Flensing Knife	C.Macadam, A.Fraser
1980	16 Aug	Prometheus (on his crag)	C.Macadam, A.Fraser
1980	16 Aug	Yellow Crack	C.Macadam, A.Fraser
1980	16 Aug	Naked Fun	C.Macadam, A.Fraser
1980	17 Aug	Guardian Angel	C.Macadam, A.Fraser
1980	23 Aug	Run Rabbit Run	C.Macadam, A.Fraser
1980	23 Sep	Devil's Daughter	C.Macadam, A.Fraser
1980	23 Sep	Mephistopheles	C.Macadam, A.Fraser
1980	24 Sep	The Python	A.Fraser, G.Macadam
1980	24 Sep	The Fin	C.Macadam, A.Fraser
1980	24 Sep	The Cutter	C.Macadam, A.Fraser
1980		The Cut	C.Macadam, G.Macadam
1981	5 Apr	Lemming's Wall	D.Austin, G.Macadam, W. Todd, D.Todd, D.Gibson
1981	5 Apr	Boozer's Chimney	A.Fraser, G.Macadam
1981	5 Apr	The Newt	W.Todd
1981	7 Aug	The Beastie	C.Macadam, A.Fraser
1981	7 Aug	Waiting for Godot	C.Macadam, A.Fraser

1981		Mirror, Mirror	I.Duckworth, C.Macadam
1981		The Changeling	C.Macadam (solo)
1981		Wild Horses	C.Macadam
1982	21 Jun	Adventures in the Skin Trade	C.Macadam, A.Fraser
1991	14 Aug	Goblin's Eyes	A.Fraser, R.McAllister
1991	14 Aug	Killer on the Loose	R.McAllister, A.Fraser

MONREITH

1987	15 May	Do Barnacles Bite	F.Stevenson, A.Long
1987	15 May	Soup Dragon	F.Stevenson (solo)
1987	15 May	Stingray	F.Stevenson (solo)
1987	15 May	Hack Crack	F.Stevenson (solo)
1987	16 May	Fireball XL 1.5	F.Stevenson (solo)
1987	16 May	Mobile-Kack	F.Stevenson (solo)
1987	7 Aug	Jelly Fish	F.Stevenson (solo)
1987	9 Aug	Mobile-Bar	F.Stevenson (solo)
1987	30 Aug	Satori	F.Stevenson
1987	5 Sep	The Big Dig	S.Smith, F.Stevenson (alts)

GARHEUGH POINT

1985		Two Tyred	A.Greig
1985		Deathwish	A.Greig
1985		Secrets of the Coast	A.Plumb, S.Aird
1987	Apr	Battle of the Bulge	D.Gibson
1987	1 Aug	Snailey-Whaley	F.Stevenson, A.Smith, B.Davison, J.Vlasto
1987	1 Aug	Flubb	A.Smith, J.Vlasto, F.Stevenson
1987	10 Aug	The E-6 Process	F.Stevenson
1987	3 Sep	Smuggler's Grill	F.Stevenson (solo)
1987	3 Sep	Landmark	F.Stevenson (solo)
1987	3 Sep	Cash n'Carry	F.Stevenson (solo)
1993	May	T Bone	A.Scougall, A.Plumb

ROADSIDE CRAG

All routes by S.Aird and A.Plumb, 1985/86

PORTOBELLO

1987	Spring	Crawford's Crackers	C.Rice, T.Prentice, R.Webb
1987	Spring	Happy Man	R.Webb, C.Rice
1987	Spring	The Man from Del Monte	T.Prentice
1987	Spring	Thunderbolt	C.Rice, T.Prentice, R.Webb
1987	Spring	Only Monsters	R.Webb, T.Prentice, C.Rice

1987	Summer	Floating Voter	S.Richardson, T.Prentice
1987	Summer	Blockhead	S.Richardson (solo)
1989	9 Dec	Puffin Nuffin	A.Fraser, J.Thomson
1989	9 Dec	Sanity Claus	A.Fraser, J.Thomson
1989	9 Dec	Riverboat Gambler	A.Fraser, J.Thomson
1989	9 Dec	Surfin' Safari	A.Fraser, J.Thomson
1989	9 Dec	Warsteiner	J.Thomson, A.Fraser
1990	18 Mar	Basking up the Wrong Tree	J.Dickson, A.Fraser
1990	18 Mar	Cutty Shark	A.Fraser, J.Dickson
1990	4 Apr	Speed Limpets	A.Fraser, J.Thomson.

Named after a speeding ticket and Lampard's broken ankle.

1990	4 Apr	Dead Sea Strolls	A.Fraser, J.Thomson
1990	17 Jul	Feeling the Pinch	R.McAllister, A.Fraser
1990	17 Jul	The Zombie	A.Fraser, R.McAllister
1990	31 Jul	Aqua Vitae	R.McAllister, A.Fraser
1990	31 Jul	Shellfish Bastard	A.Fraser, R.McAllister
1990	31 Jul	Cockle Sucker	R.McAllister, A.Fraser
1990	31 Jul	Mussel Bound	A.Fraser, R.McAllister
1990	21 Oct	Parallel Lines	A.Fraser, S.Lampard
1990	21 Oct	Hanging Duck	S.Lampard. A.Fraser
1990	21 Oct	Return of the Limpet	S.Lampard, A.Fraser

The broken ankle healed.

1990	21 Oct	Count Duckula	A.Fraser, S.Lampard
1991	3 Jul	The Water Margin	A.Fraser, R.McAllister
1991	17 Jul	The Cruel Seaside	R.McAllister
1991	7 Aug	The Ducking Stool	A.Fraser, J.Thomson
1992	29 Mar	Soul Kitchen	R.McAllister, A.Fraser
1992	10 May	Bootless	S.Lampard, J.Blyth
1992	13 May	Basic Instinct	M.Reed, A.Fraser, D.McGimpsey
1992	13 May	Winklepicker	M.Reed, A.Fraser, D.McGimpsey
1992	13 May	Silence of the Clams	A.Fraser, M.Reed, D.McGimpsey
1992	26 Jun	Acid Test	R.McAllister
1992	2 Jul	Pushed to the Limit	R.McAllister, A.Fraser, D.McGimpsey
1992	9 Jul	St Elmo's Fire	A.Fraser, R.McAllister, D.McGimpsey
1992	9 Jul	Ramplet	D.McGimpsey, A.Fraser, R.McAllister
1992	9 Jul	Critical Mass	R.McAllister, A.Fraser, D.McGimpsey
1992	1 Oct	Figget's Rest	D.McGimpsey, S.Figgit, R.McAllister
1993	26 Apr	Water Dance	R.McAllister, M.Reed
1993	8 May	Betty Blue	K.McClusky, R.McAllister
1993	9 May	Sweaty Trembler	R.McAllister
1993	20 May	Underling	M.Reed, A.Fraser, R.McAllister
1993	20 May	The Crayfish Twins	A.Fráser, M.Reed
1993	22 May	Dances with Mackerel	R.McAllister, K.McClusky
1993	12 Jul	Changeling	R.McAllister, M.Reed, K.McClusky
1993	14 Jul	Lost at Sea	R.McAllister, A.Fraser

| 1993 | 14 Jul | Horse Latitudes | R.McAllister, A.Fraser |
| 1993 | Aug | The Waster | M.Reed |

First lead without pre-placed runners: R.McAllister, S.Mearns, 4 Sep 1993

| 1993 | 5 Dec | Another.One Bites The Dust | M.McConnell, R.McAllister |

JUPITER ROCK AND KILN O' THE FUFFOCK

1993	18 Feb	Rock Lobster	R.McAllister, M.Reed, A.Fraser, D.McGimpsey
1993	18 Feb	Penguin Parade	A.Fraser, D.McGimpsey
1993	5 May	The Beauty of Flight	M.Reed, R.McAllister
1993	5 May	Bridg it	M.Reed
1993	16 Oct	Saturation Point	R.McAllister, G.Borland
1993	17 Oct	Body Swerve	S.Mearns, R.McAllister
1993	18 Oct	Burning the Boats	R.McAllister, A.Fraser
1993	18 Oct	The Pincer, Sea Fowl	R.McAllister, A.Fraser
1993	21 Oct	Echo Beach	R.McAllister, S.Mearns
1993	26 Oct	Total Immersion	R.McAllister, S.Muir
1993	28 Oct	Arc of a Diver	A.Fraser, R.McAllister
1993	28 Oct	Abide With Me	R.McAllister, A.Fraser, S.Muir
1993	28 Oct	Point Break	S.Muir, R.McAllister, A.Fraser
1993	28 Oct	Seaside Buddies	S.Muir, S.Mearns
1993	28 Oct	Water Wings	S.Mearns, S.Muir
1993	31 Oct	Breakaway	G.Borland, D.McGimpsey, A.Fraser
1993	31 Oct	Spirit Level	A.Fraser, G.Borland, D.McGimpsey
1993	31 Oct	The Bends, The Bends	R.McAllister, M.Reed, D.McGimpsey, A.Fraser, G.Borland

MONEY HEAD

1992	22 Apr	Ecu Wall	A.Fraser, R.McAllister
1992	22 Apr	Slot Machine	R.McAllister, A.Fraser
1992	22 Apr	Pay Day	R.McAllister (solo)
1992	1 May	Filthy Lucre	R.McAllister, A.Fraser
1992	1 May	Pot of Gold	R.McAllister, A.Fraser
1992	1 May	Rainbow's End	R.McAllister, A.Fraser
1992	1 May	Insider Dealing	A.Fraser, R.McAllister
1992	14 Jun	The Liquidator	A.Fraser, K.Douglas
1992	14 Jun	The Root of All Evil	R.McAllister, A.Fraser
1992	14 Jun	Bolivars	J.Thompson, D.McGimpsey
1992	14 Jun	Free Enterprise	R.McAllister, D.McGimpsey
1992	14 Jun	Tumbling Dice	A.Fraser, K.Douglas, J.Thompson
1992	14 Jun	Cash Flow	R.McAllister, D.McGimpsey
1992	14 Jun	Tax Evasion	A.Fraser, K.Douglas, J.Thompson

LAGGANTALLUCH HEAD

1987		Stingray	S.Richardson, T.Prentice
1987		Dublin Packet	T.Prentice, S.Richardson
1987		Laggantalluch Corner	S.Richardson, T.Prentice
1987		First Touch	S.Richardson, T.Prentice
1987		Seal Song	T.Prentice, S.Richardson
1987		Pillar	S.Richardson, T.Prentice
1987		Freewheeling	T.Prentice, R.Everett
1987		Irish Mist	R.Everett, T.Prentice
1987		Ape Escape	T.Prentice, R.Everett
1987		Sciatic Nerve	R.Everett (solo)
1987		Seventh Wave	S.Richardson, R.Reid
1987		Arete	R.Reid, S.Richardson
1987		Tormentil	R.Reid, S.Richardson
1987		Wave Goodbye	R.Reid, S.Richardson
1987		Rogered	R.Everett (solo)
		Direct: R.McAllister, D.McAllister 20 Sept 1991	
1987		Refusnik	T.Prentice, R.Everett
1987		Back Burner	T.Prentice
1991	1 Sep	Fish Tales	A.Fraser, C.Stenhouse
1991	1 Sep	The Fish Ladder	A.Fraser, C.Stenhouse
1991	1 Sep	Good Morning Ladies	C.Stenhouse, A.Fraser
1991	1 Sep	Little Feat	A.Fraser, C.Stenhouse
1991	1 Sep	Skating	C.Stenhouse, A.Fraser
1991	8 Sep	Heart of Darkness	R.McAllister, A.Fraser
1991	8 Sep	Bouillabaisse	A.Fraser, R.McAllister
1991	8 Sep	Darwin's Waiting Room	A.Fraser, R.McAllister
1991	8 Sep	Waiting for the Sun	R.McAllister (solo)
1991	8 Sep	Stepped Corner	R.McAllister, A.Fraser
1991	20 Sep	Mourning Rib	D.McGimpsey (solo)
1991	20 Sep	Spongonema	J.Blyth, R.McAllister, C.Stenhouse, A.Fraser
1991	20 Sep	Desert Island Discs	A.Fraser, C.Stenhouse
1991	20 Sep	The Blind Man	C.Stenhouse, A.Fraser
1991	20 Sep	The Clam Catcher	J.Blyth, D.McGimpsey
1991	20 Sep	The Origin of Species	A.Fraser, C.Stenhouse
1991	20 Sep	The Oyster Thief	J.Blyth, D.McGimpsey
1991	20 Sep	The Shaddow Line	J.Blyth, D.McGimpsey
1991	12 Oct	Aqualung	D.McGimpsey A.Fraser, R.McAllister
1991	12 Oct	Fish Fingers	R.McAllister, A.Fraser
1991	12 Oct	White Sauce	D.McGimpsey (solo)
1991	12 Oct	Tunes of Glory	A.Fraser, R.McAllister, D.McGimpsey
1991	9 Nov	A Plaice by the Sea	S.Lampard, J.Thompson
1992	May	Quick Seal	G.Dudley
1992	17 Jun	Micro Niche	R.McAllister, M.Reed

| 1992 | 29 Jul | Obliteration | R.McAllister, D.McGimpsey |
| 1992 | 19 Sep | Davy Jones's Locker | A.Fraser, R.McAllister |

POINT OF THE CLEUGH

1992	28 Aug	The Chancer	D.McGimpsey (solo)
1992	28 Aug	Cleuch Clamber	D.McGimpsey, S.Ravey
1992	28 Aug	Just Friends	S.Ravey, D.McGimpsey
1992	28 Aug	The Slot	S.Ravey (solo)
1992	29 Aug	Comatose	D.McGimpsey, R.McAllister

CRAMMAG HEAD

1992	8 Aug	Molotov Cocktail	A.Fraser, D.McGimpsey
1992	8 Aug	Kalashnikov	C.Stenhouse, R.McAllister
1992	8 Aug	Freedon Fighter	R.McAllister
1992	8 Aug	Gorilla Warfare	D.McGimpsey, A.Fraser
1992	8 Aug	Skol's Out	R.McAllister, A.Fraser, C.Stenhouse, D.McGimpsey (all solo!)
1992	16 Aug	The Soft Parade	R.McAllister, J.Freeman, D.McGimpsey
1992	16 Aug	Fallen Star	D.McGimpsey, C.Stenhouse
1992	16 Aug	Lighthouse Wall	R.McAllister, C.Stenhouse
1992	16 Aug	Hourglass Slab	C.Stenhouse, R.McAllister
1992	16 Aug	Hagar The Horrible	C.Stenhouse, D.McGimpsey, J.Freeman
1992	16 Aug	Dormouse	J.Freeman, D.McGimpsey (solo)
1992	18 Aug	Enfant Terrible	A.Fraser, D.McGimpsey, R.McAllister
1992	18 Aug	Yosemite Sam	R.McAllister, D.McGimpsey, A.Fraser
1992	18 Aug	The Ship's Cat	A.Fraser, R.McAllister, D.McGimpsey
1992	18 Aug	Mog	D.McGimpsey, A.Fraser, R.McAllister
1992	18 Aug	Funeral Pyre	R.McAllister, A.Fraser, D.McGimpsey
1992	23 Aug	Accomodations of Desire	R.McAllister, D.McGimpsey, T.Allan
1992	23 Aug	Shining Path	T.Allan, R.McAllister
1992	23 Aug	Poisoned Ocean	R.McAllister, T.Allan
1992	23 Aug	Fragile Edge	R.McAllister, D.McGimpsey
1992	23 Aug	Orabidoo	D.McGimpsey, G.Gerrard
1992	27 Aug	Pillage	D.McGimpsey, S.Ravey
1992	29 Aug	The White Rabbit	A.Fraser, R.McAllister, D.McGimpsey
1992	29 Aug	Ragnarok	A.Fraser, D.McGimpsey
1993	11 Apr	Fresh Air	R.Everett, D.Gaffney
1993	29 Apr	Anvil Chorus	R.McAllister, M.Sayers
		Down Under	R.McAllister, M.Sayers
1993	24 Sep	Sid Stingray	D.McGimpsey, S.Meffen-Main
1993	24 Sept	Bully Beef	D.McGimpsey, S.Meffen-Main (both solo)

| 1993 | 6 Nov | The Four Bees | D.McGimpsey, R.McAllister |
| 1993 | 6 Nov | The Seven Seas | R.McAllister, D.McGimpsey |

WEST TARBET

| 1991 | 1 Sep | Bible Class | C.Stenhouse, A.Fraser |
| 1991 | 1 Sep | Sundae School | A.Fraser, C.Stenhouse |

NORTH THIRD

1982		The Flying Dragon	R.Cowels
1982		Jezebel	R.Cowels
1982		Red Shift	R.Cowels, A.Kay

By the variation start and some aid.
FFA G.Latter 1984, start as described: K.Spence

CAMBUSBARRON QUARRY

1983		Big Country Dreams	A.Kay, R.Cowels
1984		Visions of Monaco	C.Macadam
1984		The Purr-Blind Doomster	C.Macadam
1984		Quasi Pulls Through	K.Spence
1984		Formica Crack	M.Hamilton
1984		Murray's Groove	M.Hamilton
1984		Fuel for Thought	R.Anderson
1984	May	Both Ends Burning	D.McCallum
1984	May	Quantum Grunt	G.Pedley
1984		Power of Endurance	G.Latter
1984		Spanking the Monkey	G.Livingstone
1985	13 May	Economy Drive	R.Anderson, J.McKenzie
1985	19 May	Adulterer's Repentence	D.McCallum, D.Simmonds
1985	14 Jun	The Crowd	D.McCallum
1986	8 Jun	Trail Blazer	R.Anderson, A.Russell
1986	7 Sep	Pathfinder	R.Anderson, N.Elstone, G.Nicoll
1988	31 Jul	Thug of War	R.Anderson

CAMBUSBARRON WEST QUARRY

1980s		Another One Bites The Dust	G.Harrison, P.Laughlan
1980s		Malky the Alky	G.Harrison, P.Laughlan
1980s		Not Easy Contract	G.Harrison, P.Laughlan
1985	1 May	Easy Contract	C.Hewitt, N.Shepherd, K.Clark
1990	17 Jul	Gobi Roof	M.Garthwaite, G.Szuca, G.Campbell
1991	21 May	Force 8, Wind Up	M.Garthwaite, G.Szuca
1991	22 May	The Doobie Brothers	M.Garthwaite, G.Szuca
1991	23 May	Slot Shot	M.Garthwaite, G.Szuca

1991	14 Jul	Scaresville	G.Szuca, P.Hyde
1991	17 Jul	Brat Attack	M.Garthwaite, G.Szuca
1993	27 Apr	Production Line	A.Wren
1993	Jul	The Ubiquitous Chip	M.Worsley, G.Urquhart
1993	Summer	Chisel	D.Gregg, G.Szuca
1993	Summer	Cha	G.Szuca, D.Gregg
1993	25 Oct	Ninety Five	G.Szuca (back rope solo)

WOLFCRAG QUARRY

1980s	Leonardo	I.Duckworth
	Ian's Wa'	I.Duckworth
	Up on the Catwalk	A.Kay
	Experiments in Incest	A.Kay
	Tribal Look	A.Kay
	Waterfront	C.Macadam
	The Outsider	C.Macadam
	Lock-it	R.Cowels
	Thirty Frames A Second	R.Cowels

CRAIG ROSSIE

All routes by R.Cowels, 1984

RATHO QUARRY

1975	Godzilla	W.Jeffrey, C.Craggs
1975	Terminal Street	C.Craggs, W.Jeffrey
1975	Terminal Case	W.Jeffrey, C.Craggs
1976	Shear Fear	W.Jeffrey
1976	Ouroborus	W.Jeffrey, C.Craggs
1976	Beanpud	M.Pettifer, W.Jeffrey
1976	Scotty Arete	J.Hutchison
1976	Spiny Norman	J.Hutchison
1976	Shoskred	W.Jeffrey, C.Craggs
1980	Doomed Oasis	P.Hunter, K.Spence

Originally E2, but harder since the loss of a flake.

1980	Diverticulitis	P.Hunter, W.Jeffrey
1980	Pettifer's Wall	P.Hunter, W.Jeffrey
1981	Ouroborus Eliminate	P.Hunter, K.Spence
1981	Pete's Wall	P.Hunter, C.Lees
1981	Up the Creek	P.Hunter, K.Spence
1981	Sedge Warbler	P.Hunter
1981	Sahara	P.Hunter

Originally E3 but harder since the loss of the flake. Re-climbed by J.Andrew, 1992

1982		Gruel Brittania	K.Spence
1982		Slow Strain	R.Anderson
1983		Wally 1	K.Spence
1983		Wally 2	K.Spence
1983		Wally 3	K.Spence
1983		Rebel Without Claws	R.Anderson
1983		The Lone Groover	G.Handren
1983		Artho	K.Spence
1983		This Septic Heil	K.Spence
1983		Welcome to the Cruise	R.Anderson

Formerly called In Memoriam

1983		Time's Last Gift	J.Melrose
1983		Ane Ledge	R.Anderson
1985	3 May	The Blob	D.McCallum, G.Pedley
1985	1 Jul	Right Under	R.Anderson, A.Russell
1985	7 Jul	Left Over	R.Anderson, R.Milne, A.Russell
1988	24 Apr	Lone Groover Alternative	R.Anderson, A.Williams
1989		So It Goes	G.MacIntyre
1990	4 Jul	Pull the Other One	G.Nicoll, K.Noble, A.Chamings
1991	20 Nov	5000 Christmas Trees	J.Andrew, N.Armstrong

Probably climbed previously in mistake for Beanpud.

1991	25 Nov	Danger No Entry	J.Andrew
1991	28 Nov	Business as Usual	J.Andrew, N.Armstrong
1992	24 Mar	In a Prickle	J.Andrew, N.Armstrong
1992	24 Mar	Thorn in my Side	N.Armstrong, J.Andrew
1992	26 Mar	Chalk and Cheese	J.Andrew, N.Armstrong
1992	26 Mar	Strongarm	J.Andrew, N.Armstrong
1992	26 Mar	Election Sickness	N.Armstrong, J.Andrew
1993	Apr	Alopecia	I.Taylor, I.Pitcairn
1993	28 Apr	Fledge	J.Inglis, J.Ritchie

DALMAHOY HILL

Many of the climbs were first done by the 'Currie Boys' in the late 1950s and early 1960s. Unfortunately, no details are available and the cliff was neglected until the late 1970s, when members of the Edinburgh JMCS re-cleaned, climbed and named most of the routes. A further burst of activity is detailed below.

1987		Scree Surfing	A.Plumb, R.Ferguson
1991	14 Aug	Elation	J.Inglis, G.Jones, C.Eilbeck
1991	22 Aug	Midgey Gem	J.Inglis, A.McCleish, C.Eilbeck
1991	31 Aug	Cleaned Sweep	J.Inglis, C.Eilbeck
1992	20 May	The Lemming	J.Inglis, D.Buchanan, C.Eilbeck

BLACKFORD HILL

Quarry Pinnacle was climbed by H.Raeburn in 1896 and the routes dated 1950s were done by members of the EUMC. The other routes were climbed recently by J.Andrew (with A.Matthewson on Burning Bush) but it is quite likely that these routes and possibly others were climbed some time ago.

HOLYROOD PARK

1897		Eastern Buttress Face Route	H.Raeburn
Later called Hackenback			
1897		Fallen Column Climb	H.Raeburn
1900	11 Jul	Cat Nick Buttress	H.Raeburn, W.Inglis Clark
1902	25 Jul	Great Buttress	W.Morrison, W.Newbigging, L.Briquet
Formerly called Eastern Buttress.			
1933	4 Sep	Hewit's Groove	J.Hewit, W.Nisbet
1935	4 Aug	Sentry Box	J.Hewit, J.Donaldson
1936	5 Jul	Initial Route	J.Hewit
1937	2 Oct	Wall Route	J.Hewit, W.Nisbet
1944	23 Apr	Pinnacle Corner	A.Hendry
1944	14 May	Hyphen Route	A.Hendry
1945		Archie's Slab	A.Hendry
1945		Harrison's Climb	A.Harrison
1945		Horne's Slab	A.Horne
1945		Red Buttress	A.Graham
1945		Question Mark Crack	J.Berkeley
1945	22 Apr	The Lift Arete	G.Scott
1945	7 Oct	Athlete's Arete	G.Scott, D.Haworth
1945	26 Oct	Overhanging Route No.1	D.Haworth
Later called Evening Pillar			
1946		Barbed Wire Route	D.Haworth, A.Myerscough, A.Dick
1946		Stomach Layback	J.Berkeley
1946		Steeplejack's Staircase	D.Haworth
A peg has recently appeared on this historic route.			
1946		Hanging Slab	P.Myerscough
1946	20 Apr	Overhanging Route No.2	D.Haworth
Later called Evening Crack			
1946	23 Apr	Pinnacle Face	D.Haworth, P.Myerscough
1946	23 Apr	The Conflict with Temptation	D.Haworth
1946	1 May	Hanging Over Gladys, Gladys' Rib, No Love Rib	All by M.Slesser
1946	12 May	Rib and Mantelshelf	D.Haworth, A.Dick

1946	15 May	Wicked Lady	D.Haworth
1946	25 May	Eureka	D.Haworth
1946	25 May	Bacchus' Buttress Route	D.Haworth
1946	16 Jun	Waverley Crack	G.Parish, D.Duff
1946	25 Oct	Tournez	D.Haworth, A.Myrescough
1946	25 Oct	Toujours	D.Haworth, A.Dick
1946	2 Nov	Moonlight Traverse	D.Haworth, I.McPhail, A.Dick
1946	13 Nov	Great Electrocardiogram Traverse	D.Haworth, I.McPhail
1946	24 Nov	Graham's Route	D.Haworth
		Later called Smoker's Slab Route	
1946	2 Dec	Cracked Slab	A.Wright
1946	9 Dec	Cracked Slab Crack	A.Liver
1947	19 Jan	Editor's Crack	G.Dutton, M.Slesser, Miss Bainton
1947	22 Jan	Doubledecker	D.Haworth, G.Parish
1947	22 Feb	Wee Chokestone Crack	D.Haworth
1947	29 May	Grand Finale Route	D.Haworth, G.Ritchie
1952		Doubledecker Variation	A.More, D.Mill
1956		Left Ribs	R.Smith
1960		Scuttle	R.Smith
1960		Black Corner	Unknown. FFA J.Andrew 1991
1982		Ginger Nympho's Lust	J.Handren, J.Melrose
1982	8 Dec	Straight Satan	J.Handren, B.Kerr
1983		The Blackdance	J.Handren, J.Melrose
1983		After the Axe	J.Handren, B.Kerr
1983		Walking on Sunshine	J.Handren, J.Melrose
1983		Transatlantic Trip	J.Handren, D.McCallum
1987	Mar	Vague Arete	A.Matthewson
1987	10 Jun	Election Special	R.Anderson, G.Taylor, D.Bond, A.Williams, K.Spence
1991	14 Aug	Second Offence	J.Andrew, J.Tout
1991	2 Dec	Walk On By	J.Andrew
1991	13 Dec	The Ragged Rascals	J.Andrew, J.Tout
1992	3 Jun	Idle Gossip	J.Andrew
1992	24 Jun	Ped Xing	J.Andrew, J.Tout, A.Matthewson, A.Tibbs

ROSLIN GLEN

1976		Centre Line	W.Jeffrey, C.Craggs, P.Buckley
1980		Beyond Traprain	P.Hunter, W.Jeffrey
1980		Gaping Gab	P.Hunter
1980		Ham Jam	W.Jeffrey
1985	Jun	Red Face	K.Spence, J.Rooney
1985	Jun	The Forty-Twa	K.Spence, J.Rooney

1985	Jun	Day of the Jockal	K.Spence
1985	Jun	The Climbist	K.Spence
1985	Jun	The Wrinklies	K.Spence, J.Rooney
1985	Jun	The Thin Crack	J.Rooney, K.Spence
1985	30 Jun	Pinky and Perky	K.Spence, J.Rooney
1985	3 Jul	Cave Crack	J.Rooney, K.Spence
1985	3 Jul	Rampo	K.Spence, J.Rooney
1985	7 Jul	Gruesome Gamboge	K.Spence, J.Rooney
1985	7 Jul	Faustus Entor	K.Spence, J.Rooney
1985	9 Jul	Rufus	K.Spence
1985	14 Jul	Rock All Over Me	K.Spence, J.Rooney
1985	14 Jul	The Slater's Revenge	J.Rooney, K.Spence
1985	15 Jul	Plunging Neckline	K.Spence, J.Rooney
1985	19 Jul	Hanging Rock	K.Spence, J.Rooney
1985	21 Jul	Panama Red	J.Rooney, K.Spence
1985	3 Aug	Brown Sugar	K.Spence
1985	5 Aug	Dusty Road	K.Spence, J.MacKenzie
1985	11 Aug	Red Wedge	K.Spence, J.Rooney
1985	6 Oct	The Cue	K.Spence, J.MacKenzie, R.Anderson
1985	6 Oct	Enzyme	R.Anderson
1985	12 Oct	No Picnic	R.Anderson, K.Spence
1985	26 Oct	Edge of Darkness	R.Anderson, K.Spence
1985	26 Oct	Piano Player	K.Spence, R.Anderson
1985	27 Oct	Ruff Stuff	R.Anderson, K.Spence
1985	2 Nov	Mein Sumph	K.Spence, R.Anderson
1985	3 Nov	Red Ringer	R.Anderson, K.Spence, J.Rooney
1985	10 Nov	Old Red Eye	J.Rooney, K.Spence, R.Anderson
1985	14 Dec	Harry Dodder's Crack	R.Anderson, K.Spence
1985	15 Dec	Robert the Moose	R.Anderson, K.Spence
1985	22 Dec	Scots Wha Hae	K.Spence, J.MacKenzie
1986	29 Mar	Two Tier Crack	J.Rooney, K.Spence
1986	29 Mar	Ruggosities	K.Spence, J.Rooney
1986	24 May	Praying Mantle	R.Anderson, J.Rooney, K.Spence
1986	24 May	Last Slap	K.Spence, J.Rooney, R.Anderson
1986	7 Jun	Duncrankin	K.Spence, R.Anderson
1986	8 Jun	Shinbones Field	J.Rooney, K.Spence
1986	14 Jun	Belly Bulger	R.Anderson, R.Milne, A.Russell
1986	7 Jul	Under Pressure	R.Anderson, K.Spence
1987	3 Mar	Voice in the Dark	R.Campbell, P.Morozzo
1988	9 Apr	Eddie the Eejit	R.Campbell, N.Craig
1988	1 Oct	Deep in Diana	R.Campbell, D.Simmonds
1988	10 Oct	Bum Fun	O.Hayward
1988	10 Oct	Monodoigtism	R.Campbell
1988	Nov	Life in the Bus Lane	R.Campbell, O.Hayward
1988	Nov	Roslin Roulette	O.Hayward

Top-roped prior to leading.

| 1988 | 24 Dec | Dangleberries | O.Hayward |
| 1989 | 27 Apr | Hezbollah | R.Campbell |

Top-roped prior to leading.

1989	16 Jun	Harry Dodder's Variation	J.Andrew
1990	Dec	The Shouting Man	P.Thorburn, R.Campbell
1991		Incarnadine	G.Cohen, D.Rubens
1991	Apr	Claymore Crack	G.Nicoll, W.Jeffrey
1991	May	Basil Brush	A.Matthewson
1991	29 Jul	Rock Lobster	A.Matthewson, J.Andrew
1991	13 Aug	Syzygy	J.Andrew
1991	13 Aug	The Flying Start	J.Andrew
1991	13 Aug	Aficionado	J.Andrew
1991	Oct	Absentee Landlord	A.Matthewson, N.Armstrong, S.Elworthy
1991	4 Dec	Hoppy's Least Favorite	J.Andrew
1991	14 Dec	Strange Apparatus	G.Nicoll
1991	15 Dec	The Golden Apple of Eternal Desire	R.Campbell, G.Latter
1992	Jan	Give 'em enough rope	P.Thorburn, R.Campbell

Top-roped prior to leading

| 1992 | Feb | Survival of the Fattest | R.Campbell |
| 1992 | 26 Mar | Walk On By | P.Thorburn |

Top-roped prior to leading.

| 1992 | 3 Apr | Jumbo's Proctoscopy | J.Andrew |

(medical advice; Dr G.Irvine) Top-roped prior to leading.

| 1992 | 3 Apr | Turn the Other Cheek | J.Andrew, N.Armstrong |

Top-roped prior to leading.

1992	7 May	Scotch Corner	J.Andrew, A.Matthewson
1992	7 May	Gadaffi's Ear	J.Andrew
1992	18 Jun	Always the Sun	J.Andrew

Top-roped prior to leading.

| 1993 | 11 Nov | The Chocolate Orgasm | J.Andrew, G.Watt |

NORTH QUEENSFERRY QUARRY

1985		Scharnhorst	R.Baker, R.Howard
1985		The Boat	R.Baker, R.Howard
1986	15 Mar	Dive Dive Dive	R.Baker, R.Howard
1987	3 Mar	Edge of Time Variation	R.Campbell, P.Morozzo
1987	14 Apr	Edge of Time	S.Jenkins, E.Cameron
1989	8 Oct	Bismark	A.Perkins, M.Duff
1989	14 Oct	Fleet Air Arm	A.Perkins, I.Tattersall, M.Duff

Andy Perkins broke an arm during the ascent.

| 1991 | Apr | Nearly an Angel | G.MacIntyre, T.Gould |

George MacIntyre broke both an arm and a leg on this route.

| 1991 | 24 May | The Vital Spark | A.Matthewson, J.Andrew, D.Kirk |

ROSYTH QUARRY

1972		Gold Foil, Route to Root	R.Baker
1972		Wireworm	R.Baker
1972		Chemical Warfare	P.De Mengle
1972		Smith's Dilemma,	M.Smith
		Sickle	M.Smith
1972		Jack's Route	J.Rice
		Broken Pillar	J.Rice
1972		Legover Groove	R.Baker
1972		Heathy, Cathy	I.Conway
1973		Iconoclast	First aided ascent unknown.

FFA W.Jeffrey, M.Plant 1975

1973		Grenville	I.Conway
1973		The Stinking Swordsman	I.Conway
		(6PA)	

Originally called Matinee Cracks. FFA I.Cropley 1986

1974		Andy's Route	A.McCord
1974		Drizzle, C.N.D	I.Conway
1974		Phillistine (6PA)	R.Baker

FFA Unknown

1974		Pogo Groove	R.Baker
1974		Fat Sam	A.McCord
1974		Serendipity	P.De Mengle
1975		Hands Off, Ram Jam	A.McCord
1975		Corner, Gift Horse	
1975		Late Night Final	R.Baker
1975	10 Aug	Grot Corner	W.Jeffrey, M.Martin
1975	16 Aug	The Beast	W.Jeffrey, A.Davidson
1975	16 Aug	Tiger Pad	W.Jeffrey
1975	25 Aug	Inspiration	W.Jeffrey, M.Plant
1975	31 Aug	The Waullie	W.Jeffrey, C.Craggs
1975	31 Aug	Corpuscle (10PA)	M.Plant, L.Linaker, M.Martin.

FFA Unknown

1975	31 Aug	The Grinder	W.Jeffrey, C.Craggs
1975	5 Sep	Changeling (5PA)	M.Plant, M.Martin, R.Columbo.

FFA Unknown

1975	10 Sep	Flakeoff (6PA)	M.Plant.

FFA Unknown

1976		The Beauty	C.Craggs, C.Binks
1976		The Flying Bink	C.Craggs, C.Binks
1977		If Pigs Could Fly	M.Hamilton
1985	28 Oct	Jagdhond	R.Howard, R.Baker
1986	May	Plod	D.Moffat
1990	May	Skinny Lizzie	S.Brown, D.Moffat
1992	10 Jun	The Rust Bucket	I.Taylor

THE HAWKCRAIG

1965		Fish Head Arete	N.MacNiven
1965		Pain Pillar	N.MacNiven
1965		Saki, Brutus	N.MacNiven
1965		Torment, Eureka	N.MacNiven
1965		Fish Head Wall, Ugh	J.Knight
1965		The Lilly, Escalator	J.Knight
1965		Tink, Shadow Corner	J.Knight
1965		Termination, The Low Girdle	J.Knight
1965		Sacrilege, Squirrel Slab	D.Bathgate
1965		Gismo, Gaucho, Diptera	D.Bathgate
1965		Urmi, The High Girdle	D.Bathgate
1965		Eech, Cranium Crack	I.MacEacheran
1965		Gaucho	I.MacEacheran
1965		Rebel's Groove	I.MacEacheran
1965		Chimney Arete	I.MacEacheran
1965		Gunga Din, Saracen, Toerag's Wall	I.MacEacheran
1965		Halleluja Wall The Whang	I.MacEacheran
1965		Flake and Wall, Destiny Groove	I.MacEacheran
1965		Maureen	I.MacEacheran
1965		Conquistador Crack	B.Robertson
1965		Stomach-Ache, Crusader	A.McKeith
1965		The High Girdle	A.McKeith
1965		Guano	J.Brumfitt
1965		Ganja, The Chimney	J.Renny
1970	24 May	Asinine	D.Edwards, A.Ford
1975		The Arete	D.Cuthbertson, R.Anderson
1975		Guano Variation	D.Cuthbertson, R.Anderson
1975		Weasel Wall	M.Hamilton
1983		Serendipity	S.Murdoch, J.Murdoch
1990	31 Jul	Where Were You?	S.Brown, J.Armour
1990	13 Oct	Psylocibie	A.Connolly, G.Szuca

BENARTY HILL

1982		Cubism	K.Spence
1983		A Fist Job	J.McKenzie, K.Spence
1983		Dolly Parton	K.Spence, J.McKenzie
1983		Ram	J.McKenzie, K.Spence
1991	Jul	Treasure Seeker	A.Matthewson

| 1991 | Jul | Hot Potato | N.Armstrong, J.Andrew, A.Matthewson |
| 1991 | Jul | Demerara, Goblin, Oat Flake | A.Matthewson |

LIMEKILNS

1981		Humbug	M.Bennett
1983	Jun	Hunter and the Hunted	A.Kay
1983	Jun	Dingley Dell	N.Paxton, N.Morrison, A.Kay
1983	Jun	Marley's Ghost	R.Cowels, A.Kay
1983	25 Jun	Cruel Summer	N.Morrison, N.Paxton
1983	27 Jun	Methods of Dance	A.Kay, N.Morrison
1983	27 Jun	New Gold Dream	N.Morrison, A.Kay, N.Paxton
1983	27 Jun	Colours Fly	N.Morrison
1984		Elgin's Crack	A.Pettit, R.Cowels
1984	Mar	The Iron Fist	J.McKenzie
1984	Mar	Velvet Glove	K.Spence, J.McKenzie, D.McCallum
1984	28 Apr	The Struggler	N.Morrison, C.McLean, A.Ross
1985		Neutral Gear	D.Moffat
1985		Forbidden Colours	A.Borthwick, M.Russell
1985	16 Apr	D-Day	D.Moffat, R.Baker
1985	21 Apr	White Ensign	R.Baker, A.McCord, D.Moffat
1985	21 Apr	Red Flag	A.McCord, R.Baker
1985	23 Apr	DT's	D.Moffat, K.Todd
1985	24 Apr	Sunsetter	A.Borthwick, M.Russell
1985	May	Link Rib	A.Borthwick, D.Forsyth
1985	May	One Ringer	A.Borthwick, D.Forsyth
1985	May	Two Ringer	A.Borthwick, D.Forsyth
1985	May	Edge of Fear	A.Borthwick
1985	May	Protectless	A.Borthwick
1985	May	The Ivy League, Yuppie	D.McCallum
1985	3 May	VE Day	D.Moffat, R.Baker
1985	31 May	Grasp the Nettle	R.Howard, R.Baker
1985	3 Jun	The Sting	D.Moffat, I.Todd
1985	5 Jun	Dead Ringer	D.Moffat, R.Baker
1985	20 Jul	The Charleston	M.Hamilton, R.Anderson
1985	10 Aug	Rock Around the Block	R.Anderson, A.Russell
1985	15 Sep	Slots	R.Anderson
1985	13 Oct	Through the Motions	R.Anderson, K.Spence
1986	3 Aug	On the Blocks	R.Anderson, K.Spence, G.Cohen
1986	5 Oct	Velvet Glove, The Satin Finish	R.Anderson

TRAPRAIN LAW

No first ascent records have been kept, however it is known that those mentioned below have played a part in the development of Traprain Law. G.Anderson, M.Anderson, J.Andrew (FFA Tipp), A.Barclay, D.Bathgate, R.Campbell, D.Cuthbertson, G.Dutton, G.Elliot, A.Ewing, M.Fleming, J.Hall, M.Hamilton (FFA Beatle Crack), D.Haston, R.Holt, B.MacDonald, N.MacNiven, A.McKeith, J.Marshall (Wobble, Piglet), R.Marshall, J.Moriarty, G.Murray, R.Phillips, G.Ritchie, B.Robertson, R.Smith (Burp, Chute), J.Stenhouse, R.Swanson, A.Taylor, G.Tiso.

NORTH BERWICK LAW

1989	9 Apr	Old Lawbreaker	R.Anderson, C.Greaves, K.Spence
1989	29 Apr	Jaws of the Law	R.Anderson, C.Anderson
1989	5 May	Law of Gravity	R.Anderson
1989	9 Sep	Necktie	B.Kerr, R.Young
1989	9 Sep	Fogtown	B.Kerr, R.Young
1989	18 Sep	Law of the Flies	R.Anderson
1989	25 Sep	Law and Disorder	R.Anderson, C.Anderson
1992		Eliminate Law	I.Pitcairn
1993	21 Apr	Igneous Intruder	N.Ashton

THE FAST CASTLE SEA-CLIFFS

1965		The Souter, Landward Side	D.Bathgate, R.Campbell
1965	Jul	Abseil Gully, Vertigo, Urinal Wall, Atlanta, The East Arete	G.Davidson, J.Binns
1966	Sep	Gannet Groove, Castle Wall	G.Davidson, P.Lockey
1970		Landward Side Direct Variant	S.Black, D.Smith
1970		The Souter, Ordinary Route	I.Clough, J.Cleare
1970		Ordinary Route Variation	D.Bathgate, R.Sharp
1970		The Skate	I.Rowe, D.Godfrey
1970		Carapus	J.Wells, P.Brian
1970		Cockle Shell Cracks	B.McDonald, R.Sharp
1970		Squid	D.Bathgate, M.Watson
1970		Sperm	D.Bathgate, I.Rowe
1970		Dayglo	S.Black, J.Porteous
1970		Purve	S.Black, T.Blenkinsop
1974	24 Aug	Cyclops	G.Davidson, M.Moran
1979	Feb	Zigzag	B.Kerr, E.Hughes

1981	Mar	Guano Corner	J.Griffiths, A.Moist
1981	Mar	Lucky Day	K.Howett
1981	Apr	Spring Shower	J.Griffiths, K.Howett
1981	Apr	Jonathan Livingstone Shitehawk	K.Howett, J.Griffiths
1981	Apr	Blue Moves, Sea Sprite, What have the Vikings... Rufus the Red, Sea Ahoy	P.Clarke, A.Hinks
1982	Feb	A Drop in the Ocean The Fish Business	J.Handren
1982	Feb	Second Sight, Fast Bleeder	J.McKenzie, R.Duncan
1982	Feb	J.P.S.	R.Anderson, K.Spence
1982	Feb	Plain Sailing	K.Spence, R.Anderson
1982	Feb	Shorty, Sweep, Sooty	A.Taylor, K.Spence, R.Anderson
1982	Feb	Chimp, Walli	A.Taylor
1982	Feb	The Great Gonzo	R.Duncan, J.Handren
1982	Feb	Moving Like a Slug	J.McKenzie, R.Duncan
1982	Mar	Bloodbath	J.Melrose
1982	Mar	Stiff Bunnies	R.Anderson, K.Spence
1982	Mar	Fraud Escort	K.Spence, R.Anderson
1982	Mar	Walnut	J.McKenzie, R.Anderson
1982	Mar	Orgasmatron	J.Handren, R.Duncan
1982	Mar	Lightning Crack	R.Young, B.Kerr
1982	Mar	Blockbuster	R.Anderson, J.McKenzie
1982	Apr	Mingy Metro	M.Hamilton, R.Anderson, R.Duncan
1982	Apr	Souterrain	K.Spence, J.McKenzie
1982	Apr	Leech	M.Hamilton
1982	May	Souterrain Direct Start	P.Hunter, K.Spence
1982	May	Pigeon Shit	M.Hamilton, R.Anderson
1982	Jun	Wallow, Wallette	K.Spence, D.Jamieson
1982	Jul	Porker's Wall	M.Hamilton, R.Anderson
1982	Sep	Return to Sender	R.Anderson, K.Spence
1983	Apr	Take it to the Limpets	K.Spence, R.Anderson
1983	Jul	Squid Vicious	K.Spence, D.McCallum
1983	Oct	Graddled, Drunk and Disorderly	J.McKenzie
1983	Oct	Quasi's Back	K.Spence, J.McKenzie
1989	4 Nov	The Twilight Hour	B.Kerr, G.MacIntyre
1989	Nov	The Bat Crack, The Buoy Wonder	G.Nicoll, K.Noble, N.McNeill
1990	24 Mar	Fated Panda	M.Smith, R.Campbell
1990	1 Apr	Seal of Approval	R.Campbell
1990		Kylie	P.Thorburn, R.Campbell
1990		Crimpanzie	M.Smith

1990		Not the HVS	P.Thorburn, I.Dawson
1990		First of Four	R.Campbell, I.Dawson
1990		The Undercut Kid	M.Smith, R.Campbell
1990		Tied up at Work	R.Campbell
1990		Psittacosis	P.Thorburn
1991		Gary's in Harry's	G.MacIntyre, G.Nicoll
1991	Apr	Bouma Sequence	A.Matthewson, D.Kirk
1991	18 Jul	The Ancient Mariner	J.Andrew, A.Matthewson
1991	28 Jul	Up-helly-aa	A.Matthewson, J.MacLaurin
1991	3 Nov	The East Arete True Finish	J.Andrew, J.Tout, A.Matthewson
1991	23 Nov	The Folly	A.Matthewson, A.Tibbs
1992	11 Jan	Rapunzel, Atlanta Direct Finish	A.Matthewson
1992	17 Mar	Coming Up Roses	J.Andrew
1992	17 Mar	Merlin and Wendy's Day Out	N.Armstrong, J.Andrew
1992	28 Apr	Edge of the Wedge	J.Andrew
1992	28 Apr	Fuzzy Stone	J.Andrew, N.Armstrong
1992		Seize the Day	B.Kerr, G.MacIntyre
1992		Drop the Pilot	G.MacIntyre, B.Kerr
1992		The Voyage of the Mad Manxman	B.Kerr, J.Reeves
1992	Oct	Curve of the Earth	G.MacIntyre, M.Davies
1993	13 Mar	Starboard Bow Turning in-tide-out	G.MacIntyre, C.McKee, B.Kerr
1993	14 Mar	Mea Culpa, Enigma	B.Kerr, R.Robertson
1993	21 Mar	Constant Hunger	G.MacIntyre, B.Kerr
1993	21 Mar	Inferno	B.Kerr, G.MacIntyre
1993	4 Apr	Welcome to the Midden	B.Kerr, G.MacIntyre
1993	4 Apr	Lunar Pull	G.MacIntyre, B.Kerr, D.Leckie
1993	4 Apr	Port Bow	G.MacIntyre, B.Kerr
1993	Summer	Brucellosis	R.Campbell
1993	18 Sep	Tidal Race, Ranald's Rant, Whitebait Can't Jump, Flounder Member, Pirrett's Progress	A.Matthewson, G.Watt, A.Hume

TEVIOTDALE

1993	7 Jul	Who youse callin' Fatlips	S.Reid, J.Campbell
		Fatlips Corner	J.Campbell, S.Reid

Graded List of Climbs

This section comes with all the usual disclaimers. We know it is incomplete, and we would welcome any suggestions, additions and corrections for incorporation into the next edition of the guide. Due to the difficulty of giving exact comparisons between bolted and traditional climbs, bolted routes have not been included in this list (except where all the routes are bolted).

DUMBARTON ROCK

Requiem	E7 6c ***
Cyclops	E5 5a,6b,5a *
Chemin de Fer	E5 6a ***
Woops	E4 6a *
Grey Wall	E4 5c *
Supple as a Brick	E4 5c *
Fever Pitch	E4 5c *
Rock of Ages	E3 6a **
Antigrav	E3 6a **
Samora	E3 5c
Datura	E3 5c
Requiem Direct Start	E3 5b
The Big Zipper	E3 5b ***
Gaucho	E2 5c
Slainte	E2 5c
Snowwhite	E2 5b ***
Rough Sea	E2 5b
Rising Power	E2 5b
Ciamar a tha Sibh	E2 5b
Gamma	E1 5c
Longbow	E1 5b ***
Crackerjack	E1 5b **
Beta	E1 5b
Big Ears	E1 5b
Banana Slide	E1 5a
The Neilweg	HVS 5b *
Route Three	HVS 5b *
Windjammer Crack	HVS 5a ***
Desperado	HVS 5a *
Alpha	HVS 5a
Drizzle	HVS 5a *
Stonefall Crack Direct	HVS 5a *
Stonefall Crack	HVS 5a **
Tag	HVS 5a
Uisge Beatha	HVS 5a
Silly Thing	HVS 4b,5b
Bobtail	HVS 5a
Bohert	HVS 5a

Boulevard	VS 5a *
Alleyway	VS 5a
Grey Slab	VS 5a
Poison Ivy	VS 5a
Dumbarton Chimney	VS 4c
Frendo	VS 4c
Ganglion Grooves	VS 4c
Banana Groove	VS 4c
Sunset Groove	VS 4c
West Face Girdle	VS 4c
Old Socks	VS 4c
Pinky	VS 4b

DUNGLAS

Steel Finger	E3 6a *
Bite them Bequerels	E3 5c
Wall of Horrors	E3 5c *
North-East Arete	E2 5c
The Nightmare	E2 5c
Overlord	E1 5c
The Cross	E1 5b *
Deviant	E1 5b *
A Feet of Arms	HVS 5b
The Gentle Touch	HVS 5b
Downfall	HVS 5b
A Dream of Brown Trousers	VS 5b
Little Gripper	VS 5a
Skirmish	VS 5a
Pullover	VS 4c
Curioser and Curioser	VS 4c
Joker's Groove	VS 4c

AUCHINSTARRY QUARRY

Carouselambra	E5 6b **
The Surf Shack	E5 6b
Surface Tension	E5 6b ***
Nijinski	E5 6a ***
Deep Throat Revived	E5 6a ***
Hopelessly Treading Water	E4 6a

Death is the Hunter	E4 6b ***
Dream Machine	E4 6a/b ***
Promontory Runner	E4 6b
Blade Runner	E4 6a **
Twilight Zone	E4 6a *
Stool Pidgeon	E3 6b
High Dive	E3 5c *
Spanking the Rustbucket	E3 5c
Race Against Time	E3 5c
Band Aid	E3 5c
The Gold Bug	E3 5c
Replicant	E3 5c
Foxy Woxy	E3 5c **
Soft Machine	E2 5c
Both Toes Burning	E2 6a
Red Snapper	E2 5c
Think of England	E2 5c **
The Seven Year Plan	E2 5c *
I-Spy	E2 5c *
After the Gold Rush	E2 5a
Cat's Whiskers	E2 5b
Harry Goes West	E2 5b
Glass	E1 5c
Mascarade	E1 5c
Midas Touch	E1 5b ***
Power Play	E1 5b *
After the Grave Dig	E1 5a **
Knock Back	E1 5b **
The Color Purple	E1 5b
Gold Rush	E1 5b ***
Shot in the Dark	E1 5a *
B.C.'s Return	E1 5b
First Footer	E1 5c **
Short Reach	E1 5b **
Newcastle Brown	E1 5b
Whiplash	E1 5b
Kelvin Way	E1 5a
Lion	HVS 5b
Walk on the Wild Side	HVS 5a ***
Mac's Wall	HVS 5a
Stir Crazy	HVS 5a
Footloose	HVS 5a
Green Onion	HVS 5b
Promontory Direct	HVS 5a ***
Sunshine	HVS 5a **
Christmas Corner	HVS 5a *

Caftan	HVS 4c
Bazaar	HVS 4c
Maypole	HVS 4c

BEN AN

Tricky Vicky	E4 6a *
Club Corner	E3 5c *
The Hook	E3 5c ***
Twilight Groove	HVS 4c *
Coriander	VS 4c **
The Rent	VS 4c *
Hanging Crack	VS 4c **
The Edge	VS 4c *

LOUDOUN HILL

Lunge	E3 6a ***
Slings	E3 5c **
Chalkster	E2 5c **
Epitaph Variation	E2 5c **
Cling	E2 5c
Automation	El 5b
The Belk	El 5b ***
The Splits	E1 5b **
Ring	HVS 5a
Dee's Crack	HVS 5a ***
Sadist's Groove	HVS 5a
Quick Skive	HVS 5a**
Cave Crack	VS 4c ***
Pulpit Crack	VS 4c **
Busman's Holiday	VS 5a
Contortion Groove	VS 4c
John's Last	VS 4c
The Edge	VS 4b ***
Epitaph	VS 4c
Mantleshelf Wall	VS 4b *
Trench Direct	VS 4b

MAUCHLINE

Bye Eck	E4 6a
Bridge Over Troubled Water	E4 5c **
Y Bother	E3 5c
Ayrheid	E2 5b,5c,5a *
Games of Chance and Sandancing	E2 5b **
Lightning Crack	E2 6a

Board Walk	E2 5b	Fingerlust	E3 6a **
Mossy Wall	E2 5a	Lemur	E3 6a *
Purism Personified	E2 5a	Beyond The Terminator	E3 5c **
Unnamed	E1 5b	The Arete	E2 5c ***
The Chimney	HVS 5a	Moonshine	E2 5c **
Green Machine	VS 4b	Aquiline	E2 5c
Dredge Bog	VS 4b	Revolver	E2 5b *
Gardeners' Corner	VS 4b *	Wall Street	E1 5b ***
		Blazing Apostles	E1 5b **
GLEN AFTON		Nebula	E1 5b
Delirium	E4 6a **	Jugular Vein	E1 5b ***
Sweet Liberty	E3 5c *	Crosswires	E1 5b
Hyacinth House	E2 5b *	Labrum	E1 5b
Stone Circle	E1 5b ***	Little Wall	E1 5a
Midnight Express	E1 5b **	Outcast	HVS 5a
Crack of Doon	HVS 5a *	The Slash	HVS 5a
Deception Slab	HVS 5a	Crackshot	HVS 5a *
Raven Slab	HVS 4c *	D.I.Y.	HVS 5a *
Magic Carpet	VS 4c	The Direct	HVS 5a
Grass Roots	VS 4b	Wiggle	HVS 5a *
		Ratten's Rest	HVS 5a *
DUNGEON HILL		Gibbon in Wonderland	HVS 5a *
Parcel of Rogues	E3 6a,5b **	Hotlips	VS 4c **
English Gold	E3 5b,5c	Sideshoot	VS 4c
Incy Wincy Spider	E2 5b **	Sunset	VS 4c
Heir Apparent Direct Finish	E2 5b	Red Slab	VS 4c
Saddle Tramp	E2 5a/b,5b *	The Groove	VS 4c
Bruce's Stone	E1 5b	Tour de Force	VS 4c **
Hammer of the Scots	E1 5b	Twin Cracks	VS 4b **
Free Land	HVS 5b	Elder's Crack	VS 4b
Cyclopath	HVS 5a,4c,4c **	Crawl Wall	VS 4b
Bannockburn	HVS 5b *	Dirl Chimney	VS 4b ***
Heir Apparent	HVS 5a,5a,5b **	Novice Crack	VS 4b
The Colonel's			
Corner	HVS 5a,4b,5a **	**MEIKLE ROSS**	
Scots Wha' Hae	HVS 5a *	Sunshine Superman	E4 6a *
The Highway Man	HVS 5a,4c,4a *	Fil d'Or	E3 6a ***
Monkey Puzzle	VS 4c,4c,4a,4b	Corridor of Power	E3 5c ***
Traitor's Gait	VS 4a,3c,4b,4c	Zugsfang	E2 5c *
Carrick Corner	VS 4c **	Ancient Mariner	E2 4b,5b **
Comyn Corner	VS 4a	A Walk on the Wild Side	E1 5b,5b **
		Back Track	E1 5a,5a
CLIFTON		Finesse	E1 5b **
Toddamundo	E4 6a ***	Scared to Dance	E1 5a **
Loneliness of the Long		Bloody Crack	E1 5b *
Distance Runner	E4 6a	Argus	E1 5b *

Compulsion	E1 5b
The Battle of Osfrontalis	HVS 4c,4b
Titan's Corner	HVS 5a *
Fats Waller	HVS 5a
Side Track	HVS 5a,5a **
Maple Leaf Rag	HVS 4b,5a,5a *
Crack Track	HVS 4a,5a,5a *
Dogleg	HVS 5a **
Accutrac	HVS 5a
Akela	HVS 5a *
Bumper Dumper	HVS 5b *
Seadog	HVS 5a *
Galloway Corner	HVS 4c,5a *
K.9.	HVS 4b,5a *
Yellow Dog	HVS 4a,4c
Limehouse Blues	HVS 3b,4b,5a *
Dolphin Groove	HVS 4c
Dolce Vita	HVS 4c
Spectrum Wall	HVS 5b
Rhythm n'Blues	HVS 5a,5a **
Pinking Sheer	HVS 5a ***
Bad Medicine Waltz	HVS 5a *
Salty Dog	HVS 4c *
Old Zawn	HVS 4c
Amnesia	VS 4c
Headcase	VS 4c
Mellow Yellow	VS 4c ***
Cairn's Cream	VS 4c *
Mental Block	VS 4c ***
Demolition Tango	VS 4c **
Alligator Crawl	VS 4c *
Evens	VS 4c *
Crack and Corner	VS 4c *
Blue Finger	VS 4c
Meikle Gorbachov	VS 4c
Grand Central Couloir	VS 4c
Sorcerer's Apprentice	VS 4b *
The Moosetrap	VS 4c
Steve's Route	VS 4b
Route Two	VS 4b
Marie Celeste	VS 4b

BURROW HEAD

Mirror, Mirror	E3 5c,5b,5a *
Adventures in the Skin Trade	E3 5c **

Naked Fun	E2 5b ***
Conquistador	E2 5b,5a
The Beastie	E1 5b
Prometheus (on his crag)	E1 5b *
Wild Horses	E1 5b
Guardian Angel	HVS 5b *
Devil's Daughter	HVS 5a
Goblin's Eyes	HVS 5a *
The Cutter	HVS 5a,4b
The Fin	HVS 5a
Waiting for Godot	HVS 4c
Mephistopheles	VS 4c
Flensing Knife	VS 4c
Watership Down	VS 4c *
Bright Eyes	VS 4c
Lemming's Wall	VS 4c
Killer on the Loose	VS 4b

PORTOBELLO

The Waster	E5 6b ***
Sweaty Trembler	E5 6b **
Changeling	E4 6a **
Pushed to the Limit	E4 6a
The Man From Del Monte	E3 6a ***
Betty Blue	E3 5c
St Elmo's Fire	E3 5c ***
The Cruel Seaside	E2 5c ***
Acid Test	E2 5c
Dances with Mackerel	E2 5c
Lost at Sea	E2 5b/c *
Underling	E2 5c
The Crayfish Twins	E2 5c **
Horse Latitudes	E1 5a **
The Water Margin	E1 5b ***
Water Dance	E1 5b *
Critical Mass	E1 5b **
Soul Kitchen	E1 5b *
Only Monsters	E1 5a
Basic Instinct	HVS 5a *
Thunderbolt	HVS 5a
Silence of the Clams	HVS 5a **
Figget's Recipe	HVS 5a
Mussel Bound	HVS 5a **
Floating Voter	HVS 5a
Crawford's Crackers	HVS 5a
Ramplet	VS 5b

The Ducking Stool	VS 4c *
Bootless	VS 4c
Riverboat Gambler	VS 4c *
Parallel Lines	VS 4b
Feeling the Pinch	VS 4b *

MONEY HEAD

The Root of All Evil	E3 5c *
Free Enterprise	E1 5b *
Filthy Lucre	E1 5a
Cash Flow	HVS 5a
The Liquidator	HVS 5a **
Slot Machine	HVS 5a *
Pot of Gold	HVS 5a *
Tumbling Dice	VS 4c *
Pay Day	VS 5a
Bolivars	VS 4b

LAGGANTALLUCH HEAD

Quick Seal	E3 6a ***
Back Burner	E3 6a
Obliteration	E3 5c
Ape Escape	E2 6a **
Freewheeling	E2 5b **
Refusnik	E2 5b **
Fish Fingers	E2 5b
Seal Song	E1 5b ***
First Touch	E1 5b **
Spongonema	E1 5b *
Seventh Wave	E1 5b *
Davy Jones's Locker	E1 5b **
Dublin Packet	E1 5a
Irish Mist	E1 5a
Rogered Direct	HVS 5a
Laggantalluch Corner	HVS 5a ***
The Oyster Thief	HVS 5a *
Micro Niche	HVS 5a
Heart of Darkness	HVS 5a *
Aqualung	HVS 5b
Pillar	HVS 5a
Tormentil	HVS 5a
The Clam Catcher	VS 4c
The Origin of Species	VS 4c
Desert Island Discs	VS 4c
Little Feat	VS 4c *
Waiting for the Sun	VS 4c

The Blind Man	VS 4c
Tunes of Glory	VS 4b *
Darwin's Waiting Room	VS 4b
A Plaice by the Sea	VS 4b

CRAMMAG HEAD

The Seven Seas	E3 5c ***
Down Under	E2 5b,5c ***
Accomodations of Desire	E2 5c **
Fresh Air	E1 5b ***
Anvil Chorus	E1 5b
The Soft Parade	E1 5b *
Mog	E1 5b *
Molotov Cocktail	E1 5b **
Funeral Pyre	E1 5b *
Freedom Fighter	HVS 5b *
Yosemite Sam	HVS 5b **
Ragnarok	HVS 5a *
Gorilla Warfare	HVS 5a *
Enfant Terrible	HVS 5a
Fragile Edge	HVS 5a
Poisoned Ocean	HVS 5a
The Ship's Cat	HVS 5a *
Lighthouse Wall	HVS 5a *
Orabidoo	VS 4c
Kalashnikov	VS 4b *
The White Rabbit	VS 4b
Shining Path	VS 4c

CAMBUSBARRON QUARRY

The Crowd	E5 6a/b
Power of Endurance	E5 6b **
Both Ends Burning	E5 6b ***
The Purr-Blind Doomster	E5 6a **
Running on Methane	E4 6a
Quasi Pulls Through	E4 6a/b
Big Country Dreams	E4 6a ***
Thug of War	E4 6b
Quantum Grunt	E3 6a **
Adulterer's Repentance	E3 5c
Fuel for Thought	E3 5c
Economy Drive	E3 6a **
Formica Crack	E3 6a **
Visions of Monaco	E3 5c
Trail Blazer	E2 5c
Murray's Groove	E2 5c

Grace Under Pressure	E2 5b
Pathfinder	E1 5b

RATHO QUARRY

Sahara	E5 6b **
This Septic Heil	E5 6b ***
Artho	E4 6a/b *
The Blob	E4 6a **
Pettifer's Wall	E4 6a **
Alopecia	E4 6a *
Wally 2	E4 5c *
Wally 3	E4 6a *
Doomed Oasis	E3 5c **
Ouroborus Eliminate	E3 5c
Strongarm	E3 6a *
The Lone Groover	E3 6a *
Gruel Brittania	E3 6a ***
Business as Usual	E3 6a
Diverticulitis	E3 6a **
Right Under	E3 6a *
Jumping Jack Splat	E3 6a
Ane Ledge	E3 5c *
Wally 1	E2 5c ***
So it Goes	E2 5c
5000 Christmas Trees	E2 5c *
Godzilla	E2 5c *
Slow Strain	E2 6a *
Left Over	E2 5c
Time's Last Gift	E2 5c **
Rebel Without Claws	E2 5c **
Shear Fear	E2 5c **
Chalk and Cheese	E2 5a *
Sedge Warbler	E2 5b **
Welcome to the Cruise	E1 5b **
Cornered	E1 5c
Up the Creek	E1 5b
Pull the Other One	E1 5b/c
Pete's Wall	E1 5b
Thorn in my Side	E1 5c
Beanpud	E1 5b **
Blue Rinse	E1 5b *
Ouroborus	HVS 5b **
Quick Pull	HVS 5a
Alan's Groove	HVS 5a
Terminal Case	HVS 5a
Shoskred	HVS 5a **

Cracking Up	HVS 5a *

ROSYTH QUARRY

The Stinking Swordsman	E4 6b *
Corpuscle	E3 5c
Phillistine	E2 6a
The Rust Bucket	E2 6a
If Pigs Could Fly	E2 5c **
Inspiration	E1 5b
The Waullie	HVS 5b *
The Beauty	HVS 5a *
Tiger Pad	HVS 5a *
Iconoclast	HVS 5a *
Skinny Lizzie	HVS 5a
Broken Pillar	HVS 5a *
Jagdhond	HVS 5a
The Grinder	HVS 4c
Plod	HVS 5a
Ram Jam Corner	HVS 5a
Flakeoff	VS 4c
The Beast	VS 5a
Hands Off	VS 4c
Changeling	VS 4c
Cathy	VS 4c **
The Flying Bink	VS 4c
Pogo Groove	VS 4c
Route to Root	VS 4c
Gold Foil	VS 4c **
Heathy	VS 4c **
Fat Sam	VS 4c
Gift Horse	VS 4b
Grenville	VS 4b
Serendipity	VS 4c *

THE HAWKCRAIG

Weasel Wall	E2 5c
Where Were You?	E2 5b
Guano Variation	E2 5b
Psylocibie	E2 5a
The Arete	E1 5b *
The High Girdle	HVS 5b *
Gaucho Variation	HVS 5a
Gaucho	HVS 5a **
Serendipity	HVS 5a
The Dwarf	HVS 5a
Gismo Variation	HVS 5a *

Guano	HVS 5a **
Conquistador Crack	VS 5a *
Squirrel Slab	VS 5a *
Toerag's Wall Variation	VS 5a *
Asinine	VS 5a **
The Groper	VS 5a
Pain Pillar Variation	VS 5a
Sacrilege	VS 5a
Cranium Crack	VS 4c **
Eureka	VS 5a *
Pain Pillar	VS 4c ***
Rebel's Groove	VS 4c
Diptera	VS 4c
Gismo	VS 4c
Saki	VS 4c *
Saracen	VS 4c *
Termination	VS 4c
The Low Girdle	VS 4c *
Urmi	VS 4c *
Eech!	VS 4c

TRAPRAIN LAW

Tipp	E2 6a
Beatle Crack	E1 5c *
Down my Street	E1 5b
The Chute	E1 5b *
Tiger Wall	HVS 5b *
Cat's Paw	HVS 5b
Piglet	HVS 5b **
Torque	HVS 5a *

Hanging Crack	HVS 5a
Slab and Tickle	HVS 5b
Dangle	HVS 5a
The Shield	HVS 4c *
Burp	HVS 5a *
The Western Girdle	VS 5a *
Retard Arete	VS 5a
Swingin'	VS 5a
Wobble	VS 5a *
Via MacNiven	VS 5a *
Sabre Cut	VS 5a *
Weech's Overhang	VS 5a
The Right Edge	VS 4c
Pip's Pillar	VS 4b
Turf Trundle	VS 4b
The Direttissima	VS 4c

NORTH BERWICK LAW

Eliminate Law	F7c
Fogtown Alternative Finish	F6c+ *
Necktie	E3 5c
Law of the Rings	F6c *
Law of the Flies	F6c **
Law of Gravity	F6c **
Fogtown	F6c **
Igneous Intruder	F6c
Jaws of the Law	F6b+ **
Old Lawbreaker	F6b **
Law and Disorder	F6a *

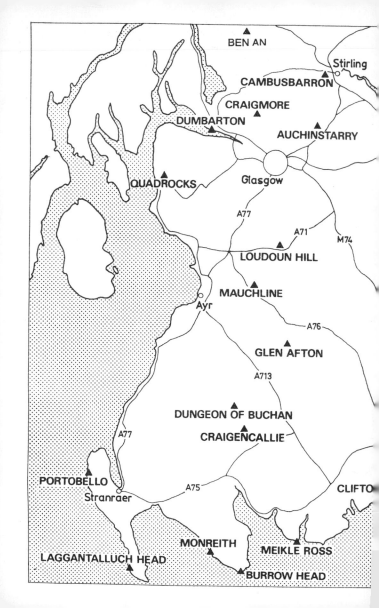